# Die Kettner Briefe

# Die Kettner Briefe

**by**
**Ilse Wurster**

**Edited**

**by**
**Charles A. Kettner, Ph.D.**

**Translations**

**by**
**Peter Benje, Ph.D. (Old Script German to Modern German)**

**Carol Okeson and Jerry Okeson, Ph.D. (Modern German to English)**

**Cover design by SuZann Kettner**

Comanche Creek Press
Wilmington, DE

Library of Congress Control Number: 2008937598

ISBN: 978-1463705985

**Published by:**

Comanche Creek Press

2411 Chatham Drive, Wilmington, DE 19803

**Printed and Distributed by:**

www.Createspace.com and www.Amazon.com, respectively

# Table of Contents / Inhaltsverzeichnis

## List of Figures / Bildverzeichnis

# About the Author and Editor/ Über den Autor und Herausgeber

**Author / Autor**

Ilse Wurster, geb. Erdrich, wurde am 23. Juni 1941 in Bremen geboren. Sie machte eine Ausbildung als Außenhandelskauffrau mit Abschluß im Jahre 1963. Die längste Zeit war sie in einer Gesellschaft für Rohtabak Im-und Export in Bremen angestellt, wo sie die Position einer stellvertretenden Direktorin erreichte. Seit 2001 befindet sie sich im Ruhestand. Ihre Anschrift ist Beckfeldstraße 7A, D-28213 Bremen, Deutschland. / Ilse Erdrich Wurster was born June 23, 1941 in Bremen. She completed her training as a Foreign Trade Clerk in 1963. Most of her professional career was in a leaf tobacco import-export company in Bremen where she rose to the level of a Vice President. She has been retired since 2001. Her mailing address is Beckfeldstrasse 7A, D-28213, Bremen, Germany.

**Editor / Herausgeber**

Charles Kettner, born October 27, 1946, grew up in Mason County, Texas on the ranch originally owned by his ancestor Franz Kettner. He currently owns the family home. He earned an undergraduate degree (1969) and a Masters degree (1971) from Southwest Texas State University (now called Texas State University) in Chemistry. He holds a Ph.D. in Biochemistry and Biophysics from Texas A&M University (1974). For most of his career, he was employed by E.I. DuPont Company, Wilmington, DE where he rose to the level of "Research Fellow." He is an author/inventor on over 100 scientific papers and patents. He is presently retired and can be reached at 2411 Chatham Drive, Wilmington, DE 19803 or skettner7@msn.com. / Charles Kettner, geboren am 27. Oktober 1946, wuchs auf in Mason County, Texas auf der Ranch, die ursprünglich im Besitz seines Vorfahren Franz Kettner war. Er ist immer noch im Besitz des Familienhauses. Er besitzt einen Abschluss (1969) und einen Master-Abschluss (1971) der Southwest Texas State University (jetzt Texas State University) in Chemie. Er hat einen Doktor in Biochemie und Biophysik von der Texas A & M University (1974). Die längste Zeit seiner Karriere war er angestellt bei E.I. DuPont Company, Wilmington, DE, wo er auf die Ebene der "Research Fellow" aufstieg. Er ist Autor und Erfinder von mehr als 100 wissenschaftlichen Publikationen und Patenten. Er befindet sich jetzt im Ruhestand und kann erreicht werden unter seiner Postadresse ist 2411 Chatham Drive, Wilmington, DE 19803 oder unter skettner7@msn.com.

# Preface / Vorwort

## Preface

Franz Kettner immigrated to Texas from Oberkirch, Baden Germany in 1848 and remained in his adopted country until his death in 1907. Fortunately for historians, Franz communicated with his father, Dr. Franz Lambert Kettner, through the exchange of letters. One quickly comes to recognize the communication skills of both individuals. Presently, I have acquired 39 of these and related letters and have published them as *Die Kettner Briefe*. I hope the reader will find the firsthand accounts of events that occurred on the Texas frontier and also in Europe during the second half of the nineteenth century as fascinating as I have.

The history of the letters is as follows. Franz Kettner was the uncle of my great-grandmother. My father, Fritz Erdrich, received the letters from other family members in Oberkirch. I am not sure of the circumstances. He realized the historical significance of the letters and shared three of the letters with Dr. Gilbert Jordan, Professor of Classical German Literature, Southern Methodist University, Dallas, Texas. These letters cover the period of 1853 to 1856. His son, Dr. Terry G. Jordan, and his wife Marlis Anderson Jordan translated the letters and published them in the *Southwestern Historical Quarterly* 69, (1966): 463 in a paper entitled "Letters of a German Pioneer in Texas." This paper is often referenced by historians interested in this era. Terry Jordan is a highly recognized expert on the roles of Germans in shaping the Texas frontier and he is widely published in this area. See for example, T.G. Jordan, *German Seeds in Texas Soil, Immigrant Farmers in Nineteenth Century Texas* (Austin, Texas: University of Texas Press, 1998). Independent of the letters translated by Dr. Jordan, two letters were published in the Renchtal Newspaper of the City of Oberkirch in 1973. I found excerpts from Letter 33 in the Homeland and Grimmelshausen Museum in Oberkirch in the Department of Revolution and Emigration of Baden. It is possible that other letters are in archives and have not been found. I am aware of a book by Kurt Klotzbach, *Wagenspur nach Westen* (Goettingen: W. Fischer-Verlag, 1974). The latter chapters of this publication describe events associated with Franz Kettner. The stories are told in the correct time frames, but I have not been able to confirm the extensive details given in this book from my research or from the references provided by Kurt Klotzbach.

Intrigued by the letters written by Franz Kettner and because of my long standing interest in family history, I undertook the translation of the letters from old script to modern German. Some expressions are different today from those in 19th century German. Also, in some cases, I shortened extremely long sentences into segments in order to facilitate translation. This was done with the help of Dr. Peter Benje, a family friend. He has had many years experience in translation of old documents from the archives and could read the old script German. Peter Benje also conducted an internet search and found a descendent of Franz Kettner, Jason T. Esquell, in the USA. He had done genealogical research and posted his Family Tree on the internet. From this site, we found that Franz Kettner had immigrated to Texas on the ship LOUIS from Antwerp and landed in Galveston November 20, 1848, with the destination of Gillespie County. Further research led us to the aforementioned Dr. Terry G. Jordan in Austin, Texas. Through Dr. Jordan, we contacted other descendents of Franz Kettner in Mason, Texas. Dr. Jordan's ancestors are from Mason, Texas (the county of origin of more than two thirds of the letters) and he is related to Joan Leifeste Kettner. Interestingly, members of the Kettner Family in Texas were not aware of relatives of Franz in Germany.

Patsy Kothmann Ziriax, a great-grandchild of Franz Kettner, had letters which had been written to Franz Kettner in Mason and gave me copies for translation and for inclusion in this publication, along with Franz Kettner's Obituary delivered by R. Runge. Finally, after compiling and translating all of the letters into modern German, Carol Okeson, with the assistance of her husband, Dr. Jerry Okeson, translated the letters from German to English. I have arranged the text of *Die Kettner Briefe* (The Kettner Letters) so that the English translation is followed by the modern German version for each letter. Figures are placed between the English and German versions. Additional supporting material has been added in footnotes. Realizing that the German and English reader will have different interests, information in the footnotes for each version was selected for the respective English and German audiences.

I have donated the original letters in old German script to the archives of the City of Oberkirch and a copy to the Mason Historical Commission. A copy of the original Letter 3 is shown in Fig. 1.

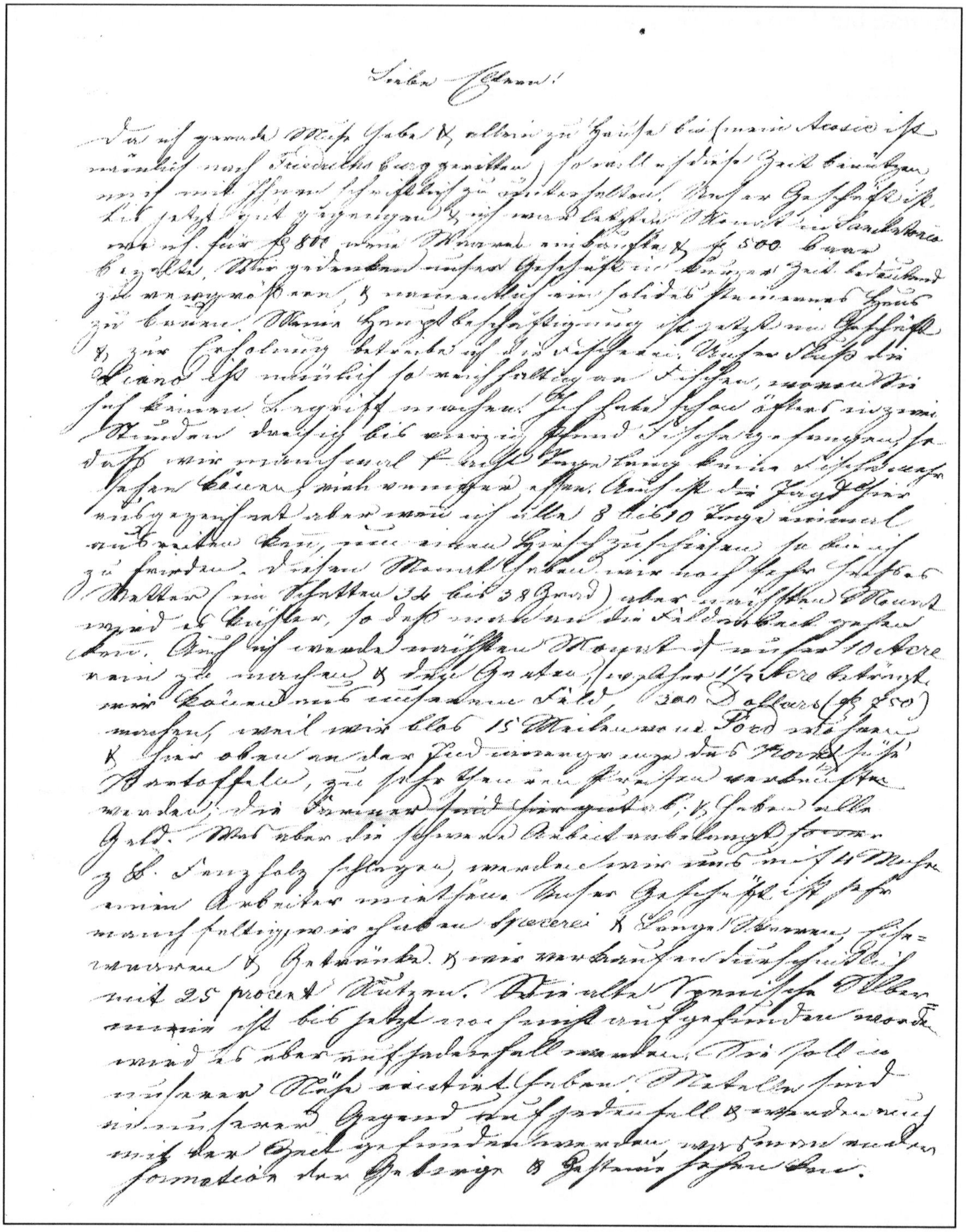

Dies ist für uns von ungeheurem Interesse, da
wir dadurch in kurzer Zeit auf einen andern [illegible]
ein Hauptstraße ist jetzt die Eisenbahn, welche von
der Küste bis San Antonio schon in Angriff genommen
ist. Die [illegible] begreift man, daß das Land
mit jedem Jahre steigt. Vor 5 Jahren bezahlte man
in der Gegend von Braunfels für Acre 1 bis 1½ Doll.
jetzt kostet der Acre 5 bis 10 Dollars. Hier aber
ist es noch billiger, wir wohnen nämlich 115 Meilen
von Braunfels & 100 Meilen von San Antonio
(nordwestlich). Wir werden auch wohl in kurzer
Zeit einige hundert Acre Land kaufen, [illegible] damit
zu speculiren. Es sind hier viele [illegible] von
in Deutschland [illegible] aufgezeichnet worden. Also
wenn dann schlimmere Zeiten, die bald in Deutschland
eintreten werden, [illegible] hier ein [illegible] zu haben.
Denn darüber sind alle in America einig, daß es
in Deutschland, ja in ganz Europa in kurzer Zeit zu
einem heftigen Zusammenstoß kommen wird [illegible]
nicht das Band [illegible] Mutterliebe geschont wird
America wird bei der künftigen Revolution nicht mehr
neutral bleiben sondern die Republicaner kräftig
unterstützen. Unser Staat wird mit jedem Jahre an
Kraft zu & es kann jetzt schon der alten Welt die
Spitze bieten. Wir werden in kurzer Zeit in Castell
ein Postamt [illegible] haben. Mein Partner
Kuevitz ist von der Regierung als Postmeister
vorgeschlagen & ich werde den Contract der Post
zu reiten [illegible] Meile
während der [illegible] es ist [illegible] zu [illegible]
So vergeht [illegible] Geschäft mit jedem Tage
& [illegible] von der Stadt
Castell am Llano finden. Was meine Gesundheit anbelangt
so bin ich immer wohl & munter, und die Leute behaupten
ich werde nie älter ich sehe immer noch aus wie ein Mann
von 23 bis 24 Jahre & besonders [illegible]
in meinem guten Humor, den ich nicht verloren habe
als ich auf dem Retour [illegible] Riogrande [illegible]
[illegible] & wir [illegible] 2 Tage [illegible]

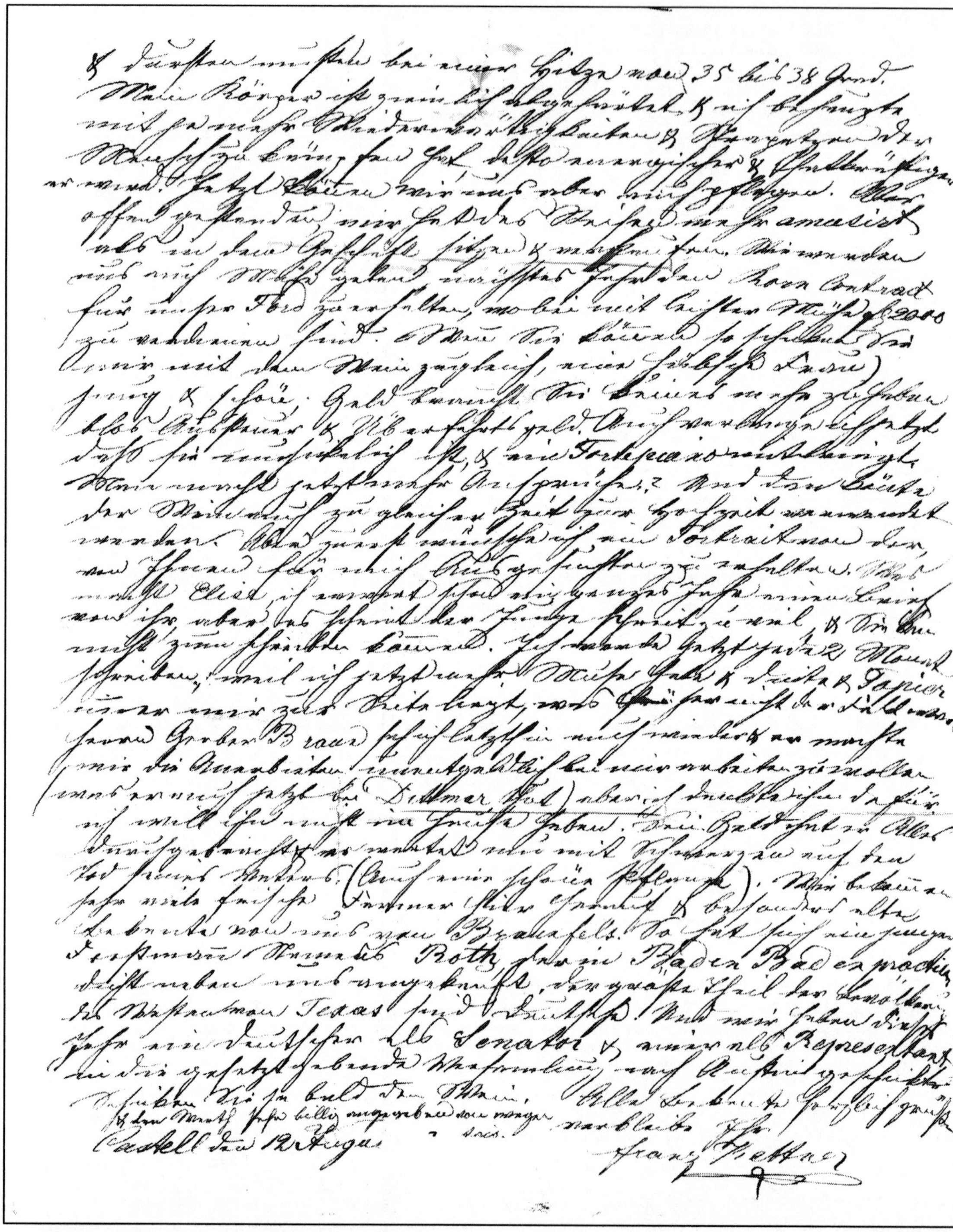

**Fig. 1. Original Letter 3 from Franz Kettner at Castell, Texas to his Parents in Oberkirch, Baden Germany.** Note the old German Script. This is the first of the three letters shared with Professor Jordan and published in the *Southwestern Historical Quarterly* (Jordan and Jordan, 463) and this publication.

**Abb. 1. Originalbrief 3 von Franz Kettner aus Castell, Texas an seine Eltern in Oberkirch, Baden.** Beachte die alte deutsche Schrift. Dieses ist der erste von drei Briefen, die Professor Jordan zur Verfügung gestellt wurden und in the *Southwestern Historical Quaterly* (Jordan and Jordan, 463) und in der vorliegenden Veröffentlichung publiziert wurden.

**Vorwort**

Franz Kettner wanderte im Jahre 1848 von Oberkirch, Baden, Deutschland nach Texas aus und blieb in seiner Wahlheimat bis zu seinem Tode im Jahre 1907. Zum Glück für Historiker kommunizierte Franz Kettner mit seinem Vater Dr. Franz Lambert Kettner mittels Briefwechsel. Beide waren brillante Berichterstatter. Gegenwärtig befinden sich 32 Briefe aus der Korrespondenz von Franz Kettner in meinem Besitz, die ich als *Die Kettner Briefe* veröffentlichen möchte. Die Berichte aus erster Hand schildern Ereignisse, die sich an den Grenzen von Texas sowie in Europa während der zweiten Hälfte des neunzehnten Jahrhunderts zutrugen. Ich hoffe, der Leser wird diese Berichte genauso faszinierend finden wie ich.

Dies ist die Geschichte der Briefe: Franz Kettner war der Onkel meiner Urgroßmutter väterlicherseits. Angefangen hat alles mit der Vererbung von insgesamt 32 Briefen in den sechziger Jahren des letzten Jahrhunderts an meinen Vater Fritz Erdrich, der als einer der nächsten noch lebenden Verwandten von Franz Kettner in Deutschland diese Briefe aus Oberkirch glücklicherweise erhalten hat. Die näheren Umstände sind mir leider nicht bekannt.

Mein Vater erkannte die historische Bedeutung dieser Briefe und hat zunächst drei dieser Briefe Dr. Gilbert J. Jordan, Professor für klassische deutsche Literatur an der Southern Methodist University, Dallas, Texas, zur Verfügung gestellt. Es handelte sich hierbei um Briefe von Franz Kettner an seine Eltern in Oberkirch aus den Jahren 1853-1856. Sein Sohn Dr. Terry G. Jordan übersetzte dieselben zusammen mit seiner damaligen Frau Marlis Anderson Jordan. Veröffentlicht wurden diese Briefe dann in *Southwestern Historical Quarterly* 69, (1966): 463 unter dem Titel "Letters of a German Pioneer in Texas". Diese Veröffentlichung wurde von historisch Interessierten dieser Zeitperiode häufig zitiert. Terry Jordan ist ein hoch anerkannter Experte über die Rollen der Deutschen bei der Gestaltung der Grenze von Texas. Von ihm gibt es zahlreiche Veröffentlichungen in dieser Region. Siehe zum Beispiel T.G. Jordan, *German Seeds in Texas Soil, Immigrant Farmers in Nineteenth Century Texas* , (Austin, Texas: University of Texas Press, 1998).

Unabhängig hiervon wurden zwei weitere Briefe im Jahre 1973 in der Renchtal Zeitung der Stadt Oberkirch veröffentlicht. Bei einem Besuch im Heimat- und Grimmelshausenmuseum in Oberkirch im September 2003 fand ich in der Ateilung Badische Revolution und Auswanderung den Auszug des Briefes 33 von Franz (Francis) Kettner an seinen Vater in Oberkirch vom 18.09.1873. Also ist es möglich, daß sich noch weitere Briefe in Kopie in badischen Archiven befinden. Wie sehr die Berichte der Kettner Briefe immer wieder zu eigenständigen Geschichten Anlaß gaben, zeigt sich ganz besonders in einem Buch von Kurt Klotzbach, *Wagenspur nach Westen* (Göttingen: W. Fischer-Verlag, 1974). Die letzten Abschnitte dieses Buches beschreiben Abenteuer von Franz Kettner. Die Geschichten werden im korrekten zeitlichen Rahmen erzählt, ich war jedoch nicht in der Lage, die umfangreichen Details in diesem Buch durch meine Erkundungen zu bestätigen, noch sind sie durch Kurt Klotzbach belegt. Ich halte sie für romanhaft überhöht.

Fasziniert von den Briefen von Franz Kettner und interessiert an unserer Familiengeschichte habe ich mich bemüht, dieselben aus der alten deutschen Schreibschrift in die lateinische Schrift zu übertragen. Geschrieben in der 2. Hälfte des 19. Jahrhunderts unterscheidet sich die Ausdrucksweise von Franz Kettner in manchem von dem heutigen Deutsch und ist daher teilweise schwer verständlich. Außerdem sind manche Sätze so lang, daß ich sie in kürzere Segmente geteilt habe, um das Lesen und die Übersetzbarkeit zu erleichtern. Rechtschreibung und Zeichensetzung sind behutsam den heutigen Gewohnheiten angepaßt. Hierbei erhielt ich Unterstützung von Dr. Peter Benje, einem Freund der Familie. Er hat langjährige Erfahrung bei der Entzifferung von alten Dokumenten aus den verschiedensten Archiven und konnte die alte deutsche Schreibschrift lesen. Auch führte Peter Benje umfangreiche Recherchen per Internet durch und fand zunächst einen Nachfahren von Franz Kettner in den USA, Jason T. Esquell. Dieser hatte genealogische Nachforschungen betrieben und seinen Familienstammbaum im Internet veröffentlicht. Von ihm erfuhren wir, daß Franz Kettner auf dem Schiff LOUIS von Antwerpen kommend nach Texas immigrierte und am 20. November 1848 in Galveston landete mit Destination Gillespie County.

Die weitere Suche führte zu dem bereits genannten Professor Dr. Terry G. Jordan in Austin, Texas. Dr. Jordan stellte den Kontakt zu noch lebenden Nachkommen von Franz Kettner in Mason, Texas her. Auch die Vorfahren von Dr. Jordan stammen aus Mason, Texas, dem Ursprungsland von gut zwei Drittel der Briefe, und er ist verwandt mit Joan Leifeste Kettner. Interessanterweise wußten die Mitglieder der Familie Kettner in Texas nichts von Verwandten von Franz in Deutschland.

Patsy Kothmann Ziriax, eine Urenkelin von Franz Kettner, besaß Briefe, die an Franz Kettner in Mason geschrieben wurden. Sie überließ mir Kopien derselben zur Übersetzung und um sie in diese Veröffentlichung einzubeziehen. Ebenfalls übersandte sie mir Franz Kettners Grabrede, die von R. Runge gehalten wurde. Nach endgültiger Zusammenstellung und Übersetzung der Briefe in modernes Deutsch, hat schließlich Carol Okeson, assistiert von ihrem Ehemann Dr. Jerry Okeson, diese Briefe vom Deutschen ins Englische übersetzt.

Ich habe den Text der Kettner Briefe so angeordnet, dass die moderne deutsche Version jedes Briefes der englischen Übersetzung folgt. Abbildungen finden sich zwischen der englischen und der deutschen Version. Zusätzliches Informationsmaterial wurde in Fußnoten eingefügt. Da deutsche und englische Leser unterschiedliche Interessen haben, wurden die Fußnoten für jede Version den entsprechenden Lesern angepaßt. Die englischen Fußnoten enthalten umfangreiche zusätzliche Informationen.

Ich habe die Originalbriefe in alter deutscher Schreibschrift dem Archiv der Stadt Oberkirch geschenkt und Fotokopien derselben der Mason Historical Commission zur Verfügung gestellt. Eine Kopie des Originalbriefes Nr. 3 wird in Abb. 1 gezeigt.

# Acknowledgements / Danksagungen


**Acknowledgements**

First, I would like to thank my husband, Dr. Juergen Wurster, for help and encouragement throughout the preparation of this book. I thank Dr. Peter Benje, Bremen, for help in translating the letters from old script German into modern German and for his extensive help with research. Similarly, Professor Terry Jordan (The Walter Prescott Webb Chair in History and Ideas, Department Geography, The University of Texas at Austin) provided help in locating members of the Kettner family and provided support and encouragement. The author is saddened by his untimely death on October 16, 2003. I thank Lois Jordan Koock, Mason, Texas, for contacts she helped me make in Texas and her research. The material she obtained from the Mason Library Genealogical Collection was valuable in compiling this manuscript. Jane Hoerster, Chairperson of Mason County Historical Commission, also provided valuable information and old photographs of Mason County.

I would like to particularly thank Patsy Kothmann Ziriax, Mason, Texas, for copies of letters Franz Kettner received in Texas from Germany. They added a number of valuable chapters to this book. Members of the Kettner family in Mason provided photos and other documents for this publication. The list includes Fred Kettner and his wife Joan Leifeste Kettner, Charles Kettner, Patsy Kothmann Ziriax, Joan Kettner Lindley, Henrietta Kettner Keener, and Emelia Grosenbacher Winjum. These are all great-grandchildren of Franz Kettner who, without a doubt, are proud of their heritage. Jason Esquell, a great-great-grandchild, shared with us genealogical information on the Kettner family which he had compiled. We also gratefully acknowledge Patty Schneider Pfister's help in searching the Texas State Archives.

I would like to acknowledge the contribution of Carol and Jerry Okeson[1] for their careful translation of the letters from modern German into English. I thank Charles and SuZann Kettner for their help in publishing this book.

Finally, in preparation of this manuscript, I have drawn heavily from several resources which have provided essential historical background information for the *Die Kettner Briefe* (The Kettner Letters). They are the *Handbook of Texas Online* and *Frontier Times*. For the latter, J. Marvin Hunter, a historian and publisher wrote "Brief History of the Early Days in Mason County" and published it in a continuing series in the *Frontier Times* (Vol. 6, No. 2, Nov. 1928 through Vol. 6, No. 6, Mar. 1929).[2] In the *Die Kettner Briefe*, I have included a number of large direct quotes from the *Frontier Times* with the kind permission of Jim Rogers at http://-www.frontiertimesmagazine.com/index.html who owns the copyrights and presently is a source for the magazine.

**Danksagungen**

Zunächst danke ich meinem Ehemann Dr. Jürgen Wurster für seine Hilfe und Ermutigung bei der Vorbereitung dieses Buches. Ich danke Dr. Peter Benje, Lübberstedter Str. 5, 28217 Bremen, Deutschland, für seine Unterstützung, die Briefe von altdeutscher Schrift in modernes Deutsch zu übersetzen, sowie für seine umfangreiche Recherche per Internet. Ebenso war Professor Terry Jordan (The Walter Prescott Webb Chair in History and Ideas, Department Geography, The University of Texas at Austin) sehr behilflich, weitere Mitglieder der Familie Kettner aufzuspüren. Ich bin ihm zu großem Dank verpflichtet für die unermüdliche Unterstützung bei allen Recherchen auf amerikanischer Seite. Zu meinem großen Bedauern verstarb Dr. Terry G. Jordan nach langer Krankheit bereits am 16. Oktober 2003. Die wenigen Monate unserer Verbindung waren eine große Freude und haben mir viele positive Impulse gebracht. Ohne sein uneigennütziges Engagement wäre die vorliegende Veröffentlichung wahrscheinlich nicht zustande gekommen. Mein Dank gilt auch Lois Jordan Koock, Mason, Texas für ihre erfolgreiche Suche und Kontakte, die sie in Texas herstellte. Die Unterlagen der Mason Library Genealogical Collection, die sie beschaffte, waren es wert, in diesem Manuskript aufgenommen zu werden.

---

[1] The addresses of the contributors are: Dr. and Mrs. Jerry Okeson, 2422 Chatham Dr., Wilmington, DE 19803 and Dr. and Mrs. Charles A. Kettner, 2411 Chatham Dr., Wilmington, DE 19803.

[2] Hunter acknowledges the contribution of Don H. Biggers of Fredericksburg, TX to this publication. According to Marvin Hunter, around 1928 the Mason Chamber of Commerce hired Biggers to write a history of Mason County. He was previously noted for writing a history of Gillespie County. After several months of research, Biggers concluded that this undertaking would require several years. He turned over all of his research material to the Chamber of Commerce which in turn, made them available to Hunter for use in the aforementioned series. Hunter states the following: "Mr. Bigger's work is to be highly commended, for he has certainly arranged his material in splendid style, and has included in his compilation the main historical points of much value to the future historians who may essay to write the history of Mason County" (J. Marvin Hunter "Brief History of the Early Days in Mason County," *Frontier Times*, 6 November 1928, 73).

Ich danke ganz besonders Patsy Kothmann Ziriax, Mason, Texas für Kopien einiger Gegenbriefe an Franz Kettner aus Deutschland. Sie tragen eine Anzahl wertvoller Kapitel zu diesem Buch bei. Außerdem lieferten Mitglieder der Kettner Familie in Mason Fotos und andere Dokumente für diese Publikation. Hierbei handelt es sich um Fred Kettner und seine Frau Joan Leifeste Kettner, Dr. Charles Kettner, Patsy Kothmann Ziriax, Joan Kettner Lindley, Henrietta Kettner Keener und Emilia Grosenbacher Winjum. Sie alle sind Urenkel von Franz Kettner, die zweifelsohne stolz auf ihre Herkunft sind. Jason Esquell, ein Ur-Urenkel stellte uns genealogische Informationen über die Kettner Familie zur Verfügung, die er gesammelt hatte. Die Hilfe von Patty Schneider Pfister bei der Suche in den Texas State Archiven wird dankbar anerkannt.

Ich möchte mich für die Beiträge der Carol and Jerry Okesons[3] bedanken, ihre sorgfältige Übersetzung der Briefe aus dem modernen Deutsch ins Englische. Ich danke Charles und SuZann Kettner für ihre Hilfe bei der Veröffentlichung dieses Buches insbesondere bei der Beschaffung und Einfügung des Bildmaterials und des einschlägigen historischen Materials in die Abschnitte der englischen Übersetzung. Auch hat Dr. Charles Kettner den Abschnitt "Einführung" in so umfassender und vorzüglicher Weise neu editiert, dass ich ihn diesbezüglich als Koautor anerkennen möchte.

Schließlich habe ich mich bei der Vorbereitung dieses Manuskriptes häufig verschiedener Quellen bedient, die wesentliche historische Hintergrundinformationen für *Die Kettner Briefe* geliefert haben. Dies sind das *Handbook of Texas History Online* und die *Frontier Times*. Für letztere hat J. Marvin Hunter, ein Historiker und Herausgeber, die Serie "Brief History of the Early Days in Mason County" geschrieben und diese in Fortsetzungen in den *Frontier Times* (Vol.6, Nr.2, Nov.1928 bis Vol.6, Nr.6, Mar.1929) veröffentlicht. In *Die Kettner Briefe* habe ich eine Anzahl umfangreicher direkter Zitate aus den Frontier Times aufgenommen mit freundlicher Erlaubnis von Jim Rogers, http://www.frontiertimesmagazine.com/-index.html, der die Copyrights besitzt und gegenwärtig eine Quelle für das Magazin ist.

[3] Die Adressen der Mitwirkenden sind: Dr. and Mrs. Jerry Okeson, 2222 Chatham Dr., Wilmington, DE 19803 and Dr. and Mrs. Charles A. Kettner, 2411 Chatham Dr. Wilmington, DE 19803.

Rock Pens by SuZann Kettner 1972

# Introduction / Einführung

## Introduction

*Die Kettner Briefe* consists primarily of letters exchanged between Franz Kettner and his father Dr. Franz Lambert Kettner over the period from 1850 to 1875. Franz, forced to leave his home in Germany, arrived in Galveston on November 20, 1848 on the ship LOUIS (See Fig. 2) from Antwerp with Gillespie County as a destination. His letters give first hand accounts of life and events on the Texas frontier. Similarly, from letters written by Dr. Franz Lambert Kettner, a physician in Oberkirch, Baden, one learns of life in Germany over the same time period.

Franz was on the forefront of the movement of German immigrants into the Texas Hill Country (See Fig. 5). The first of the Kettner letters is dated August 1850 from New Braunfels, Texas.[4] His third letter, in August 1853, is from Castell which is on

---

[4] New Braunfels is located at mouth of the Comal River on the Guadalupe River in Comal County, TX. It was founded March 21, 1845, by the Adelsverein, headed by Prince Carl Solms Braunfels. The Adelsverein was also called the "Society for the Protection of German Immigrants in Texas" and later, "The German Immigrant Company." It was established by wealthy, titled Germans to promote the colonization of Texas for profit as well as philanthropic reasons. The Adelsverein purchased the rights to establish colonies in the Fisher-Miller Land Grant in central Texas (territory north of the Llano river and south and west of the San Saba and Colorado rivers, see map Fig. 5). They acquired this tract of land without seeing it and did not realize that it was too far from their port of entry at Indianola for immediate settlement. They also did not realize that the Fisher-Miller Grant consisted of uncharted territory which was occupied by the war-like Comanche Indians. Therefore, colonies were established in New Braunfels and later at Fredericksburg in 1846 as way stations to the Fisher-Miller Grant. The latter was settled by John O. Meusebach, who succeeded Prince Solm as commissioner of the Adelsverein. Also, he was responsible for forging a peace treaty with the Comanche in 1847. However at this time, the Adelsverein went bankrupt and the only colonies established under their auspices were those in the vicinity of Castell on the southern edge of the Grant. Franz Kettner was one of the early settlers of the Fisher-Miller Grant. Franz's Letter 3 is from Castell and later, Letter 10 is from Foley's Crossing in Mason Co. In letter 10, Franz states that his nearest neighbor is an hour away and that he has no neighbors north of him. References: Terry Jordan, *German Seed in Texas Soil* (Austin, Texas: University of Texas Press, 1992), 42-46, *Handbook of Texas Online*, s.v. "Adelsverein," http:// www.tsha.utexas.edu/handbook/online/articles/AeA/ufa1.html (accessed July 30, 2006), and the *Handbook of Texas Online*, s.v. "Meusebach, John O.," http://-www.tsha.utexas.edu/handbook/online/articles/MM/fme33.html (accessed July 30, 2006).

the southeastern edge of the Fisher-Miller Grant, an area unsettled at the time. Later letters are from Fredericksburg in Gillespie County and from Mason County. Franz moved to Foley's Crossing in the western portion of Mason County in 1859 only a year after Mason County was established. He remained in Mason County until his death in 1907. Over the period of 1848-1907, Franz had many experiences and observed many changes leading to the settlement and development of this area in the Texas Hill Country. His funeral address delivered by Rudolf Runge provides an overview of many of these events (See below.). Franz describes the early development of the agriculture industry during the open range era. He describes numerous encounters with Indians including the search for Alice Todd (a story later dramatized in a novel entitled *The Searchers* by Alan LeMay). In Franz's letters in 1863 and 1865, he tells his father of the difficulties he and other German immigrants had during the Civil War due to their opposition to slavery. Franz tells of vigilante lynchings and shootings in the neighboring Gillespie County and gives first hand accounts of the role of the militia in restoring order. Many more events and details are given in the letters.

In reading *Die Kettner Briefe*, one realizes the challenges, in addition to the dangers and physical hardships, of life on the Texas frontier. Perhaps more important, we can appreciate the difficulty of being separated from one's parents and children and not learning of important family events such as the birth of children and death of loved ones for many months. Finally, one reads about small family conflicts which are characteristic of most, if not all, families. To maintain authenticity, these items have been included. One must remember that we have intruded on personal communications for the sake of history and hope that they will not mind after 150 years.

Two documents can readily serve as an introduction to the *Die Kettner Briefe*. The first is the eloquent funeral address delivered by Rudolf Runge, a long time friend of Franz. The second is the address honoring Dr. Franz Lambert Kettner upon his retirement. It provides background during his early career. However, as one reads *Die Kettner Briefe* one obtains insights into their everyday lives and into their character as well as historic events from their perspective. Life on the Texas frontier can be contrasted to life in mid-nineteenth century Europe.

Figures 7 and 8 are pictures of the principal correspondents.

Address delivered upon the Funeral of Francis Kettner on
September 9, 1907, by R. Runge[5]

Dear Friends:

Again we have marched to the city of the dead to deposit in its sacred precincts the remains of one of the best. At his request I address to you a few words, giving a short sketch of some of the principal events of his life,

[5] R. Runge "Obiturary Francis Kettner" *Mason County News*, September 13, 1907.

not to pronounce an eulogy upon him; for such is told much more eloquently by a long and noble life than words can express it. He was a man with whom "to do good" was religion. A man who by virtue of his many sterling qualities and noble character, from the early settlement of this country, has held a fond place in the hearts of the people. Coming hither when Mason County was a wilderness, infested by hostile Indians, when the few white settlers each were acquainted with the other, all soon learned to know, respect and love him. Francis Kettner was a man of indomitable courage, scrupulously honest and conscientious, pronounced in his views, indulgent toward others, imbounded in hospitality. In the perilous, early days, when none but the best would do, he was frequently called upon by the citizenship of his county to fill the office of a sheriff and other responsible positions. And the efficient and energetic manner in which he discharged the hazardous and difficult duties of those positions, under adverse circumstances, ever was a credit to himself and of untold benefit to his constituents. Nor is his good name and fame confined to the bounds of Mason County, nor to this state, nor, indeed to this continent.

Our beloved dead was born (nearly 81 years ago) in the Grand Duche of Baden, Germany, on October 12, 1826, a date which coincides with the natal day of the ruler of his native state, the venerable Grand Duke of Baden.

Our departed friend received a careful education in the celebrated institutions of learning of his fatherland. But before his education was finished, he in 1848, joined the revolutionary party, which had for its object the throwing off of the yoke of petty and greater tyrants and the unification of what is now the German Empire. This territory was then divided in about 34 separate and theoretically--independent sovereignties; the inhabitants of the smaller ones having to submit not only to the arbitrary will of their own rulers, but as well to the tyranny of the more powerful of these countries, while none of them was strong enough, single handed, to defend against any of the great powers of Europe. Some of these revolutionists had far advanced ideas, dreaming of a "Republic of Germany," while united Germany, strong enough to defend herself against any of her neighbors, with a ruler whose powers were to be limited by a constitution, was all that the more conservative and thoughtful demanded or hoped for—a hope that was realized as the result of the Franco-German War 23 years later. "Union and Liberty" was the slogan of the revolutionists of '48 with which they went to battle under Franz Sigel, later a celebrated general of the U.S. Army. And our departed friend in this fight for the oppressed people against potentates and tyrants, risked his all. The revolutionary movement was crushed by forces of the strongly disciplined armies of the princes, and our friend, to escape persecution, together with many of the nation's best, was compelled to part from his native land and sought a new home in the new state of

Texas, in 1848. He at once went to work with a will, but not acquainted with the conditions and workings of this country, it was years before he acquired a competency. In the first year of residence in Texas he tried farming in a bend of the Guadalupe in Comal County, which on account of its particular form is called "Demijohn Bend." The next year we find him in Captain Connor's company of Texas Rangers in the Rio Grande country, protecting the state against invasions of hostile Indians and Mexicans. This company was later mustered into the service of the United States from which the departed during the last few years of his life has drawn a small pension for his service in the campaigns of that company. Of the 80 and some young men that composed his company 57 years ago—so far as known, only 2 survive our departed friend, namely, Gustav Schmeltzer of San Antonio, and Charles C. Schriener of Kerrville. This period was full of adventure and dangers, and our friend would most interestingly talk of them. I regret that the limited time will not permit me to relate some of them. Robert Brodemann of New Braunfels, Mr. Kriewitz of Castell, and Captain Dosch of San Antonio, whom many of you know, were with Kettner in this service. They all preceded him in death. Upon the completion of this service, Mr. Kettner lived for a short time with this friend Kriewitz at Castell, thereupon he moved to Gillespie County, where he was elected sheriff, making one of the best sheriffs that county ever had. Still making Gillespie County his home he engaged in farming and freighting. Freighting was then done by means of large ox teams, and a single trip to the coast or to one of the military posts far off on the frontier, would often require months, while such journeys over the long and lonesome routes were not bare of charm to those who in loneliness loved to commune with nature and to some romantically inclined youths, it was full of hardship and perils incident to the early frontier life. Our friend having by this time seen considerable of the frontier life was of great service to his comrades who were new or "green" on the frontier.

On September 3, 1857, he was married to Katherine Keller at Fredericksburg. Two years later he moved with his young wife and child to Mason County, settling on the south bank of the Llano River, on the place now owned by Adolph Keller at what is now known as the Foley Crossing. Here he and his family suffered untold privations and dangers. During the Civil War the conditions were exceedingly bad. For years afterwards, the Indians were very bad, and this place seemed to be on their "trail" or route they were accustomed to travel when going on their depredations in the white settlements. It finally became so bad that to longer attempt to stay on that place would have been little short of suicide. In 1875,[6] while Mr. Kettner was at work in the field a bunch of Indians swept down upon the ranch attempting to drive off the saddle horses grazing within 75 yards of the house. The

[6] Runge is mistaken on the date. This incident occurred in 1871.

oldest, Louis, then a lad of 13, boldly attacked them, firing upon them with his six-shooter, while Mrs. Kettner took a Spencer Carbine to her husband in the field. When Mr. Kettner arrived on the scene, gun in hand, the Indians called the fight off, fleeing with all speed to the mountains, Mr. Kettner firing on them as they fled. This occurred while there was a company of rangers stationed within 2 miles of the ranch. Soon after even this supposed protection was withdrawn, when the family moved to what was then known as the McSwane place,[7] six miles below the town on Comanche Creek, where they lived until 6 years, when they moved to our town where Mr. & Mrs. Kettner have since resided.

During this residence in Mason, the departed held many important positions. He was sheriff in early days, later he was revenue officer, in the early 70's he held the then highly important office of cattle inspector and in that capacity probably did more than any other man to see that everyone got his dues. Later he was elected county commissioner and re-elected many times—so long as he could be persuaded to accept the office—and to his ability and faithful performance of the duties of that office, it is largely due that Mason County was rescued from a state of bankruptcy and placed on a cash basis.

There were born to Mr. and Mrs. Kettner 5 children: the sons, Louis, Will and Charles, and the daughters, Ida and Alice, now Mrs. August Keller, and Mrs. John Gamel, all of whom survive him and now stand at his grave; 15 grandchildren also survive him.

The departed lived to see 2 happy events, which are of rare occurrence in the short span of time allotted to man. The one was the birth of a great grandchild, the other was the 50th Anniversary of his wedding day - The Golden Wedding. It is sad to know that the latter of these 2 events was destined to be the beginning of the end. For while the day opened brightly and beautifully, shortly before noon, while the table was spread, and the happy children and grandchildren in anticipation of a most joyous time gathered around the parental board, the beloved groom, the father and grandfather suffered a paralytic stroke to which he succumbed, yielding up his life 8 days later, at 4 o'clock yesterday one week to the hour after we laid to rest the remains of his kinsman and lifetime friend, Major James Hunter.

While the departed, in his long life by industry, and economy accumulated a handsome fortune, his aim in life never was the acquisition of riches. He was one of the old school of idealist, now nearly extinct, who saw his happiness in the elevation of mankind, whose deeds were directed by his principle, "To do unto others as he would have them do unto him." Most of you have known him the greater part of your lives-speaking for myself, I for the first time grasped his hand over half a century ago. You all remember

[7] "McSwane" is a printing error. It should be "McSween."

good and noble deeds of his. No one can point to any wrong that he ever committed. You men and women of a younger generation who knew him in life, whenever you meet with an occasion where you do not know whether to do a certain thing is right or not, ask yourselves this question: "What would he have done under like circumstances?" Do what you know he would have done and a clear conscience will be your reward. While we submit his remains to the grave, surrounded by those of many friends, who have gone before, let his life be our beacon-light.

Honors for Dr. Franz Lambert Kettner Upon His Retirement
January 20, 1873

The Oberkirchener Amtsblatt regards it as its duty to report on the events which particularly concern it and it fulfills this obligation with great joy when it is able to give a worthy person his crown.

On the 20th of January of this year, the Grand Duke's Assistant Doctor Kettner at 80 years old announced his retirement. There is recognition of his long years of faithfully performed service. Because he has been in practice here for 47 years, which is a long span of world and medical history, there has been the opportunity to observe and make a judgment of him. An honorable private and public life, faithful fulfillment of duties in his office and outward circles, strong conscientiousness and honest openness in speech and deed; these are the virtues of his way of life. Though his modesty rejects it, a loud recognition of his fellow medical colleagues and his fellow citizens believe that it is a necessity for his community to declare this recognition publicly. He served twice as surgeon with the Baden troops in the field outside Strassburg in 1813 and 1815 and now he had seen with his own eyes the fulfillment of his dreams of that time come true. The Active Service Decoration and the Order of the Zaehringer Lion grace his chest and the respect of a wide family circle brightens his remaining years. May it be granted us for a long while still to enjoy with him the uplifting example of a well-lived life.

Finally, further insights into Franz (Francis) Kettner's personality were obtained from a recent communication with Emelia Winjum. She is a great-granddaughter of Franz and recalls the following events told by her mother, Estella Kettner Grosenbacher.

I remembered some things my mother told me about Francis Kettner. She was 9 years old when her grandparents, Francis and Catherine K. had their 50th wedding anniversary, so she remembered the planned festive celebration and also remembered how the festive occasion changed into one of sorrow when he suffered a stroke.

Ken, my husband, paces the floor when he is thinking. My mother said that he reminded her of her Grandfather Kettner who walked the floor and thought. On one occasion, she and some other children were playing in front of her house when he walked right past them. He was so engrossed in thought that he didn't see them. I asked her what the children did. She laughed and said that they marched behind him as if he was the Pied Piper. When he noticed what they were doing he burst out laughing and told them he hadn't seen them. She said the children loved him. Thought you might enjoy this tidbit about Francis' personality.

**Fig. 2. The Ship LOUIS.** The painting of the ship LOUIS by C. J. Fedeler, 1841, was reproduced with the permission of "Focke-Museum, Bremer Landesmuseum für Kunst und Kulturgeschichte."

**Abb. 2. Das Segelschiff LOUIS.** Ölgemälde von C.J. Fedeler 1841. Publikationsgenehmigung vom "Focke-Museum, Bremer Landesmuseum für Kunst und Kulturgeschichte."

**Fig. 3. The Harbor at Antwerp, Belgium about 1850.** This engraving is from Deutscher Kunstverlag and the original is in possession of Dr. Peter Benje. The Cathedral of Our Lady, constructed 1352-1521, is in the background. Its spire (405 feet) remains one of the tallest in the region.

**Abb. 3. Antwerpen.** Von der Spitze von Flandern. D. Kunstverlag. Originalstahlstich um 1850. Privatbesitz Dr. Peter Benje.

**Fig. 4. Galveston, Texas around 1850**. The original engraving is in the possession of Ilse Wurster and is from Kunstanstalt des Bibliograhischen Instituts, Hildburghausen.

**Abb. 4. Galveston in Texas**. Kunstanstalt des Bibliographischen Instituts, Hildburghausen. Original Stahlstich um 1850. Privatbesitz Ilse Wurster.

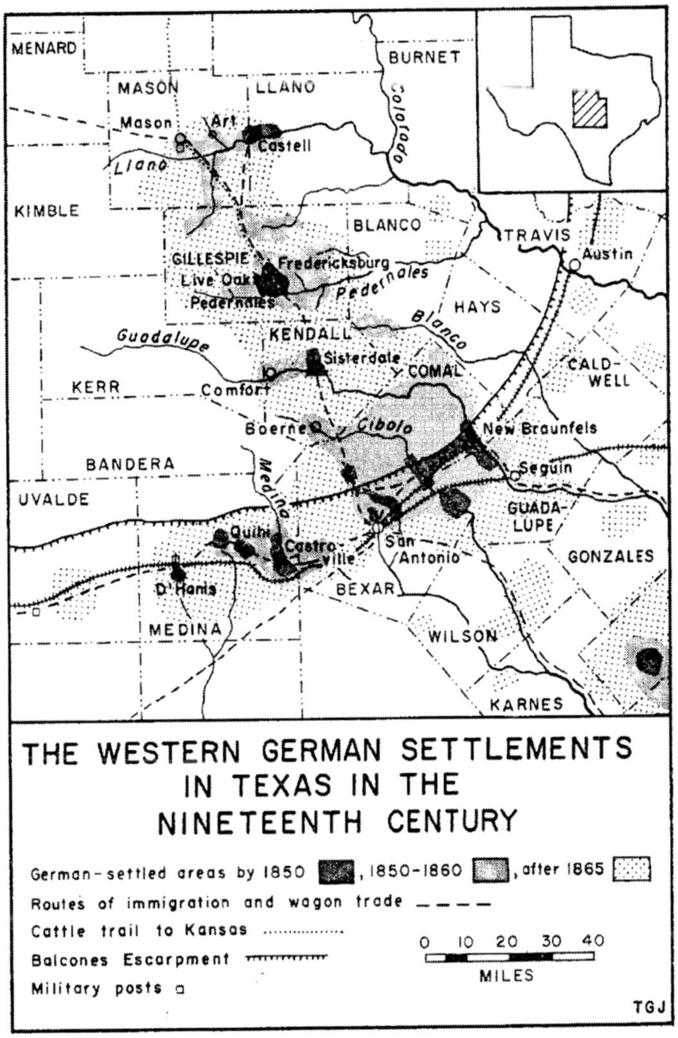


**Fig. 5. Western German Settlements.** From *German Seeds in Texas Soil: Immigrant Farmers in Nineteenth Centry Texas* by Terry G. Jordan. Copyright © 1966, renewed 1994. Courtesy of the University of Texas Press. McCulloch Co (north of Mason) and San Saba Co. (north of Llano Co) are not labeled. In later descriptions of the Fisher-Miller Grant (land between the Llano, San Saba, and Colorado Rivers) the location of the San Saba River is important. Unfortunately, it is not shown on this map. It originates in Menard Co. and flows through the northwest corner of Mason, Co., through McCulloch Co. and San Saba Co. It flows into the Colorado River close to where it intersects the top of the map. See also Fig. 21.

**Abb. 5. Westliche deutsche Siedlungen.** Aus *German Seeds in Texas Soil: Immigrant Farmers in Nineteenth Centry Texas* von Terry G. Jordan. Copyright © 1966, erneuert 1994. Mit freundlicher Genehmigung der University of Texas Press. McCulloch County (nördlich von Mason) und San Saba County (nördlich von Llano County) sind nicht bezeichnet. In späteren Beschreibungen des Fisher-Miller-Grant (Land zwischen den Flüssen Llano, San Saba und Colorado) ist die Lage des San Saba Flusses von Bedeutung. Leider ist er auf dieser Karte nicht abgebildet. Er entspringt im Menard County und fließt durch die nordwestliche Ecke vom Mason County, durch McCulloch County und San Saba County. Er mündet in den Colorado Fluß nahe dem Punkt, wo dieser den oberen Rand der Karte kreuzt.

**Fig. 6. Kettner Family on the 50th Anniversary of Francis (Franz) and Katherine Kettner.** The children, Louis, Ida Keller, Charlie (Karl), Alice Gamel, and William, are standing behind their parents.

**Abb. 6. Familie Kettner anläßlich des 50. Hochzeitstages von Franz und Katharina Kettner**. Die Kinder Louis, Ida Keller, Karl, Alice (Elise) Gamel und William stehend hinter ihren Eltern.

**Fig. 7. Dr. Franz Lambert and Maria Clara Kettner.** These pictures were recently found among Erdrich family possessions by the author in Germany. They were wrapped in paper labeled "unknown ancestors." The author identified these prints from a photograph in the possession of Charles Kettner in Texas. See the Genealogy section, upper photo p. 263. These pictures seem to be selective enlargements of the original negative, from which the print on p.263 had been taken. In letters Franz wrote to his parents, he makes a number of requests for a photograph of his parents, emphasizing how important it is for his children to know what their grandparents look like. However, from the letters one does not know when Franz received a photograph of his parents.

**Abb. 7. Dr. Franz Lambert und Maria Clara Kettner.** Diese Bilder wurden von der Autorin vor kurzem im Nachlaß der Familie Erdrich in Deutschland gefunden. Sie waren in Packpapier eingewickelt, das mit "unbekannte Vorfahren" beschriftet war. Die Autorin identifizierte diese Abzüge mit Hilfe einer Fotografie aus dem Besitz von Charles A. Kettner in Texas. Siehe Abschnitt Genealogie, oberes Bild, S. 263. Diese Fotografien scheinen Ausschnittsvergrößerungen aus dem Originalnegativ zu sein, von dem auch der Abzug auf S. 263 gemacht wurde. In den Briefen, die Franz an seine Eltern geschrieben hat, bittet er sie verschiedentlich um eine Fotografie seiner Eltern, wobei er besonders darauf hinweist, wie wichtig es für seine Kinder zu wissen sei, wie ihre Großeltern aussehen. Jedoch kann man den Briefen nicht entnehmnen, wann Franz dieses Foto erhalten hat..

**Fig. 8. Franz Kettner.** This photograph is in the possession of Henrietta Kettner Keener. The date of the photograph is unknown.

**Abb. 8. Franz Kettner.** Foto im Besitz von Henrietta Kettner Keener. Das Datum des Fotos ist unbekannt.

## Einführung

*Die Kettner Briefe* bestehen vor allem aus dem Schriftwechsel zwischen Franz Kettner und seinem Vater Dr. Lambert Kettner in der Zeit von 1850 bis 1875. Franz, der gezwungen war Deutschland zu verlassen, erreichte Galveston am 20. November 1848 mit dem Schiff LOUIS (s. Abb. 2) von Antwerpen kommend mit Destination Gillespie County. Seine Briefe geben Zeugnis aus erster Hand von dem damaligen Leben und den Ereignissen an der texanischen Grenze. Ebenso erfährt man etwas über das Leben in Deutschland zur selben Zeit aus den Briefen von seinem Vater Dr. Franz Lambert Kettner, einem Arzt aus Oberkirch, Baden.

Franz gehörte zu der ersten Welle von deutschen Einwanderern in das texanische Hügelland (s. Abb. 5). Der erste Kettner Brief datiert von August 1850 aus Neu Braunfels, Texas. Der dritte Brief von August 1853 wurde in Castell geschrieben, das an der Südwest-Ecke des Fisher-Miller-Grant liegt und zu der Zeit unbesiedelt war. Spätere Briefe stammen aus Friedrichsburg in Gillespie County und aus Mason County. Im Jahre 1859 zog Franz dann nach Foley's Crossing, in den westlichen Teil von Mason County, nur ein Jahr nachdem Mason County gegründet worden war. Er blieb in Mason County bis zu seinem Tod im Jahre 1907. In den Jahren 1848-1907 hat Franz viel erlebt und konnte manche Veränderungen beobachten, die zu der Besiedlung und Entwicklung in dem Gebiet des texanischen Hügellandes führten. Die Trauerrede, die Rudolf Runge gehalten hat, gibt einen Überblick über viele dieser Ereignisse (siehe unten).

Franz beschreibt die frühe Entwicklung der landwirtschaftlichen Industrie während der Zeit der offenen Grenzen. Er beschreibt zahlreiche Zusammenstöße mit Indianern einschließlich der Suche nach Alice Todd (einer Geschichte, die später in dem Roman *The Searchers* von Alan LeMay dramatisch verarbeitet wurde). Franz berichtet seinem Vater in den Briefen von 1863 und 1865, welche Schwierigkeiten er und die anderen deutschen Einwanderer während des Bürgerkrieges hatten auf-grund ihrer Opposition zur Sklaverei. Franz schreibt über Lynchmorde von Selbstschutzgruppen (Mitgliedern privater Milizen; Vigilanten) und Schießereien im benachbarten Gillespie County und berichtet aus erster Hand über die Rolle der Bürgerwehr zur Wiederherstellung der Ordnung. Viele weitere Ereignisse und Einzelheiten werden in den Briefen dokumentiert.

Beim Lesen von *Die Kettner Briefe* werden einem die Herausforderungen bewußt, die neben den Gefahren und physischen Härte des Lebens an der texanischen Grenze bestanden. Es ist aber vielleicht noch wichtiger, daß wir die Schwierigkeiten einschätzen können, die darin bestanden, von Eltern und Kindern getrennt zu sein, über Monate nichts über wichtige Familienereignisse zu erfahren wie der Geburt von Kindern oder dem Tod von Lieben. Schließlich liest man über kleine Familienkonflikte, wie sie für viele, wenn nicht sogar alle Familien charakteristisch sind. Um die Authentizität zu bewahren, werden diese Punkte nicht fortgelassen. Man sollte daran denken, dass wir uns der Historie zuliebe in persönliche Mitteilungen eingemischt haben und wir hoffen, dass die Betroffenen nach 150 Jahren nichts mehr dagegen haben.

Zwei Dokumente können ohne weiteres als Einführung für *Die Kettner Briefe* dienen. Das erste ist die ausdrucksstarke Trauerrede von Rudolf Runge, einem langjährigen Freund von Franz. Das zweite ist die Ehrung von Dr. Franz Lambert Kettner anläßlich seines Rückzugs aus dem Berufsleben. Sie liefert den Hintergrund seines früheren Berufslebens. Beim Lesen von *Die Kettner Briefe* erhält man auf jeden Fall Einblick in ihr Alltagsleben und ihren Charakter sowie über geschichtliche Ereignisse aus ihrer Sicht. Das Leben an der texanischen Grenze kann dem Leben in Europa während der zweiten Hälfte des 19. Jahrhunderts gegenübergestellt werden.

Abb. 7 und Abb.8 zeigen Fotos der Hauptbriefpartner.

Nachruf, gehalten von R. Runge anläßlich der Beerdigung
von Francis Kettner am 9. September 1907

Liebe Freunde:

Wieder sind wir zur Ruhestätte der Toten gegangen, um in ihre heiligen Grenzen die Überreste eines der Besten zu legen. Auf seinen Wunsch richte ich ein paar Worte an Euch, um Euch einen kurzen Abriß einiger der wichtigsten Ereignisse seines Lebens zu geben, nicht aber um eine Lobrede auf ihn zu halten; denn dieses wird weit deutlicher durch ein langes und nobles Leben gesagt, als es Worte ausdrücken können. Er war ein Mann, dem "es gut zu machen" Religion war. Ein Mann, der Dank seiner vielen echten Qualitäten und seines noblen Charakters seit der frühen Besiedlung dieses Landes einen Vorzugsplatz in den Herzen der Leute eingenommen hat. Er kam hierher, als Mason County eine Wildnis war, heimgesucht von feindlichen Indianern. Als die wenigen weißen Siedler alle miteinander vertraut waren, lernten alle schnell, ihn zu respektieren und zu lieben. Francis Kettner war ein Mann von unbeugsamem Mut, bedingungslos ehrenhaft und gewissenhaft, entschieden in seinen Ansichten, nachsichtig anderen gegenüber, der Gastfreundschaft verpflichtet. In den gefährlichen frühen Tagen, als nur die Besten gut genug waren, wurde er häufig durch die Bürgerschaft seines Landes berufen, um das Amt eines Sheriffs auszufüllen und andere verantwortliche Positionen. Und die effiziente und energische Art und Weise, in der er seinen gewagten und schwierigen Pflichten unter widrigsten Bedingungen nachkam, gereichte ihm immer zur Ehre und war seinen Wählern von unsagbarem Nutzen. Weder blieb sein guter Name und Ruhm auf die Grenzen von Mason County beschränkt, noch auf diesen Staat, noch tatsächlich auf diesen Kontinent.

Unser geliebter Verstorbener wurde vor fast 81 Jahren im Großherzogtum Baden geboren, in Deutschland, am 12. Oktober 1826, ein Datum, das mit dem Geburtstag des Herrschers seines Geburtsstaates übereinstimmt, des ehrwürdigen Großherzogs von Baden.

Unser verstorbener Freund erhielt eine sorgfältige Erziehung in den berühmten Lehranstalten seines Vaterlandes. Aber bevor seine Erziehung abgeschlossen war, schloss er sich 1848 der revolutionären Partei an, die als Ziel hatte, das Joch kleinerer oder größerer Tyrannen abzuwerfen und die Vereinigung dessen, was heute das deutsche Reich ist. Dies Gebiet war damals in über 34 separate und theoretisch unabhängige Herrschaftsgebiete geteilt; die Einwohner der kleineren mußten sich nicht nur der Willkür ihrer eigenen Herrscher unterwerfen, sondern auch der Tyrannei der Mächtigeren dieser Länder, während keines von ihnen stark genug war, sich allein gegen irgendeine der großen Mächte Europas verteidigen zu können. Einige dieser Revolutionäre hatten sehr fortschrittliche Ideen, den Traum einer "Deutschen Republik". Einerseits war das vereinigte Deutschland um so konservativer, andererseits stark genug, um sich gegen jeden ihrer Nachbarn zu verteidigen, mit einem Herrscher, dessen Macht durch eine Konstitution begrenzt sein sollte. Dies wurde achtsam gefordert oder erhofft – eine Hoffnung, die dann als Ergebnis des deutsch-französischen Krieges 23 Jahre später realisiert war. "Einheit und Freiheit" war der Slogan der Revolutionäre von '48, unter dem sie geführt von Franz Sigel in die Schlacht zogen. Jenem Franz Sigel, der später ein berühmter General der US Armee wurde. Und unser dahingegangener Freund riskierte all das Seine in diesem Kampf für die unterdrückten Menschen gegen Potentaten und Tyrannen. Die revolutionäre Bewegung wurde zerschlagen durch die Kräfte der hochdisziplinierten Armeen der Fürsten, und um Verfolgung zu entgehen war unser Freund gezwungen, zusammen mit vielen der Besten seiner Nation von seinem Heimatland Abschied zu nehmen und suchte im Jahre 1848 ein neues Heim in dem neuen Staat von Texas. Er begab sich sofort an die Arbeit mit großem Willen, aber nicht vertraut mit den Bedingungen und der Arbeitsweise dieses Landes, dauerte es Jahre bevor er diesbezüglich Kompetenz erlangte. Im ersten Jahr seines Aufenthaltes in Texas versuchte er in einer Biegung des Guadalupe in Comal County eine Farm zu betreiben. Diese Biegung wird wegen ihrer speziellen Form "Demijohn Bend" genannt. Im folgenden Jahr finden wir ihn in Captain Connor's Kompanie von Texas Rangern im Rio Grande Gebiet, wo er den Staat gegen die Invasion feindlicher Indianer und Mexikaner beschützte. Diese Kompanie wurde später in den Dienst der Vereinigten Staaten gerufen, woraus der Verstorbene während der letzten paar Jahre seines Lebens eine kleine Pension erhalten hat für seinen Dienst in den Unternehmungen jener Kompanie. Von den gut 80 jungen Männern, die diese Kompanie vor 57 Jahren bildeten – überlebten, soweit bekannt ist, nur 2 unseren dahingegangenen Freund, nämlich Gustav Schmeltzer aus San Antonio und Charles C. Schriener aus Kerrville. Dieser Lebensabschnitt war voller Abenteuer und Gefahren und unser Freund würde darüber noch äußerst interessant berichten. Ich bedauere, daß die begrenzte Zeit es mir nicht erlaubt, über einige davon zu berichten. Robert Brodemann aus Neu Braunfels, Mr. Krievitz aus Castell und Captain Dosch aus San Antonio, den viele von Ihnen kennen, waren mit Kettner in diesem Dienst. Sie alle gingen ihm im Tode voran. Nach Beendigung dieses Dienstes lebte Mr. Kettner für kurze Zeit mit seinem Freund Krievitz in Castell, darauf zog er weiter nach Gillespie County, wo er zum Sheriff gewählt wurde, einen der besten Sheriffs abgebend, den das County jemals hatte. Immer noch Gillespie County zu seiner Heimat machend, beschäftigte er sich im Farm- und im Fracht-Geschäft. Das Frachtgeschäft wurde damals mit Hilfe großer Ochsengespanne und deren Führer betrieben, und eine einzige Fahrt zur Küste oder zu einem der Militärposten weit draußen an der Grenze nahm oft Monate in Anspruch. Wenn auch solche Reisen über die langen und einsamen Routen nicht ohne jeden Reiz für jene waren, die sich in Einsamkeit in der Natur zu ergehen liebten und für einige romantische Jünglinge, so waren sie doch im frühen Grenzleben in Wirklichkeit mit Härte und Gefahren verbunden. Da unser Freund zu jener Zeit bereits beträchtliches von dem Grenzleben gesehen hatte, war er seinen Kameraden sehr zu Diensten, die neu oder "grün" an der Grenze waren.

Am 3. September 1857 wurde er mit Katherine Keller in Fredericksburg vermählt. Zwei Jahre später zog er mit seiner jungen Frau und einem Kind nach Mason County, wo er sich am Südufer des Llano River niederließ, auf jenem Platz, der sich jetzt im Besitz von Adolph Keller befindet und der heute als Foley Crossing bekannt ist. Hier erlitten er und seine Familie unsägliche Entbehrungen und Gefahren. Während des Bürgerkrieges waren die Bedingungen außerordentlich schlecht. Noch Jahre später waren die Indianer sehr schlimm, und jener Ort schien auf ihrem Pfad oder ihrer Route zu liegen, die sie gewöhnlich benutzten, wenn sie auf ihre Raubzüge in das weiße Siedlungsgebiet zogen. Schließlich wurde es so schlimm, daß es nicht weit von Selbstmord entfernt gewesen wäre, noch länger zu versuchen, an jenem Ort zu bleiben. 1875,[8] während Mr. Kettner sich bei der Arbeit auf dem Feld befand, fiel eine Horde Indianer über die Ranch her und versuchte, die Reitpferde wegzutreiben, die innerhalb von 75 yards von dem Hause grasten. Der Älteste, Louis, jenerzeit ein Bursche von 13, griff sie tapfer an, und beschoß sie mit seinem Sechsschüsser, während Mrs. Kettner ihrem Ehemann einen Spencer Karabiner auf das Feld brachte. Als Mr. Kettner mit dem Gewehr in der Hand auf der Szene erschien, gaben die Indianer den Kampf auf, indem sie mit größter Geschwindigkeit in Richtung Berge flüchteten. Mr. Kettner beschoß sie während ihrer Flucht. Dies geschah, während eine Kompanie von Rangern innerhalb von 2 Meilen von

---

[8] Runge irrt hinsichtlich des Datums. Zu diesem Vorfall kam es im Jahre 1871.

der Ranch stationiert war. Kurz darauf wurde auch noch dieser vorgesehene Schutz abgezogen. Darauf zog die Familie an jenen Ort, der damals als McSwane[9] Platz bekannt war, sechs Meilen unterhalb der Stadt am Commanche Creek, wo sie für 6 Jahre lebten, bis sie in unsere Stadt zogen, wo Mr. & Mrs. Kettner seitdem ansässig waren.

Während dieser Residenz in Mason hatte der Verstorbene viele wichtige Positionen inne. In frühen Tagen war er Sheriff , später war er Steuereinnehmer, in den frühen 70ern hatte er die damals sehr wichtige Position des Viehinspektors inne und in jener Eigenschaft tat er wahrscheinlich mehr als jeder Andere, damit jedermann sein Recht bekam. Später wurde er zum "County Commissioner" gewählt und häufig wiedergewählt – solange wie er überzeugt werden konnte, dieses Amt anzunehmen. Und seinen Fähigkeiten und dem vertrauenswürdigen Wahrnehmen der Pflichten jenes Amtes ist es weitgehend zu verdanken, daß Mason County vor dem Bankrott gerettet wurde und zahlungsfähig blieb.

Mr. und Mrs. Kettner wurden 5 Kinder geboren: die Söhne Louis, Will und Charles, und die Töchter Ida und Alice, heute Mrs. August Keller und Mrs. John Gamel, die ihn alle überlebten und jetzt an seinem Grabe stehen; auch 15 Enkel haben ihn überlebt.

Der Verstorbene sah in seinem Leben 2 glückliche Ereignisse, die nur selten in der kurzen Zeitspanne eines Menschenlebens vorkommen. Das eine ist die Geburt eines Urenkels, das andere war der 50. Hochzeitstag, die Goldene Hochzeit. Es ist betrüblich zu wissen, daß das letztgenannte dieser zwei Ereignisse zum Beginn vom Ende bestimmt war. Denn während der Tag klar und schön begann, kurz vor Mittag, während der Tisch gedeckt wurde und die glücklichen Kinder und Enkel in Vorfreude auf eine höchst erfreuliche Zeit sich um die elterliche Tafel versammelten, erlitt der geliebte Gatte, der Vater und Großvater einen Schlaganfall, dem er erlag, und der sein Leben 8 Tage später beendete, um 4 Uhr gestern, genau eine Woche nachdem wir die Überreste seines Kameraden und lebenslangen Freundes Major James Hunter zur Ruhe betteten.

Während der Verstorbene in seinem langen Leben durch Geschäftigkeit und ökonomisches Geschick ein stattliches Vermögen ansammelte, war es niemals sein Lebensziel Reichtümer anzusammeln. Er war einer von der alten Schule der Idealisten, jetzt nahezu ausgestorben, welche ihr Glück im Aufbau der Menschheit sahen, deren Taten durch folgendes Prinzip bestimmt wurden. "Andere zu behandeln, wie er wünschte, daß sie ihn behandeln würden." Die meisten von Euch haben ihn den größeren Teil Eures Lebens gekannt – ich spreche auch für mich selber, ich ergriff seine Hand zum erstenmal vor über einem halben Jahrhundert. Ihr alle erinnert

---

[9] "McSwane" ist ein Druckfehler. Es sollte "McSween" heißen.

seine guten und noblen Taten. Niemand kann auf irgend etwas Falsches deuten, daß er jemals begangen hätte. Ihr Männer und Frauen einer jüngeren Generation, die ihr ihn im Leben gekannt habt, immer wenn ihr auf eine Gelegenheit trefft, wo ihr nicht wißt, ob es richtig ist oder nicht, ein bestimmtes Ding zu tun, stellt euch diese Frage: Was würde er unter ähnlichen Umständen getan haben? "Tue, was er getan haben würde, und ein gutes Gewissen wird Deine Belohnung sein." Während wir seine Überreste in das Grab übergeben, umgeben von jenen vielen Freunden, die zuvor gegangen sind, laß sein Leben unser Leitstern sein.

Ehrung für Dr. Franz Lambert Kettner wegen Rückzug aus dem Berufsleben, Ruhesetzung[10]
Zum 20. Januar 1873

Das Oberkirchener Amtsblatt hält es für seine Pflicht, die Ereignisse zu besprechen, die es besonders angehen, und es erfüllt diese Pflicht mit um so größerer Freude, wenn es dabei gilt dem Verdienste seine Krone zu reichen.

Am 20. Januar des Jahres hat der Großh. Assistenzarzt Kettner mit zurückgelegtem achtzigsten Lebensjahr seine Ruhesetzung erbeten, und dieselbe ist ihm mit der Anerkennung seiner langjährigen und treu geleisteten Dienste zu Teil geworden. Ein Zeitraum von 47 Jahren, denn so lange ist er hier angestellt, ist ein starkes Band von Welt und Artsgeschichte und die Beobachtung hat Gelegenheit gehabt, ihr Urteil festzustellen. Ehrenhaftes häusliches und öffentliches Leben, treue Pflichterfüllung im amtlichen und außeramtlichen Kreise, strenge Gewissenhaftigkeit und biedere Offenheit in Rede und Tat, das sind die Zierden seines Wandels, und wenn auch seine Anspruchslosigkeit es ablehnte, ein geräuschvolles Anerkenntnis seiner Amtsgenossen und Mitbürger anzunehmen, so ist es doch ein Bedürfnis seiner Umgebung, dieses Anerkenntnis öffentlich auszusprechen. Zweimal im Feldzuge 1813 und 1815 mit den badischen Truppen vor Straßburg als Chirurg gelegen, haben nun die Erfüllung der damaligen Wünsche unter seinen Augen sich verwirklichen gesehen. Die Feldienstauszeichnung und der Zähringer Löwenorden zieren seine Brust und die Verehrung eines weiten Familienkreises erheitert seinen Lebensabend. Möge es uns noch lange vergönnt sein, uns mit ihm, dem erhebenden Beispiele eines gut geführten Lebens, eines heiteren Verkehrs zu erfreuen.

[10] Handschriftliche Vorlage für Transcription und Übersetzung befindet sich bei Patsy Kothmann Ziriax, Mason, Texas.

Schließlich haben wir noch weitere Einblicke in die Person Franz Kettner anläßlich einer kurzen Unterhaltung mit Emelia Winjum erhalten. Sie ist eine Urenkelin von Franz und berichtete über folgendes Erlebnis, das ihre Mutter Estella Kettner Grosenbacher ihr erzählt habe.

> Ich habe mich an einige Dinge erinnert, die meine Mutter mir über Franz Kettner erzählt hat. Sie war 9 Jahre alt, als ihre Großeltern Franz und Catherine Kettner ihren 50. Hochzeitstag gefeiert haben. Sie erinnerte sich an die geplante Festlichkeit und auch daran, wie dieser feierliche Augenblick sich aufgrund seines Schlaganfalls in Kummer verwandelte.
>
> Mein Mann Ken schreitet durch die Räume, wenn er nachdenkt. Meine Mutter sagte, dass er sie an ihren Großvater Kettner erinnere, der auch immer durch die Gegend streifte um nachzudenken. Einmal, als sie mit anderen Kindern vor ihrem Haus spielte, lief er rechts an ihnen vorbei. Er war so in seine Gedanken vertieft, dass er sie nicht bemerkte. Ich fragte sie, was die Kinder gemacht hätten. Sie lachte und sagt, dass die Kinder hinter ihm hergegangen seien wie hinter dem Rattenfänger. Als er die Kinder bemerkte, brach er in Lachen aus und sagte, er habe sie nicht gesehen. Sie sagte, dass die Kinder ihn geliebt hätten. Ich dachte mir, diese kleine Anekdote über Franz' Persönlichkeit könne den Leser erfreuen.

# Letter / Brief 1

### Letter 1 (August 27, 1850) from Franz Kettner in Comal County,[11] Texas to his Parents in Oberkirch, Baden

Dear Parents,

I have both of your letters from May 20 and 30 and am pleased with their contents. At the same time I received the discussed money order from New York which I was able to exchange for money in New Braunfels.

In order to give you again an accurate overview of my business prospects here, I must say that a person doesn't have the possibility of becoming rich here immediately. One can, however, improve his situation each year with the result of a secure livelihood after several years. Every year one can develop more acreage under cultivation. The cattle, cows, swine, and chickens breed more. One breeds horses. In this manner one develops a secure livelihood.

The everyday needs here are so few. For example, a man wears only cotton pants here which he can buy ready-made for one dollar. Likewise, a pair of shoes costs one dollar, colored shirts cost 75 cents each. Jackets are seldom worn here. People laugh at finery here because they are all so sensible that they only look for practicality. However, that's why it suits me so well.

The setting in which our land is located is one of the finest. Surrounded by two large hills, we lie in a valley, elevated from the Guadalupe River by steep banks. There stand our buildings. Near the water lies our cultivated land and the garden which was particularly fine this year. We grew all the German vegetables.

Across from us on the other side of the river (which is only half the size of the Neckar) are a saw mill, flour mill, shingle machine, a cotton gin, and a large boat (ferry) to transport wagons across the river. All these have made our land 50% more valuable.

---

[11] Franz Kettner arrived in Galveston on November 20, 1848, on the ship LOUIS from Antwerp with Gillespie County as a destination. It is not known if he came directly to New Braunfels from Galveston. The exact location of Franz's farm on the Guadalupe River is uncertain. One can assume that it is in the vicinity of New Braunfels in Comal Co. The farm mentioned in this letter is different from the farm at the Demijohn Bend on the Guadalupe River described in Letter 2.

I also own a small boat which is very useful to me for fishing or hunting alligators.

The temperature between the months of July and September often rises to 88 degrees in the shade. So far it hasn't gone higher. In the other months it can be so varied that one day it is extremely hot and the next day, when the wind comes from the north, it is very cold. Concerning fruit varieties, here we have wild plums, various sorts of nuts, wild grapes, mulberries, and persimmons (when cooked, these taste like cooked prunes).

The forests here are quite beautiful, especially the oak forests.

For the past few months the Indians have made themselves noticed through stealing and murder so that an Indian war is probable. When an Indian is seen, he is shot down like a wild (game) animal. They are said to be gathering together again up in the hills to plan some sort of attack against the soldiers. There are approximately 20,000 Indians still in Texas from the different tribes. They are almost all mounted which is what makes their pursuit so exceedingly difficult. Not long ago near San Antonio there occurred a small skirmish between the Texas Rangers (volunteers) and the Indians (who left 5 dead on the field in addition to a large number of stolen horses).

The Texas Rangers are exceedingly well-armed. They all have excellent American rifles which shoot very small bullets. In addition, there are pistols which can shoot seven shots by means of one cylinder that holds the cartridges.[12] They shoot accurately up to 60 paces. The volunteers are also well-mounted.

Our normal food this summer consists of: Mornings – potatoes, bread, butter and fried beef or venison. (A Texan normally eats meat for breakfast as well.) Noontime – either sour milk or buttermilk, vegetables (for example, beans, peas, spinach, kohlrabi, cabbage, cucumbers, red (?); beef, fried or boiled, or some catch from hunting such as rabbit, deer, turtle or fish. The very best food which I have eaten is turtle soup or bear ham.

We built a double log cabin this summer. On one side is the fireplace with a passage to a stable for the horses (only for the winter.) The other part is for a chicken house. All was built by our own hands.

This winter we intend to bring 6 more acres into cultivation. Then we'll have 10 acres. Except for two acres which we need for our own use, the land produces 30 bushels of grain per acre. That is the minimum which an acre grows. Figuring at the lowest price of one half dollar per bushel, this brings 120 dollars, which approximates 280 florins.[13]

We have very few purchased supplies other than coffee, salt, sugar, and the necessary clothing. Also we're expecting 6 new milk cows next spring. One of them is a young cow which I have raised from a calf that I won't sell at any price. Every

---

[12] Franz probably was mistaken. At the time, there were no 7 cartridge pistols, only 5 or 6 cartridge.

[13] The florin was the former currency from Florence, Italy, abbreviated fl. This abbreviation was transferred to the Dutch gulden, which was the currency for the Grand-Duchy of Baden.

summer we can slaughter a beef and in winter as many pigs as we need. And we can still sell a good many since we presently already own 20 pigs. They come each evening to the house and spend the night in a pen especially built for them. They receive some grain there so that they will come home regularly each evening.

In winter our meals consists mainly of fried pork, sweet potatoes, coffee, (in evenings) tea.

Lambrecht, with his family, has moved into his newly built log cabin across from us so close that we can wave to one another.

I have three large dogs. They're very good watchdogs and at night keep everyone more than 15 minutes away from the house. Our cattle, which sleep at night near the house, are well-protected from wolves and panthers by the dogs.

July 4$^{th}$, the day the United States became independent from England, is the biggest holiday here. It is splendidly celebrated in all of Texas, especially in Braunfels, where I had gone. On the morning of the 4$^{th}$, the guard marched with music and flags to a designated open place in the forest. There was a large meal along with games and singing. Many women were also present. We spent our time there until evening. Then we rode to the meeting place of the singing club who also camped out in the open.

Tents had been set up around a circle and we danced there almost the entire night. The remainder of the night we slept outside in the open air. That is easy to do here since everyone carries a blanket (rolled behind the saddle) on his horse and the nights are not cold. In the morning we rode home. The city had wonderfully prepared and invited almost all the farmers in the entire area.

The majority of the population in Braunfels belongs to the educated classes. They include all sorts of craftsmen, brewers, pharmacists, two churches, two pastors, a large number of stores, four German doctors with families, cigarette factories, candy factories, and several flour and saw mills. The city is also laid out in squares beautifully like Mannheim. And you can find gardens in Braunfels as lovely as anywhere in Germany.

The population now reaches between 3,000 to 4,000 people. The number of German settlers will soon equal the number of Americans.

Many awful bureaucrats have arrived here recently. They find themselves better off behind a plow than with a pen. Their bellyaching is over and their heads are not dizzy in the morning. In short, they are free from all repression and laugh about the old world customs and methods. Here they do not need to compliment or serve anyone and do not have to bow down to anyone. We are a long way away from the highly touted civilization of Europe. Here we always have dealings with reasonable and unaffected people.

I have not been sick at all this summer, and I think that I am used to this climate now. I speak English fluently.

The legislative laws here are outstanding. Every year the civil servants are elected. Every half year there is a so-called jury court, which is presided over by a head judge elected by the citizens to serve three years. The current one is my closest neighbor who is also a farmer. The accused chooses 6 men and the plaintiff also 6. These men are sworn in and comprise the jury. With every trial, different men are chosen to be the jury.

I am curious how long it will still take until the Germans tell their so-called idols to go to hell. When one speaks to an American about politics, he can scarcely think how it is possible that a people keep a king and allow themselves to be ruled against their will.

North America is now the most powerful country on earth, on the sea as well as on land. American ships are recognized as the best. The Americans are also very brave, and in addition, cool-headed.

I would like to know all the news from Oberkirch in your next letter. All the other news I can get out of the newspaper. How is Elise and how does she like being married? I'm not at all surprised with the news about ...., I have considered him to be a big windbag for a long time.

I want to let you know that you do not need to address my letters to my former house. I am well-known to the postmaster. When he gets the chance, he tells me if there are letters for me when I have not been to Braunfels for a long time.

Tell Emil hello for me and tell him that I invite him to go on a bear hunt, which he certainly would like to do. What is the Schauenburg family[14] doing these days? I am also interested in the family of refugees and would like to know how they are doing.

In general, tell all of my friends hello for me. If one or the other of them has a desire to immigrate to Texas, he can learn my whereabouts in Seguin or Braunfels. Then I could be very helpful to him. Someone familiar with the circumstances in the country can buy things much cheaper and the newcomer can save a lot of money.

Give August and Elise my regards many times and I remain your son Franz Kettner.

August 27, 1850

Recently I received a letter from a former childhood friend from Mannheim who is presently in Texas. I have not seen him yet. His name is Herrmann Hengenius von Mueller.

Wegner is still out in the country with his wife where he has rented a farm. I think he will soon come here, however.

Texas indeed had a small fight with New Mexico on account of Santa Fe which probably could lead to hostilities. The New Mexicans are cowardly. That means that peace can be reached by means of a few thousand men who will march here shortly.

My address is as written down.

Again I send you heartfelt greetings. Franz Kettner

---

[14] Franz is referring to the family of Baron Emil von Schauenburg.

**Fig. 9. Photograph of New Braunfels in mid 1850s.** This photograph was obtained through the courtesy of the Sophienburg Museum & Archive, New Braunfels, Texas.

**Abb. 9. Foto von Neu Braunfels Mitte der 1850er Jahre.** Dies Foto wurde großzügigerweise durch das Sophienburg Museum & Archive, Neu Braunfels, Texas zur Verfügung gestellt.

**Fig. 10. Etching of New Braunfels,Texas about 1850.** Original steel-engraving is in the possession of Ilse Wurster and is from Kunstanstalt des Bibliographischen Instituts, Hildburghausen.

**Abb. 10. Neu Braunfels in Texas.** Kunstanstalt des Bibliographischen Instituts, Hildburghausen. Original Stahlstich um 1850. Privatbesitz Ilse Wurster.

**Fig. 11. Oberkirch**. Etching by Weber del Nilson 1823. This was taken from Hans-Martin Pillin, *Oberkirch, Die Geschichte der Stadt von den Anfängen bis zum Jahre 1803,* Volume I (Oberkirch: Die Stadt Oberkirch, 1976), page 17. Volume I in this series was published in 1976 to commemorate the 650th anniversary of the founding of the township of Oberkirch.

**Abb. 11. Oberkirch.** Radierung von Weber del Nilson 1823. Entnommen Hans-Martin Pillin, *Oberkirch, Die Geschichte der Stadt von den Anfängen bis zum Jahre 1803,* Band I (Oberkirch: Die Stadt Oberkirch, 1976), S. 17. Band I dieser Serie wurde 1976 veröffentlicht anläßlich des 650. Jahrestages der Verleihung der Stadtrechte an das Gemeinwesen Oberkirch.

**Oberkirch**
von Butschbach aus gesehen im Jahre 1836.

**Blick von der Ruine Schauenburg bei Oberkirch ins Rheintal**
Im Hintergrund die Vogesen und das Straßburger Münster.

**Fig. 12. Northeastern View of Oberkirch in the Year 1836 (top etching) and the Southwestern View from the Ruine Schauenburg (Castle) near Oberkirch into the Rhein Valley( bottom etching).** [*Festschrift zum 600=jährigen Jubiläum der Stadtgemeinde Oberkirch.* (Oberkirch: Die Stadt Oberkirch, 1926), 69] Also see Letter 25, Fig. 44.

**Abb. 12. Oberkirch von Butschbach aus gesehen im Jahre 1836 (oberes Bild) und Blick von der Ruine Schauenburg bei Oberkirch ins Rheintal (unteres Bild).** *Festschrift zum 600=jährigen Jubiläum der Stadtgemeinde Oberkirch.* Herausgegeben von der Stadt Oberkirch 1926. Seite 69. Siehe auch Brief 25, Abb. 44.

## Brief 1 (27. August 1850) von Franz Kettner aus Comal County/Texas an seine Eltern in Oberkirch/Baden

Liebe Eltern!

Ihre beiden Briefe vom 20. und 30. Mai 1850 habe ich richtig erhalten und freue mich über deren Inhalt. Zu gleicher Zeit erhielt ich von New York aus den besagten Wechsel, den ich in Neu Braunfels[15] auch an Geldeswert umsetzen konnte.

Um Ihnen noch einmal genaue Übersicht geben zu können über den Erwerbszweig hier, so muß ich Ihnen sagen, daß man keine Aussicht hat auf einmal reich zu werden. Allein man kann doch mit jedem Jahre weiter vorankommen, so daß man sich in einigen Jahren eine sichere Existenz gegründet hat. Mit jedem Jahre bringt man einige Acre[16] mehr in Kultur. Das Vieh, Kühe, Schweine, Hühner vermehren sich. Man zieht Pferde. So hat man ein ganz sicheres Auskommen.

Die Bedürfnisse sind hier so gering. Man trägt hier z.B. nur baumwollene Hosen, die man fertig für 1 Dollar das Stück kauft. Ebenso 1 Paar Schuhe für 1 Dollar, farbige baumwollene Hemden 75 ct. Röcke werden hier wenig getragen. Über Luxus lacht man hier, denn die Menschen sind hier alle so vernünftig, daß sie nur auf Zweckmäßigkeit sehen. Aber deshalb gefällt es mir so gut.

Die Lage, wo unser Land liegt, ist eine der reizendsten. Umgeben von zwei großen Hügeln liegen wir in einem Tale, welches sich gegen die Guadalupe[17] zu sehr steilen Ufern erhebt. Dort stehen unsere Gebäude. Am Wasser liegt unser in Kultur gegebenes Land nebst Garten, welcher dieses Jahr besonders schön war. Wir zogen alle deutschen Gemüse.

Vis à vis von uns über dem Fluß, welcher halb so groß wie der Neckar ist, sind jetzt eine Sägemühle, Mehlmühle, Schindelmaschine und Baumwoll-Reinigungsmaschine errichtet worden, mit einem großen Boote, um Wagen überzusetzen. Dadurch hat unser Land um die Hälfte an Wert gewonnen.

Ein kleines Boot besitze ich selbst, welches mir beim Fischfang und der Alligatorjagd sehr dienlich ist.

Die Temperatur ist im Monat Juli bis September sehr oft im Schatten bis zu 31 Grad Celsius gestiegen. Höher noch nicht. In den übrigen Monaten ist sie so verschieden, daß wir es einen Tag sehr heiß, den anderen Tag sehr kalt haben, wenn der Nordwind kommt. Was die Obstarten betrifft, so gibt es hier wilde Pflaumen,

---

[15] Neu Braunfels wurde am 21. März 1845 (Karfreitag) von einer Gruppe deutscher Siedler, dem "Verein zum Schutze deutscher Einwanderer in Texas" auch "Adelsverein" genannt, unter Führung von Friedrich Wilhelm Carl Ludwig Georg Alfred Alexander, Prinz von Solms, Lehnsherr von Braunfels, Grafenstein, Münzenberg, Wildenfels, und Sonnenwalde gegründet an der Mündung des Comal river in den Guadalupe river. Quelle: *Handbook of Texas Online,* unter dem Stichwort "Adelsverein," http:/www.tsha.utexas.edu/handbook/online/articles/AeA/ufa1.html (Zugriff am 30. Juli 2006).

[16] 1 Acre = 4046,8 $m^2$

[17] Guadalupe. Fluß in Texas, der im westlichen Kerr County entspringt und kurz vor dem Golf von Mexiko in den San Antonio Fluß mündet.

verschiedene Arten Nüsse, wilde Trauben, Maulbeeren, Persimonen,[18] welches Obst gekocht gerade wie gekochte Zwetschgen ist. Waldungen gibt es sehr schöne, besonders Eichwaldungen. Die Indianer haben sich seit einigen Monaten wieder bemerkbar gemacht durch Morden und Stehlen, so daß ein Indianerkrieg in Aussicht steht. Wo sich einer sehen läßt, wird er wie ein Stück Wild zusammengeschossen. Sie sollen sich aber in den Gebirgen weiter oben im Land zusammengezogen haben, um etwas Entscheidendes gegen die Soldaten zu unternehmen. Es befinden sich in Texas ungefähr noch 20.000 Indianer von den verschiedensten Stämmen. Diese sind sämtlich bis auf einige Mann beritten, weshalb ihre Verfolgung so ungeheuer schwierig ist. Bei San Antonio fand letzthin ein kleines Treffen statt zwischen Texas Rangern (Freiwilligen) und den Indianern, wobei letztere 5 Tote auf dem Platze ließen, nebst einer Menge gestohlener Pferde.

Die Bewaffnung der Texaner Freiwilligen ist aber auch ausgezeichnet. Sie haben alle ausgezeichnete amerikanische Büchsen, welche ganz kleine Kugeln schießen. Ferner eine Pistole,[19] welche siebenmal abgeschossen werden kann mittels eines Zylinders, welcher die Patronen enthält. Sie trägt sicher auf 60 Schritte. Auch sind alle Freiwilligen sehr gut beritten.

Unsere Kost hat diesen Sommer bestanden aus: Morgens Kartoffeln, Brot, Butter und gebratenes Ochsenfleisch oder Hirschbraten. (Der Texaner ißt nämlich morgens ebenfalls Fleisch). Mittags entweder dicke Milch oder Buttermilch, Gemüse, z.B. Bohnen, Erbsen, Spinat, Kohlrabi, Weißkraut, Gurken, Rot...?, Ochsenfleisch gebraten oder gekocht, oder sonst etwas auf der Jagd Erbeutetes, wie Hasen-, Hirsch-, Schildkröten- oder Fischfleisch. Das ausgezeichnetste, was ich gegessen habe, ist Schildkrötensuppe oder Bärenschinken.

Gebaut haben wir diesen Sommer ein doppeltes Blockhaus, die fain? Seite für den Kamin, mit Durchgang zu einem Stall für die Pferde (nur für den Winter). Den anderen Teil für ein Hühnerhaus. Alles mit eigener Hand.

Diesen Winter beabsichtigen wir 6 Acre mehr in Kultur zu bringen. Dann haben wir 10 Acre. Nach Abzug von zwei Acre, welche wir für unseren eigenen Bedarf nötig haben, tragen diese jährlich 30 Büschel Korn den Acre. Das ist das wenigste was ein Acre trägt. Den Büschel zu dem niedrigsten Preise à ½ Dollars berechnet ergibt 120 Doll. entspricht fl[20] 280.

Auslagen haben wir sehr wenige, z.B. Kaffee, Salz, Zucker und die nötigen Kleidungsstücke. Auch bekommen wir nächstes Frühjahr 6 frische Melkkühe. Davon ist mir eine junge Kuh, welche ich als Kalb aufgezogen habe, um keinen Preis feil. Jeden Sommer können wir einen Ochsen schlachten und im Winter Schweine, so

---

[18] Englisch "persimmon" = Dattelpflaume.

[19] Das Wort Pistole wurde seinerzeit im Englischen wie im Deutschen für alle kurzläufigen Handfeuerwaffen benutzt. Vergleiche den Aufdruck einer Zündhütchenschachtel aus dem Jahre 1851 "COLT'S PATENT REVOLVING BELT PISTOL". Damals gab es allerdings keine 7-schüssigen Revolver, nur 5-schüssige und 6-schüssige.

[20] Die Abkürzung fl steht für Florin, die vormalige Währung aus Florenz, Italien. Die Abkürzung wurde auf holländische Gulden übertragen, die damalige Währung im Großherzogstum Baden.

viel wir bedürfen. Und wir können noch eine hübsche Menge verkaufen, da wir gegenwärtig schon 20 Stück besitzen. Diese kommen jeden Abend nach Hause und bringen die Nacht in der für sie bestimmten Fenz zu. Dort erhalten sie etwas Korn, damit sie jeden Abend regelmäßig nach Hause kommen.

Im Winter besteht unsere Nahrung hauptsächlich aus Schweinefleisch (gebratenes), süßen Kartoffeln, Kaffee, abends Tee.

Lambrecht ist mit seiner Familie in sein neugebautes Blockhaus uns vis à vis eingezogen, so daß wir einander zuwinken können.

Hunde habe ich 3 große Stück. Diese sind sehr wachsam und lassen bei Nacht auf eine 1/4 Stunde Wegs nichts ans Haus. Unsere Kühe und Ochsen, welche in der Nähe von unserem Hause ihren Schlummer halten, sind hier vor Wölfen und Panther durch die Wachsamkeit der Hunde gesichert.

Als Tag der Befreiung der Vereinigten Staaten von England ist der 4. Juli der größte Feiertag. Er wurde in ganz Texas auf das glänzendste gefeiert und besonders in Braunfels, wo ich zugegen war. Nämlich morgens zog der Schützenverein mit Fahnen und Musik zu dem dazu bestimmten Platz im Gehölz. Dort wurde ein Essen gegeben, abwechselnd gab es Gesang und Spiele, sehr viele Damen waren zugegen. Dort verweilten wir bis zum Abend.Dann ritten wir in das Lokal des Gesangvereins, welcher ebenfalls im Freien campierte. Zelte waren ringsum aufgeschlagen, wo wir beinahe die ganze Nacht tanzten. Die übrige Zeit der Nacht haben wir Auswärtigen im Freien geschlafen, was hier ein Leichtes ist, da jeder seinen Teppich immer auf dem Pferd ...trägt und die Nächte nicht kalt sind. Den anderen Morgen ritten wir nach Hause. Alles gab die Stadt zum Besten und es waren sämtliche Farmer in der ganzen Nachbarschaft dazu eingeladen.

Was die Bevölkerung von Braunfels betrifft, so gehört diese meistens dem gebildeten Stande an. Es befinden sich daselbst alle nur möglichen Handwerker, Bierbrauereien, Apotheke, zwei Kirchen, zwei Geistliche, Kaufläden in Menge, 4 deutsche Ärzte, mit Familien, Zigarrenfabrik, Schokoladenfabrik, mehrere Mehl- und Sägemühlen. Auch ist die Stadt wie Mannheim sehr schön in Quadraten angelegt. Und man findet in Braunfels Gärten so schön wie irgendwo in Deutschland.

Die Bevölkerung beträgt jetzt zwischen 3.000 bis 4.000. Überhaupt wird die Kopfzahl der Deutschen bald der der Amerikaner gleichstehen.

Sehr viel gräßliche Beamte sind in der letzten Zeit hier eingetroffen, welche sich nun beim Pfluge besser befinden, als bei der Feder. Ihre Unterleibsbeschwerden sind vergangen, sie fühlen sich morgens nicht mehr schwindelig im Kopfe. Kurzum sie sind von allen Übeln befreit und lachen über die alte Welt und deren Mittel und Gebräuche. Hier brauchen sie keine Komplimente und Diener zu machen und mit Kratzfüßen den Leib in eine ..... Position zu bringen. Die gepriesene Zivilisation von Europa bleibe uns ja recht lange fern. Dann haben wir immer mit natürlichen, vernünftigen Menschen Umgang.

Mit Krankheiten habe ich diesen Sommer nichts zu tun, und ich glaube, daß ich nun akklimatisiert bin. Englisch spreche ich schon geläufig.

Die Gesetzgebung hier ist ausgezeichnet. Jedes Jahr werden die Beamten gewählt. Alle halbe Jahr ist sogenanntes Geschworenengericht unter dem Vorsitz eines vom Volke auf 3 Jahre gewählten Oberrichters. (Der jetzige ist mein nächster Nachbar und ebenfalls Farmer). Der Verklagte wählt sich 6 Männer und der Kläger ebenfalls 6. Diese werden beeidigt und bilden die Juri. Also werden bei jeder Klage andere Männer als Geschworene gewählt.

Neugierig bin ich, wie lange es noch dauert, bis die Deutschen ihre sogenannten Götzenbilder zum Teufel jagen. Wenn man mit einem Amerikaner über Politik spricht, so kann sich dieser gar nicht denken, wie es möglich ist, daß ein Volk noch einen König erhalten will und sich wider Willen regieren läßt.

Nordamerika ist nun der mächtigste Staat auf Erden, sowohl zur See wie zu Land. Die amerikanischen Schiffe sind als die besten anerkannt. Der Amerikaner ist auch sehr tapfer und äußerst kaltblütig.

Nun möchte ich im nächsten Briefe alle Neuigkeiten von Oberkirch wissen. Die anderen erfahre ich alle aus der Zeitung. Wie es der Elise geht und wie es ihr im Ehestand behagt. Die Nachricht von dem .... hat mich nicht im mindesten überascht, denn ich halte ihn schon längst für einen schlechten Schwätzer.

Was das frühere Haus anbelangt, wohin Sie meine Briefe adressierten, so diene Ihnen zur Nachricht, daß dies gar nicht notwendig ist. Ich bin mit dem Postmeister sehr gut bekannt, und er läßt mir, wenn ich gerade längere Zeit nicht nach Braunfels komme, bei Gelegenheit sagen, wenn Briefe an mich da sind.

Grüßen Sie mir den Emil und sagen Sie ihm ich lade ihn ein auf eine Bärenjagd, wozu er gewiß Lust hätte. Was macht überhaupt die Familie Schauenburg.[21] Auch nahm ich Anteil an den Familien der Flüchtlinge und möchte wissen, wie es ihnen geht.

Grüßen Sie mir überhaupt alle Bekannten. Und sollte der Eine oder der Andere Lust haben nach Texas auszuwandern, so kann er in Seguin oder Braunfels meinen Aufenthalt erfahren. Wo ich ihm dann behilflich sein werde, da ein mit den Verhältnissen im Land Bekannter alles viel billiger kaufen kann und so dem Unbekannten große Summen ersparen kann.

Grüßen Sie mir August und Elise vielmal und bleibe Ihr Sohn Franz Kettner

Monat August, den 27ten 50

Letzthin bekam ich einen Brief von meinem ehemaligen Jugendfreund aus Mannheim, welcher sich gegenwärtig in Texas befindet. Zu sehen habe ich ihn noch nicht bekommen. Sein Name Herrmann Hengenius von Müller.

Wegner ist mit seiner Frau noch unten im Lande, wo er eine Farm gepachtet hat. Ich denke er wird aber bald heraufkommen.

Texas hat wirklich einen kleinen Streit mit Neu Mexiko wegen Santa Fe, was wahrscheinlich zu einigen Feindseligkeiten führen kann. Die Neu Mexikaner sind

[21] Es handelt sich um die Familie von Freiherr Emil von Schauenburg.

aber lauter Mexikaner und diese sind feig, weshalb es mit einigen tausend Mann, welche nächstens dahin abmarschieren, zur Ruhe gebracht werden wird.

Meine Adresse ganz wie schon geschrieben. Nochmals grüße Sie herzlich

Franz Kettner

# Letter / Brief 2

### Letter 2 (December 25, 1851) from Franz Kettner at the Demijohn Bend on the Guadalupe River in Comal County, Texas to his Parents[22,23]

Dear Parents,

I found your last letter waiting for me at the post office just when I returned from an expedition against the Indians. You had to make unnecessary worry over my dear life because you had not heard from me in over a year. The cause was not me, but the mail and also, the fact that for a year I have been away from all deliveries.

I wrote you in my last letter that Joseph Braun had taken over Schuchardt's share of the farm which had been called Kettner and Braun. I decided, however, to sell the farm and we obtained the same amount of money from the sale that the land and the equipment had cost.

You indicated in your last letter that you wanted to know more about the lives of the Indians. Because I came into close contact with them since that time, it will be more interesting to you. There are about 40,000 Indians in Texas. They live primarily from hunting, particularly buffalo hunting. They are all mounted with the exception of one tribe. They raise some of their horses themselves and try to steal others. Their skin color is reddish brown, their faces are usually painted and their clothing is

---

[22] A shortened version of this letter was published August 23, 1973 in the Renchtal newspaper in Oberkirch.

[23] The Demijohn Bend is eighteen miles northwest of New Braunfels in northern Comal County. The name derived from a demijohn-shaped bend in the Guadalupe River that formed a 400-acre peninsula that was nearly encircled by the stream.

According to the *Handbook of Texas Online*, this area was a German farming and ranching community that was settled in the 1850s by the Pantermuehl and Baetge families. (Franz's letter indicates that a Mr. Theusen was also an early settler in this community, possibly preceding others. See latter portion of this letter.) (*Handbook of Texas Online*, s.v. "Demijohn Bend, Texas" http://-www.tsha.utexas.edu/handbook/online/articles/DD/hvd20.html (accessed July 28, 2006)).

made out of leather. They know how to tan leather very well. They are armed mainly with bows and arrows and lances but some also possess firearms.

The German immigrants moved deeply into the farthest points of (the Indians') land so that the Indians were continually driven back and robbed of parts of their best hunting grounds. The Indians sought to make it difficult and to stop the settlers in any way possible. They stole horses, shot work oxen, and even murdered whenever they could find a single person by himself without endangering themselves. This was easier for them since the Indians are sly as cats.

In recent times the Indians had become so bold that the few regular militia men who remained at the border were not sufficient. In general, the regular militia isn't suitable to fight the Indians since they never battle out in the open unless in an emergency. Overall we need (fighters) people who are at home in the forests and mountains. Here they are called "woodsmen" who can take care of themselves everywhere because there are no trails and bridges over the border and one finds direction by the sun. Therefore, the Texas governor assembled four companies of volunteers to find the Indians and force them to make a peace treaty.

This happened exactly at the time when I sold the farm. All of the young Texans took up their weapons, I among them. Each company was a hundred men strong. We voted for our captain from among ourselves, also all the remaining officers, and provided our own horses. The weapons consisted of a revolver that you can shoot 60 paces (six times without reloading), and a rifle which was issued to us by the government. In addition (we were issued) feed for our horses, tents, food supplies, two 6-span horse wagons, and around 30 mules which were loaded with the supplies. Our company was made up of 26 Germans, many of whom were my former ship mates, and the rest were Americans.

Our company made its camp on a small river. If you look at a map of Texas, our camp was located about 20 hours north of the settlement on the Medina. We maintained our base camp and stored supplies there for half a year while we made our excursions against the Indians. It is truly a romantic area. We wore our normal clothing, had very good American horses (English type), received oats, and were given very good food supplies. We had absolutely no military discipline and received 25 dollars a month from the state of Texas, somewhat more than a lieutenant receives in Germany.

Our principal mission was to pursue the Indians who had stolen horses or broken the laws. I was in two battles which I came out of covered with honors without getting wounded. Each time we drove the Indians into retreat through a courageous attack, our horses in full gallop and with hot shooting revolvers. Each time, some Indians were killed, but we also had some losses.

I cannot describe completely enough to you how the life in camp was. I will put it off until I come to Germany and tell you about it personally. I have plenty of material since I have already experienced many adventures. After we served for a year, a peace was made. We were let out of the service on July 17, 1851 and paid. Each man returned once again to peaceful occupations.

I leased a piece of land north of Braunfels in the Guadalupe Mountains with two men. They are Mr. von Kriewitz,[24] a former Prussian forester candidate, and Mr. Specht, a Husar lieutenant from Braunschweig. Both served at the same time in the company with me. We are busy plowing right now. We are bringing about 30 acres into cultivation. An acre is a piece of land 210 feet long and 210 feet wide. Therefore, it is somewhat larger than a German "Morgen."[25] We are planting corn, tobacco, and potatoes this year. Next year probably cotton.

We have leased for two years. The first year we pay no rent, the second year we turn over a third of the harvest. Mr. Theusen, from whom we have rented, also lives here with his wife. He is from Cologne; his dignified wife is the daughter of a wealthy manufacturer on the Rhine, by the name of Rhodin_________.[26]

Since I am more disposed to writing today than I was yesterday, I will describe the area that we live in for you. The place lies directly on the Guadalupe exactly where the river makes a great bend. The land is enclosed on all sides with the exception of one entrance. The land consists of some 600[27] acres and cost Mr. Theusen one thousand dollars because it is fenced in by nature. We live eight hours from Braunfels. The land is mostly hilly with very beautiful valleys.

Hunting is very productive. We have very many bears which are so fat in winter that they are worth a lot. There are also a large number of buffalo and wild horses

---

[24] Emil von Kriewitz de Czepry (1822-1902) immigrated to Texas in 1846 and played a large role in the settlement of the area. After serving the US army in the war with Mexico, he was hired by the Adelsverein to form a company of men to guard John O. Meusebach on his excursion into the Fisher-Miller Land Grant to make a peace treaty with the Comanche Indians. However, he met the party returning from successful negotiations at San Saba. His company guarded the surveying party in the area north of the Llano River in present day Mason and Llano counties as agreed on by the treaty with the Comanche Indians. [See Handbook of Texas Online, s.v. "Meusebach, John O." http://-www.tsha.utexas.edu/handbook/online/articles/MM/fme33.html (accessed July 28, 2006).]

According to von Kriewitz, the Comanche requested that a German live with them at their camp as a "guarantee of the peaceable intention of the Germans." He accepted this dangerous assignment and lived in the camp of Santa Anna at San Saba. His presence helped assure good relationships with the Indians and helped assure the safety of the early settlers.

Later von Kriewitz charted a road and led settlers to Bettina, a short lived colony of German intellectuals on the Llano River near present day Castell. He also led settlers to the colonies of Castell, Leiningen, and Schoernbuerg in the same area in 1847. Ref: *Handbook of Texas Online*, s.v. "Kriewitz, Emil" http://www.tsha.utexas.edu/handbook/online/articles/KK/fkr12.html (accessed July 28, 2006); Emil Kriewitz "Recollections from Indian Times" in *Fredericksburg, Texas, The First Fifty Years*, trans. C. L Wisseman, Sr. 48-49 (Fredericksburg, TX: Fredericksburg Publishing Co., Inc, 1971).

In the period around 1851, Emil Kriewitz served in the Texas Rangers with Franz and later was engaged in farming with him. In Letter 3 (August 1853), Franz describes their continued partnership in opening a store at Castell and von Kriewitz's role as postmaster.

[25] A land measure (local variations from 0.6 to 0.9 acre) from *Cassell's German-English, English-German Dictionary*, ed. H.T. Betteridge (New York: Macmillan Publishing Co., 1979), s.v. "Morgen." This is not to be confused with a Dutch and South African morgen which is equal to 2.116 acres.

[26] This is an incomplete name due to partial damage to the letter.

[27] Franz probably over estimated the acreage.

as well as wild turkey and deer. What is quite rare is that a short time ago Kriewitz shot a magnificent spotted tiger cat.

All the letters that you write me, even those under the old address, I always receive from Braunfels. Each month one of the three of us travels there. I ride out from our place about two in the afternoon and arrive in Braunfels in the evening. It takes eight hours. Braunfels is always lovely. We have two breweries with bowling lanes where I play rambo each time I am there.

I have not heard anything from Christian Schrempp and have not received the little chest that you described. Be careful then with such agreements. Do not send me any more letters through chance opportunities but send them all through the mail. When you send them collect, they only cost me 14 (cents). I also forbid you to send me small gifts of money. It does not help me and you can use it.

I have firmly decided to choose Texas as my new homeland, so I am therefore ready to apply for citizenship.[28] I would like to marry now. It is hard here to find an educated young woman. I think that it would be best to try to marry in Germany when I visit you in two years. Without a wife, it is difficult to make a decent living.

Write me in detail what you think about this matter, whether it is possible to find an educated woman who would move to Texas with me for about 2,000 to 3,000 guldens in savings. What is Lyssette doing? Tell her hello for me and ask her to forgive me since writing two letters is not possible for me. Send her my letter to read and tell her that I am also waiting to hear her opinion about my important life question.

We were invited by Mr. Theusen to celebrate the first Christmas holiday there together.

How are things going in Oberkirch? I have often thought that it must be lonesome for you without anyone at home who makes noise, unless it is sometimes Papa when he is in a foul mood. Has he gotten over complaining about little things? I want Papa to share interesting news with me and wish he would spare me his warnings and good advice that take up half the letter each time. Since he is unfamiliar with the conditions in Texas he cannot advise me. Regarding his warnings, I simply repeat that I am twenty-five years of age and probably already have more experiences than a European, for America is the school for experiences and knowledge about people.

How is Welle doing (from Oedsbach)? Tell her hello for me along with the Schauenburg family, in general all friends. I do not want to extend my trip for a long visit when it actually happens because I do not think I can take myself into those ridiculous social engagements. Here I am free as a bird and find pleasure in hunting bear or buffalo on horseback instead of going to balls and tea parties.

I cannot stand to walk anymore and it seems to me as if I were born on horseback.

Traveling is my greatest pleasure here. A person takes two wool blankets, one goes under the saddle and the other is tied on behind, then a tin drinking cup is

---

[28] Franz was nationalized in 1856. See Figures 14 & 15. One of the conditions for receiving citizenship was a 5 year residency in the state of Texas.

fastened to the saddle, some bread and roasted coffee and good flints/tinder to start a fire. The rifle is tied in front of the saddle horn. You also carry along a long hemp rope with which to tie the horse at night so that it can feed. Both of the blankets serve as bedding. Then you make a small fire, boil the coffee and roast the meat (which can always be shot on the way) over the coals. And while the climate here is always somewhat warm, it is very pleasant to sleep out in the open. So traveling here is certainly very cheap.

I will write you the next letter in two or three months when the harvest results can be estimated. I want to give you an exact report, particularly what we will earn from tobacco - which grows here exceptionally well. We work the land some with oxen (we own four span) and some with two strong work horses. Each of us plows with his own plow so that we always work with three plows. It is now time for our noon meal and Mr. Theusen has invited us and we'll drink punch and French wine in the evening so I need to stop writing.

It just occurred to me that Papa would enjoy knowing what grows here. First of all, cotton and tobacco - in short, everything that thrives in Germany and, in addition, the southern varieties of plants. Wine grapes thrive very well. This I have seen in the Braunfels' gardens where most people have planted wine grapes. Then sugar, wheat, two types of potatoes, and all garden vegetables only with the difference that here one has two harvests of vegetables, in spring (mostly nothing grows in summer on account of the high heat and drought). However, there is a second planting late in the year so that one gets double the yield as in Germany. Also, all varieties of fruit trees grow here.

Although at this time I wish you good luck and contentment in the New Year, I will not neglect to write you again regularly.

With love to you, Franz Kettner

**Fig. 13. Emil von Kriewitz.** This photograph was taken from an old photo album in the possession of Henrietta Kettner Keener and labeled Kriewitz.

**Abb. 13. Emil von Kriewitz.** Dies Foto wurde einem alten Fotoalbum aus dem Besitz von Henrietta Kettner Keener entnommen, das mit Kriewitz beschriftet war.

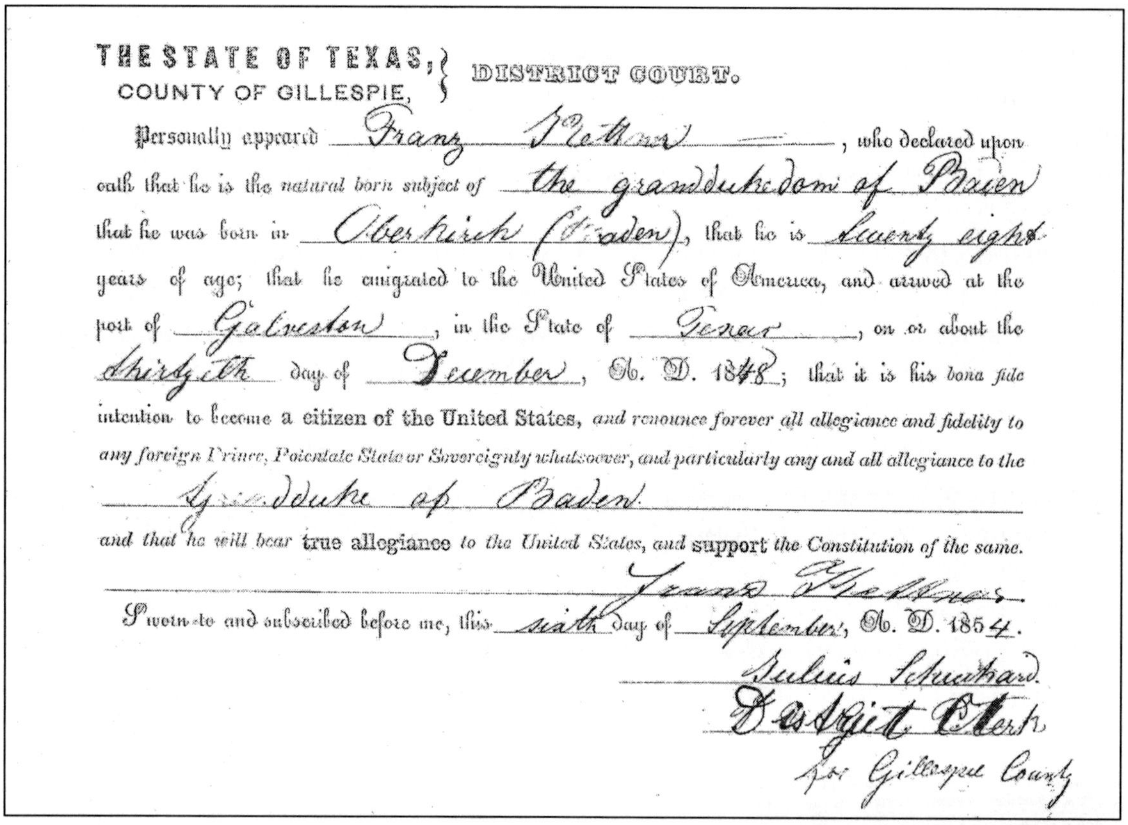
THE STATE OF TEXAS, }
COUNTY OF GILLESPIE, } DISTRICT COURT.

Personally appeared Franz [illegible], who declared upon oath that he is the *natural born subject of* the grandukedom of Baden that he was born in Oberkirch (Baden), that he is twenty eight years of age; that he emigrated to the United States of America, and arrived at the port of Galveston, in the State of Texas, on or about the thirtieth day of December, A. D. 1848; that it is his *bona fide* intention to become a citizen of the United States, *and renounce forever all allegiance and fidelity to any foreign Prince, Potentate State or Sovereignty whatsoever, and particularly any and all allegiance to the* Grandduke of Baden

*and that he will bear* true allegiance *to the United States, and* support *the Constitution of the same.*

Franz [illegible]

Sworn to and subscribed before me, this sixth day of September, A. D. 1854.

Julius Schuchard
District Clerk
for Gillespie County

**Fig. 14. Declaration of Intent.** Franz filed his Declaration of Intent to become a citizen of the United States on September 6, 1854. This is the first step in obtaining U.S. citizenship. This document is archived in the Gillespie County Court House (Nat. File Box No. 2 #260). A copy of this declaration was entered in the District Court Minutes (Vol. A, p 137B).

**Abb. 14. Absichtserklärung.** Franz gab seine Absichtserklärung, ein Bürger der Vereinigten Staaten zu werden, am 6. September 1854 zu den Akten. Dies ist der erste Schritt, um die US Staatsbürgerschaft zu erlangen. Dies Dokument befindet sich in dem Archiv im Gillespie County Court House (Nat. File Box No. 2#260). Eine Kopie dieser Erklärung wurde in das Protokoll des Distriktgerichtes aufgenommen (Vol. A, p 137B).

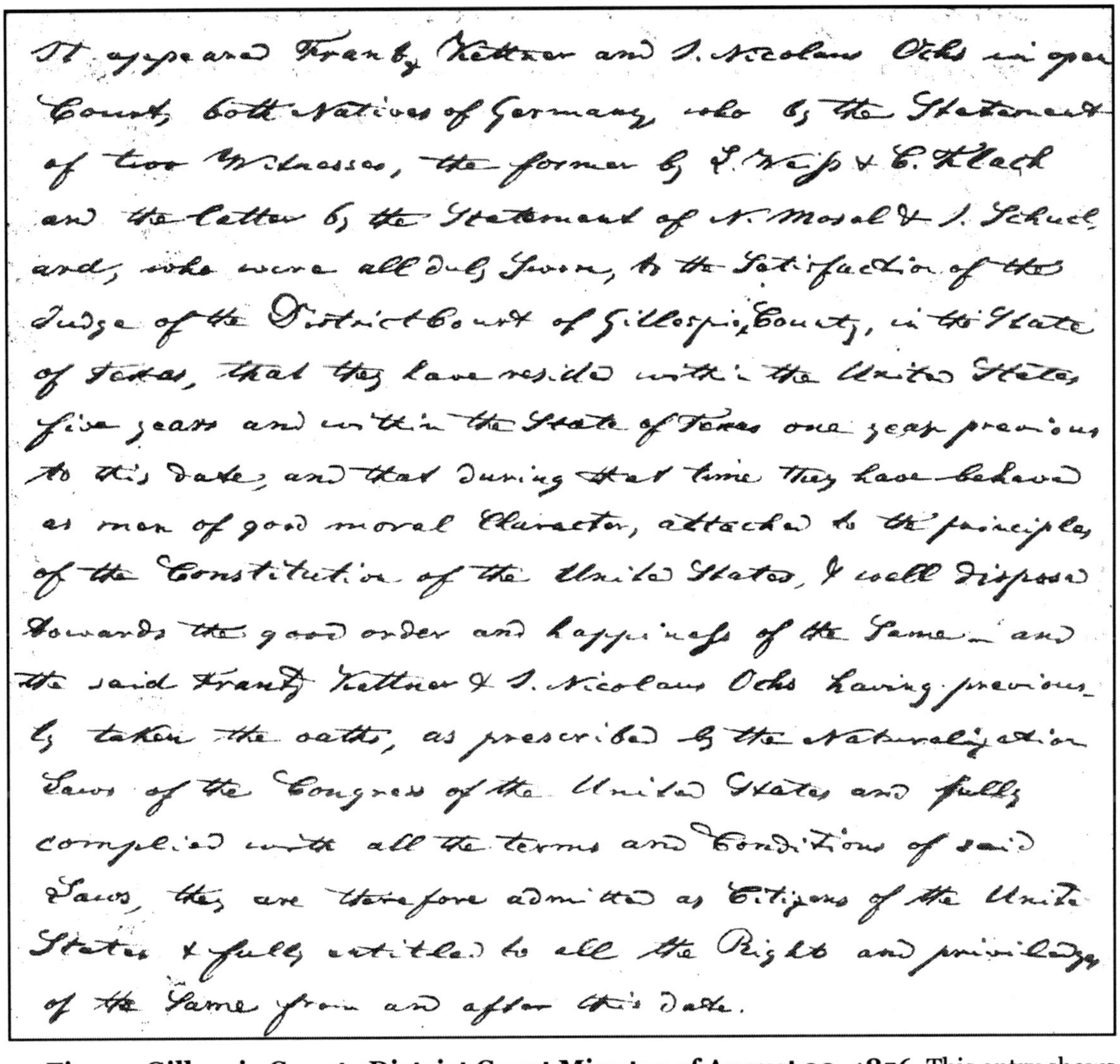

It appeared Franz Kettner and J. Nicolaus Ochs in open
Court, both Natives of Germany, who by the Statement
of two Witnesses, the former by J. Weiss & C. Klach
and the latter by the Statement of N. Mosel & J. Schuch
and, who were all duly sworn, to the satisfaction of the
Judge of the District Court of Gillespie County, in the State
of Texas, that they have resided within the United States
five years and within the State of Texas one year previous
to this date, and that during that time they have behaved
as men of good moral Character, attached to the principles
of the Constitution of the United States, & well disposed
towards the good order and happiness of the Same — and
the said Frantz Kettner & J. Nicolaus Ochs having previously taken the oaths, as prescribed by the Naturalization
Laws of the Congress of the United States and fully
complied with all the terms and Conditions of said
Laws, they are therefore admitted as Citizens of the United
States & fully entitled to all the Rights and privileges
of the Same from and after this date.

**Fig. 15. Gillespie County District Court Minutes of August 30, 1856**. This entry shows that Franz appeared in court and was granted citizenship (Volume B, p 47 and 47B). However, this information was not recorded in The Index to Naturalization Records until September 16, 1856.

**Abb. 15. Gillespie County Bezirksgericht, Protokoll vom 30. August 1856**. Dieser Eintrag zeigt, dass Franz vor Gericht erschien und ihm die Staatsbürgerschaft verliehen wurde (Volume B, p 47 und 47B). Dagegen wurde diese Information im Index der Einbürgerung nicht vor dem 16. September 1856 aufgegenommen.

## Brief 2 (25. Dezember 1851) von Franz Kettner aus Demijohn Bend am Guadalupe River in Comal County/Texas an seine Eltern[29]

Liebe Eltern!

Soeben zurückgekommen von einer Expedition gegen die Indianer fand ich Ihren letzten Brief auf der Post, worin Sie seit einem Jahre keine Nachricht mehr von mir erhielten und deshalb sich unnötigerweise Sorge um mein zartes Leben machten. Die Ursache liegt nicht bei mir, sondern bei der Post und andererseits in meiner einjährigen Abwesenheit von allem Verkehr.

Ich zeigte Ihnen in meinem letzten Brief an, daß Joseph Braun den Schuchardt'schen Teil der Farm übernahm, mithin die Firma Kettner & Braun hieß. ..... Ich drang aber darauf, die Farm zu verkaufen, welches auch geschah Und wir schlugen dasselbe Geld heraus, was das Land gekostet hatte und die Einrichtung.

Da Sie in Ihrem letzten Brief besonders über die Verhältnisse der Indianer etwas zu wissen wünschten und ich während der Zeit in nähere Berührung mit ihnen kam, so wird es um so interessanter für Sie sein. Die Indianer, deren es in Texas ungefähr 40.000 gibt, leben bloß von der Jagd, besonders Büffeljagd. Sie sind alle beritten, einen Stamm ausgenommen, ziehen teils ihre Pferde selbst auf, teils suchen sie solche zu stehlen. Ihre Gesichtsfarbe ist rötlichbraun, ihr Gesicht meistens bemalt und die Kleidung besteht aus Lederzeug, welches sie sehr gut zu gerben verstehen. Ihre Bewaffnung besteht meistens aus Bogen und Pfeilen und Lanzen. Auch besitzen einige Feuergewehre.

Durch die deutsche Ansiedlung, welche ganz aufwärts ins Land geht, immer nach den äußersten Punkten, wurden die Indianer immer weiter zurückgedrängt, und teils auch ihrer besten Jagdreviere beraubt. Sie suchten deshalb, den vordersten Ansiedlungen es auf alle mögliche Art zu erschweren, sich zu halten, durch Stehlen der Pferde, durch Totschießen von Zugochsen und selbst durch Morden, wenn sie ohne Gefahr einzelne überfallen konnten. Dies war für sie um so leichter, da der Indianer so schlau wie eine Katze ist.

In der letzten Zeit trieben die Herren es jedoch zu frech, so daß das wenige reguläre Militär, was an der Grenze steht, nicht hinreichend war. Überhaupt paßt reguläres Militär für Indianer nicht, weil sich diese ohne Not nie in ein offenes Gefecht einlassen. Überhaupt mußten es Leute sein, die in den Wäldern und Gebirgen zu Hause waren. Man nennt sie hier Wudsmänner,[30] die sich überall zurecht zu finden wissen, da man hier keine Wege und Stege über der Grenze findet und immer nach der Sonne reitet. Deshalb ließ der Gouverneur von Texas schnell 4 Kompanien Freiwilliger errichten, um die Indianer zu züchtigen und sie dann zu einem Frieden geneigt zu machen.

---

[29] Dieser Brief wurde am 23.08.1973 in der Renchtal Zeitung in Oberkirch in leicht gekürzter Form veröffentlicht.

[30] Englisch "woodsmen" = Waldläufer.

Dies fiel gerade in die Zeit, als ich die Farm verkaufte. Alle jungen Texaner ergriffen nun die Waffen, und auch ich. Jede Kompanie war hundert Mann stark. Wir wählten unseren Hauptmann aus unserer Mitte, sowie alle übrigen Offiziere und stellten unsere Pferde selbst. Die Waffen, welche aus einer Pistole bestand, mit welcher man auf 60 Gänge 6mal schießen konnte, ohne zu laden, und einer Büchse, wurden uns vom Gouvernement geliefert. Ebenfalls Furage für unser Pferde, Zelte, Proviant, zwei sechsspännige Pferdewagen und circa 30 Stück Maultiere, welche mit Gepäck beladen wurden. Unsere Kompanie bestand aus 26 Deutschen, die übrigen waren Amerikaner, worunter sehr viele von meiner ehemaligen Schiffsgesellschaft waren.

Unsere Kompanie schlug ihr Lager an einem Flüßchen auf. Wenn Sie die Karte von Texas zur Hand nehmen, ungefähr 20 Stunden oberhalb der Ansiedlungen an der Medina,[31] in einer wirklich romantischen Gegend, wo wir unseren Vorrat für ein halbes Jahr hatten und von wo aus wir unsere Exkursionen gegen die Indianer machten. Wir trugen unsere gewöhnlichen Kleider, hatten alle sehr gute amerikanische Pferde (englisch), bekamen Hafer, sehr guten Proviant für uns geliefert. Wir hatten gar keine militärische Zucht und bekamen vom Staate Texas monatlich 25 Dollars, etwas mehr als in Deutschland ein Leutnant.

Unsere Hauptbeschäftigung war, die Indianer, die Pferde gestohlen hatten oder über die vorgeschriebene Linie gingen, zu verfolgen. Ich war in zwei Gefechten gegenwärtig, wo ich mit Ruhm bedeckt durchkam, aber ohne verwundet zu werden. Wir schlugen die Indianer jedes Mal in die Flucht durch einen mutigen Angriff mit der heiß schießenden Pistole und im vollen Rennen der Pferde, wobei jedesmal einige Indianer blieben, aber auch wir mitunter einigen Verlust hatten.

Das Leben, wie es in einem Lager ist, kann ich Ihnen so ausführlich nicht beschreiben. Ich verschiebe es, bis ich nach Deutschland komme, Ihnen mündlich zu berichten. Stoff habe ich genug, denn ich habe schon manches Abenteuer bestanden. Nach einem Jahr, in welchem wir in Aktivität standen, wurde Frieden gemacht. Wir wurden am 17. Juli 1851 entlassen und ausbezahlt. Jeder kehrte wieder zu friedlicher Beschäftigung zurück.

Ich pachtete mit einem Herrn von Kriewitz[32] und einem Herrn Specht, der eine ehemaliger preußischer Forstkandidat, der andere braunschweigischer Husarenleutnant, die mit mir zu gleicher Zeit in der Kompanie standen, ein Stück Landes oberhalb Braunfels in den Gebirgen der Guadalupe. Und wir sind wirklich am Pflügen. Wir bringen circa dreißig Acre in Kultur. (Ein Acre ist ein Stück Land von 210 Fuß lang und ebenso 210 Fuß breit, also etwas größer als ein deutscher Morgen.)

---

[31] Es handelt sich um das Flüßchen Medina westlich von San Antonio, das in den San Antonio River mündet.

[32] Emil von Kriewitz de Czepry, 18.01.1822-21.05.1902. Nähere Angaben über seinen Lebenslauf finden sich im: *Handbook of Texas Online*, unter dem Stichwort "Kriewitz, Emil", http://www.-tsha.utexas.edu/handbook/online/articles/KK/fkr12.html (Zugriff 28. Juli 2006).

Wir ziehen dieses Jahr Korn, Tabak und Kartoffeln. Nächstes Jahr wahrscheinlich Baumwolle Wir haben auf zwei Jahre gepachtet. Das erste Jahr haben wir es unentgeltlich, das zweite Jahr geben wir ein Drittel der Ernte ab. Herr Theusen, von welchem wir gepachtet haben, wohnt mit seiner Frau auch hier. Er ist von Köln, seine liebenswürdige Frau eine Tochter von einem reichen Fabrikanten am Rhein, der Name ist Rhodin...

Da ich heute etwas mehr aufgelegt bin wie gestern, so will ich Ihnen die Gegend etwas beschreiben, in welcher wir wohnen. Die Lage ist dicht an der Guadalupe und sogar, da der Fluß eine furchtbare Biegung macht, von allen Seiten eingeschlossen, ausgenommen einer Einfahrt.[33] Das Land besteht aus circa 600 Acre[34] und kostet Herrn Theusen[35] 1.000 Dollars, weil das Land von der Natur eingefenzt ist. Wir wohnen 8 Stunden von Braunfels, meistens gebirgig, mit sehr schönen Tälern versehen.

Die Jagd ist sehr ergiebig. Wir haben sehr viele Bären, welche im Winter so fett sind, daß ein ungeheurer Wert daraus entspringt. Büffel und wilde Pferde gibt es auch in großer Anzahl, sowie diese wilden Puter und Hirsche. Auch schoß Kriewitz, was aber zur Seltenheit gehört, vor kurzer Zeit eine prachtvoll gefleckte Tigerkatze.

Alle Briefe, die Sie auch ferner mir schreiben, unter der alten Adresse, da ich sie immer in Braunfels abholen werde, wo jeden Monat einer von uns dreien hinkommt. Ich bin schon um 2 Uhr nachmittags von unserem Platze aus fortgeritten und war abends in Braunfels. Das sind 8 Stunden. Braunfels wird immer schöner. Wir haben 2 Bierbrauereien mit Kegelbahnen, wo ich jedesmal, bei meinem Dortsein Rambo spiele.

Von Christian Schrempp und dem beschriebenen Kistchen habe ich nie etwas gehört. Seien Sie also vorsichtiger mit solchen Aufträgen. Schicken Sie mir keine Briefe mehr per Gelegenheit, sondern alle per Post, da sie mir, wenn Sie solche frei machen, circa 14 ? kosten. Auch verbitte ich mir solche Kleinigkeiten an Geld zu schicken, da es mir nichts nützt, Ihnen aber.

Ich habe mich nun fest entschlossen, Texas als neues Vaterland zu betrachten, bin auch bereits schon um das Bürgerrecht eingekommen.[36] Ich werde mich nun zu verheiraten suchen. Hier hat es einige Schwierigkeit, ein gebildetes Mädchen zu

---

33 Diese Biegung wird heute Demijohn Bend genannt. Sie liegt 18 Meilen nordwestlich von Neu Braunfels im nördlichen Comal County. Hier lag eine deutsche Farm- und Ranchgemeinschaft, die in den 1850er Jahren durch die Pantermuehl und Baetge Familien besiedelt wurde. Der Name wird abgeleitet von einer korbflaschen-förmigen Biegung des Flusses Guadalupe, die eine 400 Acre große Halbinsel formt, welche von dem Fluß fast vollständig eingeschlossen wird. Siehe: *Handbook of Texas Online*, unter dem Stichwort "Demijohn Bend, Texas," http://www.tsha.utexas.edu/handbook/online/articles/DD/hvd20.html. (Zugriff 19.10.2003).

34 Man beachte die großzügige Flächenschätzung Kettners.

35 Der Brief Kettners ergänzt die Informationen über die Pächter des Demijohn Bend, die der Universität Texas vorliegen, um einen Pächter/Käufer Theusen im Jahre 1851, der möglicherweise sogar den dort genannten Familien voranging.

36 Der Antrag auf Einbürgerung erfolgte am 06.09.1854. Vgl. Abb. 14. Voraussetzung für die Einbürgerung war u.a. ein Mindestaufenthalt von 5 Jahren im Staate Texas. Vgl. auch Abb. 15.

bekommen. Deshalb glaube ich, wird es das Beste sein, wenn ich Sie in zwei Jahren besuche, und mich in Deutschland zu verheiraten suche. Denn ohne Frau ist keine geregelte Wirtschaft zu führen.

Schreiben Sie mir über diesen Punkt ausführlich, was Sie dazu glauben, ob es möglich sei, ein gebildetes Mädchen von circa 2 bis 3000 Gulden Vermögen zu finden, welche mit nach Texas geht. Ohne verheiratet zu sein, werde ich keine eigene Haushaltung mehr anfangen. Was macht Lyssette? Grüßen Sie mir alle und entschuldigen Sie mich bei ihr, aber zwei Briefe zu schreiben ist mir nicht möglich. Schicken Sie ihr meinen Brief zum Lesen und sagen Sie ihr, ich erwarte auch ihre Ansicht zu hören über meine wichtige Lebensfrage.

Wir sind heute bei Herrn Theusen eingeladen und feiern daselbst den ersten Weihnachtsfeiertag. Wie sieht es in Oberkirch aus? Ich habe schon oft gedacht, es muß bei Ihnen sehr einsam sein. Niemand mehr im Hause, der Lärm macht, höchstens vielleicht manchmal der Papa, wenn er übler Laune ist. Hat er sich das Schimpfen über Kleinigkeiten noch nicht abgewöhnt? Ich wollte, der Herr Papa würde mir interessante Neuigkeiten mitteilen, und mich mit seinen Ermahnungen und guten Ratschlägen verschonen, die er mir jedesmal in seinen Briefen mitteilt und die jedesmal über die Hälfte derselben einnimmt. Da er mir als ein mit den Verhältnissen von Texas Unbekannter nicht raten kann. Und was die Ermahnungen anbelangt, da erwidere ich bloß, daß ich 25 Jahre passiert habe, und wahrscheinlich schon mehr Erfahrungen gemacht habe als ein Europäer, denn Amerika ist die Schule für Menschenkenntnis und Erfahrungen.

Was macht Welle (Oedsbach)? Grüßen Sie mir sie sowie Schauenburgs Familie, überhaupt alle Bekannten. Lange werde ich meinen Besuch, wenn er wirklich zustande kommt, nicht ausdehnen, denn ich glaube nicht, daß ich mich in diese lächerlichen Verhältnisse schicken könnte. Hier bin ich frei, lebe wie der Vogel, statt Bälle und Teegesellschaften finde ich mehr Vergnügen, wenn ich zu Pferd Bären jage oder Büffel.

Das Zu-Fuß-Gehen kann ich gar nicht mehr vertragen, und es kommt mir vor, als wenn ich auf dem Pferd geboren wäre. Das Reisen gefällt mir hier am besten. Man nimmt sich zwei wollene Decken, die eine unter den Sattel die andere hintenauf geschnallt, dann ein blechener Becher an den Sattel gebunden, etwas Brot und gebrannten Kaffee und gutes Feuerzeug. Vorn auf dem Sattelknopf ist die Büchse befestigt. Auch führt man ein langes hänfenes Seil mit sich, woran nachts das Pferd angebunden wird und fressen kann. Die beiden Decken dienen als Nachtlager. Dann wird ein kleines Feuerchen angemacht, Kaffee gekocht und Fleisch, das man unterwegs immer schießen kann, auf Kohlen gebraten. Und da wir es hier immer ziemlich warm haben, so ist es sehr angenehm, im Freien zu schlafen. Also das Reisen ist hier gewiß sehr billig.

Von heute in zwei Monaten bis drei Monaten später werde ich Ihnen den nächsten Brief schreiben, wenn das Ergebnis der Ernte zu mutmaßen ist, worüber ich Ihnen genau Auskunft geben werde, besonders was wir in Tabak, welcher hier ausgezeichnet gerät, machen werden. Wir bearbeiten das Land teils mit Ochsen, deren wir 4 Joch besitzen und 2 starken amerikanischen Zugpferden. Jeder führt seinen Pflug, so daß wir immer mit 3 Pflügen arbeiten.

Da es Zeit ist zum Mittagessen und Herr Theusen uns eingeladen hat und wir auf den Abend Punsch und französischen Wein trinken, so muß ich den Brief zu schließen suchen.

Soeben fällt mir ein, daß Papa wissen möchte, was hier wächst. Zuerst Baumwolle und Tabak ausgezeichnet, kurzum alles, glaube ich, was in Deutschland gedeiht und die südlichen Früchte ebenfalls. Wein gedeiht sehr, das habe ich in den Gärten von Braunfels gesehen, wo die meisten Leute Wein gepflanzt haben. Dann Zucker, Weizen, zweierlei Arten von Kartoffeln, alle Gartengewächse, nur mit dem Unterschied, daß man zweimal des Jahres Gartengewächse hat, nämlich Frühjahr (Sommer wächst meistens wegen zu großer Hitze und Trockenheit nichts), aber im Spätjahr wird wieder gepflanzt, so daß man hier den doppelten Ertrag als wie in Deutschland hat. Auch alle Arten von Obstbäumen geraten hier.

Indem ich Ihnen zu gleicher Zeit zum neuen Jahre Glück und Zufriedenheit wünsche, werde ich nicht ermangeln, Ihnen wieder regelmäßig zu schreiben.

Ihr Sie liebender
Franz Kettner

Guadalupe, 25. Dezember 1851
Brief senden Sie mir unter der alten Adresse.

# Letter / Brief 3

### Letter 3 (August 12, 1853) from Franz Kettner at Castell, Texas to his Parents[37]

Dear Parents,

Since I have some leisure time right now and am at home alone (my partner has gone on horseback to Fredericksburg), I will use this time to talk with you in a letter. Our store is doing well so far, and I was in San Antonio last month, where I bought new wares for $320 and paid $200 of this amount in cash. We are thinking about considerably enlarging our store very soon, that is, to build a large, solid stone house.[38] My main occupation now is in the store, but for relaxation I go fishing. Our river, the Llano, is so very full of fish that you could not image it. Many times I have caught thirty to forty pounds of fish in two hours, so much that we cannot stand to look at, much less eat, any more fish for a week. Hunting is also excellent, and I am quite content if I can ride out every eight or ten days to shoot a buck. This month we are still having very hot weather (93° F. to 100° F. in the shade), but next month it will be cooler, so that we can start working in the fields. I will also attempt to clear our ten acres and the garden of one and one-half acres. We can make $300 from our field, since we live only fifteen miles from the fort, and up here on the Indian border, grain and sweet potatoes are sold at very high prices. All the farmers around here

---

[37] This letter as well as the letters in chapters 4 and 5 were translated and published by Professor Terry G. Jordan and Marlis Anderson Jordan. (Terry G. Jordan and Marlis Anderson Jordan "Letters of a German Pioneer in Texas," *Southwestern Historical Quarterly* 69 (1966): 463-472.) I have used the Jordan's translations with the permission of Dr. Jordan and the Texas State Historical Association. I did not include footnotes or photographs from this publication, but rather added those relevant to the complete set of letters. Note that Professor Jordan deleted purely personal references from the letters.

[38] See the maps in Figures 5 and 25 (Letter 10) for the location of Castell. According to Patty Schneider Pfister "Castell, Texas, One Hundred Sixty Years, 1847 – 2007" *in preparation*, the first store and postoffice was built in the early 1850 and was operated by Emil Kriewitz and Franz Kettner in 1853. It was located on the north side of the Llano River across from the present day town of Castell, but its exact location is not known. Kriewitz returned to Castell after the Civil War in 1865 and bought property on the north side of the river and ran a two room log store and mail post on what is now CR 104. This may have been the location of the first store and post office.

are well-off and have enough money. For the heavy work, like cutting wood for fences, we will hire a worker for four weeks. Our store is very diverse; we have groceries, dry goods, hardware, and beverages, and we sell at a profit of 25 per cent on the average. The old Spanish silver mine has not been found yet, but soon will be. It is supposed to have existed in our vicinity. There are minerals in our surroundings in any case, as can be seen by the formation of the mountain ranges and rocks, and they will be found in time. This is of very great interest to us, since we could get rich in a short time.

One of the main things right now is the railroad which is already being built from the coast to San Antonio. You cannot imagine how much the land values rise each year. Five years ago, one had to pay only $1.50 per acre in the vicinity of New Braunfels, and now one acre costs five to ten dollars. Up here, land is still cheap, since we live 115 miles from New Braunfels and 100 miles northwest of San Antonio. In a short time, we will also buy several hundred acres, just to speculate in land values. Much land around here has been bought by people still living in Germany who want a place of refuge to come to during the bad times which will soon come to Germany. All people in America are agreed that there will be a mighty clash in Germany, yes in all of Europe, in which not even the child in the mother's womb will be safe. America will not remain neutral in the coming revolution, but will help the republicans. Our country gains strength every year and could show the Old World who is boss.

In a short time, we will have a post office in Castell. My partner Kriewitz has been nominated postmaster by the people, and I will take over the contract to ride the mail on horseback, that is, I will hire a man to ride the mail. Some profit can be made that way. This one increases one's business every day, and you will be able to send your letters directly to the town of Castell on the Llano.

Concerning my health, I am still well and happy, and people insist that I never grow older and still look like a man of twenty-three or twenty-four years. They envy especially my good humor, which I did not lose even when we ran out of food on the way back from the Rio Grande. We had to go hungry and thirsty for almost two days, and the temperatures were between 95° F. and 100° F. My body is somewhat hardened, and I maintain that the more stresses and strains a person has to endure, the stronger and more energetic he becomes. But now we are able to take better care of ourselves. If I may say so, I liked travelling better than sitting in the store and selling.

We will try to get the grain contract for our fort next year, by which we can easily earn $800.

If you can, send some wine and with it a pretty woman, young and beautiful. She does not have to have much money, only a dowry and enough for the trip over here. I also expect that she will be musically inclined and will bring with her a pianoforte. I require more in a prospective wife now. The wine could also be used at the wedding. First, however, I want a portrait of the one you have chosen for me.

I will write every two months now because I have more leisure time and there is always some ink and paper at hand, which was not the case before.

We are getting many new farmers up here, especially old friends of ours from New Braunfels. The majority of the population of western Texas is German,[39] and now this year we have a German senator and one representative in the congress at Austin.

Be sure to send the wine as soon as possible.

My greetings to all my acquaintances.

Yours, Franz Kettner

Castell, August 12, 1853

**Fig. 16. Historical Marker at Castell.** This marker is on the north bank of the Llano River.

**Abb. 16. Historische Gedenktafel in Castell.** Diese Gedenktafel befindet sich am Nordufer des Llano River.

**Fig. 17. Llano River at Castell.**

**Abb. 17. Llano River bei Castell.**

[39] According to Jordan (Jordan and Jordan, 463), Kettner's "Western Texas" only meant the western settled part of Texas, and the German counties were the westernmost ones that were settled in 1853.

## Brief 3 (12. August 1853) von Franz Kettner aus Castell/Texas[40] an seine Eltern[41]

Liebe Eltern!

Da ich gerade Muße habe und allein zu Hause bin (mein Associé ist nämlich nach Fredericksburg[42] geritten), so will ich diese Zeit benutzen, mich mit Ihnen schriftlich zu unterhalten. Unser Geschäft ist bis jetzt gut gegangen und ich war letzten Monat in San Antonio, wo ich für fl 800 neue Waren einkaufte und fl 500 bar bezahlte. Wir gedenken unser Geschäft in kurzer Zeit bedeutend zu vergrößern und namentlich ein solides steinernes Haus zu bauen. Meine Hauptbeschäftigung ist jetzt im Geschäft und zur Erholung betreibe ich die Fischerei. Unser Fluß, der Llano,[43] ist nämlich so reichhaltig an Fischen, wovon Sie sich keinen Begriff machen. Ich habe schon öfters in zwei Stunden dreißig bis vierzig Pfund Fische gefangen, so daß wir manchmal acht Tage lang keine Fische mehr sehen können, viel weniger essen. Auch ist die Jagd hier ausgezeichnet, aber wenn ich alle 8 bis 10 Tage einmal ausreiten kann, um einen Hirsch zu schießen, so bin ich zufrieden. Diesen Monat haben wir noch sehr heißes Wetter (im Schatten 34 bis 38 Grad), aber nächsten Monat wird es kühler, so daß man an die Feldarbeit gehen kann. Auch ich werde nächsten Monat unsere 10 Acre rein machen und den Garten, welcher 1½ Acre beträgt. Wir können aus unserem Feld 300 Dollars (fl 750) machen, weil wir bloß 15 Meilen vom Fort entfernt wohnen. Hier oben an der Indianergrenze werden das Korn und süße Kartoffeln zu sehr teuren Preisen verkauft. Die Farmer sind hier gut dran und haben alle Geld. Was aber die schwere Arbeit anbelangt, z.B. Fenzholz schlagen, werden wir uns für 4 Wochen einen Arbeiter mieten. Unser Geschäft ist sehr mannigfaltig. Wir haben Spezerei und Lange Waren, Eisenwaren und Getränke. Wir verkaufen durchschnittlich mit 25 Prozent Nutzen.

---

[40] Castell = Deutsche Siedlung am Llano River, die bis heute überlebt hat.

[41] Der vorliegende Brief sowie die Briefe 4 und 5 wurden von Professor Terry G. Jordan und Marlis Anderson Jordan ins Englische übersetzt und publiziert (Terry G. Jordan and Marlis Anderson Jordan "Letters of a German Pioneer in Texas," *Southwestern Historcial Quarterly* 69 (1966): 463-472.) Bemerke: Rein persönliche Bemerkungen wurden von Prof. Jordan dort fortgelassen. Ich habe die Übersetzungen der Jordans mit der Genehmigung von Dr. Jordan und der Texas State Historical Association verwendet. Die Fußnoten und Fotos dieser Publikation wurden nicht übernommen, sondern durch jene ersetzt, die für den kompletten Satz von Briefen wichtig sind.

[42] Fredericksburg wurde 1846 von deutschen Angehörigen des Adelsvereins gegründet. Siehe: *Handbook of Texas Online*, unter dem Stichwort "Fredericksburg, Texas", http://www.tsha.utexas.-edu/handbook/online/articles//FF/hff3.html. (Zugriff 19.10.2003). Heute an dem Interstate Highway 290 gelegen.

[43] Der Llano entsteht aus zwei Quellflüssen, dem Nord-Llano und dem Süd-Llano. Der Nord-Llano entspringt im westlichen Zentral Sutton County. Der Süd-Llano entsteht im nordwestlichen Edwards County und verläuft für 55 Meilen in nordöstlicher Richtung bis er den Nord-Llano östlich von Junction im Kimble County trifft. Der entstehende Llano River fließt in fast genau östlicher Richtung für ca. 100 Meilen durch Kimble County, Mason County und Llano County, bis er in den Colorado River mündet. Siehe: *Handbook of Texas Online*, unter dem Stichwort "Llano River", http://-www.tsha.utexas.edu/handbook/online/articles/LL/rnl11.html. (Zugriff 11.10.2003).

Die alte spanische Silbermine ist bis jetzt noch nicht aufgefunden worden, wird es aber auf jeden Fall werden. Sie soll in unserer Nähe existiert haben. Metalle gibt es in unserer Gegend auf jeden Fall. Sie werden auch mit der Zeit gefunden werden, was man an der Formation der Gebirge und Gesteine sehen kann. Dies ist für uns von ungeheurem Interesse, da wir dadurch in kurzer Zeit reich werden könnten.

Eine Hauptsache ist jetzt die Eisenbahn, welche von der Küste bis San Antonio schon in Angriff genommen ist. Sie machen sich keinen Begriff, wie das Land mit jedem Jahre im Wert steigt. Vor 5 Jahren bezahlte man in der Gegend von Braunfels per Acre 1 bis 1 ½ Doll. Jetzt kostet der Acre 5 bis 10 Dollars. Hier oben ist es noch billiger, wir wohnen nämlich 150 Meilen von Braunfels und 100 Meilen von San Antonio (nordwestlich). Wir werden uns auch in kurzer Zeit einige Hundert Acre Land kaufen, bloß um damit zu spekulieren. Es sind hier viele Ländereien von in Deutschland Wohnenden aufgekauft worden, bloß um in den schlechten Zeiten, die bald in Deutschland eintreten werden, hier einen Zufluchtsort zu haben. Denn darüber sind alle in Amerika einig, daß es in Deutschland, ja in ganz Europa in kurzer Zeit zu einem heftigen Zusammenstoß kommen wird, in dem nicht das Kind im Mutterleibe geschont wird. America wird bei der künftigen Revolution nicht mehr neutral bleiben, sondern die Republikaner kräftig unterstützen. Unser Staat nimmt mit jedem Jahr an Kraft zu und es kann jetzt schon der alten Welt die Spitze bieten. Wir werden in kurzer Zeit in Castell eine Postverbindung haben. Mein Partner Kriewitz ist von der Bevölkerung als Postmeister vorgeschlagen und ich werde den Kontrakt übernehmen, die Post zu reiten (d.h., ich werde einen Mann einstellen, der sie reitet). Es ist etwas daraus zu machen, so vergrößert man sein Geschäft mit jedem Tage, und dann können Sie auch die Briefe direkt nach der Stadt Castell am Llano senden.

Was meine Gesundheit anbelangt, so bin ich immer wohl und munter. Die Leute behaupten, ich werde nie älter. Ich sähe immer noch aus wie ein Mann von 23 bis 24 Jahren und besonders beneiden sie mich um meinen guten Humor. Den habe ich auch nicht verloren, als uns auf dem Rückweg vom Rio Grande die Lebensmittel ausgingen und wir beinahe 2 Tage hungern und dursten mußten bei einer Hitze von 35 bis 38 Grad. Mein Körper ist ziemlich abgehärtet, und ich behaupte, mit je mehr Widerwärtigkeiten und Strapazen der Mensch zu kämpfen hat, desto energischer und tatkräftiger wird er. Jetzt können wir uns aber auch pflegen. Aber offengestanden, hat mich das Reisen mehr amüsiert, als im Geschäft zu sitzen und zu verkaufen. Wir werden uns auch Mühe geben, nächstes Jahr den Kornkontrakt für unser Fort zu erhalten, wobei mit leichter Mühe fl 2000 zu verdienen sind.

Wenn Sie können, so schicken Sie mir mit dem Wein zugleich eine hübsche Frau, jung und schön, Geld braucht sie keines mehr zu haben, bloß Aussteuer und Überfahrtsgeld. Auch verlange ich jetzt, daß sie musikalisch ist und ein Fortepiano mitbringt. Man macht jetzt mehr Ansprüche? Und dann könnte der Wein auch zu gleicher Zeit zur Hochzeit verwendet werden. Aber zuerst wünsche ich ein Portrait von der von Ihnen für mich Ausgesuchten zu erhalten.

Was macht Elise? Ich erwarte schon ein ganzes Jahr einen Brief von ihr, aber es scheint, der Junge schreit zuviel und sie kommt nicht zum Schreiben.

Ich werde jetzt alle 2 Monate schreiben, weil ich jetzt mehr Muße habe und Tinte und Papier immer mir zur Seite liegen. Das war früher nicht der Fall.

Herrn Gerber Braun sah ich letzthin auch wieder.......

Wir bekommen sehr viel frische Farmer hier herauf und besonders alte Bekannte von uns von Braunfels. So hat sich ein junger Forstmann namens Roth, der in Baden-Baden praktizierte, dicht neben uns eingekauft. Der größere Teil der Bevölkerung des Westens von Texas sind Deutsche. Wir haben dieses Jahr einen Deutschen als Senator und einen als Repräsentanten in die gesetzgebende Versammlung nach Austin geschickt.

Schicken Sie ja bald den Wein......

Alle Bekannte herzlich grüßend verbleibe Ihr

Franz Kettner

Castell, 12. August 1853

# Letter / Brief 4

## Letter 4 (April 23, 1855) from Franz Kettner at Fredericksburg to his Parents

Dear Parents,

Since your last letter, which I received in December of last year, I have had no news from you. I am rushing this letter to tell you about my military service, since I have been discharged. Our whole military expedition consisted only of escorting wagon transports for the regular army. We had six companies and escorted about 400 six-span mule-wagons to a fort that lies a little below El Paso, about 600 miles from San Antonio.[44] It took us, going and coming, about three months. Other than the fact that many died due to the bad weather, nothing of interest happened. It was a wild, rocky land, deficient of water, and we sometimes had to travel for two days before reaching water again. I myself bore the hardships very well and did not get sick a single time.

Concerning the Indians and their attacks, they lasted until the middle of March, and many people, mostly Germans, were killed in sneak attacks, even in the immediate vicinity of Fredericksburg.[45] The losses in horses and cattle that were stolen cannot be measured. Now we have peace once again, and Congress has granted 100,000 dollars (700,000?)[46] for the feeding of the Indians. In addition, an attempt will be made to resettle them in an area designed for that purpose and to

---

[44] According to Jordan (Jordan and Jordan, 463), Franz most likely is referring to Fort Bliss, founded in 1848.

[45] Jordan (Jordan and Jordan, 463) also points out that the German settlements experienced increasing trouble with the Indians in the mid-1850's. Until this time the two groups had lived in peace under the terms of the renowned treaty made by J. O. Meusebach in 1847. See R. L. Biesle, "The German Settlers and the Indians in Texas, 1844-1860." *Southern Historical Quarterly* 31, (1927) 116-129.

[46] Remark of the author: Professor Terry G. Jordan is uncertain if the transcription of this number is 100,000 or 700,000. To a German it is quite clear that this number is 100,000. But I know by personal experience that the Americans handwrite their number seven as the Germans write their number one.

encourage them to adopt agriculture, so that I think we will see them completely banished from our area within two months.

My own affairs have changed considerably. When I left the Llano with my wares because of the Indians, I was forced to sell them in order to be able to meet other obligations incurred in a lawsuit with a merchant in Fredericksburg over some grain, and I suffered considerable losses in this sale. I had delivered a large amount of grain to A. G. Wolff in Fredericksburg, who had taken over the grain contract with the fort,[47] and it was picked up at my house by his teamsters. It happened that en route to the fort six wagons full of grain were stopped and robbed by the Indians. Of course, I demanded my money from Wolff, but he said I should deal with the teamsters. I told him that I could not do that, since I had nothing to do with them and that he had hired them and was therefore responsible. In short, I was forced to sue. I won in the first, second, and last stages of appeal, but there is one disadvantage in Texas, the plaintive party has to underwrite the court expenses. This put me into great financial difficulties. If I had lost, I would have had to start again from scratch, for the court costs amounted to $160. As it is, I have no expenses, except $20 to my lawyer. I am to receive $100, which will be paid to me within two weeks.[48]

I have sold my house on the Llano and have bought a piece of land, 160 acres in size, near Fredericksburg, perhaps as pretty as any to be found in Texas. I will start a farm. It is four hours from Fredericksburg, has water, wood, in short, everything. For this year I have rented a farm of sixteen acres ready for cultivation about an hour from here, and I will start to farm this summer.

The land I bought cost me $160 in cash, two yoke of oxen cost me $110, a breaking plough $16. In short, I have had quite a few expenses. My money on hand after expenses amounts to about $200. In addition, I own a good horse worth $80 and all the riding gear. But half a year earlier, I owned over double that amount.

The prospect for this year's crop is bad, since there is a severe drought. My visit to Germany will have to be postponed again for several years.

I have received the cherry brandy and the wine. The wine was a little sour, but the cherry brandy was very good. Incidentally, the expenses of shipping the liquor were equal to the price I received for selling it, after, of course, I had taken some for my own use.

My only wish would be that you would decide to immigrate to Texas. We could live together very happily, especially since you no longer have any children in Germany. I have not found a wife yet, although that is the first requirement for getting anywhere in Texas. I still think you will have to send me one.

I am quite familiar with European happenings, since I continually read the newspaper. I view the storming of Sebastopol with impatience.[49]

---

47 Fort Mason.

48 The jury's verdict in this case, Kettner vs Wolff, is shown in Fig. 18.

49 The reference is to the Crimean War (Jordan and Jordan, 469).

Upon receipt of this letter, buy me a half-dozen pairs of glasses with frames No. 9 and No. 10, pack them well in a letter, and send them to me by mail, not by opportunity.[50] The last things that were sent by opportunity, I think there were some glasses among them did not arrive, even though two years have passed, and I do not think they will ever come. This sending by opportunity is the unsafest means one can imagine. I think you sent the last package by Christian Schrempp, and I have seen none of all those persons who wanted to come here from Oberkirch and its surroundings. They probably let themselves be diverted in the port towns, for this is a big business in America. My last pair of glasses, which I am wearing, is in bad condition, and I have not been able to find others, although I have made great effort.

I have dreamed very often lately about home.

In the hope that you are all still healthy, I remain your thankful son,

Franz Kettner

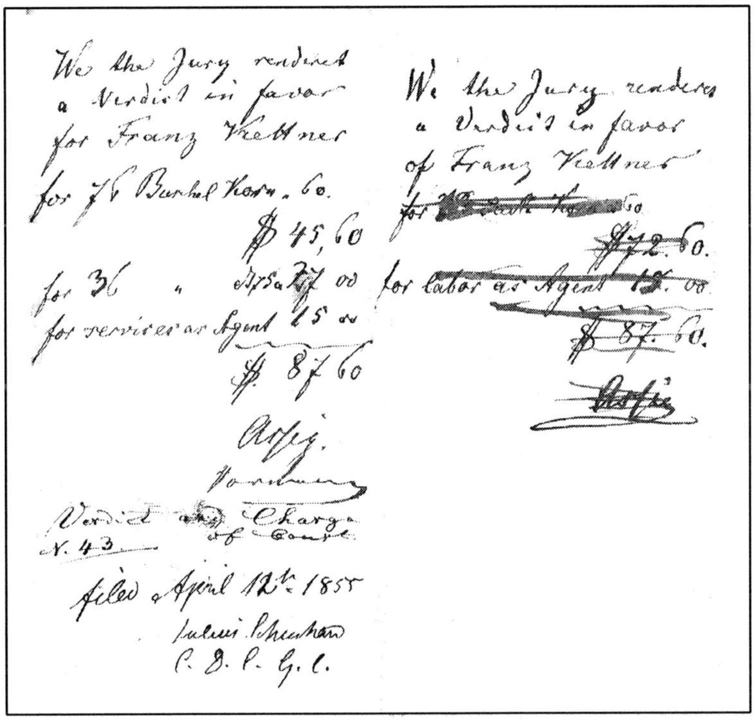
We the Jury render a Verdict in favor for Franz Kettner for 76 Bushel Korn . 60.

$ 45,60

for 36 " 27 00

for services as Agent 15 00

$ 87 60

We the Jury renders a Verdict in favor of Franz Kettner

$72.60.

for labor as Agent 15. 00

$ 87. 60.

Verdict Charge of Court

N. 43

filed April 12th 1855

**Fig. 18. Handwritten Jury Verdict in Kettner *v* Wolff Aug. 12, 1855.** This case is described in the District Court Minutes of Gillespie County. (Book A, 1849-1855, p 172-172B). Extensive documentation for this case, including an itemized list of expenses, are archived in the Court House.

**Abb. 18. Handschriftliches Gerichtsurteil in der Angelegenheit Kettner gegen Wolff vom 12. August 1855.** Dieser Fall wird im Protokoll des Bezirksgerichtes von Gillespie County beschrieben. (Buch A, 1849-1855, p 172-172B). Eine ausführliche Dokumentation dieses Falls, einschließlich einer spezifizierten Liste von Ausgaben, ist im Gerichtshaus archiviert.

50 *Per Gelegenheit*, or "sending by opportunity." referred to the practice of sending via other emigrants who were coming from Oberkirch to Texas (Jordan and Jordan, 469).

## Brief 4 (23. April 1855) von Franz Kettner aus Friedrichsburg/Texas an seine Eltern

Liebe Eltern!

Seit Ihrem letzten Brief, den ich gelegentlich im Dezember vorigen Jahres erhielt, habe keine Nachricht mehr von Ihnen erhalten. Ich beeile mich, da ich wieder vom Militär frei bin, Ihnen sofort Nachricht darüber zu geben. Unser ganzer Kriegszug beschränkte sich nämlich bloß darauf, Wagentransporte für das reguläre Militär zu eskortieren. Wir waren sechs Kompanien stark und eskortierten ungefähr 400 6-spännige Maultierwagen nach dem etwas unterhalb El Paso angelegten Fort, ungefähr 600 Meilen von San Antonio,[51] und gebrauchten dazu hin und zurück ungefähr 3 Monate. Außer, daß sehr viele infolge schlechter Witterung starben, fiel gar nichts Interessantes vor. Es war eine wilde, felsige Gegend, welche sehr viel Mangel an Wasser hat, so daß wir manchmal zwei Tagereisen gebrauchten, um wieder an Wasser zu gelangen. Ich für meinen Teil ertrug die Strapazen sehr gut und war nicht ein einziges Mal krank.

Was die Indianer-Räubereien anbelangt, so haben solche bis Mitte März fortgedauert und es wurden sehr viele Menschen, meistens Deutsche, sogar in unmittelbarer Nähe von Friedrichsburg heimlicherweise getötet. Der Schaden an Feldern und Rindvieh, was gestohlen wurde, ist nicht zu berechnen. Jetzt hat sich Ruhe eingestellt, da der Kongreß 100.000 Dollars zur Fütterung für die Indianer bewilligt hat. Außerdem wird jetzt der Versuch gemacht, dieselben auf einem dazu bestimmten Gebiet niederzulassen und zu kultivieren, namentlich zum Ackerbau anzuhalten, so daß ich glaube, daß wir in ungefähr zwei Monaten dieselben gänzlich aus unserer Gegend verbannt sehen werden.

Was meine eigenen Angelegenheiten anbelangt, so haben sich diese sehr verändert. Als ich nämlich mit meinen Waren der Indianer wegen Llano verließ, so war ich durch einen Kornprozeß, welchen ich mit einem Kaufmann in Friedrichsburg hatte, gezwungen, die Waren auszuverkaufen, um andererseits meiner Verbindlichkeit nachkommen zu können und verlor ziemlich viel daran. Ich hatte nämlich an A. C. Wollff in Friedrichsburg, welcher den Kontrakt für das Fort übernommen hatte, eine große Anzahl Korn geliefert. Es wurde von dessen Fuhrleuten in meinem Hause abgeholt. Nun ergab sich daß sechs Wagen voll Korn unterwegs von Indianern abgefaßt und sämtliches Korn gestohlen wurde. Ich verlangte natürlicherweise mein Geld von Wollff und dieser sagte mir, ich sollte mich an die Fuhrleute halten. Ich erklärte ihm, daß ich dieses nicht könnte, indem ich mit denselben nichts zu tun hätte und er dieselben engagiert, deshalb auch dafür verantwortlich wäre. Kurz, ich wurde gezwungen zu klagen. Ich gewann es in erster, zweiter und letzter Instanz. Nun ist dieser Übelstand in Texas, daß der klagende Teil sämtliche Unkosten auszulegen hat, was mich in große Geldverlegenheit brachte. Der letzte Termin war in Friedrichsburg den 10. April 1855 und ich wollte deshalb

[51] Nach Professor Terry G. Jordan (s. Jordan and Jordan, 463) kann Kettner sich hier nur auf Fort Bliss bezogen haben, das 1848 gegründet wurde.

nicht eher schreiben als bis diese Sache entschieden war. Wenn ich verloren hätte, dann hätte ich gerade wieder von vorne anfangen können, denn die Unkosten belaufen sich auf 400 Gulden; so habe ich jetzt keine Auslagen als meinen Advokat mit fl 50. Der Betrag macht fl 250, welche ich binnen 14 Tagen ausbezahlt bekomme.

Mein Haus am Llano habe ich verkauft und habe mir in der Nähe von Friedrichsburg ein Stück Land, 160 Acre groß, so schön wie es vielleicht in Texas zu finden ist, gekauft und werde mir eine Farm einrichten. Ich habe 4 Stunden nach Friedrichsburg, Quellen, Holz, kurzum alles vereinigt. Für dieses Jahr habe eine Stunde davon eine Farm gemietet von 16 Acre in Kultur. Werde diesen Sommer ans Bauen[52] gehen. Das Land kostet nur in bar 160 Dollars, zwei Joch Ochsen 110 Dollars, einen Brechpflug 16 Dollars, kurzum ich habe schon schöne Ausgaben gemacht. Meine Barschaft außer den gemachten Ausgaben wird sich ungefähr noch auf 200 Dollars belaufen. Außerdem besitze ein feines Pferd 80 Dollars wert und sämtliche Einrichtung.[53] Ein halbes Jahr vorher hatte aber über das Doppelte mehr. Die Aussicht für die diesjährige Ernte ist schlecht, wir haben große Trockenheit. Der Besuch nach Deutschland wird jetzt allerdings wieder einige Jahre weiter hinausgeschoben werden.

Das Kirschenwasser und Wein habe erhalten. Der Wein war sauer, das Kirschenwasser sehr gut. Übrigens haben sich die Unkosten gerade so hoch belaufen, als ich daraus machte, einiges für meinen eigenen Gebrauch abgerechnet. Mein einziger Wunsch wäre, daß Sie sich entschließen möchten, nach Texas auszuwandern. Wir könnten hier sehr glücklich zusammen leben, besonders, da Sie keine Kinder mehr in Deutschland besitzen. Zu einer Frau bin ich immer noch nicht gekommen, obgleich es die erste Bedingung ist, um zu etwas zu kommen in Texas. Ich glaube doch noch, daß Sie mir eine schicken müssen.

Mit den europäischen Angelegenheiten bin ich vollkommen bekannt, da ich beständig die Zeitung lese, und ich sehe mit Ungeduld der Erstürmung von Sebastopol entgegen.[54]

Lassen Sie mir die Tante von Mannheim[55] einmal grüßen und sagen, daß ich ihrer stets gedenke mit dem frommen Wunsch, auch meiner zu gedenken. Von meinem toten Schwesterchen habe schon oft geträumt und ich muß gestehen, daß mich Ihr Tod mehr angegriffen hat wie Idas.[56] Dieses mag vielleicht daher rühren, daß es mich zu plötzlich überraschte, während ich auf den der Ida vorbereitet war. Unterlassen Sie ja nicht, mir einen Ring zum Andenken von Ihr zukommen zu lassen.

---

[52] Gemeint ist Bauen im Sinne von Anbauen.

[53] Wie Professor Jordan anmerkt, ist es interessant zur Kenntnis zu nehmen, daß der Wert für ein gutes Pferd dem Gegenwert von achtzig Acres Land entsprach (s. Jordan and Jordan, 468).

[54] Kettner bezieht sich auf den Krim-Krieg (s. Jordan and Jordan, 469).

[55] Maria Magdalena Sartorius, geb. Kettner, wohnhaft Mannheim.

[56] Ida Leopoldine Kettner, verh. Kissel , geb. 19.07.1821, gest. 10.11.1845. Von einer zweiten Schwester ist der Autorin nichts bekannt.

Ich habe überhaupt auf meinen Brief von Friedrichsburg Antwort erwartet, und ich vermute, daß entweder mein Brief oder Ihre Antwort verloren gegangen sein muß. Wagner und seine liebe Frau habe auch einmal besucht. Es geht ihnen sehr gut und ich glaube, sie leben sehr glücklich. Bei Ankunft dieses Briefes besorgen Sie mir ein halbes Dutzend Brillen mit Gestellen Nr. 9 und 10, verpacken solche gut in meinen Brief und schicken mir solche per Post. Ja nicht per Gelegenheit hierher. Die letzten Sachen per Gelegenheit, ich glaube es waren Brillen dabei, habe nicht erhalten. Es sind nun zwei Jahre, und ich glaube, ich werde es nie mehr erhalten. Dieses per Gelegenheit schicken ist das Unsicherste was man sich denken kann. Ich glaube per Christian Schrempp schickten Sie es damals. Und von allen denen, die hier herkommen wollten von Oberkirch oder Umgegend bekam noch keinen zu sehen, weil sie sich wahrscheinlich in den Hafenstädten wieder abwendig machen lassen, denn dieses wird in Amerika als großes Geschäft betrieben.[57] Meine letzte Brille, die ich auf habe, ist in schlechtem Zustand und ich konnte trotz vieler Mühe noch keine auftreiben.

Gestern träumte ich von Welle aus Oedsbach, ob sie wohl noch jeden Donnerstag kommen mag. Ich habe überhaupt in letzter Zeit viel von zu Hause geträumt.

In der Hoffnung, daß Sie noch alle wohl und gesund sind verbleibe ich

Ihr dankbarer Sohn Franz Kettner.

Friedrichsburg, 23. April 1855

---

[57] Nach Professor Jordan hingen zwielichtige Charaktere aller Sorten in den Docks herum, die auf die Emigranten-Schiffe warteten. Diese hatten viele Methoden, um die Emigranten um ihr Geld zu erleichtern, speziell der Verkauf wertlosen Lands (s. Jordan and Jordan, 469).

# Letter / Brief 5

## Letter 5 (April 2, 1856) from Franz Kettner in Fredericksburg, Texas to his Parents

Dear Parents,

I finally received the glasses, but I am sorry to report that they are completely useless. The glasses are much too ordinary and badly ground. They must not have been made by an optician, but by a dabbler in that specialty. I have been able to obtain a good pair of glasses with much hard-earned money.

Concerning my present living conditions, I am happy to be able to tell you that they have improved considerably. After I had my farm half established, I found a buyer for it who gave me $250 more than I had paid. Besides the cash, I took four yoke of oxen in payment. With the oxen, I earned $175 within a month and a half by hauling a wagon to a fort 150 miles above Fredericksburg.[58] I let my oxen rest near the Llano during March and went to look for another piece of land, not far from that I sold earlier. I found it. I have already made a contract for the work on the farm, and I myself will only break the land and make the necessary trips with my ox-wagon in order to earn a few hundred dollars in cash. Later on I will rent my wagon for half its profits, on which I could live very well even without the farm. The only loss I have had was that the Indians once again stole my horse, but I was consoled by the fact that I can buy another one at any time, since my finances are in very good condition.

One week before I sold my farm in the vicinity of which fifteen families now live, I shot six deer in one morning, and we went out with a horsedrawn wagon to get them. During the three-quarter year stay there, I also found twenty bee trees, of which the best one had thirty bottles of honey. I shot more deer in this nine month

---

[58] The Germans were quite active in the freighting business in West Texas. Kettner apparently misjudged the distance and meant Fort McKavett, founded in 1852 in present-day Menard County, some 100 miles from Fredericksburg. (Jordan and Jordan, 470)

period than I usually shoot in two years, without spending much time at it, except on Sundays and early in the mornings when I went to look for the oxen.

We now have a large German beer brewery, which turns out a splendid product. Now one has something decent to drink when one comes to town. I must admit that I really filled myself up drinking the last time I was in town.

This year at Pentecost, we will have a big singing festival in Fredericksburg, and in the evening a dance where I, as an eligible bachelor, must of course not be missing.

Fredericksburg has really progressed in the last few years, and only strong, well-built stone houses are built now.

In the United States, people believe there will be a war with England and France, and the younger people are even hoping for this war. The French and English will find a small difference between Russia and the United States, for while in Russia the soldiers must be forcibly recruited, here millions of volunteers rush to enlist at the beginning of a war. Each of them will fight for home, freedom, and independence.

The reason for my not writing earlier was the glasses. I did not want to write until they had arrived. Please answer my letter soon and tell me all the news of my old hometown. ...

I am healthy and doing well and am leaving tomorrow with a wagon load for Fort Mason.

I remain your loving son,
Franz Kettner

**Fig. 19. Replica of One of the Officer's Quarters of Fort Mason.** Fort Mason was established in July of 1851 as one of a line of forts to protect the frontier from Indians. It was at its maximum occupancy in 1856 when it was the headquarters for the U.S. Second Cavalry and Companies B, C, D, G, H, and I under Col. Albert Sidney Johnston. The fort was abandoned to the Confederacy during the Civil War and was reoccupied in 1866. It was abandoned 1869 and fell into disrepair. The fort consisted of approximately 30 buildings surrounding a parade ground. The replica of the officers's Quarters was built by the Mason Historical Society in 1976. The state marker was installed in 1936. Note the fort was located on Post Hill, a high vantage point where the surrounding country side can be observed and today the town of Mason. *Handbook of Texas Online*, s.v. "Fort Mason," http://www.tsha.utexas.edu/handbook/online/articles/FF/qbf34.html (accessed July 30, 2007).

**Abb. 19. Nachbildung eines Offiziersquartiers in Fort Mason.** Fort Mason wurde im Juli 1851 gegründet als eines einer Reihe von Forts, um die Grenze vor Indianern zu schützen. Es hatte seine maximale Besatzung im Jahre 1856, als es das Hauptquartier für die 2. US Kavallerie war und für die Kompanien B, C, D, G, H und I unter Colonel Albert Signey Johnston. Das Fort wurde den Konföderierten während des Bürgerkrieges überlassen und 1866 zurückerobert. Es wurde 1869 aufgegeben und verfiel. Das Fort bestand aus ca. 30 Gebäuden, die einen Paradeplatz umgaben. Die Nachbildung des Offiziersquartiers wurde durch die Mason Historical Society im Jahre 1976 gebaut. Der Gedenkstein wurde im Jahre 1936 errichtet. Bemerke, dass das Fort auf Post Hill lag, einem hohen günstigen Punkt, von dem aus die Umgebung beobachtet weren kann und heute die Stadt Mason. *Handbook of Texas Online*, s.v. "Fort Mason," http://www.tsha.utexas.edu/handbook/-online/articles/FF/qbf34.html (Zugriff am 30. Juli 2007).

## Brief 5 (2. April 1856) von Franz Kettner aus Friedrichsburg/Texas an seine Eltern[59]

Liebe Eltern!

Die Brillen habe ich endlich erhalten, aber leider sind dieselben für mich ganz und gar untauglich. Die Gläser sind viel zu ordinär und schlecht geschliffen. Dieselben müssen von keinem Opticus herstammen, sondern von einem Stümper in diesem Fache. Außerdem sind dieselben nicht hohl geschliffen. Ich habe mir aber mit schwerem Geld eine gute Brille zu verschaffen gewußt, und der Schaden wäre damit ausgeglichen.

Was meine jetzigen Lebensverhältnisse anbelangt, so freut mich sehr Ihnen melden zu können, daß dieselben sich sehr gebessert haben. Nachdem ich nämlich meine Farm halb eingerichtet hatte, so fand sich ein Käufer, welcher mir 250 Dollar mehr gab, als es mich kostete. Außer barem Geld, nahm ich einen Ochsenwagen mit 4 Joch Ochsen mit in den Kauf. Mit diesem erwarb ich mir in einem Monat und in einem Halben 175 Dollars mittels einer Ladung, welche ich nach einem Fort brachte, 150 Meilen oberhalb Friedericksburg. Im Monat März gab ich meinen Ochsen Ruhe an der Llano, und suchte mir ein anderes Stück Land. Nicht sehr weit von meinem verkauften Land, fand sich ein schöner Fleck und ich erwarte jeden Tag den Feldmesser, um es vermessen zu lassen. Die Arbeiten zu dieser Farm habe bereits in Accord gegeben und ich werde bloß das Land brechen und die nötigen Fuhren tun, denn ich glaube, ich stelle mich besser. Den Monat April, Mai und Juni werde ich noch einige kleine Touren mit meinem Ochsenwagen machen, um noch einige hundert Dollars bar in die Hand zu bekommen: Später werde ich meinen Frachtwagen vermieten gegen die Hälfte, wovon ich ohne Farm sehr gut leben könnte. Den einzigen Verlust den ich hatte, ist, daß die Indianer mir wieder einmal mein Pferd stahlen. Habe mich aber sehr rasch getröstet, indem ich mir zu jeder Zeit für Geld wieder eines kaufen kann, und meine Cassa im Augenblick sehr gut ist.

Acht Tage bevor ich meinen Platz, in dessen unmittelbarer Nähe jetzt mehr als 15 Familien wohnen, verkaufte, habe ich an einem Vormittage 6 Stück Hirsche geschossen, so daß wir mit einem Pferdewagen hinausfuhren, um dieselben zu holen. Ebenso fand ich während meines ¾-jährigen Aufenthaltes daselbst mehr als 20 Stück Bienenbäume, wovon der beste ungefähr 30 Flaschen Honig gab. Diese ¾ Jahre habe ich mehr Hirsche geschossen als sonst in zwei Jahren, ohne extra Zeit darauf zu verwenden, außer am Sonntag, sondern immer morgens früh beim Ochsensuchen.

---

[59] Anmerkung der Autorin: Der folgende Brief, in dem Franz Kettner seine Verheiratung mit Katherine Keller mitteilt, liegt heute nicht mehr vor. Die Eltern müssen ihn erhalten haben, da sie ihrem Sohn zur Vermählung gratuliert haben. Die Heirat fand am 3. September 1857 in der Vereins-Kirche in Fredericksburg statt. Die Schwiegereltern waren Johann Peter Keller (1802-1872) und Anna Maria Keller, geb. Mohr (1817-?). Quelle: *Mason County Historical Book*, 135 (Mason, Texas: Mason County Historical Commission, 1976).

Gesund und munter bin ich noch immer und die Leute behaupten, daß ich noch nicht gealtert habe seit ich in Texas bin. Die meisten Menschen halten mich auch bloß für 24 Jahre alt.

Wir haben jetzt eine große deutsche Bierbrauerei, welche einen herrlichen Stoff liefert, so daß man etwas ordentliches zu trinken hat, wenn man in die Stadt kommt. Ich muß ehrlich gestehen, daß ich mich das letzte mal, als ich in der Stadt war, ordentlich satt getrunken habe.

Diesen Pfingsten haben wir in Friedrichsburg ein großes Gesangsfest und abends Ball, wo ich natürlicherweise als Heirats-Kandidat nicht fehlen darf. Friedrichsburg hat sich in den letzen Jahren ungemein gehoben. Es werden jetzt bloß noch massive Steinhäuser gebaut.

In den Vereinigten Staaten glaubt man an einen Krieg mit England und Frankreich; und die junge Bevölkerung wünscht sogar den Krieg. Die Franzosen und Engländer würden übrigens doch einen kleinen Unterschied finden zwischen Rußland und den Vereinigten Staaten, denn während in Rußland die Rekruten mit Gewalt ausgehoben werden müssen, so strömen hier bei Ausbruch eines Krieges Millionen von Freiwilligen zu den Fahnen und ein jeder schlägt sich für seine Heimat und für die Freiheit und Unabhängigkeit. Übrigens haben die Alliierten, trotz ihrer Prophezeiung, daß sie niemals Sebastopol nehmen könnten und würden, dasselbe doch eines schönen Morgens genommen? Wo bleibt denn der Krieg?

Die Ursache meines langen Stillschweigens waren die Brillen. Ich wollte nicht eher schreiben, als bis dieselben angekommen waren. Haben Sie die Güte und beantworten Sie mir diesen Brief bald. Schreiben Sie mir alle Neuigkeiten, die es in meiner alten Vaterstadt gegeben hat. Und ich werde nicht verabsäumen, Ihnen alsdann sogleich einen sehr ausführlichen Brief zu schreiben über mein neu gekauftes Stück Land, was ich jetzt noch nicht kann, da ich die Grenzen noch nicht kenne und es erst sicher weiß, wenn es vermessen ist.

Alle diejenigen, die nach mir fragen, grüßen Sie von mir. Dieser kurze Brief hat den Zweck, erstens Vorwürfe zu ersparen wegen meinem zu langen Nichtschreiben, zweitens um Ihnen Gewißheit zu geben, daß ich gesund bin und daß es mir gut geht. Denn freie Zeit habe ich im Augenblick wenig, da ich morgen mit einer Ladung wieder nach Fort Mason fahre.

Antworten Sie mir sogleich und Sie werden alsdann einen ausführlichen Brief erhalten.

Indessen verbleibe Ihr Sie liebender Sohn
Franz Kettner

Friedrichsburg, 2. April 1856

# Letter / Brief 6

### Letter 6 (March 15, 1858) from Franz Kettner in Fredericksburg, Texas to his Parents

Dear Parents,

I just received your letter of December 29, 1857 in early March and am hurrying in order to answer it. We thank you kindly for your congratulations concerning our wedding.[60] Concerning your good advice on how I should treat my wife, I can assure you that my wife is very satisfied with me and I believe that I have become a considerate husband. Concerning the marriage of my childhood friend Schauenburg, it delights me that he has married the same year as I. Give him my greetings and I will send him a letter soon. That my dear mother is completely well again makes me exceedingly happy.

Although it concerns you that I could become exhausted because of my hard work with good Mother Earth, I can assure you that this winter (which was so mild that we hardly had any frost at night) I plowed up 40 acres of land (the acre here is considerably larger than a German morgen) together with a hired man. In addition, I have often been riding out to gather cattle. Up to today, I have rounded up twenty cows with calves.

In addition, you wanted to know whether one could build a saw mill on a small river. Certainly, when a person has enough money in order to build it! However, the wages here are so high that the costs to build a simple saw mill when one counts in all the costs including land on which the saw mill could be built is not less than 10,000 German guldens. My father-in-law has a hired man who earns 265 German guldens yearly in wages. Now you can imagine approximately just how much it costs

---

[60] Franz married Catherine Keller on September 3, 1857 in the Vereins-Kirche in Fredericksburg [Mary Kothmann, "Francis (Franz) Kettner," in *Mason County Historical Book,* 135 (Mason, Texas, Mason County Historical Commission, 1976)]. The Vereins-Kirche is shown in Fig. 20. Franz's in-laws were Johann Peter Keller (1802-1872) and Anna Maria (Mohr) Keller (1817- unknown). Franz's letter to his parents telling of his marriage and their response are missing.

in German money in order to establish some business here. Also, a person can buy more for a gulden in Germany than here with a dollar, which is worth about 2 gulden and 50 kreuzer.

Concerning your desire to support me at this time with money – we do not want to talk about it. What the reciprocal agreement between Baden and the state of Texas is, I simply cannot tell you. There are scarcely any people from the state of Baden who live here and the Texas government perhaps believes, due to the small number, that an agreement is not worth the trouble. It also does not matter to me because I surely know being here in Texas that I will not get anything after your death. I am unaffected whether estate property is taken away or not. I think that by then, it will no longer be very necessary. I would not be in need of it at all if my father-in-law had not had to pay the government for his land claims this year, which cost him 800 florin. I am not so in need now overall since my father-in-law will make an amount of over 800 florins from his land claims which do not have to be cashed in to the government this year. In addition, we had a bad harvest so we had to buy our flour for bread. If my father-in-law had not had this expense, he could have helped me without a strain. Regarding the two gold rings, send them to me through the mail, packed in the following manner: between two pieces of paper lids, sewn together, and in a very good letter envelope. Have them made according to the enclosed size. The larger one is for me, the smaller for my wife.

My father-in-law is from the Prussian area on the Rhine. He is in his fifties[61] and weighs over 300 pounds. My household possessions consist of a large bed (the most luxurious item here and which cost me 30 florins), a table and chairs, a mirror, etc.,etc.

You know that I still live with my in-laws.

People do not need a lot of room here because they spend almost all of the year on the porch. My wife and I have a beautiful room which we hardly use except to sleep and to house our belongings.

My personal work this winter, as I have mentioned above, is plowing and planting, for example, corn, wheat, Chinese sugar beets, sweet potatoes, and a type of horse feed similar to clover. That is what we plant in the fields. In addition, in a garden of about 3 acres, we plant all the vegetable varieties that are found in Germany. So far we have planted one third of the fields in addition to having the garden all completed. I will be planting until the end of March or the middle of April. From then on, my work will be to round up the cattle. This work lasts until the end of June. Then the heat will be pretty strong and the Texas time for loafing around begins.

My father-in-law has already sold 17 head of three-year-old cattle the beginning of March for 220 dollars and he can still sell about another 30 head. Because of the poor harvest, however, he must make a living from cattle proceeds and also freight hauling.

[61] Johann Peter Keller is 56 years old at this time.

I have received four span of oxen from my father-in-law so you can easily understand that I need a wagon so that I can earn money from the capital received from the cattle rather than let it lie around. In addition, when I have a good wagon and can hire a boy, I can earn enough to pay for household expenses and clothing for my wife and myself. All of this, so to say, is an existential question until my cattle are grown enough that I can sell them as ready-for-slaughter cattle that are shipped by steamer from Texas to New Orleans.

You are speaking though of the future. Now, I will put out this case, you receive (from 500 florins at 5 percent interest) 25 florins in interest. When your financial situation is such that your entire future depends on 25 florins in interest more or less, I believe that in five years at the latest, I will be able to add an additional 50 florins to your yearly 25 florins in interest.

Regarding your further wish, to be with me only 8 days in order to be helpful to me with your experience – I can only tell you plainly: We call all the people who come here directly from Europe with the expression "greenhorns" because they act so foolish until they have learned to adapt to the conditions here. That happens only after they have lost all the money that they have brought with them. The same thing would happen to you despite all your experience. I also understand very well what is possible to do here with speculation and the hatching of plans. However, I have been held back only through the lack of funds. It is easy to make money when you have capital in hand. However, without capital, it goes exactly the same as in Germany.

You wanted to know about the varieties of trees. Of the ones known to you there are oak, elm, walnut, and black walnut. In addition, there are cedar and cypress from which shingles are made. Then there is a type of resinous wood. There are saw mills driven by man power as well as steam power.

A railway is being built from Indianola[62] on the coast to San Antonio. I talked to Lambrecht in Fredericksburg a while ago. He is also not doing so well. He had counted on a good harvest but had a poor harvest. He is earning his living by making shingles.

Concerning Mr. Wegner, I can assure you that his account of making money is the biggest exaggeration that I have ever heard. He earns his living and lives very well, so far as I could see three years ago. However, to save money is unthinkable. He lacks all the possibilities. I ask you not to make a fuss about this with his relatives. The expression here in Texas is that when someone has a son, he says that he is already a thousand dollars richer because the labor costs here are so expensive and

---

[62] Indianola (called Karlshafen initially and founded in 1846) is located on Matagorda Bay in Calhoun County, TX. It was the origin of the military road running from the coast to San Antonio and Austin and was the initial port of entry for German immigrants into western Texas. It also served as a supply depot for the western forts. Indianola was destroyed by a hurricane in 1875. It was rebuilt and destroyed again by a hurricane and accompanying fire in 1886 to be abandoned. *Handbook of Texas Online*, s.v. "Indianola, Texas," http://www.tsha.utexas.edu/handbook/online/articles/-II/hvi11.html (accessed July 30, 2006). See Fig. 21.

the father will soon have help. Perhaps Mr. Wegner, who has a fairly large batch of children, figures them to be his saved capital.

No one spends any effort here to raise bees. They are all wild and hide in hollow trees or cliffs. They are found by taking honey and some aniseed – when the bees come they are slowly followed until one reaches the place. Then the honey is taken but the bees are not further cared for because they can find food here the entire year.

I have described to you in my last letter how the cattle are raised here. Fodder grows here the whole year and one does not think about feeding horses. Raising sheep has increased a lot here, and I think that there will be a significant trade in wool here in a few years. They flourish here exceptionally well.

You also want to know my way of life. I live exactly as you so in Germany with the exception that I eat for breakfast either fried meat or sausage or eggs. We slaughtered two cattle and about twelve pigs this winter.

Almost all the fashion extravagance here, principally due to the feminine sex, is as much as in Germany.

In addition to the bad harvest that we had last year there was still greater damage. We had a hard frost at the time the oak trees were in full bloom. This meant the trees grew no acorns and the feed for the pigs was ruined. It was a big loss for my father-in-law who is accustomed to selling 200 dollars worth of bacon and lard every year.

Every man here in Texas has his own brand. Usually it is one or two letters or a number made out of iron with which the cow is branded, usually on the back hip. Likewise, there is a marking on the ear so that each can recognize his animal. All the calves are now held in fenced enclosures. The cows come home in the evening to be partly milked, the rest the calves get. In the evenings, the cows are fenced in and the calves let out so that they can eat some grass. The next morning the calves are again in the vicinity of the fenced pen and are allowed to go to the cows. Each cow is again milked, only a little, so that they remain tame.

The young animals and oxen come every evening along with the milk cows to the house and sleep in the vicinity of the house or lay near the corral. When all the animals come together every evening in the area around the house, there are 500 head. It is an impressive sight when the animals, in groups of 60 head come from different directions in the evening toward home. They are all fat, hardy, and lively. It is the same with the horses when they come home each evening at full run, their tails straight in the air, making all sorts of jumps, in order to receive their grain.

Enclosed you will find the measurements for both rings, that is, the circumference of the inside of the rings. Get one with decorations for my wife, she owns a plain one, the other, however, with a small capsule in which the hair of both of my dead sisters[63] can be saved. My wife wishes, additionally, that you, when the opportunity presents itself, have daguerreotype portraits taken of yourselves and send them to us. She very much desires to know you at least by pictures.

---

[63] See letter 4.

News, such as the Mainz gunpowder works and the grenade assassination attempt on Louis Napoleon,[64] in general all the European news, we know in detail and extremely fast, since we receive two New York newspapers and one Texas newspaper. We receive two newspapers from New York each week.

My father-in-law asks a favor from you. He read in the New York newspaper about a railroad lottery in Baden of 400,000 tickets in which someone has to win. The tickets were priced through the agents at 2 dollars here or 5 German guldens and the drawing was each quarter year. He wishes to have tickets for each of the three drawings which remain for this year, when that is possible. He would like you, therefore, to purchase a ticket for him under the name J.P. Keller from America and in the next letter to write what the cost is for these three drawings. He will either pay you the amount by money order or pay me here, which ever you prefer.

I will write my aunt in Milwaukee[65] in the next few days. Because it is rainy weather, I am using this time to answer your letter. My wife and I, as well as my in-laws, send you our best greeting and remain yours.

Franz Kettner

[64] Napoleon III, Emperor of France (1852-1870).

[65] No information is available on this individual.

**Fig. 20. Vereins-Kirche (Society Church).** The Adelsverein established the colony of Fredericksburg on May 8, 1846. Streets and lots were laid out and a site for a church in the middle of Main Street (Market Square) in the center of town was selected. The church was established in 1847 and was considered common property for all settlers in Gillespie County. It served as a school and meeting house as well as a church for early Fredericksburg. However, it fell into disrepair and was torn down in 1897. The Gillespie County Historical Society constructed a replica of the Vereins-Kirche on the site of the original building in 1934 which stands today. [Handbook of Texas Online, s.v. "Vereins Kirche," http://www.tsha.utexas.edu/habook/online/articles/VV/ccv1.html (accessed July 8, 2007)]. The photograph of the original Vereins-Kirche was obtained through courtesy of the Gillespie County Historical Society. Special thanks are extended to Natasha Atkins, Curator, for her generous help in selecting the image and also in finding the map in Fig. 21.

**Abb. 20. Vereins-Kirche (Society Church).** Der Adelsverein gründete die Kolonie von Fredericksburg am 8. Mai 1846. Straßen und Grundstücke wurden abgesteckt und ein Platz für eine Kirche in der Mitte der Main Street (Marktplatz) im Zentrum der Stadt wurde ausgewählt. Die Kirche wurde im Jahre 1847 errichtet und wurde als Gemeinschaftseigentum aller Siedler in Gillespie County angesehen. Sie diente als Schule und Treffpunkt sowie als Kirche für das frühe Fredericksburg. Allerdings geriet sie in Verfall und wurde 1897 abgerissen. Die Gillespie County Historical Society errichtete einen Nachbau der Vereins-Kirche auf dem Gelände des ursprünglichen Gebäudes im Jahre 1934, der heute noch steht. [Handbook of Texas Online, s.v. "Vereins-Kirche," http://www.tsha.utexas.edu/habook/online/articles/VV/ccv1.html (zugegriffen 8. Juli 2007)]. Das Foto der Original Vereins-Kirche wurde mit freundlicher Genehmigung der Gillespie County Historical Society zur Verfügung gestellt. Besonderer Dank gebührt der Kuratorin Natasha Atkins für ihre großzügige Hilfe bei der Auswahl der Bilder und auch bei der Suche nach der Karte in Abb. 21.

**Fig. 21. Immigrant Route to Castell.** The Adelsverein map (full map) has the following legend:

**Map of the State of**
**TEXAS**
*According to the new borders in Washington in September 1850 and confirmed by the Texas legislature in Austin*
*Issued by the "Society for the Protection of German Emigration", in Wiesbaden, together with special maps of the Society's properties, a panorama of New Braunfels and an instruction for emigrants*
*In the Society's own publishing house in Wiesbaden*
***1851***

The locations of towns (Indianola, Victoria, Gonzales, New Braunfels, Fredericksburg, and Castell) along the immigrant route were added to the expanded map. The distance from New Braunfels to Fredericksburg is about 60 miles and from Fredericksburg to Fort Mason is approximately 40 miles.

The Adelsverein Map was provided courtesy of the Texas General Land Office, P.O. Box 12873, Austin, TX 78711-2873 (www.glo.state.tx.us). Thanks are extended to Jerry Patterson and Susan Smith Dorsey of the Land Office for their help. Note that theTexas General Land Office has archived a number of historic Texas maps which are available to the public. (Continued on the next page.)

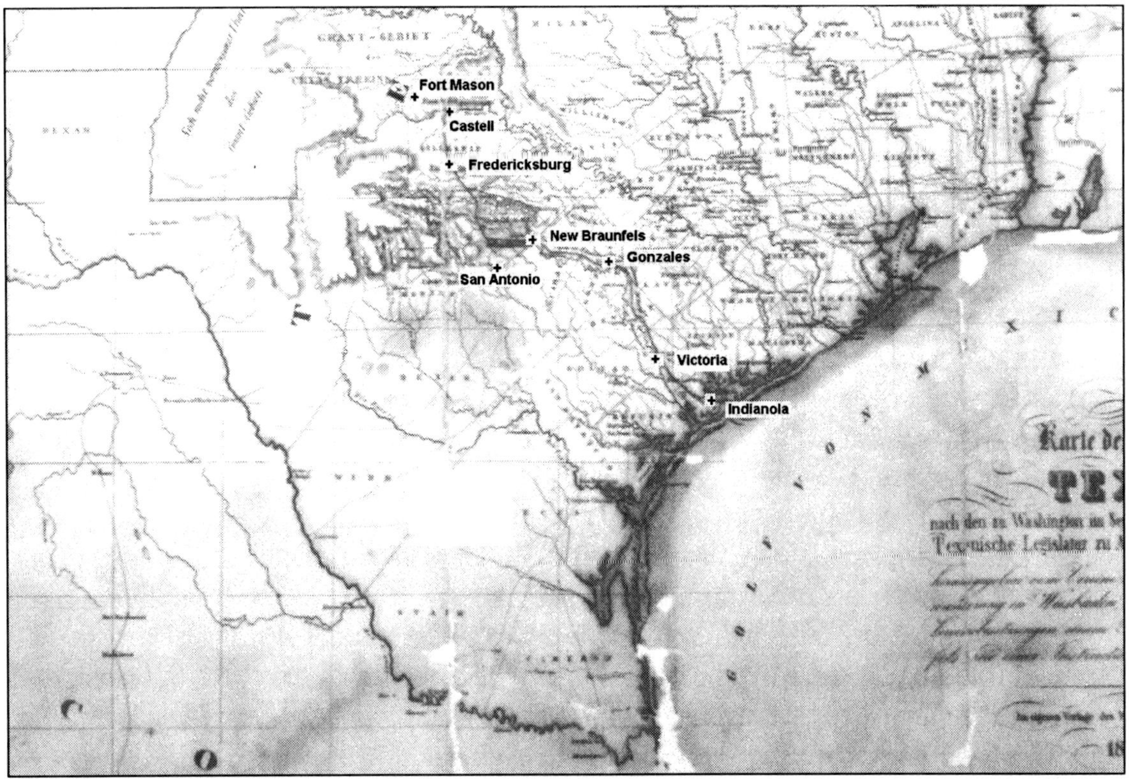


**Abb. 21. Immigrationsweg nach Castell.** Die *Karte des Adelsvereins* (ganze Karte) hat folgende Legende:

**Karte des Staates**
**TEXAS**
*Nach den zu Washington im September 1850 regulierten und durch die Texanische Legislatur zu Austin bestätigten neuen Grenzen*
*Herausgegeben vom Verein zum Schutz deutscher Auswanderung in Wiesbaden, nebst Spezialkarten der Vereinsbesitzungen, einem Panorama von Neu Braunfels und einer Instruktion für Auswanderer.*
*Im eigenen Verlage des Vereins zu Wiesbaden*
***1851***

Die Standorte der Städte (Indianola, Victoria, Gonzales, Neu Braunfels, Fredericksburg, und Castell) entlang der Route der Einwanderer wurden in der erweiterten Karte ergänzt. Die Entfernung von Neu Braunfels nach Fredericksburg beträgt ungefähr 60 Meilen und von Fredericksburg nach Fort Mason ist etwa 40 Meilen.

Die Karte des Adelsvereins wurde mit freundlicher Genehmigung vom Texas General Land Office, PO Box 12873, Austin, TX 78711-2873 (www.glo.state.tx.us) zur Verfügung gestellt. Dank gebührt auch Jerry Patterson und Susan Smith Dorsey vom Land Office für ihre Hilfe. Beachten Sie, dass das Texas General Land Office eine Reihe von historischen Karten von Texas archiviert hat, die der Öffentlichkeit zur Verfügung stehen.

## Brief 6 (15. März 1858) von Franz Kettner aus Friedrichsburg/Texas an seine Eltern

Liebe Eltern!

Ihren Brief vom 29. Dezember 1857 habe erst anfangs März erhalten und beeile mich, denselben sofort zu beantworten. Was Ihre Glückwünsche zu unserer Verheiratung anbelangen, so danken wir Ihnen verbindlichst. Was die guten Ermahnungen anbelangen, wie ich meine Frau behandeln soll, so kann ich Ihnen Versicherung geben, daß meine Frau mit mir sehr zufrieden ist und ich glaube, daß ich einen aufmerksamen Ehemann abgegeben habe. Was die Verheiratung meines Jugendfreundes Schauenburg anbelangt, so hat es mich gefreut, daß er in demselben Jahr mit mir geheiratet hat. Und ich lasse ihn grüßen und werde ihm nächstens einen Brief senden. Daß meine liebe Mutter sich wieder ganz wohl befindet, hat mich außerordentlich gefreut.

Was Ihre Sorge anbelangt, daß durch meine starken Anstrengungen der guten Mutter Erde zu viele Kräfte entzogen werden könnten, so kann ich Ihnen doch die Versicherung geben, daß ich diesen Winter, welcher sehr gelind war, so daß wir bloß einigemal kleine Nachtfroste hatten, mit einem Knecht zusammen 40 Acres Land (der hiesige Acre ist bedeutend größer als der deutsche Morgen) herumgepflügt habe. Dabei bin ich aber auch sehr viel nach Vieh geritten, denn ich habe bis auf den heutigen Tag schon zwanzig Kühe mit Kälbern eingetrieben.

Außerdem wünschten Sie zu wissen, ob sich an einem Flüßchen nicht eine Sägemühle anbringen ließe? O ja, wenn man Geld genug hat, um eine bauen zu lassen. Aber da die Arbeit so teuer bezahlt wird, so läßt sich eine einfache Schneidemühle, wenn man alles rechnet, Land, worauf die Sägemühle gebaut werden könnte, nicht unter 10.000 deutscher Gulden bauen. Mein Schwiegervater hat einen Knecht, welcher jährlich 265 deutsche Gulden Arbeitslohn erhält. Nun können Sie sich ungefähr vorstellen, wie viel nach deutschem Gelde dazu gehört, um hier etwas anzufangen. In Deutschland kommt man aber auch mit einem Gulden weiter als hier mit einem Dollars, welches fl 2.50 Kreuzer[66] sind.

Was meinen Wunsch anbelangt, mich im Augenblick etwas mit Geld zu unterstützen, wollen wir jetzt ganz mit Stillschweigen übergehen. Was den abzuschließenden Staatsvertrag Texas einerseits mit Baden anbelangt, so kann ich Ihnen bloß erwidern, daß beinahe gar keine Badenser in Texas wohnen, und wegen der geringen Zahl, die Regierung vielleicht glaubt, daß es die Mühe nicht wert ist. Außerdem ist mir auch gar nicht daran gelegen, denn ich weiß doch, daß ich hier in Texas nach Ihrem Tode nichts erhalte.[67] Also bleibt es mir ganz gleichgültig, ob Liegenschaften abgezogen werden oder nicht. Ich glaube auch, daß ich es bis dahin nicht mehr sehr nötig hätte. Ich hätte es überhaupt nicht sehr nötig, wenn mein Schwiegervater, nicht dieses Jahr seine Landpatente bei der Regierung einlösen muß, welches eine Summe von über fl 800 ausmacht. Außerdem war die letzte eine

---

[66] fl 2,50 Kreuzer heißt 2 Gulden 50 Kreuzer.

[67] Franz Kettner irrt. Siehe Briefe 37 und 39.

totale Mißernte, so daß wir das Mehl für Brot kaufen mußten. Wenn mein Schwiegervater diese Ausgaben nicht hätte, so würde er mir unaufgefordert genug helfen. Was die beiden goldenen Ringe anbelangen, so senden Sie dieselben per Post, folgendermaßen verpackt: zwischen zwei Stückchen Papendeckel aufgenäht, und in einem guten Briefcouvert nach folgendem inliegenden Maß. Das größere für mich, das kleinere für meine Frau.

Mein Schwiegervater ist aus dem Rheinpreußischen, ist ein fünfziger[68] und wiegt über 300 Pfund. Was meine häusliche Einrichtung anbelangt, so besteht diese in einer großen Bettstelle, worauf hier der meiste Luxus verwendet wird, und welche mich fl 30 kostete. Tisch und Stühle, Spiegel, etc. etc. Daß ich bei meinen Schwiegereltern noch wohne, wissen Sie.

Große Räumlichkeiten hat man hier nicht, da man sich beinahe das ganze Jahr unter den Galerien der Häuser aufhält. Ich habe mit meiner Frau ein hübsches Zimmer, welches wir aber beinahe zu nichts benützen als zum Schlafen und um unsere Sachen aufzubewahren.

Was meine persönliche Beschäftigung anbelangt, so bestand diese diesen Winter, wie schon oben erwähnt, im Pflügen und Pflanzen, z. B. Korn, Weizen, chinesisches Zuckerrohr, süße Kartoffeln, außerdem eine Art Pferdefutter, ähnlich wie Klee. Das ist es, was wir in das Feld pflanzen. Außerdem in einem Garten, der ungefähr 3 Acre hält, welcher mit allerlei Gemüse, wie auch in Deutschland, bepflanzt wird. Bis auf den heutigen Tag haben wir ein Drittel des Feldes bepflanzt, außerdem den Garten in die Reihe gebracht. Mit dem Pflanzen habe ich zu tun bis Ende März oder Mitte April. Von da an ist meine beständige Beschäftigung, das Vieh zusammenzutreiben. Diese Arbeit dauert bis Ende Juni, wo dann die Hitze ziemlich stark wird und das texanische Faulenzen anfängt.

Mein Schwiegervater hat Anfang März schon 17 Stück 3-jährige Ochsen zu 220 Dollars verkauft und er kann ungefähr noch 30 weitere Stück verkaufen. Er muß aber wegen Mißernte auch vom Ochsenerlös und vom Frachtwagen leben. Da ich 4 Joch Ochsen von meinem Schwiegervater erhalten habe, so können Sie sich leicht denken, daß ich eines Wagens sehr bedarf, damit sich das Kapital rentiert, das in den Ochsen steckt, und nicht ruhig daliegt. Außerdem, wenn ich einen guten Wagen habe, so bringt er mir, wenn ich mir einen Jungen dazu halte, soviel ein, als ich mit meiner Frau an Haushaltungsausgaben und Kleidern brauche. Also ist dieses sozusagen eine Existenzfrage, bis mein Vieh soweit herangewachsen ist, daß ich Schlachtochsen verkaufen kann, welche von Texas per Dampfschiff nach New Orleans kommen.

Sie sprechen allerdings von der Zukunft. Nun, ich setze den Fall, Sie erhielten (fl 500 à 5 Prozent) fl 25 Zinsen das Jahr weniger. Wenn Ihre pekuniären Verhältnissen so sind, daß Ihre ganze Zukunft von fl 25 jährlich Zinsen mehr oder weniger abhängt, so glaube ich, in längstens 5 Jahren soweit zu sein, daß ich Ihnen zu diesen fl 25 Zinsen jährlich noch weitere 50 fl zukommen lassen kann.

[68] Johann Peter Keller ist zu diesem Zeitpunkt 56 Jahre alt.

Was Ihren weiteren Wunsch anbelangt, nur 8 Tage bei mir sein zu können, um mir mit Ihren Erfahrungen nützlich sein zu können, so kann ich Ihnen bloß erwidern: Wir bezeichnen hier alle Menschen, welche direkt von Europa hierher kommen, mit dem Ausdruck 'Grüne', weil sie sich so albern anstellen, bis sie sich in die Verhältnisse eingearbeitet haben. Das geschieht erst dann, wenn ihr mitgebrachtes Geld auf die Neige geht. Und so würde es Ihnen trotz Ihrer alten Erfahrungen auch gehen. Pläne schmieden und von Spekulationen sprechen, welche hier zu machen sind, verstehe ich auch recht gut. Aber an der Ausführung bin ich nur durch Mangel an Kapital gehindert. Geld ist hier sehr leicht zu machen, wenn jemand Kapital in Händen hat. Aber ohne Kapital geht es gerade wie in Deutschland auch.

Was die Gattungen des Holzes anbelangt, welches Sie zu wissen wünschen, so gibt es hier von den Ihnen bekannten Holzarten Eichen, Ulmen, Nußbaum, schwarze Walnuß, außerdem gibt es Zedern, Zypressen, wovon die Schindeln gemacht werden. Dann eine Art harziges Holz. Schneidemühlen gibt es genug, durch Menschenkraft getrieben, sowie auch durch Dampfkraft.

Auch ist eine Eisenbahn von Indianola[69] an der Küste bis San Antonio in Arbeit genommen worden. Lam(brecht?)[70] habe ich vor einiger Zeit in Friedrichsburg gesprochen.

Es geht ihm auch nicht am besten. Er hatte sich auf eine sichere Ernte verlassen und es gab eine Mißernte. Er machte sein Leben mit Schindelmachen.

Was Herrn Wegner anbelangt, so kann ich Ihnen die Versicherung geben, daß sein Geldmachen die größte Aufschneiderei ist, die mir je vorgekommen ist. Er macht sein Leben und lebt ganz gut, so viel ich vor 3 Jahren gesehen habe. Aber daran Geld zu sparen, ist gar nicht zu denken. Es fehlt ihm noch an allem Möglichen. Ich bitte mir aus, bei seinen Verwandten keinen Gebrauch davon zu machen. Die Redensart ist hier in Texas, wenn jemand einen Jungen bekommt, so sagt er, schon wieder tausend Taler reicher, weil die Arbeitskräfte hier teuer sind, und ein Vater dann bald Hilfe hat. Vielleicht rechnet Herr Wegner, welcher ein ziemlich großes Häuflein Kinder hat, diese zu seinem ersparten Kapital.

Auf Bienenzucht wird hier gar keine Aufmerksamkeit verwendet, sondern sie sind alle wild und stecken in hohlen Bäumen oder Felsen und werden aufgesucht, nämlich mit Honig und etwas Anis, wonach die Bienen kommen und immer langsam verfolgt werden, bis man den Aufenthalt erreicht. Dann wird der Honig

---

[69] Indianola Hafenstadt an der Matagorda Bay im Calhoun County, Texas. Gegründet im August 1846. 1844 wurde ein Küstenstreifen ausgewählt von Carl, Prinz von Solms Braunfels, Generalbeauftragter des sog. Adelsvereins, als Landeplatz für die deutschen Emigranten, die unter der Sponsorschaft des Vereins für West-Texas bestimmt waren. Die Landestelle wurde ursprünglich mit Karlshafen bezeichnet. Im Februar 1849 wurde der Name der wachsenden Stadt in Indianola geändert. Quelle: *Handbook of Texas Online*, unter dem Stichwort "Indianola, Texas," http://www.tsha.utexas.edu/handbook/online/articles/II/hvi11.html (Zugriff 21.10.2003). S. Abb.21.

[70] Name abgekürzt bzw Spitzname, Ergänzung nach Vermutung der Autorin.

genommen und um die Bienen wird sich weiter nicht bekümmert, da die Bienen das ganze Jahr hindurch Futter finden.

Auf welche Art die Viehzucht hier betrieben wird, habe ich Ihnen in meinem letzten Brief geschrieben. Futter wächst hier das ganze Jahr hindurch und an Fütterung unserer Pferde wird hier nicht gedacht. Die Schafzucht kommt jetzt sehr in Aufnahme und ich glaube, in einigen Jahren wird hier ein bedeutender Wollhandel sein. Sie gedeihen außerordentlich gut.

Außerdem wünschen Sie meine Lebensweise zu wissen. Ich lebe gerade so wie Sie in Deutschland, ausgenommen daß ich morgens zum Frühstück entweder gebratenes Fleisch oder Wurst oder Eier esse. Wir haben diesen Winter 2 Ochsen und ungefähr 12 Schweine geschlachtet.

Der Luxus ist hier beinahe, namentlich unter dem weiblichen Geschlecht, so groß wie in Deutschland.

Letztes Jahr hatten wir außer Mißernte noch einen großen Schaden. Wir bekamen nämlich einen starken Nachfrost, nachdem die Eichbäume schon in voller Blüte standen, wodurch die Bäume keine Eicheln trugen und die Mast für die Schweine ruiniert war. Das machte meinem Schwiegervater einen großen Schaden, welcher gewohnt war jährlich für 200 Dollars Speck und Schmalz zu verkaufen.

Hier in Texas hat jeder Mann sein Brandzeichen. Gewöhnlich ein oder zwei Buchstaben oder eine Zahl aus Eisen, womit das Vieh gebrannt wird, gewöhnlich auf die hintere Hüfte. Ebenso eine Markierung an den Ohren, damit jeder sein Vieh kennt. Die Kälber werden jetzt alle in Umzäunungen gehalten. Abends kommen die Kühe nach Haus, werden etwas gemolken, das andere bekommen die Kälber. Die Nächte bleiben die Kühe eingesperrt und die Kälber kommen heraus, damit sie etwas Gras fressen können. Den nächsten Morgen befinden sich die Kälber alle wieder in der Nähe der Umzäunung, werden zu den Kühen gelassen und es wird abermals etwas gemolken von jeder Kuh, nur eine Kleinigkeit, damit sie zahm bleiben. Wenn dann die Kälber gegen Spätjahr hin so groß sind, daß die Kühe nicht mehr danach kommen, so werden sie gebrannt und gemarkt und mit den Kühen laufengelassen. Jedes Frühjahr wird der ganze Viehstock nach Hause getrieben.

Das junge Vieh und Ochsen kommen jeden Abend mit den Milchkühen nach Hause und schlafen in der Nähe vom Hause oder liegen bei der Umzäunung, so daß, wenn das Vieh alles wieder beisammen ist, jeden Abend an 500 Stück Vieh in der Umgegend vom Hause liegen. Es ist ein prachtvoller Anblick, wenn das Vieh, abends in Truppen von 60 Stück aus verschiedenen Richtungen nach Hause kommt. Alle fett, munter und tanzend. So auch die Pferde, wenn sie abends in vollem Jagen, die Schwänze schnurgerade in die Höhe, alle Arten von Bocksprünge machend, nach Hause kommen, um ihr Korn in Empfang zu nehmen.

Beiliegend finden Sie das Maß der beiden Ringe, nämlich den Umfang der inneren Seite des Ringes. Für meine Frau nehmen Sie einen mit Verzierungen, einen einfachen besitzt sie. Der andere aber mit einer Kapsel, wo das Haar von meinen beiden verstorbenen Schwestern[71] aufbewahrt werden kann. Meine Frau wünscht außerdem, daß Sie, wenn sich einmal eine sichere Gelegenheit darbietet, uns Ihre beiden Portraits als Daguerreotypie ausgeführt senden mögen. Sie verlangt sehr, Sie wenigstens per Bild kennen zu lernen.

Neuigkeiten, wie Mainzer Pulvergeschäfte, das Granatenattentat auf Louis Napoleon,[72] überhaupt alle europäischen Neuigkeiten, erfahren wir sehr ausführlich und ungeheuer rasch, da wir 2 New Yorker Zeitungen und eine Texas-Zeitung halten. Wir erhalten wöchentlich 2 Zeitungen von New York.

Ein Anliegen hat mein Schwiegervater an Sie. Er las nämlich in der New Yorker Staats-Zeitung von der badischen Eisenbahn-Lotterie, von den 400000? Losen, wovon ein jedes gewinnen muß. Das Los war durch den Agenten zu 2 hiesigen Dollars oder nach deutschem Gelde zu 5 Gulden angerechnet und vierteljährige Ziehung. Er wünscht, wenn sich die Sache so verhält, für diese drei Ziehungen, welche dieses Jahr noch vorkommen, jedesmal ein Los zu nehmen; Er ersucht Sie deshalb, ein Los für ihn zu nehmen unter dem Namen I. P. Keller aus Amerika und in dem nächsten Brief zu schreiben, was der Betrag eines Loses für die drei Ziehungen ist. Entweder wird er Ihnen den Betrag per Wechsel oder an mich hier bezahlen; wie es Ihnen dann beliebt.

An meine Tante in Milwaukee[73] werde ich nächsten Tage schreiben. Da wir gerade Regenwetter hatten, so benutze ich diese Zeit, um Ihren Brief zu beantworten.

Meine Frau und ich sowie meine Schwiegereltern grüßen Sie bestens und verbleiben Ihre

Franz Kettner

Friedrichsburg, 15. März 1858

---

[71] Vgl Brief Nr 4.

[72] Napoleon III., Kaiser der Franzosen (1852-1870).

[73] Die Daten der Tante in Milwaukee sind der Autorin bisher nicht bekannt.

# Letter / Brief 7

## Letter 7 (June 8, 1858) from Franz Kettner in Fredericksburg, Texas to his Parents

Dear Parents,

Because I have a secure opportunity offered to me to get some things from Germany, I am taking the liberty to burden you with some requests. Because fine clothing is so difficult to find and is also very expensive here (also my wife loves finery and is somewhat vain) send us a black silk fringed scarf, two white, embroidered collars, and a pair of white, well-embroidered cuffs, a gold clasp and what else Mama might sacrifice from her own finery. In addition, do not forget baby clothing because we are expecting a little one in the fall. My wife also wants the daguerreotype portrait of Papa and Mama and if possible one of the children.

Say hello to Nicolai and tell him he could send me a fine Meerschaum pipe as a keepsake.

Mr. Rexroth, who had bought some cattle stock here in the neighborhood and who travels back to Germany will spend four weeks there and then again return. He has promised me this totally secure opportunity to bring back a small chest with him if you will send one to him.

In addition, send me a bit and snaffle, however, from German silver.

In particular, send me finery for my wife for she is somewhat vain, which I gladly support and such items are very expensive here. They are nevertheless worn. Even high fashion makes progress here in Texas.

You can rely on Mr. Rexroth very certainly. He will send this letter on to you upon his arrival in Germany with the addition of his address, but he will be there at the longest four to five weeks.

My wife and in-laws greet you and I remain your son.

Franz Kettner
Fredericksburg, June 8, 1858

**Fig. 22. Catherine Keller Kettner.** This photograph is in the possession of Henrietta Kettner Keener and was labeled Grandma Kettner. We have no indication of her age.

**Abb. 22. Catherine Keller Kettner.** Dieses Foto befindet sich im Besitz von Henrietta Kettner Keener und wurde mit “Großmutter Kettner” bezeichnet. Wir haben keinen Hinweis auf ihr Alter.

## Brief 7 (8. Juni 1858) von Franz Kettner aus Friedrichsburg/Texas an seine Eltern

Liebe Eltern!

Da sich mir eine sichere Gelegenheit dargeboten hat, einiges von Deutschland zu erhalten, so bin ich so frei, Sie mit einigen Aufträgen zu belästigen. Da Putzsachen so schwer zu bekommen und auch hier sehr teuer sind, meine Frau sich außerdem gerne putzt und etwas eitel ist, so senden Sie uns eine seidene schwarze Mantille mit Fransen, zwei weiße gestickte Kragen und ein Paar weiße ausgestickte Vorärmel; eine goldene Agraffe.[74] Was immer Mama vielleicht noch von ihren Putzsachen entbehren will. Außerdem die Kindersachen ja nicht zu vergessen; denn wir erwarten etwas Kleines bis Herbst. Außerdem wünscht meine Frau die (Daguerreotypie) Abbildung, vom Papa und Mama und wo möglich von den Kindern.

Grüßen Sie Nicolai und sagen ihm, er möchte mir eine schöne Meerschaumpfeife zum Andenken schicken.

Herr Rexroth, welcher einen Stock Vieh hier in der Nachbarschaft gekauft hat, und welcher nach Deutschland zurückgeht, wird sich bloß 4 Wochen dort aufhalten und alsdann wieder hier zurückkehren. Es ist eine ganz sichere Gelegenheit Derselbe versprach mir, ein kleines Köfferchen mit hierher zu bringen, welches Sie an ihn senden wollen.

Außerdem senden Sie mir eine Stange und Trense, aber von Neusilber.

Namentlich schicken Sie für meine Frau Luxusgegenstände, denn sie ist etwas eitel, was ich ganz gerne sehe und solche Gegenstände sind hier sehr teuer; werden aber dennoch getragen. Da sogar der Luxus auch in Texas Fortschritte macht.

Auf Herrn Rexroth können Sie sich ganz sicher verlassen. Derselbe wird sofort bei Ankunft in Deutschland diesen Brief an Sie absenden, mit Hinzufügung seiner Adresse, wird sich aber höchstens 4 bis 5 Wochen dorten aufhalten.

Meine Frau und Schwiegereltern grüßen Sie und ich verbleibe

Ihr Sohn

Franz Kettner

Friedrichsburg, 8. Juni 1858

---

[74] Schmuckspange

# Letter / Brief 8

### Letter 8 (January 3, 1859) from Franz Kettner in Fredericksburg, Texas to his Parents[75]

Dear Parents,

Since my last letter many new things have happened to me. The main news is that I have a baby son who is a completely true image of me. He was born on December 16, 1858, a healthy child without flaws. My wife had to endure much pain since the labor pains followed very closely together but were not strong enough. The labor lasted from afternoon until the next morning at 2 o'clock. It was, however, without a doctor's help, only the midwife and my little bit. Since he looks so extremely similar to me, he has been blessed with the name Franz.[76]

Like I say, since my last letter a lot has changed. First, my wife and I no longer live with my in-laws but in the city and I practice my old occupation again. The disagreement developed because my in-laws kept back their promised dowry until my wife would have delivered the baby. They were afraid that she could die in child-birth and perhaps the baby, too, and then they would have lost the entire dowry for their other children. And then probably when they saw from my letter from Germany that I had no hope of an inheritance from you, they believed they had me totally in hand. I showed them, however, that I have a good future without their wealth.

The citizens of Fredericksburg, by whom I'm quite well-liked (without flattering myself) nominated me as candidate for sheriff in the election last August. There were three candidates, an American, a German, and my small self. It was a very exciting election and despite all the conceivable efforts my in-laws made to have me fail, I was elected for a two-year term by a majority of 200 votes.[77] I earn approximately

---

[75] This letter was published August 27,1973 in the Renchtal Newspaper in Oberkirch in a slightly shortened form.

[76] Apparently, Franz decided later to name his son Louis rather than Franz.

[77] County Records [B. Blum, "The History of the Development of Gillespie County According to Information Taken from the County Records" in *Fredericksburg, Texas, the First Fifty Years,* trans. C.L. Wisseman, 52 (Fredericksburg, TX: Fredericksburg Publishing Co., Inc, 1971)] indicated the

400 to 500 dollars a year. My duties as sheriff are to appoint and to summon the jurors. The jail is my responsibility as well as to maintain the public peace. Each citizen has to obey me and when I request help, each must help me or face a punishment in jail for refusing.

The militia is directly under my command should it be necessary to call them out. The position is quite similar to that of a director of police in Germany. The difference is simply that we have no policemen and when the sheriff needs to arrest a criminal, he takes the best citizens or does it himself. The sheriff has the right to shoot anyone who is a danger to him. In addition, he can keep someone in prison without chains or with chains, according to his own desire or judgment. He can also set someone immediately free against the citizens' wishes when the sheriff judges that they were carried away (in their decision).

The sheriff stands under no supervision; everything depends upon his own judgment. The only authority that is over him is the jury who convenes every six months in each county in order to decide everything. There is one other high authority. Because the office of sheriff is so important, I must put up a security of six thousand dollars. In addition, I still have a beer saloon.

I am now in a shaky situation with my in-laws. Since we had our little son, they come to our home each time they come to the city and want to make everything right again. I myself still have no desire to do so. They are very obsessed with money and I am not, thank God.

My wife gave our little son a present of a cow and calf. I think that by the time he is grown up that he will have raised a large number of animals from them. My wife's shawl unfortunately looks rather shabby since she always wraps our son in it. I am sure you can still manage to put a pretty shawl in the packed chest as a Christmas present for my wife. Just something reasonable (priced), however, preferably an embroidered shawl with a blue background.

You mentioned to me concerning the riding gear that you are already old and have never used a silver-plated bridle. I surely believe that, but can say in reply that I do not ride an old nag but a fine horse (English breed). My horse, the kind which I need for my position, cost me 250 German gulden[78] in spite of the fact that horses are cheap here. You can understand that this kind of horse needs a fine bridle. The main point is that a person cannot buy separate gear here (that is bit and snaffle separately) but the bit and snaffle are attached.

---

following: "The following officers which were elected in 1858 were: Wm. Wahrmund, Chief Justice; F. Wrede, County Clerk. F. Fresenius, J.M. Caldwell, Wm. Marschall, Wm. Feller: Commissionsers. A. Erlemeyer, District Clerk. Francis Kettner, Sheriff. Georg Max, Assessor and Collector. Conrad Wehmeyer, Treasurer." "On July 27, 1859 Louis Weisz took the oath of office for sheriff and on October 10, 1859 Herman Ochs as county clerk. On February 6, 1860 Ed. Maier was sworn in as sheriff."

[78] 250 Gulden is equivalent to 100 dollars.

A reliable opportunity has come about since a very good acquaintance of mine is returning to Bremen to spend some time with his brother-in-law. As soon as you receive a letter from Mr. Seeger from Bremen, send the chest by railroad to him at his enclosed address. Mr. Seeger will send it on a ship which goes directly to Galveston so that the chest will come into my hands very certainly.

I am sending you this letter in the mail and at the same time writing one to Seeger in Bremen so that he will send you his address under which you can securely send him the chest. From then on, Seeger is responsible himself. He is a very reliable young man and has been a close friend of mine for two years. I have put this matter on his conscience before he left for Bremen.

Once again to return to our little boy; I never thought I could be so crazy over little children. First, he is so tremendously similar to me and second, we share at least our name. He is very well-behaved so far; he sleeps and drinks and drinks and sleeps. He is a beautiful child. The Fredericksburg Singing Club drank two kegs of beer (on my account) in my beer salon the next evening to celebrate the safe birth of the little boy. My wife is also once again completely recovered.

I hope that you are healthy and happy when this letter reaches you. My wife and I greet you many times and I love you.

Your grateful son, Franz Kettner

**Fig. 23. View of Fredericksburg, 1880's.** Note the Vereins-Kirche is in the center of the picture. This picture was obtained from the archives of the Gillespie County Library. It is also published in in the "Appendix" of *Fredericksburg, Texas, The First Fifty Years*, trans. C. L Wisseman, Sr., 116 (Fredericksburg, TX: Fredericksburg Publishing Co., Inc, 1971).

**Abb. 23. Blick auf Friedrichsburg um 1880.** Bemerke die Vereins-Kirche im Zentrum des Bildes. Dieses Bild stammt aus den Archiven der Gillespie County Bücherei. Es ist ebenso veröffentlicht im "Appendix" of *Fredericksburg, Texas, The First Fifty Years*, trans. C. L Wisseman, Sr., 116 (Fredericksburg, TX: Fredericksburg Publishing Co., Inc, 1971).

**Fig. 24. Gillespie County's First Court House.** Construction of the Court House was authorized on October 3, 1854. Its location was on the corner of Main and Crockett Streets. The structure served as a Court House until 1882. This information and the picture were taken from the Fredericksburg Newspaper (Elise Kowert, "First Court house Remembered," *Fredericksburg Standard Radio Post*, June 23, 1993).

**Abb. 24. Das erste Gerichts-gebäude des Gillespie County.** Der Bau des Gerichtsgebäudes wurde am 3. Oktober 1854 genehmigt. Es befand sich an der Ecke von Main Street und Crockett Street. Das Bauwerk diente als Gerichtsgebäude bis 1882. Diese Information und das Bild wurden der Friedrichsburger Zeitung entnommen (Elise Kowert, "First Court house Remembered," *Fredericksburg Standard Radio Post*, June 23, 1993).

## Brief 8 (3. Januar 1859) von Franz Kettner aus Friedrichsburg/Texas an seine Eltern[79]

Liebe Eltern!

Seit meinem letzten Brief hat sich viel Neues bei mir zugetragen. Die Hauptneuigkeit ist die, daß ich einen kleinen Jungen habe, ganz das getreue Ebenbild von mir. Der Junge wurde geboren am 16. Dezember 1858, ein gesundes Kind ohne Fehler. Meine Frau hatte viele Schmerzen auszustehen, da die Wehen sehr rasch aufeinander folgten, aber zu kurz waren. Es dauerte von mittags bis den nächsten Morgen 2 Uhr, aber ohne ärztliche Hilfe, bloß die Hebamme und meine Wenigkeit. Derselbe soll, da er mir so ungeheuer ähnlich sieht, mit dem Namen Franz[80] beglückt werden.

Seit meinem letzten Brief hat sich, sage ich, vieles verändert. Erstens wohne ich mit meiner Frau nicht mehr bei meinen Schwiegereltern, sondern in der Stadt, und betreibe meine alte Beschäftigung wieder. Die Uneinigkeit entstand namentlich daraus, daß meine Schwiegereltern ihre versprochene Mitgift (Aussteuer) zurückhielten, bis meine Frau niedergekommen wäre. Denn Sie hatten Angst, sie könnte im Kindbett sterben, vielleicht das Kind auch, und dann wäre die ganze Aussteuer verloren für ihre anderen Kindern. Und da Sie wahrscheinlich einen Brief von Deutschland an mich in die Hand bekamen, woraus Sie sahen, daß ich von Ihnen keine Unterstützung zu hoffen hatte, so glaubten Sie, mich vollständig in der Hand zu haben. Ich zeigte Ihnen aber, daß ich mein gutes Auskommen habe ohne Ihren Reichtum.

Die Friedrichsburger Bevölkerung, bei der ich, ohne mir zu schmeicheln, ziemlich beliebt bin, stellte mich als Kandidaten bei der letzten Augustwahl auf, als Kandidat für das Sheriffsamt. Wir waren zu dreien, ein Amerikaner, ein Deutscher und meine Wenigkeit. Es war eine sehr aufgeregte Wahl, und ich wurde, obgleich meine Schwiegereltern sich alle erdenkliche Mühe gaben, mich durchfallen zu machen, mit einer Majorität von 200 Stimmen für die Dauer von zwei Jahren für dieses Amt erwählt. Es bringt mir ungefähr 400 bis 500 Dollars jährlich ein. Mein Geschäft als Sheriff besteht darin, die Geschworenen bei Gericht selbst zu ernennen und vorzuladen. Außerdem steht das Gefängnis unter meiner Aufsicht, sowie für den öffentlichen Frieden Sorge zu tragen. Ein jeder Bürger hat mir zu gehorchen, und wenn er aufgefordert wird von mir, Hilfe zu leisten bei Strafe von Zuchthaus, wenn er sich weigert.

Sollte es bei Aufruhr nötig sein, Militär zu gebrauchen, so steht das Militär direkt unter meinem Befehle. Die Stellung ist beinahe ähnlich, wie die eines Polizeidirektors in Deutschland sein würde. Der Unterschied ist bloß, daß wir keine Polizeidiener haben und der Sheriff zur Festnahme von Verbrechern sich die ersten besten Bürger nimmt oder es selbst tut. Der Sheriff hat das Recht, einen jeden

---

[79] Dieser Brief wurde am 27.08.1973 in der Renchtal Zeitung in Oberkirch in leicht gekürzter Form veröffentlicht.

[80] Der erste Sohn wurde Louis genannt und nicht Franz.

niederzuschießen, wer sich ihm zu Wehr setzt. Außerdem kann er ihn frei im Gefängnis halten oder auch in Ketten schmieden lassen, je nach seinem Belieben oder seiner Ansicht, oder aber er kann denselben gegen hinreichende Bürgschaft sofort in Freiheit setzen, das heißt, wenn sie dem Shcriff hinreichend scheint.

Der Sheriff steht beinahe unter keiner Kontrolle, es hängt sozusagen alles von seiner eigenen Meinung ab. Die einzige Kontrolle, die über ihn da ist, sind die Geschworenengerichte, die alle 6 Monate in einem jeden County abgehalten werden, wo über alles entschieden wird. Außerdem haben wir noch eine höhere Instanz. Da das Amt eines Sheriffs sehr wichtig ist, so mußte ich selbst eine Bürgschaft stellen von sechstausend Dollars.[81] Außerdem habe ich noch einen Biersalon.

Mit meinen Schwiegereltern stehe ich jetzt auf einem sehr gespannten Fuße. Seit wir den kleinen Jungen haben, kommen sie zwar jedesmal in unser Haus, wenn sie in die Stadt kommen und wollen wieder alles gut machen. Allein bis jetzt hatte ich noch keine Lust dazu. Dieselben sind zu sehr Geldmenschen und Gott sei Dank, bin ich keiner davon.

Meine Frau schenkte unserem Söhnchen eine Kuh mit Kalb, und ich denke, bis er groß wird, hat er sich einen hübschen Stock Vieh davon gezogen. Da meine Frau den Jungen immer in ihren Schal einwickelt, so sieht dieser leider etwas schlecht aus. Und ich bin überzeugt, Sie fügen dem eingepackten Kistchen noch einen hübschen Schal als Weihnachtsgeschenk für meine Frau bei. Aber nur etwas Ordentliches, am liebsten hätte Sie einen gewirkten Schal mit blauem Grund.

Was die Reitstange anbelangt, so erwiderten Sie mir, sie wären schon alt, und hätten keine silberplattierte Stange geritten. Das glaube ich gerne, aber dagegen habe ich einzuwenden, daß ich auch keine Schindkraken reite, sondern feine Pferde (englische Rasse).

Mein Pferd, ich gebrauche nämlich ein solches für mein Amt, kostet mich 250 deutsche Gulden,[82] trotzdem die Pferde hier billig sind. Da können Sie sich wohl denken, daß zu einem solchen Pferde auch ein feines Gebiß gehört. Die Hauptsache ist die, man kann hier kein separiertes Gebiß, (nämlich Stange und Trense separiert) zu kaufen bekommen, sondern Stange und Trense sind fest miteinander verbunden.

Da ein sehr guter Bekannter von mir nach Bremen zurückging, wo er sich bei seinem Schwager einige Zeit aufhalten wird, so ist dieser die zuverlässigste Gelegenheit. Sobald Sie einen Brief von Mr. Seeger von Bremen werden erhalten haben, so schicken Sie das Kistchen per Eisenbahn an die von ihm Ihnen beigelegte Adresse. Mr. Seeger wird es von da durch ein Schiff besorgen, welches direkt nach Galveston geht, so daß es ganz sicher ist, daß es in meine Hände kommt.

Diesen Brief sende ich Ihnen per Post und zu gleicher Zeit schreibe ich einen an Seeger in Bremen, damit er Ihnen die Adresse zuschickt, unter welcher er das Kistchen sicher nach Bremen erhalten kann. Von da an besorgt Seeger selbst. Er ist

---

[81] Es wäre interessant zu wissen, wie es F.K. möglich war, eine Bürgschaft in dieser Höhe zu stellen.

[82] 250 Gulden = 100 Dollar. Gemäß Brief Nr. 4 kostete 1855 ein Pferd noch 80 Dollar.

ein zuverlässiger junger Mann, außerdem seit zwei Jahren ein intimer Bekannter von mir. Und ich habe es ihm, ehe er nach Bremen abreiste, sehr an das Gewissen gebunden.

Nochmals auf den kleinen Jungen zurückzukommen, so habe ich nicht gedacht, daß ich so verrückt auf kleine Kinder werden könnte. Allein er ist mir so ungeheuer ähnlich, und dann wird doch wenigstens unser Name erhalten. Er ist bis jetzt sehr artig, er schläft und trinkt und trinkt und schläft. Es ist ein sehr schönes Kind. Der Friedrichsburger Gesangverein hat den nächsten Abend sofort in meinem Biersalon zwei Fäßchen Bier auf meine eigene Rechnung getrunken auf das Wohlergehen des kleinen Jungen. Meine Frau ist jetzt auch wieder ganz munter.

In der Hoffnung, daß auch dieser Brief Sie gesund und glücklich antrifft, grüßt Sie meine Frau und ich vielmals und ich verbleibe Ihr

dankbarer Sohn Franz Kettner.

Friedrichsburg, 3. Januar 1859.

Viel Glück im neuen Jahr und bald einen Brief.

# Letter / Brief 9

### Letter 9 (May 1859) from Franz Kettner in Fredericksburg to his Parents

Dear Parents,

It is incomprehensible to me that I have not received a letter from you for a long time and that my letters remain unanswered. Have you not received my letter from December 1858 telling you that I have a baby son? I will tell you again that on December 16, 1858 my wife delivered a baby boy who is the picture of his father. The boy is five months old today and very healthy, lively, and is named Julius.[83] He is not baptized yet.

At the same time I wrote you about an acquaintance of mine by the name of Seeger who returned about 7 months ago and will stay for some time in Bremen. I requested that he send you his address in Bremen so that you could send him the chest for him to transport here. I am worried that this letter, which I sent at the same time as yours, did not reach him. Therefore, I am writing another letter to Seeger at the same time as this letter to request that he send you his address in order for you to send him the chest which he can bring back with him.

Because my wife's shawl has become unwearable due to the baby, you would bring her great pleasure when you include an embroidered shawl with a blue background. The opportunity[84] is completely safe. As soon as he sends you his address, send the chest to Seeger in Bremen for further transport and let me know about it in a letter.

Today I received a letter from Louise Huber who now lives on the coast of Texas in Indianola. Her husband is John C. Maag who introduced himself and inquired how I was getting along. I plan to answer her. Things are still going well for me, my wife is very healthy as is my little boy who only laughs and never cries.

---

[83] Apparently, the Kettners changed their minds several times in naming their son (Louis). In Letter 8, Franz says that they had named him Franz after his father and grandfather.

[84] When Franz says "opportunity", he is referring to "sending by opportunity". See Letter 4, footnote 50.

I had a dispute with my in-laws after they learned from one of your letters that they had read secretly in which you informed me that so far I could not receive any financial support from you. This had the result that they kept back the promised dowry for my wife until her delivery confinement was over. It has now passed that all the promised funds have been given and we are again on good terms.

I have now made a legal contract with my father-in-law to take care of all his stock for four years for a payment of every third calf each year which nets me as my share about sixty calves each year.

According to the newspapers, there will be a war in Italy in which perhaps all of Europe will be pulled in.[85]

My little boy weighs 18 pounds and is very strong.

When you have the opportunity to send us your portrait in a daguerreotype, it will make us very happy. You will receive sometime during this year a portrait of me, my wife, and the little boy.

The harvest outlook for this year is very bad due to the great drought. Raising sheep is coming to the forefront in Texas. We have received a settler from the northern states who owns 20,000 sheep. Also, the breeding of horses is becoming important. The wheat harvest last year came out very well. Additionally, we try to graft the wild grapes that grow here. The wine that is made from the wild grapes is very strong and red hued. A great quantity was made last year.

In the hope that I will soon receive a letter from you and that this letter finds you still hearty and healthy. I remain your son. Franz Kettner.

May 4, 1859 Fredericksburg

My wife and little boy greet you.

Unfortunately, I cannot write any more because I have much to do for the upcoming grand jury courts but I will write a detailed letter as soon as I receive an answer from you.

---

[85] Italian War of Independence. The Italian people (Garibaldi, Cavour) supported by France were victorious against Austria and the Church State. Source: Arno Peters, *Synchronoptische Weltgeschichte* (München-Hamburg: Universum-Verlag, 1965), see years 1859-1861.

### Brief 9 (4. Mai 1859) von Franz Kettner aus Friedrichsburg/Texas an seine Eltern

Liebe Eltern!

Es ist mir unbegreiflich, daß ich so lange Zeit keinen Brief von Ihnen erhalte und meine Briefe unbeantwortet bleiben. Haben Sie denn meinen Brief vom Dezember 1858 nicht erhalten, worin ich Ihnen anzeigte, daß ich einen kleinen Sohn habe? So zeige Ihnen nochmals an, daß am 16 Dezember 1858 meine Frau mit einem kleinen Jungen niederkam, ganz das Ebenbild seines Vaters. Der Junge ist auf den heutigen Tag 5 Monate alt und sehr gesund und munter und heißt Julius.[86] Getauft ist er zwar noch nicht.

Zu gleicher Zeit beauftragte ich (brieflich) einen Bekannten von mir namens Seegers, welcher vor ungefähr 7 Monaten zurückkehrte und sich einige Zeit in Bremen aufhalten wird, die Besorgung des besagten Kistchen zu übernehmen; und Ihnen von Bremen aus seine Adresse anzugeben. Ich befürchte, daß auch dieser Brief, welchen ich zu gleicher Zeit fortschickte, seine Bestimmung nicht erreicht hat. Deshalb sende ich mit diesem Brief einen Brief an Seegers, worin ich ihn ersuche, Ihnen seine Adresse anzugeben, damit Sie das Kistchen an denselben senden können, welcher mir dasselbe sicher hierher besorgen wird.

Da meiner Frau Ihre Schals durch den Jungen etwas sehr unbrauchbar geworden ist, so würden Sie Ihr eine große Freude bereiten, wenn Sie eine gewirkte Schal mit blauem Grund beilegen würden. Die Gelegenheit ist ganz sicher. Sobald er Ihnen also seine Adresse angegeben hat, so schicken Sie das Kistchen zur weiteren Beförderung an Seegers in Bremen und zeigen mir es aber in einem Briefe an.

Heute erhielt ich einen Brief von Louise Huber[87] jetzt wohnhaft in Indianola an der Küste von Texas. Ihr Mann heißt John C Maag, worin dieselbe sich erkundigt, wie es mir geht. Ich werde ihr antworten. Es geht mir immer noch sehr gut, meine Frau ist sehr gesund, so auch der kleine Junge, welcher bloß lacht und nie schreit.

Ich hatte Zwistigkeiten mit meinen Schwiegereltern, die durch heimliches Lesen eines Ihrer Briefe hervorgebracht waren, worin Sie mir anzeigten, daß ich vorderhand keine Unterstützung von Ihnen erhalten könnte. Das hatte zur Folge, daß dieselben das meiner Frau versprochene Vermögen zurückhielten, bis die Niederkunft vorbei war. Das hat sich jetzt gegeben, indem dieselben alles Versprochene herausgaben und wieder um gut Wetter anhielten.

Ich habe jetzt einen gerichtlichen Kontrakt mit meinem Schwiegervater gemacht, wonach ich seinen sämtlichen Stock Vieh auf vier Jahre übernehme, gegen das 3. Kalb jedes Jahr, was auf mein Teil ungefähr 60 Stück Kälber jedes Jahr ausmacht.

Nach den Zeitungen wird es wohl in Italien zu einem Kriege kommen, in den vielleicht ganz Europa hineingezogen wird.[88]

---

[86] Auch hier ist Louis Kettner gemeint.

[87] Die Beziehung zu Louise Huber ist der Autorin nicht bekannt.

[88] Befreiungskampf Italiens. Gegen Österreich und den Kirchenstaat siegt das von Frankreich unterstützte italienische Volk. (Garibaldi, Cavour). Quelle: Arno Peters, *Synchronoptische Weltgeschichte* (München-Hamburg: Universum-Verlag, 1965), s. Jahre 1859-1861.

Mein kleiner Junge wiegt 18 Pfund und ist sehr stark.

Wenn Sie Gelegenheit haben sollten, Ihr Portrait als Daguerreotypie senden zu können, so würde uns das sehr freuen. Sie werden im Laufe dieses Jahres mein, meiner Frau und des kleinen Jungen Portrait erhalten.

Die Ernteaussichten stehen sehr schlecht für dieses Jahr wegen zu großer Trockenheit. Die Schafzucht gewinnt jetzt in Texas die Oberhand. So haben wir einen Ansiedler erhalten aus den Nordstaaten mit 20.000 Stück Schafen. So auch die Pferdezucht. Die Weizenernte war letztes Jahr sehr gut ausgefallen; außerdem wird der wilde Wein, der hier wächst, zu veredeln gesucht. Der Wein von den wilden Trauben gemacht ist sehr stark und rot von Farbe. Es wurde eine Unmasse letztes Jahr gemacht.

In der Hoffnung, daß ich bald eine Nachricht von Ihnen erhalte und dieser Brief Sie noch munter und gesund antrifft,

verbleibe Ihr Sohn
Franz Kettner

Meine Frau und der kleine Junge lassen Sie grüßen.

Wegen der bevorstehenden großen Schwurgerichte, wobei ich sehr viel zu tun habe, kann ich leider nicht mehr schreiben, werde aber sobald ich eine Antwort von Ihnen erhalten habe, einen ausführlichen Brief schreiben.

Friedrichsburg, 4. Mai 1859

# Letter / Brief 10

## Letter 10 (July 8, 1860) from Franz Kettner at Foley's Crossing, Mason County, Texas to his Parents[89,90]

Dear Parents,

I received both of your letters but did not want to reply until we had received the chest. It arrived in good shape with all the items. The rings have pleased us very much. Concerning the children's things, we cannot use them for our little Louis but we are expecting another child this winter and the items will have good use. If we have a little girl, we will name her Ida. Our son walks and has begun to speak. He is large and strong for his age. He looks exactly like his grandfather in Germany. He makes us very happy.

Concerning the shawl, I must say honestly that we expected one somewhat better, that is with embroidery. My wife already has a similar one. You probably have little concept of the finery that prevails here and is, however, quite common. The sleeve cuffs and collar please us very much.

We now live on the Llano River because my service time is through.

---

89 Foley's Crossing is a location on the Llano River near the mouth of James River in Mason County approximately 8 miles southwest of the town of Mason, TX. Its present location is where Farm Rd 2389 crosses the Llano River. His house was later destroyed by flood waters from the Llano River in 1935. See Fig. 25.

90 During this period, Franz served as sheriff of Mason. Mason Co., founded in 1858. According to Stella Gibson Polk, *Mason and Mason County: A History* (Burnet, TX: Eakin Press, 1980), 166 using Kathryn Buford Eilers's thesis "A History of Mason County, Texas, Thesis August 1939," T.S. Milligan was the first sheriff and T.R. Cox was elected Sheriff in 1860. In May 1861, Francis Kettner was elected sheriff and served until the election in August 1862. However, J. Marvin Hunter ["Brief History of the Early Days in Mason County" *Frontier Times*, 6 January 1929, 153-166)] states that T.S. Milligan was the first sheriff and that he was killed by Indians on the outskirts of the town of Mason and that Franz Kettner replaced him. He says that Franz was probably appointed to this position.

We now have over 100 head of stock, among these 35 cows and calves this year. Next spring I will get 20 more cows, particularly young cows which are fertile so that I will have 55 head of cows and calves the following spring. In addition, I will sell 20 head of two-year-old steers for 10 dollars per head. The animals reproduce marvelously and are the most secure livelihood a person can have here, and also the most independent.

The slaughter steers are picked up from the house for the New Orleans market.

The only unpleasant thing is that one must live far from neighbors. My closest neighbor is an hour away from me and no one else lives north of me.

The Indians were very bad last winter and stole a large number of horses. About everyone south of me had lost horses. However, by chance I did not lose a single one although I came across Indians twice. The first time I was with my wife and child when I was bringing them to the cattle ranch with the ox wagon. We met five Indians who were herding about 40 stolen horses and they passed about 50 steps from our wagon. My only weapon consisted of my rifle. My revolver, which next to the rifle is the principal weapon in Texas (which fires its 6 bullets with accuracy up to a hundred paces), I had to leave behind with the bricklayer who worked in my place because Indians had been seen shortly before. Also, I had thought there would be little danger because the places where I took my wife always went by farms. Because I stopped the wagon immediately and grabbed my rifle, preparing for a desperate fight (and the Indians did not know that I was without my revolver), they went by me without attacking. You can scarcely imagine the fear of my wife since, shortly before, the Indians had killed some white men and scalped them (which means to cut the skin off the scalp and carry it with them as a trophy).

The second time, two red scoundrels were seen nearby my home who had the pious intention to steal my horses. I saw them, however, early enough and kept my horses in the house each night. In the daytime, I took them to the meadow myself and remained there. The Indians stayed in the vicinity for two days. On the third day they became bored and left; they visited my closest neighbor and had the luck to steal three horses.

Last winter was a very dangerous time for Texas. I took my revolver off in the evening and as soon as I got up in the morning, strapped it back on my side. It became quiet again in the spring time because large expeditions were undertaken against the Indians. I never risked leaving my wife alone, however, even for only an hour. I have hired a former Prussian artillery captain whom I can rely on to round up my cattle when I sometimes have to be away from my house for three or four days.

I am making good progress raising pigs. I now have about 70 pigs and in a year will have perhaps several hundred. My expenses are very low since we cannot consume (all) the butter as well as cheese and eggs. I slaughter my steers in winter as well as the needed number of pigs so that with 150 dollars I can operate my household. I can sell my steers for 200 dollars now and each year the number increases. As soon as my stock reaches over a hundred milk cows (which should at the most be in three years), I will lease the stock and care for only one half of them myself.

My wife is very cross that you have not sent her the daguerreotype of yourselves. She says that this would give her more pleasure than anything else. Therefore, I am asking you to send us another chest in the same manner by Mr. Seeger in Bremen and with the following articles: 3 good dresses for my wife, two made from muslin and one from linen, but somewhat elegant. Furthermore, a pair of golden earrings.

I would like to see, moreover, what sort of progress my niece Marie[91] has made in the convent. Therefore, I would like her to make my wife a fine embroidered slip, a pair of embroidered cuffs and a collar, and 6 linen handkerchiefs.

A dozen good knives and forks, as well as spoons and coffee spoons.

Furthermore, do not forget the daguerreotype of yourselves as well as one of Franz, Marie, Nicolai and little Klara.[92]

Several boxes of genuine Prussian primer caps, a good pocket knife with several blades. Regarding the trousers which you have sent me, I regret to say that I have very little use for them. First, I am not so wide, and second, I am taller than the pants are long.

I will let you design the chest, but not heavier or larger than the last one. The last one cost me 14 florins in German money which is very cheap for Texas. Corsets are very hard to find here and my old lady has a great fondness for laces.

When we have the opportunity, you will receive our daguerreotype by mail so that you will get to know my wife and little Louis better.

Concerning my health, I am still as spry as I was ten years ago, and I ride from morning to evening without becoming tired. To ride after cattle is a different type of riding than how you or someone else in Germany rides. It changes from all out galloping to trotting, right and left, through brush as well as over cliffs and rocks, similar to a hunting course in Germany.

Moreover, I am also still youthful in my behavior. In Texas, a person is old in years but still remains young. One does not become like a philistine as in Germany. That comes from natural living instead of forced living.

Within you will find a few lines attached for Mr. Fisher which you may want to take care of if necessary.

If Franz has the desire, send him to me. He can, when he desires, follow his inclination to be a merchant or become an animal breeder. I could well use a breeder.

---

[91] Maria Kissel was born June 28, 1844, and died October 2, 1879, in Oberkirch. She was the daughter of Ida Leopoldine Kissel (Franz's sister) and Karl Friedrich Kissel. Maria Kissel married Leopold Erdrich (born May 4, 1838, died February 2, 1877, in Oberkirch). Maria and Leopold Kissel are the great grandparents of Ilse Wurster, the author.

[92] Franz Lambert Xaver Friedrich Kissel, the brother of Maria Kissel, was born November 28, 1842 in Mannhein. The date of his death is not known. Specific information on Nicolai and Klaerchen is unavailable.

I have given my little boy a cow and her calf. When he is 15 years old, he will already have a fine small stock of animals. I will follow the same practice for all of my children. If I am able to do more for them when they are older, I will do it.

Tell Marie that if she has the desire to come to Texas, excellent opportunities are open to her. Available women are still rare here, particularly educated ones. I have only my good looks and abilities to thank that I got a wife. I was over 30 years old when I married, but my wife still believed that I was only 24 or 25.

On Sundays my wife and I usually ride over to visit the neighbors. Little Louis already rides a horse, also.

Before you prepare the chest, write to Seeger in Bremen to see whether he is willing to care for it and give him many greetings from me and my wife.

Give Welle many greetings and tell her that I often have thought about her.

Do not neglect little Louis in the chest. When the chest arrives, he will be over 2 years old and so already needs pants and little jackets.

In the hope that this letter finds you still healthy and hearty, we greet Marie and Franz, little Klara and Nicolai and remain your thankful children.

Franz Kettner and Wife

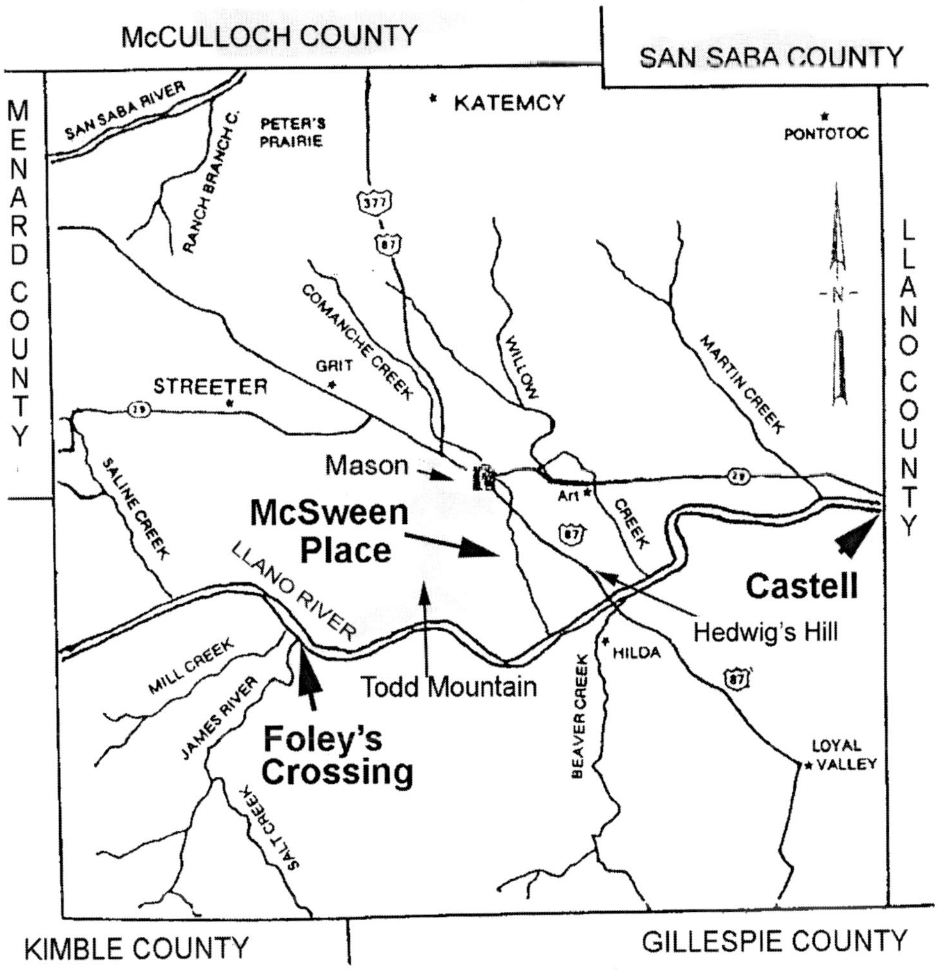


**Fig. 25. Map of Mason County.** Franz moved to Castell around 1852, which is 1 mile east of the present day Llano County line. He lived in Fredericksburg and the surrounding Gillespie County from 1856-1859. (Note Fredericksburg is 40 miles from Mason on US 87 and Loyal Valley is midway between the two towns.) He then moved to Foley's Crossing in 1859-1860 and to the McSween Place on Comanche Creek in 1871 and finally to the town of Mason in 1901. Larger arrows were used to indicate these approximate locations.

**Abb. 25. Karte von Mason County**. Franz zog 1852 nach Castell, das 1 Meile östlich der heutigen Llano County Grenze lag. Er lebte in Friedrichsburg und dem umgebenden Gillespie County von 1856-1859. (Bemerke: Friedrichsburg liegt 40 Meilen von Mason entfernt an der US 87 und Loyal Valley befindet sich auf halbem Wege zwischen den beiden Städten.) Dann zog er nach Foleys Crossing in 1859-1860 und zum McSween Place am Comanche Creek in 1871 und schließlich in die Stadt Mason in 1901. Große Pfeile markieren die ungefähren Positionen.

General Sam Houston.
Governor of the State of Texas

Your Excellency,

We feel very grateful to You for having sent two companies of rangers to our aid. But as the Indians continue to make their depredations most daily right in our neighborhood, — the other day they killed Tom Milligan, who lived two miles from Fort Mason on the main route to Camp Colorado, right at the door of his house. — Your Excellency would oblige us very much, Captain Conner having his station already near Camp Colorado and having a particular interest to stay there, by ordering Captain Burleson, to put up his station in our vicinity for the purpose of giving sufficient protection to the Counties of Mason, Llano, San Saba, Gillespie, Kerr and Medina.

Hedwigshill, Mason County
Feb 25, 1860.

Your Excellency's
obdt servts.

Francis Kellner.
Emil Kriewitz
John Deatz
August Marks
H Hasse

Louis Martin
John G. Durst
Jacob Durst
H Hörster

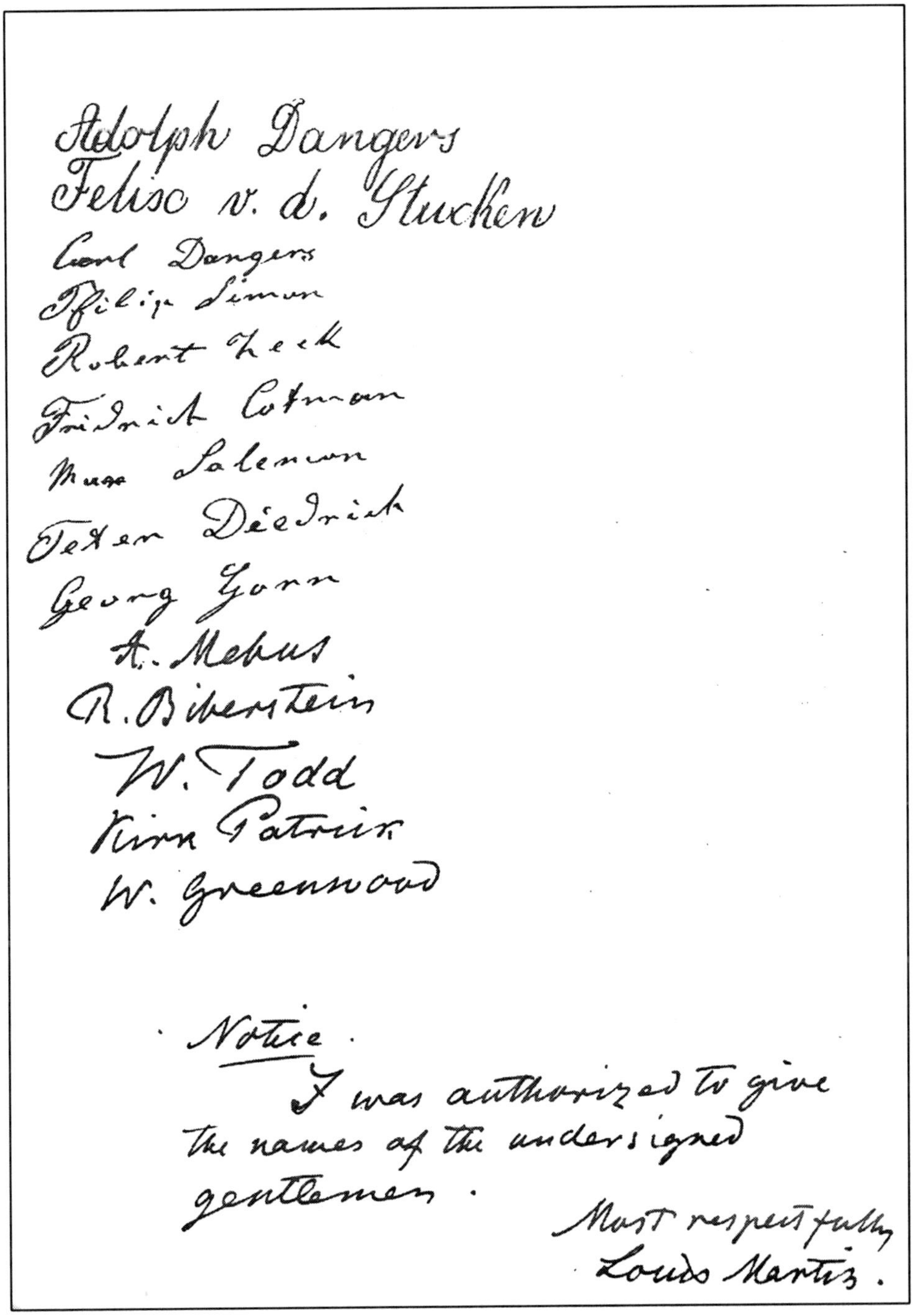

Adolph Dangers
Feliso v. d. Stucken
Carl Dangers
Filip Simon
Robert Zeck
Fridrich Cotman
Max Saleman
Peter Diedrich
Georg Gorn
A. Mebus
R. Biberstein
W. Todd
Kirn Patrick
W. Greenwood

Notice.
I was authorized to give the names of the undersigned gentlemen.

Most respectfully
Louis Martin.

**Fig. 26. Letter to Sam Houston, Governor of Texas 1860.** This letter was reproduced from Margaret Bierschwale's *History of Mason County Texas through 1964* (Mason, Texas: Mason County Historical Commission, 1998), 550-551. The letter was written by Louis Martin and Francis Kettner's signature is first.

**Abb. 26. Brief an Sam Houston, Gouverneur von Texas 1860.** Dieser Brief wurde der von Margaret Bierschwale verfaßten *History of Mason County Texas through 1964* (Mason, Texas: Mason County Historical Commission, 1998), 550-551 entnommen. Der Brief wurde von Louis Martin geschrieben und die Unterschrift von Franz Kettner steht an erster Stelle.

## Brief 10 (8. Juli 1860) von Franz Kettner aus Foley's Crossing in Mason County/Texas an seine Eltern

Liebe Eltern!

Ihre beiden letzten Briefe habe ich erhalten, wollte aber nicht eher antworten als bis wir das Kistchen erhalten hatten. Dasselbe ist gut angekommen, mit allen Gegenständen. Die Ringe haben uns viel Vergnügen gemacht. Was die Kindersachen anbelangt, so können wir dieselben für unseren kleinen Louis nicht gebrauchen, aber diesen Winter erwarten wir weitere Nachkommenschaft und dieselben werden uns gute Dienste tun. Sollten wir ein kleines Mädchen bekommen, so wird dasselbe Ida heißen. Unser Junge läuft und fängt an zu sprechen. Er ist groß und stark für sein Alter. Er sieht seinem Großvater in Deutschland auf ein Haar ähnlich. Er macht uns viel Vergnügen.

Was den Schal anbelangt, so muß ich ehrlich gestehen, so hätte ich etwas besseres erwartet, nämlich einen gewirkten, da meine Frau einen ähnlichen schon besitzt. Wahrscheinlich machten Sie sich sehr geringe Vorstellungen von dem Luxus, der hier herrscht, welcher aber ziemlich groß ist. Die Unterärmel und Kragen kamen uns sehr gut zustatten.

Wir wohnen jetzt am Llano, da meine Dienstzeit aus ist.

Unser Viehstock beläuft sich nämlich jetzt über 100 Köpfe, darunter für dieses Jahr 35 Kühe und Kälber. Das nächste Frühjahr werde ich 20 Kühe mehr bekommen, nämlich junge Rinder, die Kälber machen, so daß ich nächstes Frühjahr 55 Stück Kühe und Kälber habe. Außerdem verkaufe ich 20 Stück 2-jährige Schlachtochsen à 10 Dollars pro Stück. Das Vieh vermehrt sich fabelhaft und ist die sicherste Existenz, die man hier haben kann, und ebenfalls die Unabhängigste. Die Schlachtochsen werden am Hause für den New Orleans Markt abgeholt.

Das einzige Unangenehme ist, daß man weit von Nachbarn wohnen muß. Mein nächster Nachbar ist eine Stunde von mir und oberhalb von mir wohnt niemand mehr.

Die Indianer waren letzten Winter sehr schlimm und haben eine Unmasse Pferde gestohlen. Unterhalb von mir hat beinahe jedermann Pferde verloren. Aber wie durch Zufälligkeit habe ich nicht eines verloren, obgleich ich zweimal auf Indianer gestoßen bin. Und zwar das erstemal mit meiner Frau und Kind, als ich dieselben mit dem Ochsenwagen nach dem neuen Viehrancho brachte. Wir begegneten 5 Indianern, welche ungefähr 40 gestohlene Pferde vor sich hertrieben und dieselben passierten auf 50 Schritte an unserem Wagen vorbei. Meine ganze Bewaffnung bestand in meiner Büchse. Meinen Revolver, welcher neben der Büchse die Hauptwaffe in Texas bildet, welcher die 6 Kugeln mit ziemlicher Sicherheit bis auf hundert Schritte weit treibt, hatte ich dem Maurer zurücklassen müssen, welcher auf meinem Platze arbeitete. Denn kurz vorher waren Indianer gesehen worden. Auch dachte ich an keine Gefahr, weil von dem Platze, wo ich meine Frau abholte, der Weg immer an Farmen vorbeiging. Da ich meinen Wagen sofort anhielt, meine Büchse zur Hand nahm, mich für einen verzweifelten Kampf zurechtmachte, und außerdem die Indianer nicht wußten, ob ich mit einem von ihnen sehr gefürchteten

Revolver versehen war, so passierten dieselben, ohne mich zu belästigen. Die Angst meiner Frau können Sie sich leicht vorstellen, da die Indianer kurz vorher einige Weiße getötet und skalpiert hatten, das heißt die Kopfhaut abgezogen, welche dieselben als Trophäe mit sich führen.

Das andere Mal hatten sich zwei rote Kanaillen ganz nahe an meinem Hause sehen lassen in der frommen Absicht, mir meine beiden Pferde zu stehlen. Ich erblickte dieselben aber früh genug und stellte meine Pferde jede Nacht in das Haus. Am Tage brachte ich dieselben auf die Weide und blieb dabei. 2 Tage blieben dieselben in der Nähe. Am dritten wurde es Ihnen zu langweilig und sie machten sich auf, meinen nächsten Nachbarn zu besuchen, welchem sie auch glücklich 3 Stück Pferde stahlen.

Es war letzten Winter eine sehr gefährliche Zeit für Texas. Meinen Revolver zog ich abends aus und morgens, so wie ich aufstand, schnallte ich denselben wieder an meine Seite. Seit Frühjahr wurde es wieder ruhig, da großartige Expeditionen gegen die Indianer unternommen wurden. Allein trotzdem habe ich nie gewagt, meine Frau allein zu lassen und wenn es auch bloß eine Stunde lang war. Ich habe einen ehemaligen preußischen Artilleriehauptmann in Diensten, auf welchen ich mich verlassen kann, da ich manchmal auf 3 bis 4 Tage von Hause abwesend war, um mein Vieh zusammenzutreiben.

Meine Schweinezucht macht jetzt gute Fortschritte. Dieselbe beläuft sich auf 70 Stück und in einem Jahre vielleicht mehrere Hundert. Meine Ausgaben sind sehr gering, da wir die Butter nicht verkonsumieren können, sowie Käse und Eier. Im Winter schlachte ich meine Ochsen, sowie die betreffende Anzahl Schweine; so daß ich mit 150 Dollars meinen Haushalt betreiben kann. Ich kann jetzt schon für 200 Dollars Ochsen verkaufen und jedes Jahr vermehrt sich jetzt die Zahl. Sobald mein Stock sich über hundert Milchkühe beläuft, was in längstens 3 Jahren der Fall sein wird, so verpachte ich den Stock und besorge bloß die Hälfte selbst.

Meine Frau ist sehr böse, daß Sie Ihre Daguerreotypie nicht gesandt haben. Sie sagt, daß ihr dieses mehr Vergnügen gemacht haben würde wie alles andere.

Ich ersuche Sie deshalb, uns auf dieselbe Art durch Herrn Seeger in Bremen ein anderes Kistchen zu senden, und zwar mit folgenden Gegenständen.

3 gute Kleider für meine Frau und zwar 2 Stück Mousseline de laine und ein leinenes, aber etwas elegantes.

Ferner ein Paar goldene Ohrenringe.

Ferner möchte ich sehen, was für Fortschritte meine Nichte Marie[93] im Kloster gemacht hat. Deshalb möchte dieselbe meiner Frau einen feinen gestickten Unterrock und ein Paar fein gestickte Unterärmel und Kragen, 6 Stück leinene Taschentücher (machen).

---

[93] Maria Kissel, geb. 28.6.1844 in Oberkirch, gest. 10.2.1879 in Oberkirch. Tochter von Karl Friedrich Kissel und Ida Leopoldine Kissel, geb. Kettner, der Schwester von Franz Kettner. Maria Kissel war verheiratet mit dem Urgroßvater der Autorin, Leopold Erdrich, geb. 4.5.1838, gest. 20.2.1877 in Oberkirch. Franz nennt Maria Kissel in seinen Briefen meist Marie, mit ihrem Rufnamen.

1 Dutzend gute Messer und Gabeln, sowie Löffel und Kaffeelöffel.

Ferner ja nicht zu vergessen die Daguerreotypie von Ihnen, sowie von Franz,[94] Marie und Nicolai und Klärchen.[95]

Einige Boxen echte preußische Zündhütchen, ein gutes Taschenmesser mit mehreren Klingen. Was die Hosen anbelangt, welche Sie mir geschickt haben, so muß ich bedauern, daß ich sehr wenig Gebrauch dafür habe. Erstens bin ich nicht so umfangreich, und zweitens bin ich größer als wie die Hose lang ist.

Ich überlasse es Ihnen das Kistchen auszustatten, aber nicht schwerer und größer als wie das letzte. Dasselbe kostete mich nach deutschem Geld fl 14; was sehr billig ist für Texas. Korsetten sind sehr schwer zu bekommen hier und meine Alte hat große Liebhaberei am Schnüren.

So wie wir Gelegenheit haben, so erhalten Sie per Post unsere Daguerreotypie, dann werden Sie meine Frau und den kleinen Louis näher kennenlernen.

Was meine Gesundheit anbelangt, so bin ich noch gerade so rüstig, wie vor zehn Jahren und ich reite von morgens bis abends, ohne müde zu werden. Hinter Vieh zu reiten ist eine andere Reiterei, als wenn Sie oder jemand in Deutschland reitet. Es wechseln größter Galopp, Trab, rechts und links, über Büsche hinweg, sowie über Felsen und Steine, ähnlich wie eine Parforcejagd in Deutschland.

Außerdem bin ich auch noch so jugendlich in meinem Betragen. Man wird in Texas wohl alt an Jahren, aber sonst bleibt man jung. Man wird nicht philisterhaft wie in Deutschland. Das macht aber das Naturleben, das ungezwungene.

Inliegend finden sich einige Zeilen für Herrn Fischer beigefügt, welche Sie ggf. besorgen wollen.

Sollte Franz Lust haben, so schicken Sie denselben zu mir. Er kann, wenn er Lust hat, hier seiner kaufmännischen Neigung folgen oder aber Viehzüchter werden. Ich könnte denselben sehr gut gebrauchen.

Meinem Jungen habe ich eine Kuh mit Mutterkalb geschenkt. Bis er 15 Jahre ist, hat er schon einen hübschen kleinen Stock Vieh. Und auf diese Art werde ich es mit all meinen Kindern halten. Was ich dann mehr für dieselben tun kann, wenn sie groß sind, das werde ich tun.

Sagen Sie Marie, daß wenn dieselbe Lust nach Texas hätte, ihr vorzügliche Partien offenständen. Frauenzimmer sind hier noch immer rar, namentlich gebildete. Ich habe es bloß meiner Schönheit und Liebenswürdigkeit zu verdanken, daß ich eine Frau bekommen habe. Wie ich heiratete, war ich über 30 Jahre, und meine Frau glaubte immer noch, ich wäre erst 24 bis 25.

Sonntags reiten ich und meine Frau gewöhnlich aus, um die Nachbarn zu besuchen. Auch der kleine Louis muß schon zu Pferde sitzen.

---

[94] Franz Lambert Xaver Friedrich Kissel, Bruder von Maria Kissel, geb. 28.11.1842 in Mannheim, Todesdatum unbekannt.

[95] Die Daten von Nicolai und Klärchen sind der Autorin unbekannt.

Ehe Sie das Kistchen besorgen, so schreiben Sie an Seeger in Bremen, ob er dasselbe zu besorgen willens ist und grüßen Sie denselben vielmals von mir und meiner Frau.

Grüßen Sie Welle vielmals und sagen Sie ihr, daß ich schon oft an sie gedacht habe.

Vernachlässigen Sie den kleine Louis nicht in dem Kistchen. Derselbe ist, bis das Kistchen ankommt, über 2 Jahre alt, braucht also schon Hosen und Jäckchen.

In der Hoffnung, daß dieser Brief Sie noch gesund und munter antrifft, grüßen wir Marie und Franz, Klärchen und Nicolai und verbleiben Ihre dankbaren Kinder

Franz Kettner und Frau

Llano, 8. Juli 1860

(Die alte Adresse)

# Letter / Brief 11

## Letter 11 (October 6, 1863) from Franz Kettner at Foley's Crossing, Mason County, Texas to his Parents

Dear Parents,

I have finally found a fairly secure opportunity to send you a few lines by way of Mexico. We are so far still all healthy and our family has grown with the little Elise. She is now 15 months old. Louis will be 5 years old in December and Ida is 3 years old. The children so far have always been healthy and have grown strongly. Hopefully these lines will also find you still in good health.

Concerning our political conditions, they are extremely sad. The war[96] still rages on and we are expecting from hour to hour an attack on Texas by the northern side. Our conscription extends up to 45 years old but the militia up to 50. My small self has also been drafted. I am, however, now still on leave because the border cannot be left unguarded on account of Indian attacks. I hope that I will remain spared, except if the northern troops move over from Arkansas to Texas and come through our area. In this case, not even the militia will be spared.

This war is waged on both sides with the greatest bitterness. Our small state of Texas with a white population of 500,000 people has up to now already sent 70,000 men as soldiers to war, of which I am firmly convinced 15,000 are no longer alive. Diseases have taken away most of the people.

---

[96] The American Civil War, 1861-1865. After the election of Abraham Lincoln as president of the USA in 1861, 11 southern states, Virginia, North and South Carolina, Georgia, Florida, Alabama, Tennessee, Mississippi, Louisiana, Arkansas and Texas seceded from the Union to form the Confederate States of America. In April, 1865, the war ended with defeat of the Confederacy and the reestablishment of the Union.

Franz, like most residents of Mason County, was against secession from the Union. The vote was 75 to 2 against secession on February 1861. The 1860 census indicates that there were 18 slaves in Mason County out of a total population of 630. *Handbook of Texas Online*, s.v. "Mason County" http://www.tsha.utexas.edu/handbook/online/articles/MM/hcm4.html (accessed June 25, 2006).

Food supplies and slaughter cattle are taken by force. The most arbitrary government is in charge now. Gillespie County with the little town of Fredericksburg (my former hometown, populated mainly by Germans) had suffered terribly at the start of the revolution. They hanged people who supported the old government and who wanted not to participate. And a group of younger people who were to be conscripted fled instead toward Mexico.[97] They were overtaken by a large troop and lost 35 men out of 70 in a murderous battle. The remainder escaped to Mexico. Many good acquaintances of mine were among them.

Even my own life stood many times in great danger and I had already made all preparations to flee to Mexico. I thank God that I was not too hasty. I also had little desire to leave my family even for a short time. Instead, I was determined to make my life as expensive as possible to sell.

The population of Texas is also divided into two parties. That is, one that remains loyal to the old Union and this other fire-eating pigs' party. I am afraid that when the northern troops tread on the soil of Texas, a civil war will begin even in Texas.

The end of the war is in front of the door, and I hope that we will all be northerners again. The southern troops have indeed fought brilliantly; however, what they are fighting for is, for Europeans who were raised to be against slavery and remain against it, much too bad a thing.

Now our state has already been blockaded for two years. Supplies of goods are not to be found in our states. Additionally, a Texas family never purchases more than what is immediately necessary. The consequences are that we almost have nothing to wear, everything is torn. The only goods that we see are those smuggled from Mexico. We trade at unbelievable prices for only the most essential goods with steers which are probably intended for the French. So I had to give a 4 year-old ox for 15 yards of unbleached cotton material. I traded a 4-year-old ox for 10 yards of striped cotton material for a dress for my wife. And so it goes on. All of my 2 and 4 year-old oxen have gone in this manner to the devil and afterward wewere totally demolished. We only possess the bare necessities of clothing.

This war has brought at least a two year reversal to my family. I was so far along that I had created a totally carefree existence. I am not allowing my courage to sink, however. If the southern government (as long as it still exists) just leaves me alone and does not require my service as a soldier, I hope that we will part in peace.

What a piece of luck it was that I had left the town of Fredericksburg and looked after my animals myself. In the other case, I would now be a poor man. All the

---

97 This event is referred to as the Battle of Nueces. According to *Handbook of Texas Online*, s.v. "Nueces, Battle of the," http://www.tsha.utexas.edu/handbook/online/articles/NN/qfn1.html (accessed July 30, 2006), Unionists, mostly German intellectuals from Gillespie County, had camped on the Nueces River in Kinney County while en route to Mexico to avoid conscription. They were attacked by 94 Confederates led by Lt. C.D. McRae on August 10, 1862. Nineteen of the 61-68 Unionists were killed and 9 were wounded. The wounded were executed at the site. Eight additional Unionists were killed while trying to cross into Mexico, 11 returned home and most of the others escaped to Mexico and California. Franz also describes these events in Letter 12.

businesses, all trade has stood totally still for two years. The businessmen have to live out of their own pockets and when necessary draw out everything which they had saved in earlier years. My animal stock has still increased despite the bad times. I own 67 cows now, not counting the young animals, in all about 200 head.

In two years I will have over 100 head of cows, if I do not have to sell too many cows in order to provide me and my family with clothing. My 3 and 4 year-old steers have been sold. The 1 and 2 year-old steers will not be sold for slaughter because they are not heavy enough.

We suffer the greatest shortage in shoe leather and cooking salt. On my part, I wear mostly leather clothing now, made from tanned deer hides. Even little Louis has leather pants now since he tears up many pants terribly. I hunt now mainly on account of hides when before it was for meat. A person does not see gold or silver any more and our Confederate paper money is worth 10 cents on the dollar (100 cents), thus almost completely worthless.

My wife is always healthy and hearty and in March comes another birth again, hopefully with a little boy.

You will receive this letter through the kindness of Mr. Groos from Prussia who has a business now in Mexico (earlier in Texas) and who again travels here. If you are in the position to send me some support, I would be very thankful. If you are not in the position, however, I would wish for a negative reply.

You have truly no idea what a horrible time we have come through and what we still have to go through. The fanaticism of the southern people is terrible. Earlier, there was a shortage of women; now however, there is a shortage of men. A young man can make the most brilliant marriage here now. There are millions of young widows and no men. I think that there will soon be a law to allow each man to take more wives in order that Texas will be repopulated quickly.

Louis speaks often about his grandfather and grandmother in Germany, also little Ida. I believe that when the boy is a couple of years older, I will send him to you to remain for a couple of years. Should you be inclined to want to send me a chest with clothing, I believe that Mr. Carl Groos from Prussia,[98] who will himself stay there a while, affords a good opportunity. We also possess no more bedding. We have, unfortunately, no factories in Texas, except for one prison; indeed, the little bit which is produced there goes primarily to the military.

I have provided my bread this year through our usual living. Considering our food supplies, we have up till now no difference in regard to our earlier years. Otherwise, there are many families who suffer even a shortage of bread, including the residents of the cities because the farmers have no desire or trust to sell their butter, eggs, vegetables, etc. for paper money. Therefore, these people do not lead an

---

[98] Groos, Carl Wilhelm August (1830-1893). Carl immigrated to Texas with his brothers and sisters and widowed father on the ship LOUIS November 21, 1848. *Handbook of Texas Online*, s.v. "Groos, Carl Wilhelm August," http://www.tsha.utexas.edu/handbook/online/articles/GG/-fgr88.html (accessed July 30, 2006). Franz was on the same ship with Carl Groos. Galveston Immigration Database, Family # 10494.

enviable life. We always have an abundance of butter and eggs, cheese and meat. We also raised a lot of vegetables this summer, in particular many melons.

Some days ago I was in a hunting party with a Mr. von Marschall who was earlier an aide to the Duke of Nassau and now a hunter and good friend of mine. (He is related to the von Marschalls from Baden.) We had talked about how the relatives in Germany could not begin to make a correct conception of our circumstances. I told them (they were our four friends) your reproach in your last letter that you had put out so much for my education and had never believed that I could turn out to become an animal herder. This produced a common burst of laughter.

The cattle are not protected here on the land but walk about freely and keep fairly well together. When I ride out and find cows which have calves, I drive them to the house. They are kept in a corral until the calves are at least five months old and the cows are milked. Then the calves are branded and their ears notched. My brand is 100[99] on the ribs. This burns very prettily. And then when the calves are old enough, they are again allowed to run freely.

Our main work time is from spring until June. Then we ride out together in large parties of 10 to 12 neighbors and drive our animals (that is, those which during the winter wandered somewhat far off) back to their home grounds where they calmly maintain their area until the next winter. From June on, I ride out two or three times weekly but return home each evening. When I find cows with calves, I drive them home. Calves are born through the entire year.[100]

The entire western part of Texas is only useful for raising cattle and sheep. I would have sold all of my cattle already and occupied myself with sheep except that sheep require protection against wolves. It is not so hard to find a shepherd but it is difficult to keep one because people want to make their life easier and this job is so boring. I have no desire to herd them myself and have too good of an education to play at being a shepherd. Sheep also are subjected to more diseases which occur seldom in cattle. Grown cattle have not yet died on me with the exception of a few calves which I castrated in too hot a time. Overall, I have planned not to let my stock of cattle reach over a hundred which with calves and 1, 2, 3, and 4 year-old oxen makes about 500 head. This stock I can care for myself with the requisite number of good horses. When the Indians are eliminated, I will sell the offspring of the cows and begin to raise either sheep or horses. I have the greatest hope, therefore, when this war is won that the red scoundrels will be exterminated at any price. When they catch a white person alone or when the number (of Indians) is far greater, the white

[99] The Mason County court house burned in 1877 and early brand registrations were lost. Francis Kettner's brand was registered as "110" in 1877 (Bierschwale 199 and 591).

[100] During the winter, cattle would drift south each time a norther (cold front accompanied by a strong north wind) would blow in and usually stop at a river. With the next severe norther, they would cross the river and move further south to the next river. (J. Marvin Hunter "Brief History of the Early Days in Mason County" *Frontier Times*, 6 December 1928, 113-134). The footnotes to Letter 22 give much more details about the open range era including descriptions of the "cattle drifts" and the big round-ups. Note that the spring round-ups that Franz describes here were probably on a much smaller scale than the big round-ups that Wheeler describes after the Civil War.

person does not escape with his life. As the Turks did earlier, they pull off the scalp skin with the hair which they take home as the greatest trophy.

I have not lost any horses in the last two years because I have built a stable and keep the horses under lock and key. I have the most pleasure in raising horses. Horses prosper here excellently; in addition, we have good breeds. The old Spanish horse is best suited for the cattle drives. They are short in stature, fast in their movements, turn and change quickly on their hind quarters and stop quickly from a full gallop, which is the main quality for cattle round-ups. In addition, we have the American or English breed, a much too fine a horse to use for cattle drives. We have now begun to mix the two breeds and to make a so-called half-blooded horse. This is a very good-looking, powerful horse suited to be a riding horse. I have a very beautiful white Spanish mare which was bred to a fine English stallion and she will have a foal (intended for Louis) in the spring.

Louis' stock now consists of two cows, two yearling steers, and this year finally a female calf. The yearling steers were branded as mine until now. By 1864 he will own four cows and a foal. He is very intelligent, indeed too intelligent for his age and totally fits in our family. Likewise for Ida. The scholars are not yet united about Elise.

When times are better, I will have a daguerreotype portrait of my whole family taken and send it to you. I have requested that Mr. Carl Groos send you his address in Germany so that you can perhaps send something to me.

Since you have often wished to know how my financial circumstances stand, I will tell you what I could realize from a possible redemption:

| | | |
|---|---|---|
| 200 head of cattle at 7 dollars per head | = | 1,400 dollars |
| 2 horses at 50 dollars | | 100 |
| oxen and wagon | | 100 |
| land and house | | 200 |
| Swine | | 25 |
| furnishings, equipment | | 200 |
| 2 saddles | | 25 |
| Six shooter and rifle | | 50 |
| | | 2,000 dollars |

At 2.30 florins, in German money, 5,000 Gulden.

This much I could realize any day in other times. This is all not precisely described and many items such as plows and chains, chickens, etc., are left out. You can see, therefore, that I have not gone backwards since I have lived in Texas.

I have not received anything yet from my in-laws of the 13 head of cattle and 3 yoke of oxen that my wife was given. In addition, I do not stand on good terms with them. They believe that I should remain living with them and help them maintain their property and give up becoming independent. I have no desire to do that, however. I and my family stand with no more connection with them for three years. This is completely necessary in order to not disturb our unity since my mother-in-law is not good to deal with.

If you should happen to have a good prescription for stomach cramps which my wife has had since her last childbirth when shc eats hard or hot meals, write it for me. Earlier she ate that way frequently but now very seldom. We have gone to several German doctors without any great success.

I would write more but my horse stands saddled and I will quickly drive my oxen away because we have received news that the government will take away the oxen for paper money with which you can buy nothing. This letter will go with my oxen to Mexico and will be handed over to relatives of Mr. Carl Groos. In addition, will write a few lines to Mr. Groos so that he will send you his address in Germany and tell you the length of his stay.

All of us, wife and children greet you many times and I remain your son,
Franz Kettner.

Llano, October 6, 1863

Many greetings to all my relatives and friends.

You will find my address on the other side.

~~My old address was~~
~~Franz Kettner~~
~~Friedrichsburg~~
~~Gillespie County, Texas~~

~~My address reads now~~
~~Franz Kettner~~
~~Hedwigshill~~[101]
~~Mason County~~
~~Texas~~

You will find my address on this envelope.[102] Write me by the post service under this address, the opportunity[103] by Groos has become not possible.

---

[101] Hedwig's Hill is located on the present day US 87, approximately 1 mile north of the Llano River. It is about 12 miles east of Foley's Crossing. (See Letter 10, Fig. 25). Hedwig's Hill was established by Louis Martin prior to 1853 and named for his mother. One of the first post offices in Mason County was established there June 1858. The community was centered around the post office and a general store opened by Louis Martin's nephew. *Handbook of Texas Online*, s.v. "Martin, Louis," http://www.tsha.utexas.edu/handbook/online/articles/MM/fma61.html (accessed July 30, 2006). *Handbook of Texas Online*, s.v. "Hedwigs hill, Texas," http://www.tsha.utexas.edu/handbook/-online/articles/HH/hnh16.html (accessed July 30, 2006).

**Fig. 27. Llano River at Foley's Crossing.** This photo was taken northwest of Foley's Crossing at dusk. The branch of water to the left is James River and the branch to right is the Llano River.

**Abb. 27. Llano Fluß bei Foleys Crossing.** Dieses Foto wurde bei Sonnenuntergang nordwestlich von Foleys Crossing aufgenommen. Der Wasserlauf nach links ist der James Fluß und nach rechts der Llano Fluß.

[102] The two addresses in the letter were crossed out. The actual address on the envelope is unknown. It is possible that Franz wanted his parents to send his mail to the town of Mason which also had a post office established March 1858.

[103] See Letter 4, footnote 50 and Letter 9, footnote 84.

**Fig. 28. Llano River at Foley's Crossing.** This photo was taken downstream from Foley's Crossing. Note Franz's home was on the south bank (right side of the photograph).

**Abb. 28. Llano Fluß bei Foley's Crossing.** Dieses Foto wurde flußabwärts von Foley's Crossing aufgenommen. Bemerke: Das Haus von Franz stand auf dem südlichen Ufer (rechte Seite der Fotografie).

## Brief 11 (6. Oktober 1863) von Franz Kettner aus Foley's Crossing in Mason County/Texas an seine Eltern

Liebe Eltern,

Endlich habe ich eine ziemlich sichere Gelegenheit gefunden, Ihnen per Mexiko einige Zeilen zukommen zu lassen. Wir sind bis jetzt noch alle gesund, und unsere Familie hat sich um eine kleine Elise vermehrt. Dieselbe ist jetzt 15 Monate alt. Louis wird im Dezember 5 Jahre alt und die Ida 3 Jahre. Die Kinder sind bis jetzt immer gesund gewesen und kräftig gewachsen. Hoffentlich werden Sie diese Zeilen auch noch bei guter Gesundheit antreffen.

Was unsere politischen Zustände anbelangt, so sind dieselben höchst traurig. Der Krieg[104] wütet noch fort und wir erwarten in Texas stündlich einen Angriff von nördlicher Seite.

Unsere Conscription[105] erstreckt sich bis zum Alter von 45 Jahren, die Miliz aber bis zu 50. Meine Wenigkeit ist ebenfalls der Conscription verfallen. Ich bin aber jetzt noch auf Urlaub, da die Grenze der Indianereinfälle wegen nicht entblößt werden kann. Ich hoffe auch, daß ich verschont bleiben werde, ausgenommen die nördlichen Truppen rücken von Arkansas nach Texas und kommen durch unsere Gegend. In diesem Fall bleibt selbst die Miliz nicht verschont.

Dieser Krieg wird auf beiden Seiten mit der größten Erbitterung geführt. Unser kleiner Staat Texas, mit einer weißen Bevölkerung von 500.000 Seelen, hat bis jetzt schon 70.000 Mann Soldaten nach dem Kriegsschauplatz gesendet, wovon, wie ich fest überzeugt bin, keine 15.000 Mann mehr am Leben sind. Die Krankheiten raffen die meisten Leute hinweg.

Lebensmittel und Schlachtochsen werden mit Gewalt gepreßt. Es herrscht bis jetzt die größte Willkürherrschaft. Gillespie County mit dem Städtchen Friedrichsburg, meinem früheren Aufenthalt, meistens von Deutschen bewohnt, hat am Anfang der Revolution fürchterlich gelitten. Das Hängen von Menschen, welche der alten Regierung ergeben waren, wollte kein Ende nehmen. Und eine Partie junger Leute von da, welche der Conscription verfallen waren, sich aber nach Mexiko flüchten wollten, wurden von einer bedeutenden Truppenmacht eingeholt. In einem mörderischen Gefecht verloren dieselben 35 Mann von 70. Der Rest entkam nach Mexiko. Sehr viele gute Bekannte von mir waren darunter.

Selbst mein Leben stand mehrmals in großer Gefahr, und ich hatte schon alle Vorbereitungen getroffen, um mich nach Mexiko zu flüchten. Ich danke Gott, daß ich nicht zu voreilig war. Ich hatte auch wenig Lust, meine Familie auch nur auf

---

[104] Amerikanischer Sezessionskrieg 1861-65. Nach Wahl von Abraham Lincoln zum Präsidenten der USA traten 1861 die 11 Südstaaten, Virginia, North- und South Carolina, Georgia, Florida, Alabama, Tennessee, Mississippi, Louisiana, Arkansas und Texas aus der Union aus und gründeten die "Konföderierten Staaten von Amerika." Im April 1865 konnten die Nordstaaten die bedingungslose Kapitulation ihres Gegners erzwingen. Die Existenz der Union blieb dadurch erhalten. Quelle: *Der Große Knaur*, Band 4, S.159.

[105] Allgemeine Wehrpflicht

kurze Zeit zu verlassen. Lieber war ich entschlossen, mein Leben so teuer als möglich zu verkaufen.

Die Bevölkerung von Texas ist auch in zwei Parteien geteilt. Nämlich in eine, die der alten Union treu geblieben ist, und diese andere feuerfressende Schweinepartei. Ich befürchte, so wie nördliche Truppen den Boden von Texas betreten, nimmt der Bürgerkrieg in Texas selbst seinen Anfang.

Das Ende dieses Krieges ist jetzt vor der Tür, und ich hoffe, wir werden alle wieder nördlich werden. Die südlichen Truppen haben sich zwar brillant geschlagen, aber wofür sie fechten, ist für Europäer, welche von wegen Ihrer Erziehung gegen Sklaverei eingenommen sind, und auch immer bleiben werden, eine viel zu schlechte Sache.

Nun ist unser Staat schon zwei Jahre blockiert. Vorräte an Waren befanden sich keine in unserem Staate. Außerdem schafft sich eine texanische Familie nie mehr an, als dieselbe gerade notwendig gebraucht. Die Folgen sind die, daß wir beinahe nichts mehr anzuziehen haben, total abgerissen. Die einzigen Waren, die wir sehen, werden von mexikanischen Schmugglern, welche uns für Schlachtochsen, wahrscheinlich für die Franzosen bestimmte, das Allernotwendigste zu den unmenschlichsten Preisen verhandelten. So mußte ich für 15 Yards[106] Ellen ungebleichtes Baumwollenzeug einen 4-jährigen Ochsen geben. Meiner Frau erhandelte ich ein gestreiftes baumwollenes Kleid von 10 Yards[107] für einen 4-jährigen Ochsen. Und so ging es fort. Alle meine 2- und 4-jährigen Schlachtochsen hat auf diese Art der Teufel und dennoch sind wir total abgerissen. Nur das Allernotwendigste an Kleidung besitzen wir.

Dieser Krieg hat meine Familie um wenigstens zwei Jahre retour gebracht. Ich wäre jetzt so weit, daß ich eine ganz sorgenfreie Existenz mir gegründet hätte. Ich lasse aber den Mut nicht sinken. Wenn die südliche Regierung (so lange dieselbe noch existiert) mich bloß in Ruhe läßt, meine Dienste als Soldat nicht verlangt, so werden wir, hoffe ich in Frieden scheiden.

Was für ein Glück war es, daß ich die Stadt Friedrichsburg verließ, und mein Vieh selbst besorgte, im anderen Falle wäre ich jetzt ein armer Mann. Alle Geschäfte, aller Handel steht seit zwei Jahren total still. Die Geschäftsleute müssen ganz aus ihrer Tasche zehren und womöglich alles zusetzen, was Sie in den früheren Jahren sich erspart hatten. Mein Viehstöckchen hat sich aber trotz der schlechten Zeiten immer noch vermehrt. Ich besitze jetzt 67 Stück Kühe ohne das junge Vieh, im ganzen ungefähr 200 Stück Köpfe.

In zwei Jahren habe ich über 100 Stück Kühe, wenn ich nicht zu viele Kühe verkaufen muß, um mich und meine Familie mit Kleidern zu versehen. Meine 3- und 4-jährigen Schlachtochsen sind verkauft. 1- und 2-jährige sind als Schlachtochsen nicht zu verkaufen, weil dieselben nicht schwer genug sind.

---

[106] Einzelnes unbekanntes Zeichen.

[107] Dito.

An Leder für Schuhe, sogar an Kochsalz leiden wir den größten Mangel. Ich für meinen Teil trage jetzt ausschließlich Lederkleidung, von Hirschfellen gegerbt. Selbst der kleine Louis bekommt jetzt eine Lederhose, der Junge zerreißt fürchterlich viel Hosen. Die Jagd betreibe ich, früher des frischen Fleisches wegen, jetzt aber der Felle wegen. Silber und Gold bekommt man keines mehr zu sehen und unser konföderiertes Papiergeld steht in Texas 10 Cents den Taler (100 Cents ein Dollars) also beinahe ganz wertlos.

Meine Frau ist immer gesund und munter und kommt bis März wieder einmal nieder, hoffentlich mit einem kleinen Jungen.

Diesen Brief erhalten Sie durch die Güte eines Herrn Groos von Preußen,[108] welcher sein Geschäft jetzt in Mexiko hat (früher in Texas) und wieder hierher zurückreist. Sollten Sie in der Lage sein, mir etwas Unterstützung senden zu können, so wäre ich Ihnen sehr dankbar dafür. Sollten Sie aber nicht in der Lage sein, so wünsche ich eine abschlägige Antwort.

Sie haben wahrhaftig keinen Begriff, was für schauerliche Zeiten wir durchgemacht haben, und welche wir noch durchzumachen haben. Der Fanatismus unter dieser südlichen Bevölkerung ist schrecklich. Früher war hier Mangel an weiblicher Bevölkerung, jetzt aber Mangel an der männlichen. Ein junger Mann kann jetzt hier die brillantesten Heiraten machen. Junge Witwen zu Millionen und keine Männer. Ich glaube, daß bald ein Gesetz durchgeht, daß jeder Mann mehrere Frauen nehmen darf, damit Texas rasch wieder bevölkert wird.

Louis spricht oft von seinem Großpapa und Mama in Deutschland, auch die kleine Ida. Ich glaube, wenn der Junge einige Jahre älter ist, werde ich ihn zu Ihnen schicken, um einige Jahre daselbst zu bleiben. Sollten Sie geneigt sein, mir eine Kiste mit Kleiderzeug senden zu wollen, so glaube ich, würde sich durch Herrn Carl Groos von Preußen, welcher sich einige Zeit daselbst aufhalten wird, eine schöne und gute Gelegenheit bieten. Bettücher besitzen wir auch keine mehr. In Texas haben wir leider keine Fabriken, außer einer Strafanstalt, doch das Wenige, was darin fabriziert wird, bekommt ausschließlich das Militär.

Mein Brot habe ich dieses Jahr gezogen in unserem gewöhnlichen Leben, doch was die Lebensmittel anbelangt, haben wir bis jetzt keine Änderung gegen frühere Jahre gehabt. Sonst soll es sehr viele Familien geben, welche sogar an Brot Mangel leiden. So auch die Bevölkerung der Städte. Denn die Farmer haben keine Lust und zuwenig Zutrauen, um ihre Butter, Eier, Gemüse etc. für Papiergeld zu verkaufen. Deshalb führen dieselben kein beneidenswertes Leben. An Butter und Eier, Käse und Fleisch haben wir immer Überfluß. Auch hatten wir diesen Sommer ziemlich Gemüse, namentlich viele Melonen gezogen.

---

[108] Groos, Carl Wilhelm August (1830-1893). Carl immigrierte nach Texas mit seinen Geschwistern und seinem verwitweten Vater. Er kam mit dem Schiff LOUIS am 21.11.1848 in Texas an. Quelle: *Handbook of Texas Online*, unter dem Stichwort "Groos, Carl Wilhelm August," http://-www.tsha.utexas.edu/handbook/online/articles/GG/fgr88.html. (Zugriff 22.10.2003). F.K. befand sich auf demselben Schiff. Quelle: Galveston Immigration Database, Family # 10494.

Ich war dieser Tage mit einem Herrn von Marschall auf einer Jagdpartie, dem früheren Adjutanten des Herzogs von Nassau, jetzt Viehzüchter und guter Bekannter von mir. (Derselbe ist mit den badischen von Marschall verwandt). Wir sprachen darüber, daß die Verwandten in Deutschland sich nie eine richtige Vorstellung von unseren Verhältnissen machen könnten. Ich erzählte denselben (es waren nämlich unser vier Bekannte) Ihren Vorwurf in Ihrem letzten Brief, daß Sie so viel an meine Erziehung gewandt hätten, und nicht geglaubt hätten, daß ein Viehhirt aus mir werden sollte. Es erzeugte allgemeines Gelächter.

Das Vieh wird hier zu Lande nicht gehütet, sondern läuft frei herum; und hält sich ziemlich beisammen. Wenn ich ausreite und finde von meinen Kühen welche, die Kälber haben, so treibe ich dieselben nach Hause. Sie werden in der Schlafstätte gehalten bis die Kälber wenigstens 5 Monate alt sind, die Kühe gemolken; und alsdann die Kälber mit Ohrmarkierung und Brandzeichen versehen. Mein Brandzeichen ist 100 auf den Rippen.[109] Dasselbe brennt sich sehr hübsch. Und alsdann, wenn die Kälber zahm genug sind, werden sie wieder laufen gelassen.

Unsere Hauptarbeit ist das Frühjahr bis zum Juni. Alsdann reiten wir in großen Partien von 10 bis 12 Nachbarn beisammen, und treiben unser Vieh, nämlich solches, welches sich im Winter etwas weit entfernt hat, in seine alte Heimat zurück; worin es alsdann bis nächsten Winter ruhig seinen Gang behält. Von Juni an reite ich vielleicht wöchentlich 2 bis 3 mal aus, bin aber jeden Abend zu Hause, und treibe alsdann, wenn ich Kühe mit Kälbern finde, dieselben nach Hause. Die Kälber fallen nämlich das ganze Jahr hindurch.

Der ganze Westen von Texas ist bloß durch seine Vieh- und Schafzucht bedeutend. Ich hätte mein Vieh schon verkauft und mir Schafe angeschafft, allein dieselben müssen der Wölfe wegen gehütet werden. Einen Schafhüter zu bekommen, ist nicht so schwer, aber denselben zu halten, ist eine Schwierigkeit, da die Menschen ihr Leben zu leicht machen können, und ihnen diese Beschäftigung zu langweilig ist. Zum Selbsthüten habe ich keine Lust und auch eine zu gute Erziehung, um Schafhirt zu spielen. Die Schafe sind auch mehr Krankheiten unterworfen, was bei Vieh eine Seltenheit ist. Erwachsenes Vieh ist bis jetzt mir keines krepiert, ausgenommen einige Kälber, welche ich in zu heißer Zeit verschnitten habe.

Übrigens habe ich mir vorgenommen, meinen Viehstock nicht über 100 Kühe kommen zu lassen; was eine totale Summe mit Jungvieh und 1-, 2-, 3-, 4-jährigen Ochsen von beinahe 500 Stück ausmacht. Diesen Stock kann ich mit der hinreichenden Anzahl guter Pferde selbst besorgen. Die Zuzucht von Muttervieh werde ich alsdann verkaufen und entweder in Schafen oder in Pferdezucht anlegen, wenn die Indianer beseitigt würden. Dazu habe ich große Hoffnungen, wenn dieser Krieg erledigt ist; denn vertilgt werden müssen diese roten Kanaillen um jeden Preis.

---

[109] Das Gerichtsgebäude von Mason County brannte im Jahre 1877 ab und die Registrierung der frühen Brandzeichen war verloren. Franz Kettners Brandzeichen wurde im Jahr 1877 als "110" registriert. (Bierschwale 199 und 591)

Erwischen Sie einen Weißen allein, oder sind Sie überhaupt denselben an Zahl hinreichend überlegen, so kommt er nicht mit dem Leben davon. Sie ziehen ihm nämlich, wie es die Türken in früheren Zeiten taten, die Kopfhaut mit den Haaren ab, welches Sie als großes Triumphzeichen mit nach Hause nehmen.

Ich habe die letzten zwei Jahre keine Pferde verloren, weil ich mir einen Stall gebaut habe und sie nachts unter Schloß und Riegel habe. An Pferdezucht hätte ich den meisten Spaß. Die Pferde gedeihen hier vorzüglich, außerdem haben wir gute Rassen. Die alte spanische eignet sich am besten für den Gebrauch zum Viehtreiben. Dieselben sind kurz gebaut, schnell in ihren Bewegungen, drehen und wenden sich rasch auf dem Hinterteil und stoppen rasch in völligstem Jagen; was bei Viehtreiben die Hauptsache ist. Außerdem haben wir die Amerikanische oder Englische Rasse, ein zu feines Pferd, um zum Viehtreiben zu gebrauchen. Wir haben aber jetzt angefangen, diese beiden Rassen zu mixen und das sogenannte Halbblut-Pferd zu ziehen. Ein sehr schöner Schlag Pferde, zum Reitpferde geeignet. Ich habe eine sehr schöne spanische Schimmelmähre, welche von einem feinen Englischen Hengste belegt ist, und bis zum Frühjahr ein Fohlen (für den Louis bestimmt) bringen wird.

Der Viehstock von Louis beläuft sich jetzt auf 2 Kühe, 2-jährige Rinder und dieses Jahr hat er bloß ein Mutterkalb. Die Ochsenkälber werden bis jetzt für mich gebrannt. 1864 wird er also 4 Stück Kühe besitzen und ein Fohlen. Derselbe ist sehr klug, eigentlich zu klug für sein Alter und ganz in unsere Familie geschlagen. Ebenso die Ida. Von der Elise sind die Gelehrten noch uneinig.

Bei besseren Zeiten werde ich meine ganze Familie daguerreotypieren lassen und Ihnen dasselbe zuschicken. Herrn Carl Groos werde ich anempfehlen, daß Ihnen derselbe in Deutschland seine Adresse schickt, damit Sie mir vielleicht etwas zuschicken können.

Da Sie schon oft zu wissen gewünscht haben, wie meine Vermögensverhältnisse stehen, so werde Ihnen angeben, was ich bei etwaiger Verwertung erlösen könnte:

| | |
|---|---|
| 200 Stück Vieh pro Kopf 7 D = | 1,400 Doll |
| 2 Stück Pferde zu 50 D | 100 |
| Ochsen und Wagen | 100 |
| Land und Haus | 200 |
| Schweine | 25 |
| Einrichtung | 200 |
| 2 Stück Sättel | 25 |
| Sixshooter und Büchsflinte | 50 |
| | 2,000 Dollars à 2.30[110] |
| Der Dollars à fl 2.30 ? in deutschem Gelde | 5,000 Gulden. |

Dieselben könnte ich bei anderen Zeiten jeden Tag erlösen. Das ist noch alles spottbillig angeschlagen und manches wie Pflug und Kette, Hühner etc. ausgelassen.

---

[110] Schreibfehler, gerechnet wurde mit fl 2.50.

Also werden Sie ersehen, daß ich noch nicht rückwärts gekommen bin, seit ich in Texas wohne.

Von meinen Schwiegereltern habe ich bis jetzt bis auf die 13 Stück Kühe, welche meine Frau mitbekam und 3 Joch Ochsen nichts erhalten. Außerdem stehe ich auch auf keinem grünen Fuß mit ihnen. Dieselben glaubten, ich sollte bei ihnen wohnen bleiben, und sein Vermögen zusammenhalten helfen und darauf verzichten, selbständig zu sein. Dazu hatte ich aber durchaus keine Lust. Ich und meine Familie stehen seit 3 Jahren in gar keiner Verbindung mehr mit ihnen. Das ist durchaus notwendig, um unsere Eintracht nicht zu stören, denn meine Schwiegermutter ist ein böses Stück Fleisch, mit der nicht gut zu kramen ist.

Sollten Sie ein Rezept wissen gegen Magenkrampf, welchen meine Frau seit ihrem letzten Kindbett beim Essen von harten oder heißen Speisen hat; so schreiben Sie mir dasselbe. Damit zu tun hatte sie früher öfter, seit aber in anderen Umständen nur mehr sehr wenig. Wir haben schon bei mehreren deutschen Ärzten hier mediziniert, aber ohne großen Erfolg.

Ich würde noch mehr schreiben, allein mein Pferd steht gesattelt, und ich will rasch noch einige Ochsen verhandeln, da wir Nachricht haben, daß die Regierung uns dieselben wegnimmt gegen Papiergeld, für welches man nichts kaufen kann. Dieser Brief geht mit meinen Ochsen nach Mexiko und wird daselbst durch Verwandte dem Herrn Carl Groos eingehändigt werden. Außerdem lege ich noch einige Zeilen bei an Herrn Groos, damit er Ihnen in Deutschland seine Adresse und die Länge seines Aufenthaltes angibt.

Wir alle Frau und Kinder grüßen Sie vielmal und ich verbleibe Ihr Sohn,
Franz Kettner.
Llano, 6. Oktober 1863

Viele Grüße an alle meine Verwandten und Bekannten.

Meine Adresse finden Sie an der anderen Seite.

~~Meine Adresse bleibt die alte~~
~~Franz Kettner~~
~~Friedrichsburg~~
~~Gillespie County, Texas.~~

~~Meine Adresse lautet jetzt~~
~~Franz Kettner~~
~~Hedwigshill~~
~~Mason County,Texas.~~

Meine Adresse findet sich in diesem Briefcouvert.

Schreiben Sie mit der Post unter dieser Adresse, die Gelegenheit per Groos ist zunichte geworden.

# Letter / Brief 12

### Letter 12 (December 1865) from Franz Kettner at Foley's Crossing to his Parents

(an old dressing material with adhesive plaster and a shaving razor, also a sharpening stone would be very necessary for me, likewise a good pocket knife)

Dear Parents,

Finally, after four and a half years, I have the opportunity to send you a letter by a private person since our mail until now is not yet organized. I hope that this letter finds you both still in good health. I have in fact sent you a letter by way of Mexico during this war but I do not believe it succeeded in reaching your address. I have received no letters from you during this time.

I can say that I was fortunate to have left the town of Fredericksburg before the start of this war and settled in Mason County by the Llano River with my then small herd of animals. All the businesses went under during this time and the business people have all their earnings, until then, paid out. Whoever came through with their lives can be satisfied.

The start began with the conscription law for 18 through 35 year-olds. Approximately 60 young men from Fredericksburg and the surrounding area tried to get away by taking off for Mexico. They were overtaken by a greater number of militia and lost in a two hour battle in which they fought against a twice-as-large number. Fifteen were dead on the battlefield. The rest, with the wounded, struck out to Mexico and enlisted from there in the United States Army in the so-called Texas Calvary Brigade. I lost five very good friends in this combat.[111]

This was the beginning from which the fanaticism between the native-born Americans and the immigrants grew to the highest degree. The end of the matter was that we got martial law, likewise the necessary number of soldiers, under whose jurisdiction the most horrible murders were committed. I myself was no longer certain of my life and for a long time kept myself hidden. This situation lasted a long

[111] These events are also described in Letter 11.

half year in which I was often prepared to take off for Mexico. Only my family kept me back. During this time approximately 25 people were killed, some drowned and others captured and executed without any sort of trial, naturally all secretly in the night. In the morning the men would then be found hanged from the trees.

After this time the conscription law went through for 35 to 45 year-olds. At the same time, however, the border settlers' county organized a service against the Indians.[112] Our county had to provide 120 men. In the vote for officers I was elected as captain by the greater majority of votes against a very fanatical fire eater. Since I immediately noticed, however, that this would be construed as a political demonstration, I resigned the next day and put forward my neighbor von Bieberstein,[113] the former Prussian lieutenant. Two companies were organized, each with 60 experienced hunters. I myself joined as a member of the German company of von Bieberstein.[114] The other commander was an American by the name of Hunter[115] who is related to me through the marriage of my sister-in-law. The brother of this man, who lived in Fredericksburg, is my brother-in-law. My brother-in-law Hunter was named by the Governor to be Major of our county, that is, over the companies. Our county, however, does not belong in his district. Both of these Hunters were decided Union people, as well as our entire county with the exception of a dozen people.

---

[112] *Handbook of Texas Online*, s.v. "Frontier Organization," http://www.tsha.utexas.edu/-handbook/online/articles/GG/fgr88.html (accessed July 30, 2006) provides a description of the Frontier Organization. On December 15, 1863, the Texas legislature passed legislation allowing the transfer of the state-supported Frontier Regiment to the Confederate service. This legislation required that all persons liable for military service who were residents of frontier counties (59 counties) to enroll into companies of 25-65 men. It divided the frontier into 3 districts and the governor appointed three men to head these districts with a rank of major of cavalry. The first district was headquartered in Decatur under William Quayle, the second was headquartered at Gatesville under George B. Erath, and the third was at Fredericksburg under James M. Hunter. (Note the muster rolls indicate that Franz was from the second district.) The Frontier Organization usually used 15 men per squad or patrol duty. Most squads stayed out on patrol for 10 days. The Frontier Organization provided protection against the Indians. However, they also enforced Confederate conscription, rounded up deserters, and provided protection to settlers from renegades and bandits. The Organization consisted of nearly 4,000 men when the transfer to the Confederacy occurred on March 1, 1864.

[113] Hermann R. von Bieberstein was elected County Surveyor for Mason Co. numerous times over the period of 1858-1872. [Stella G. Polk, *Mason and Mason County: A History* (Burnet, TX: Eakin Press, 1980), 166-170.] He was a county judge in Gillespie County from 1890-1892. [B. Blum "The History of the Development of Gillespie County According to information taken fom the county records" in *Fredericksburg Texas:First Fifty Years*, trans. C. L. Wisseman, 50-56 (Fredericksburg: Fredericksburg Publishing Co., Inc. 1971)].

[114] The Texas State Archives Muster Rolls reads as follows: Kettner, Francis, Pvt; Commissioned Officer: Hunter, Alf , Capt.; Company from Mason County. Precinct Number 1, 2nd Frontier District, Texas State Troops; Enlisted February 1864; Description: Age 37; Remarks: Rank & File 73; Enrolling/enlisting officer: G.W. Todd & W.C. Lewis, 1 rifle & 1 pistol, Company organized for local defense by W. Chas. Lewis, 2 Muster Rolls dated Dec 6, 1863 & Feb. 13, 1864. Franz's name appears only on the roll dated Feb 13, 1864.

[115] Franz's brother-in-law is Major James M. Hunter. He was born in Buncombe County, North Carolina in 1827 and came to Texas in 1851. He married Phillippe Keller in 1860. They had 11 children. (J. Marvin Hunter, "Major James M. Hunter", *Frontier Times*, 6 October 1928, 1-2).

At this time, a secret society of fanatical robbers and murderers was formed under the name of "Soldiers' Friends." This society stretched over 4 to 5 counties. The purpose of the group was to get every Union man out of the way by hanging him. Robbery was also not to be forgotten.

The beginning happened in Fredericksburg.[116] Two Germans were taken from their homes at night and found hanged the next day near the city. Some of the murderers were known, however. The court people were so intimidated that they did nothing. Eight days after that, four Germans were once again found hanged near Fredericksburg. Then, my brother-in-law Hunter rode to Austin to present this matter before the Governor. The Governor ordered a suitable number of troops to go to Fredericksburg and interview witnesses and then return to give him exact information. At the same time, however, this fine society made threats that they would next clean out the Union people from Mason County.

We received the information that the troops would be concentrated in Fredericksburg at four in the afternoon on Saturday and that 30 men from our county under Captain Hunter from the American Company were already there. Bieberstein decided immediately to break out voluntarily with 30 men; it was voluntarily because we did not stand under the command of my brother-in-law. Since we live very isolated, we were not able to bring 30 men together until it was already night. We set out at night, rode through the entire night without dismounting and arrived in Fredericksburg at the break of day, 40 English miles.

There were approximately 500 men all together. The inhabitants took us gladly into their homes and the hearing of witnesses could proceed undisturbed. At that time, one could not determine how strong the Society was. I estimate it was about 100 men. Hunter took the results of the hearing to Austin with a strong escort and we marched home again. Now the entire rage of the Society was directed toward our county because of the voluntary participation of the men from Mason County and I was again strongly compromised. My brother-in-law sent me an express message one day from Fredericksburg that on the first of April 1864 I would be captured along with a dozen others. A crying shame that the bunch of crooks did not capture

---

[116] The *Frontier Times*, 6 October 1928, 1-2. also describes James M. Hunter's role in settling the Texas frontier. This article provides a brief description of the events that Franz describes to his father.

> Minute Men were organized in 1864 to protect the frontier and Major James M. Hunter was placed in command of the men from Gillespie and several adjacent counties. There were large numbers of lawless men in Gillespie Co. who instituted a reign of terror. A school teacher was dragged to death outside of Fredericksburg and 4 peaceable farmers on South Grape Creek were hung. The outlaws spread the word the people killed were Union people and that they were zealous Confederated patriots. In Major Hunter's attempt to restore order, some of his rangers mutinied. One major serving under Major Hunter claimed he would not arrest anyone for killing Union men. Hunter brought his men from Kendall, Comal, and Medina counties, quieted the mutinous company, and brought offenders to justice.

themselves. Preparations for this were good and the reception would teach them a lesson for the future.

Bieberstein established a defensible camp of 20 men a half mile from my home for all those who did not feel safe at home. I hired a woman since I did not feel safe at home and we expected a baby in our family in the coming days. Major Hunter returned from Austin with a proclamation from the Governor in which every good citizen was commanded to support the civil courts and catch the murderers.

Bieberstein, a very close friend of mine, advised me against remaining at home despite my family situation. Both of our companies armed themselves to go to Fredericksburg for a longer time in order to take part in the capture of the thieves. During this time our county would be undefended, which meant danger for me personally. I took my entire family to my neighbor who did not have to serve due to physical disability and marched with half of our company to Fredericksburg. A camp was set up close to the city. One of the Society was captured immediately the first day. He made everything known in a freely given confession. The next day under Bieberstein we rode off with a strong group of about 30 men and captured some of the best-known ones at daybreak.

Now the running away began. As deputy sheriff with 50 men, I followed a party, which had left for Mexico, for more than 100 miles. We found one and one was immediately shot. After we had served 21 days, we were replaced by the other half of our company and we returned home.

During this time I received a small son named Rudolph.[117]

The prisoners were taken care of by the people because our laws for such crimes are very favorable, primarily through postponement, during which time the prisoners would perhaps have the opportunity to escape. That is, they were all shot in prison one night.[118]

---

[117] Rudolph was later renamed William Kettner.

[118] Information on these events is sparse. The following description of this period is published in *Fredericksburg the First 50 Years*, [H.R. v. Biberstein "The First Lynching in Fredericksburg" in *Fredericksburg the First 50 Years*, trans. C.L Wisseman, 47-48 (Fredericksburg: Fredericksburg Publishing Co., Inc, 1971)]. The following is a direct quote from this book:

> The history of Fredericksburg for the Civil War period is probably even more interesting and touching than the preceding accounts:
>
> The arrival of Duff with his company in the town which remained loyal to the Union, his reign of terror and , after his departure, the scandalous murders by the fanatical "sons of the South" who received their main support from the Texas Ranger Company stationed at the White Oak Creek.
>
> The night ride of the "Llano Leatherjackets" to come to the aid of the inhabitants and partisans of Fredericksburg against the threatened burning and plundering.
>
> The calling of the militia by the district commander, James Hunter, as a protective measure and stationing them at Live Oak Creek.
>
> Their pursuit or flight of the ringleaders of the above-mentioned band of murderers and the attack on the jailed criminals.
>
> The period of relative quiet under the moderate rule of General McAdoo to the end of the war, interrupted only by occasional Indian atrocities.

Now we have survived all the suffering. Our land is occupied by at least 60,000 men. In San Antonio, where I was a few days before in order to sell the rest of my cattle that the Confederation had left over for me, were 12,000 cavalry. Every day 50 head of cattle are slaughtered.

The first year during the Confederation was fairly reasonable. The price of goods which were still available in the land rose very high. A person by himself could still buy the most necessary items for money. However, during the last three years was truly a terrible poverty. The entire coast was completely blockaded and nothing could come in. All that we were able to get came through Mexico which began with a trade in cattle. I had to pay 25 dollars (approximately 60 florins) for a housedress for my wife. In addition, our cattle were confiscated for which we received a piece of paper which was called Confederate money. There was nothing we could buy with it, that is, not in our entire region.

Taxes were terribly high. I had to pay 60 dollars in tax every year in addition to a tenth of everything that a person harvested or sold. The southern gentlemen were truly inventive in inventing taxes. I am convinced that if the swindle had lasted half a year longer, taxes would have been demanded from all the children who were born.

My family now consists of
Louis, December 1865, 7 years old
Ida, December 1865, 5 years old
Elise, last June 65, 3 years old
Rudolph, last May 65, 1 year old.

Both of the little girls, who look very much alike and are stamped in the same pattern as the rest of the children in our family, could be seen as twin sisters in sight of their size and strength. Louis speaks a lot about his grandparents in Germany. The region in which we have lived for six years is very healthy. We have not had to get through any illnesses with the children, except for the eye teeth.

My number of animals has well increased despite the fact that for the last four years I was not able to pay sufficient attention because the border service took up 10 days from each month. I branded and notched 70 head of calves this year. By the end of the year, I hope to brand another 10 head so that I would have 80 calves, half steers and half cows. The calves come, half steers, half cows. In my cattle book I have over 100 head cows but the large steers for the market, the Confederation has eaten up. Had this unholy Civil War not occurred, I would have been so far along at last that I could live worry free. However, we are, as one says, all torn up.

---

A comprehensive and impartial portrayal of these incidents is not advisable because many of those who experienced theses difficulties are still living and the cause of the South also had many eager, sincere followers. It would merely inflame healing wounds again and renew old enmities.

But a new generation has arrived, the graves of the old Union supporters have caved in, their purpose has perhaps been atoned and they themselves are probably half-forgotten by their descendants in their own struggle for their daily bread.

For the last three years I have worn on my body for everyday only leather pants and leather shirts, as has Louis. I ride out no longer to hunt for meat but for the pelts. I tan this myself, similar to the chamois gloves in Germany and my wife sews. The girls cost me the most trouble to keep them in clothing. In addition, they are a pair of wild animals who cannot keep from climbing. Things are better with them now.

You will receive this letter from a certain Clamor Brockman who lives in Fredericksburg and is making a trip to Germany for family business. He will share with you his address in Germany as well as the length of his stay.

If you should be in the circumstance to support me with things that we very much need, this would be the best and safest opportunity.

During this war, my wife has cut up all of her good clothing for the children so that one black silk dress which has become too tight for her (principally in the body) is her entire wardrobe. I would like, therefore, some yards of black silk material in order to make a wider blouse for the shirt. My wife, who has become heavier, likes to wear this clothing the best. The material for dresses, half woolen and half mousseline de lain. For the two girls, for each 2 Sunday dresses, a dozen linen sheets, a dozen towels, a dozen handkerchiefs, one or two dish towels, and one or two white bedspreads to hang over the bed. When you would like to give both girls a pleasure, then send each a pair of earrings with a small piece hanging down. For Louis and me, material for summer pants. I would most like cotton. A small Meerschaum pipe for me would also be nothing to despise. Two boxes of Prussian primer caps would also be very good for me. Also, I do not have any more silk neckties. Some yards of pink calico for children's clothing because the end of February, our family will again grow larger.

Should you be inclined to send us a chest with supplies, then pack everything that you wish to send me in a case and send it to the address that Mr. Clamor Brockman gives you. I have not yet spoken myself to Mr. Brockman while I write these lines. Should it not come to pass that he wishes to take care of this for me, then Mr. Frank van der Stucken in Antwerp will give you his address and he will take care of things safely. He lived in Fredericksburg 15 years but fled from there with his family during the war.

If Mr. Brockman cannot take care of things, then I will write Frank van der Stucken in Antwerp immediately, so that he can give you his address himself from there. Send the photographs along that I have already long requested.

My friend Braubach, who also came through, returned to Texas as Captain in the Texas Cavalry[119] and I met with him in San Antonio. My horse and I had a free stay with him which was very convenient for me since San Antonio is a very expensive boarding.

In a few days, I and many other people from the neighborhood will drive cattle to San Antonio in order to purchase all the most necessary items for the winter.

---

[119] See Letter 13.

We suffered a lot from the Indians during this war. A neighbor of mine, an American, was attacked two and a half miles from my farm. The wife was killed as well as a negress. And his daughter, a 13-year-old girl, was taken by the Indians. We followed the Indians for 300 miles but could not catch up with them despite all the energy we developed. It was, you see, in wintertime. We could not carry supplies in the fast pursuit. We lived only from meat that was held on sticks over the fire and roasted. There was no bread, no salt, we lacked even tobacco. Snow fell abnormally hard so that at times we had to follow the tracks on foot until after three days (it never remained longer) it began to melt. We had to make do at night with a saddle blanket on the wet ground or in the snow and a woolen blanket for cover. Until now, still nothing more has been heard about the girl.[120]

At least 30 to 40 people in 2 or 3 counties were murdered by the Indians. I rode away no more without rifle and revolver and in the spring when the cattle roundup began, we were sometimes 20 men together and had watchmen by night over our horses so that they would not be stolen. Many Indians were also killed. At present, this plague has stopped and we are keeping a strong force on the borders.

Mr. Wuelfing, once a captain in the Prussian artillery, who earlier worked two years for me and whom I paid in cattle, is again with us, however, without salary because I cared for his cattle from which he can provide for his few needs that he

---

[120] J. Marvin Hunter ("A Brief History of Early Days in Mason County," *Frontier Times*, 6 December 1928, 113-134) describes the events associated with the massacre of the Todd family. See below. The incident occurred near Todd Mountain off of Farm Road 2389. A historical marker is located here. According to family lore, Mrs. Kettner cared for Mrs. Todd who survived several days after the attack. Later these events were dramatized in the Alan Le May novel, *The Searchers* (New York: Curtis Publishing Co., 1954) and in the 1956 John Ford movie of the same name.

From the *Frontier Times*:

> It was during the later part of 1865 that the Indians on one of their raids, killed Mrs. G.W. Todd and a Negro girl belonging to the Todd family, and captured and carried away Miss Alice Todd, daughter of G.W. Todd. It seems that G.W. Todd, who was the first county clerk of Mason county, and Mrs. Todd were coming from their home about four miles south of Mason, their daughter riding behind her father and the negro girl riding behind Mrs. Todd, when they were attacked by a band of Indians. Mrs. Todd was badly wounded and lived only a few days, the Negro girl was killed instantly, and the white girl captured. Todd made his escape and notified the community of what had happened. A searching party was quickly organized, and started in pursuit of the Indians, whom they trailed to the Bauer crossing. Here they met parties who had seen the Indians pass, and these parties were sure, as they had watched the Indians closely from a hiding place, that there was no white girl in the party. The pursuing party then returned to the place where the attack had been made on the Todd family. There they discovered the tracks of a mule and horse that had left the main party of Indians and traveled west. Confident that these tracks were the trail of the Indians that had left the main body of the raiding party and taken the girl to the main Indian camp, it was followed for many miles. But it was winter time, bitter cold, and snow of several inches covered he ground, and fresh falling snow frequently obliterated the trail, so the chase was abandoned.

has. Additionally, he had inherited 1000 taler from Germany. He is now in his sixties but a very sprightly man.

Put some toys for the children in the trunk, some collars and cuffs for my wife. Miss Marie Kissel could herself show on this occasion what she has to offer with her embroidery.

Two hairnets would also stand very well for my girls. Put in whatever you think, what you can spare, and what is necessary for a demolished household.

In the future, address your letters exactly like the address shown below because the last letter that I received four years ago had a wrong address regarding the county. I received the letter only by pure chance.

In the hope that this letter after four long years reaches you still in good health and sprightly, I remain your son

Franz Kettner

(Marie should embroider me a pair of slippers and a cap.)

Have you received a letter by way of Mexico during this war?

My two little girls ask the grandparents for a pair of beautiful hair nets. My wife as well wishes for a corset.

What I am thinking to do later when the traffic again is restored, quiet and peace and trust again rule, will be in the next letter. I am thinking that when the cattle are marketable, to make 2000 dollars from the cattle and then set myself up with business in my city, because my children soon must have school.

Say hello to Franz and Marie and the little Klara and tell all of them that I expect letters. Greet all the relatives and friends. Regarding the material, my wife is my height and has become fairly heavy. Do not send too little material. Upon receiving this letter, in any case, write me through the postal service, I will await then the second letter through Mr. Brockman.

Address

Mr. Franz Kettner

Hedwigshill

Mason County

Texas

**Fig. 29. Major James M. Hunter.** Photograph was provided by Jane Hoerster from the archives of the Mason County Historical Commission.

**Abb. 29. Major James M. Hunter.** Das Foto wurde von Jane Hoerster aus den Archiven der Mason County Historical Commission zur Verfügung gestellt.

**Fig. 30. Phillippe Hunter.** Photograph copied from an old album in the possession of Henrietta Kettner Keener. The photo is labeled Hunter. Her resemblance to Mrs. Kettner leaves little doubt to her identity.

**Abb. 30. Philippe Hunter.** Fotografie kopiert aus einem alten Album im Besitz von Henrietta Kettner Keener. Das Foto ist bezeichnet mit Hunter. Die Ähnlichkeit mit Mrs. Kettner läßt wenig Zweifel an ihrer Identität.

**Fig. 31. Todd Mountain.** This is the view from Farm Road 2389. The Todd Mountain Marker and grave sites are at the base of the mountain, between the mountain and the road.

**Abb. 31. Todd Mountain.** Dieses ist der Blick von der Landstraße 2389. Die Todd Mountain Gedenktafel und die Gräber befinden sich am Fußc des Berges zwischen dem Berg und der Straße.

**Fig. 32. Todd Mountain Marker:** Dizenia Peters Todd, Aug 5, 1826-Jan 1865. Born in Mississippi, Dizenia Peters moved to Texas with her parents about 1835. She married William P. Smith in 1844, and had a son, James. After Smith's death, she married George W. Todd (1827-1901) in 1851; they had 3 daughters. Todd and members of his wife's family settled this area in the 1850's and were among the first Mason County officials. Mrs. Todd and a black servent girl were fatally wounded in an Indian attack near this site and buried in adjacent unmarked graves. Recorded 1975

**Abb. 32. Todd Mountain Gedenktafel:** Dizenia Peters Todd, 5. August 1826 – January 1865. Geboren in Mississippi, Dizenia Todd zog 1835 mit ihren Eltern nach Texas. Sie heiratete William P. Smith 1844 und hatte einen Sohn, James. Nach dem Tode von Smith heiratete sie George W. Todd (1827 – 1901), im Jahre 1851. Sie hatten drei Töchter. Todd und die Mitglieder seiner Frau siedelten sich in dieser Gegend in den 1850er Jahren an und gehörten zu den ersten Offiziellen des Mason County. Mrs. Todd und eine schwarze Angestellte wurden bei einem Indianerangriff tödlich verwundet nahe diesem Platz und in benachbarten unmarkierten Gräbern beederdigt. Berichtet 1975

## Brief 12 (Dezember 1865[121]) von Franz Kettner aus Foley's Crossing an seine Eltern

(Ein altes Verbandszeug mit Heftpflaster und Rasiermesser, auch ein Abziehstein dazu wäre für mich sehr nötig, ebenfalls ein gutes Taschenmesser)

Liebe Eltern!

Endlich nach vier und ½ langen Jahren ist mir die Gelegenheit dargeboten, einen Brief durch Privatperson, da unsere Posten[122] bis jetzt noch nicht reguliert sind, an Sie absenden zu können. Ich hoffe, daß dieser Brief Sie beide noch in guter Gesundheit antreffen wird. Ich habe zwar während dieses Krieges einen Brief per Mexiko an Sie gesandt, glaube aber nicht, daß derselbe je an seine Adresse gelangt ist. Briefe von Ihnen habe keine während dieser Zeit erhalten.

Es war für mich ein Glück, kann ich sagen, daß ich vor Anfang dieses Krieges das Städtchen Friedrichsburg verlassen habe, und mich mit meinem damals noch kleinen Viehstöckchen nach Mason County an dem Fluß Llano niedergelassen habe. Denn alle Geschäfte lagen während dieser Zeit danieder und die Geschäftspersonen haben all ihr bis dahin Erworbenes zugesetzt. Wer mit dem Leben davonkam, konnte zufrieden sein.

Der Anfang begann mit dem Conscriptions Gesetz für 18 bis 35 Jahre. Ungefähr 60 junge Leute von Friedrichsburg und Umgegend suchten sich desselben zu entziehen, indem sie sich nach Mexiko aufmachten. Sie wurden aber von überlegener Anzahl Militär überholt, und verloren in einem zweistündigen Gefecht, in welchem dieselben gegen doppelt überlegene Zahl kämpften, 15 Mann Tote auf dem Kampfplatze. Der Rest mit den Verwundeten schlug sich durch nach Mexiko und trat von da aus in die Vereinigten Staaten Armee, in die sogenannte Texas Kavallerie Brigade. In diesem Gefecht verlor ich 5 sehr gute Freunde.

Dieses war der Anfang, der den Fanatismus zwischen geborenen Amerikanern und eingewanderten zum höchsten Grade steigerte. Das Ende vom Liede war, daß wir Militär-Gerichtsbarkeit bekamen, ebenso die nötige Anzahl Militär, unter welcher Gerichtsbarkeit die scheußlichsten Morde verübt wurden. Ich selbst war meines Lebens nicht mehr sicher und hielt mich lange Zeit heimlich. Dieser Zustand dauerte ein langes halbes Jahr, in welchem ich mehrmals im Begriffe stand, nach Mexiko mich aufzumachen. Bloß meine Familie hielt mich zurück. Ungefähr 25 Personen wurden während dieser Zeit teils gefangen, teils ersäuft, ohne irgendein Gericht, natürlich alles heimlich in der Nacht, morgens wurden alsdann die Menschen in den Bäumen aufgehangen gefunden.

Nach dieser Zeit ging das Conscriptions Gesetz durch für 35 bis 45 Jahre. Zu gleicher Zeit wurden aber die Grenzsiedler County zum Dienst gegen Indianer organisiert. Unser County hatte 120 Mann zu stellen. Bei der Wahl der Offiziere wurde ich gegen einen sehr fanatischen Feuerfresser mit großer Stimmenmehrheit

---

[121] Datum nach Vermutung der Autorin.

[122] Lies: Poststationen.

zum Captain erwählt. Da ich aber gleich bemerkte, daß dies als eine politische Demonstration ausgelegt wurde, so resignierte ich schon den nächsten Tag; und schob meinen Nachbarn von Bieberstein[123] vor, ehemaliger preußischer Leutnant. Außerdem wurden zwei Kompanien organisiert, jede 60 Mann berittene Jäger. Ich selbst trat als Gemeiner in die deutsche Kompanie von Bieberstein, die andere Amerikanische befehligte ein Amerikaner namens Hunter, durch Heirat meiner Schwägerin etwas verwandt mit mir. Der Bruder desselben, wohnhaft in Friedrichsburg, ist mein Schwager. Mein Schwager Hunter[124] wurde vom Gouverneur zum Major unseres County ernannt, d.h. über die Kompanien. Unser County gehörte aber nicht in seinen Distrikt. Diese beiden Hunter waren entschiedene Unionsleute, sowie unser ganzes County, mit Ausnahme von 1 Dutzend.

Zu dieser Zeit wurde von fanatischen Räubern und Mördern eine heimliche Gesellschaft ins Leben gerufen unter dem Namen "Soldatenfreunde." Diese Gesellschaft erstreckte sich über 4 bis 5 County. Der Zweck derselben war, jeden Unionsmann durch Hängen aus dem Wege zu schaffen. Dabei aber auch das Stehlen nicht zu vergessen.

Der Anfang geschah in Friedrichsburg. Zwei Deutsche wurden nachts aus dem Hause geholt, und man fand dieselben den nächsten Tag aufgehangen in der Nähe der Stadt. Einige der Mörder aber wurden erkannt. Die Gerichtspersonen waren aber so eingeschüchtert, daß sie nichts taten. Acht Tage darauf wurden abermals 4 Deutsche in der Nähe von Friedrichsburg gehangen gefunden. Nun reiste mein Schwager Hunter nach Austin zum Gouverneur und stellte demselben die Sache vor. Der Gouverneur befahl, die geeignete Truppenmacht nach Friedrichsburg kommen zu lassen und die Zeugen zu verhören und alsdann ihm genaue Information zukommen zu lassen. Zu gleicher Zeit hatte aber diese feine Gesellschaft Drohungen fallen lassen, sie würden nächstens in Mason County auch aufräumen unter den Unionsleuten.

Wir erhielten die Nachricht, daß Truppen in Friedrichsburg konzentriert wurden auf einen Samstag 4 Uhr nachmittags, und daß 30 Mann von der Amerikanischen Kompanie von unserem County unter Captain Hunter schon dahin abgegangen waren. Bieberstein beschloß, sofort ebenfalls freiwillig mit 30 Mann aufzubrechen; es war nämlich freiwillig, weil wir nicht unter dem Kommando meines Schwagers standen. Da wir sehr vereinzelt wohnen, so konnten die 30 Mann nicht eher zusammengebracht werden, als bis es schon Nacht war. Wir brachen in der Nacht

---

[123] Hermann R. von Bieberstein war ein bekannter texanischer Vermessungsingenieur. Quelle: Stella G. Polk, *Mason and Mason County: A History* (Burnet, TX: Eakin Press, 1980), 166-170. Er war "County Judge" im Gillespie County von 1890-1892. [B.Blum "The History of the Development of Gillespie County. According to information taken from the county records" in *Fredericksburg Texas: First Fifty Years*, trans. Charles L. Wissemann, 50-56 (Fredericksburg: Fredericksburg Publishing Co., Inc. 1971).]

[124] Major James M. Hunter, geb. in Buncombe County, North Carolina 1829. Kam nach Texas im Jahre 1851. Er heiratete 1860 Phillippine Keller. Sie hatten 11 Kinder. Hunter starb in Mason am 31.8.1907. Quelle: J. Marvin Hunter, "Major James M. Hunter," *Frontier Times*, 6 October 1928, 1-2.

auf, ritten die ganze Nacht hindurch ohne abzusteigen und rückten bei Tagesanbruch in Friedrichsburg ein, 40 englische Meilen.

Es waren daselbst ungefähr 500 Mann beisammen. Die Einwohner nahmen uns hoch erfreut in Ihren Häusern auf, und das Zeugenverhör konnte ungestört vor sich gehen. Wie stark die Gesellschaft war, konnte man damals nicht ermitteln. Ich schätze dieselbe auf ungefähr 100 Mann. Hunter brachte das Resultat des Zeugenverhörs unter starker Eskorte nach Austin, und wir marschierten wieder nach Hause. Nun wurden durch das freiwillige Beteiligen der Masoner die ganze Wut der Gesellschaft auf unser County gerichtet und meine Persönlichkeit war wieder stark kompromittiert. Mein Schwager schickte mir eines Tages von Friedrichsburg einen Expressboten, daß auf den ersten April 1864 meine Person nebst einem Dutzend Anderer gefangen werden sollten. Jammerschade, daß die saubere Gesellschaft sich nicht einfand. Die Vorbereitungen dafür waren gut und der Empfang würde ihnen eine Lehre für die Zukunft gegeben haben.

Bieberstein etablierte ein beständiges Camp von 20 Mann, ½ Meile von meinem Hause, wohin sich alle diejenigen begaben, die sich zu Hause nicht sicher fühlten. Ich mietete eine Frau, da ich mich zu Hause nicht sicher fühlte, und wir nächster Tage einen Zuwachs in unserer Familie erwarteten. Major Hunter kam von Austin retour mit einer Proklamation vom Gouverneur, worin jeder gute Bürger aufgefordert wurde, die Civil-Gerichte zu unterstützen und die Mörder einzufangen.

Bieberstein, ein sehr intimer Freund von mir, riet mir trotz meinen Familienverhältnissen ab, zu Hause zu bleiben. Denn unsere beiden Kompanien rüsteten sich, auf längere Zeit nach Friedrichsburg zu gehen, um sich tätlich beim Einfangen der Räuber zu beteiligen. Unser County sei während dieser Zeit schutzlos und für meine Person namentlich Gefahr vorhanden. Ich brachte daher meine ganze Familie zu meinem Nachbarn, welcher durch Körperschaden frei vom Dienste war, und marschierte mit der Hälfte unserer Kompanie abermals nach Friedrichsburg. In der Nähe der Stadt wurde ein Camp aufgeschlagen. Den ersten Tag wurde gleich einer von der Gesellschaft gefangen genommen, welcher in einem freiwilligen Geständnisse alles bekannte. Den nächsten Tag brachen wir unter Bieberstein circa 30 Mann stark auf und fingen bei Tagesanbruch einige der Besten.

Nun ging aber das Ausreißen los. Ich verfolgte als Deputy-Sheriff mit 50 Mann mehrere 100 Meilen eine Partie, welche sich nach Mexiko aufmachte. Wir fingen aber bloß einen und einer wurde gleich erschossen. Nachdem wir 21 Tage daselbst gelegen hatten, wurden wir von der anderen Hälfte unserer Kompanie abgelöst, und gingen nach Hause.

Während dieser Zeit erhielt ich einen kleinen Sohn mit Namen Rudolph.[125]

Die Gefangenen wurden, da unsere Gesetze für solche Verbrechen sehr günstig sind, nämlich durch Hinausschieben, während welcher Zeit denselben vielleicht Gelegenheit sich darbietet zu entkommen, durch das Volk ausgeführt. Sie wurden nämlich in einer Nacht alle im Gefängnis erschossen.

---

[125] Rudolph wurde William Kettner genannt.

Nun haben wir alle Leiden überstanden. Unser Land ist von wenigstens 60,000 Mann besetzt. In San Antonio, wo ich selbst vor einigen Tagen war, um den Rest meiner Ochsen, die mir die Konföderation übriggelassen hat, zu verkaufen, liegen 12,000 Mann Kavallerie. Jeden Tag werden 50 Stück Ochsen geschlachtet.

Während der Konföderation ging es das erste Jahr so leidlich. Die Waren, welche noch im Land waren, stiegen sehr hoch. Allein man konnte doch noch für Geld das Notwendigste erhalten. Aber die letzten 3 Jahre war wirklich eine schreckliche Armut. Die ganze Küste war streng blockiert, nichts konnte herein. Alles was wir erhalten konnten, war durch Mexikaner, welche einen Tauschhandel mit Ochsen anfingen. Ich mußte ein Hauskleid für meine Frau mit 25 Dollars (ungefähr fl 60) bezahlen. Außerdem wurden unsere Ochsen gepreßt, wofür wir ein Stück Papier erhielten, das konföderiertes Geld genannt wurde. Dafür war aber nichts zu kaufen, namentlich nicht in unserer Gegend.

Die Steuern waren fürchterlich hoch. Ich mußte jedes Jahr 60 Dollars Steuer bezahlen, außerdem den zehnten Teil von allem, was man erntete oder verkaufte. Die südlichen Herren waren wirklich erfinderisch im Erfinden von Steuern. Ich bin fest überzeugt, daß wenn der Schwindel noch ein halbes Jahr länger gedauert hätte, so würden sie Steuern verlangt haben für alle Kinder, die geboren wurden.

Meine Familie besteht jetzt aus
Louis Dezember 1865 7 Jahre alt
Ida Dezember 1865 5 Jahre alt
Elise letzten Juni 65 3 Jahre alt
Rudolph letzten Mai 65 1 Jahr alt
Die beiden Mädchen, welche sich überhaupt sehr ähnlich sehen und so wie alle übrigen Kinder in unsere Familie geschlagen sind, können wir hinsichtlich ihrer Größe und Stärke als Zwillingsschwestern ausgeben. Der Louis spricht viel von seinen Großeltern in Deutschland. Die Gegend in welcher wir seit 6 Jahren wohnen ist sehr gesund. Krankheiten mit Kindern haben wir keine durchzumachen gehabt, außer mit den Augenzähnen.

Mein Viehstock hat sich, trotzdem ich während dieser 4 Jahre nicht die nötige Aufmerksamkeit darauf verwenden konnte, da der Grenzdienst jeden Monat 10 Tage in Anspruch nahm, doch hübsch vermehrt. Ich hatte dieses Jahr 70 Stück Kälber gebrannt und gemarkt. Außerdem hoffe ich bis Ende dieses Jahres noch 10 Stück zu brennen, so daß ich auf 80 Stück Kälber komme, halb Ochsen halb Mutterkälber. Meinem Viehbuch nach habe ich über 100 Stück Kühe, aber die großen Ochsen für den Markt, die hat die Konföderation gefressen. Wäre dieser unselige Bürgerkrieg nicht entstanden, so wäre ich endlich so weit, sorgenfrei leben zu können. So aber sind wir, was man sagt, abgerissen.

Die letzten 3 Jahre habe ich für meine Person, für alle Tage bloß Lederhosen und Lederrock getragen, so auch Louis. Ich ritt nicht mehr des Fleisches halber auf die Jagd, nein der Felle wegen. Diese gerbte ich selbst, ähnliches Leder als wie die gamsledernen Handschuhe in Deutschland, und meine Frau schneiderte. Die

Mädchen kosteten mich am meisten Mühe, in Kleider zu unterhalten.[126] Außerdem sind es ein paar Wildfänge, die das Klettern nicht lassen können. Jetzt geht es besser mit ihnen.

Diesen Brief erhalten Sie durch einen gewissen Clamor Brockmann, welcher in Friedrichsburg wohnt und in Familiengeschäften eine Reise dorthin macht. Derselbe wird Ihnen seine Adresse in Deutschland mitteilen sowie die Länge seines Aufenthaltes.

Sollten Sie in Verhältnissen sein, mich mit Zeug, was wir sehr notwendig brauchten, unterstützen zu können, so wäre das die schönste und sicherste Gelegenheit.

Meine Frau hat während dieses Krieges ihre sämtlichen guten Kleider für die Kinder verschnitten, so daß ein schwarzseidenes Kleid, welches ihr außerdem zu eng geworden ist, (nämlich der Leib), ihren ganzen Staat ausmacht. Ich wünschte deshalb einige Ellen schwarzes Seidenzeug, um eine weite Jacke zu dem Rock machen zu können. Meine Frau, welche etwas korpulent geworden ist, trägt diese Kleidung am liebsten. Das Zeug für Kleider, ein halb-wollenes und in Mousseline de lain. Außerdem für die beiden Mädchen, jedem für 2 Sonntagskleider, 1 Dutzend leinene Bettücher, 1 Dutzend Handtücher, 1 Dutzend Taschentücher, ein oder zwei Tischtücher, ebenso 1 oder 2 weiße Bettdecken über das Bett zu hängen. Wenn Sie nun beiden Mädchen ein Vergnügen machen wollen, so legen Sie jeder 1 Paar Ohrringe bei mit kleinen Anhängern. Für mich und Louis Zeug zu Sommerhosen, Nanke[127] wäre mir das Liebste. Eine kleine Meerschaumpfeife wäre für mich auch nicht zu verachten. 2 Boxen preußische Zündhütchen würden mir auch sehr gut tun. Seidene Halsbinden besitze ich auch keine mehr. Einige Ellen rosa Callico[128] für Kinderkleidchen; denn unsere Familie wird sich bis Ende Februar ebenfalls vermehren.

Sollten Sie geneigt sein, uns eine Kiste mit Zeug zukommen zu lassen, so packen Sie alles, was Sie mir zu schicken wünschen, in einen Koffer und schicken denselben, nach der Ihnen von Herrn Clamor Brockmann angegebenen Adresse. Ich habe den Herrn, während ich diese Zeilen schreibe noch nicht selbst gesprochen. Sollte es aber nicht passen, mir dieses besorgen zu wollen, so wird Ihnen Frank van der Stucken in Antwerpen, welcher in Friedrichsburg 15 Jahre gewohnt, während des Krieges aber mit seiner Familie dorthin geflüchtet ist; Ihnen seine Adresse mitteilen, und derselbe wird es ebenso sicher besorgen.

Wenn Herr Brockmann es nicht besorgen kann, werde ich sofort an Frank van der Stucken nach Antwerpen schreiben, damit er Ihnen seine Adresse von dort selbst mitteilt. Schicken Sie die Fotografien mit, die ich schon längst verlangt habe.

Mein Freund Braubach, welcher auch durchgegangen war, kam als Captain in der Texas Kavallerie nach Texas zurück, und ich traf denselben in San Antonio. Mein

[126] Gemeint ist, mit Kleidern zu versorgen.

[127] Englisch nankeen = deutsch Nanking, rötlichgelbes, festes Baumwollzeug.

[128] Englisch calico = deutsch Kattun.

Pferd und ich hatten freie Station bei ihm, was mir sehr gelegen kam, da San Antonio ein teures Pflaster ist.

In einigen Tagen werde ich und mehrere andere Leute aus der Nachbarschaft Ochsen nach San Antonio treiben, um das Allernötigste für den Winter anzuschaffen.

Von Indianern hatten wir während dieses Krieges viel zu leiden. Ein Nachbar von mir, ein Amerikaner wurde 2 ½ Meilen von meiner Farm von Indianer überfallen, die Frau wurde getötet. Ebenso eine Negerin. Und seine Tochter, ein Mädchen von 13 Jahren, wurde von den Indianern mitgenommen. Wir verfolgten die Indianer 300 Meilen, konnten dieselben aber nicht einholen trotz aller Energie, welche wir entwickelten. Es war nämlich im Winter. Proviant konnten wir in der Schnelligkeit auch keinen mitnehmen. Wir lebten bloß von Fleisch, das an Stöcken über das Feuer gehalten und gebraten wurde, kein Brot, kein Salz, sogar der Tabak war uns ausgegangen. Der Schnee fiel ausnahmsweise so stark, daß wir teilweise zu Fuß die Spuren verfolgen mußten, als es am dritten Tage (länger bleibt er niemals liegen) anfing zu schmelzen. Wir mußten nachts auf der nassen Erde oder im Schnee, mit einer Satteldecke und einer wollenen Decke zum Zudecken vorlieb nehmen. Bis jetzt ist auch nichts mehr von dem Mädchen gehört worden.[129]

So sind wenigstens 30 bis 40 Personen in 2 bis 3 Counties von den Indianern ermordet worden. Ich ritt nicht mehr aus ohne Büchse und Revolver und im Frühjahr als das Viehsuchen anging, waren wir manchmal 20 Mann zusammen und hatten nachts Wachtposten bei unseren Pferden, damit dieselben nur nicht gestohlen wurden. Indianer wurden auch manche getötet. Im Augenblick hat auch diese Plage aufgehört und wir werden starke Besatzungen an die Grenze erhalten.

Herr Wülfing, früher Captain bei der Artillerie in Preußen, welcher früher schon 2 Jahre bei mir war, und welchen ich in Vieh bezahlte, ist jetzt wieder bei uns. Jedoch ohne Bezahlung, da ich sein Vieh mitbesorge, wovon er seine wenigen Bedürfnisse bestreiten kann, die er hat. Außerdem hat er 1000 Taler von Deutschland geerbt. Er ist jetzt ein sechziger aber sehr rüstiger Mann.

Legen Sie in den Koffer einige Spielsachen für die Kinder, einige Kragen und Unterärmel für meine Frau. Fräulein Marie Kissel könnte sich bei dieser Gelegenheit hervortun und zeigen, was sie in der Stickerei zu leisten vermag.

Zwei Stück Haarnetze würden meinen Mädchen auch sehr gut stehen. Legen Sie bei, was Sie denken, das Sie entbehren können, und was notwendig für eine abgerissene Haushaltung ist.

In Zukunft adressieren Sie Ihre Briefe genau nach der unten angezeigten Adresse; da der letzte Brief, den ich etwa vor 4 Jahren erhalten habe, eine falsche Adresse hinsichtlich des County hatte. Ich erhielt den Brief bloß durch reinen Zufall.

In der Hoffnung, daß dieser Brief nach 4 langen Jahren, Sie noch gesund und rüstig antrifft, verbleibe Ihr Sohn

Franz Kettner

---

[129] Siehe Abb. 31 und 32.

(Marie möchte mir ein Paar Pantoffeln und Mütze sticken.)

Haben Sie einen Brief während dieses Krieges via Mexiko erhalten?

Meine beiden Mädchen bitten die Großeltern um ein paar schöne Haarnetze. Ebenfalls wünschte meine Frau ein Korsett.

Was ich später zu tun gedenke, wenn der Verkehr wieder hergestellt, Ruhe und Frieden und Vertrauen wieder herrscht, davon im nächsten Brief. Ich denke bis das Vieh verkäuflich wird, 2000 Dollars aus meinem Vieh zu machen, und dann in meiner Stadt mich dem Handel zu ergeben, da meine Kinder bald Schule haben müßten.

Grüßen Sie Franz und Marie und die kleine Klärchen und sagen Sie allen, daß ich Briefe erwarte. Grüßen Sie alle Verwandten und Bekannten. Wegen des Zeugs, meine Frau ist in meiner Größe und ziemlich korpulent geworden. Schicken Sie nicht zuwenig Zeug. Bei Empfang dieses Briefes schreiben Sie auf jeden Fall per Post an mich; durch Herrn Brockmann erwarte ich alsdann den zweiten Brief.

Adresse
Mr. Franz Kettner
Hedwigshill
Mason County
Texas

# Letter / Brief 13

## Letter 13 (December 17, 1865) from Franz Kettner at Foley's Crossing to his Parents

Dear Parents!

I had the opportunity to send a detailed letter by Mr. Clamor Brockman who wanted travel to Germany shortly but he has not left yet, so I will try to send you these lines through our not yet regulated postal service.

We are all still healthy and alive and have the terrible war times behind us. You will receive a detailed letter through Clamor Brockmann over all the events that we have gone through during these four and a half years.

My family consists of Louis 7 years old, Ida 5 years old, Elise 3 and ½ years old, and a little boy of 1 and ½ named William. The children are all healthy and strong for their age. In my detailed letter which you will receive somewhat later through Clamor Brockmann, I ask you for several small items that you might send me here through the same man. We became somewhat impoverished through the war, at least in our household, because almost all of our slaughter cattle from which we have lived were confiscated and we have never received payment.

We are lacking now in household linens. Therefore I wish that you send me a dozen linen sheets, towels, handkerchiefs, collars and cuffs, a large white bedspread for a double bed, 2 pair embroidered slips for both my girls, some dish towels, some good half woolen dresses or linen material for dresses for my wife and children, some good trousers for me and both my sons, an apron for my wife, not too small.

Also a first aid kit with accessories and a good pocketknife for me, some small tobacco pipes, when possible small wooden or Meerschaum pipes. Furthermore, a corset big enough to fit my wife because she has become heavy and is the same size as I. Your pictures especially and that of the children. You will receive all of our daguerreotypes as soon as we have again somewhat recovered. I have written everything in detail in the other letter. I am traveling to the capitol Austin in order to take an office as a good citizen of the United States. That is, to estimate in three different counties the worth of the property upon which the war taxes are adjusted. I received the job through my old friend Braubach. He fled at the beginning of the war and enlisted in the northern army. He returned to Texas as captain of United States troops[130] and had recommended me. With this opportunity, I will take the letter to Austin and put it in the mail and I hope it will arrive.

I will recover to some degree from the losses through this position, which I can hold for many years. I still live on the Llano. My number of stock has not increased so quickly as it would have if peace had remained. While I had to serve so much time as soldier on the border, I had only 70 calves in the year 1865 branded and marked and I should have had at least 100. Nevertheless, we are content that we at least kept alive.

I am giving you this address because one letter was wrongly addressed and only by chance came into my hands. I have received no letters from you since the year 1861.

Your son Franz Kettner
F. Kettner
Hedwigshill
Mason County Texas

What is cholera doing?
Write me immediately upon the receipt of this letter.

---

[130] The First Texas Cavalry Regiment was the first of two regiments that served in the Union Army. A total of 1915 individuals were in these Union regiments. A portion of the regiments was made up of German immigrants from the Hill Country. It was organized in New Orleans November 6, 1862. It participated in the defense of New Orleans and was involved in military operations in Louisiana. The regiment was involved in the Rio Grande expedition and occupied Brownsville, Texas October, 1863. During this time the Second Texas Cavalry regiment was formed. Both regiments returned to Louisiana and in November 1864 they merged to form the First Texas Volunteer Cavalry. They were mainly involved in reconnaissance until the end of the war. The regiment was ordered back to Texas and they were mustered out of the service November 1864. *Handbook of Texas Online*, s.v. "First Texas Cavalary, USA," http://www.tsha.utexas.edu/handbook/online/articles/FF/qlf3.html (accessed June 25, 2006).

**Fig. 33. Captain Braubach.** This photograph is included in the album in the possession of Henrietta Kettner Keener and is labeled Captain Braubach.

**Abb. 33. Captain Braubach.** Diese Fotografie befindet sich im Album im Besitz von Henrietta Kettner Keener und ist mit Captain Braubach bezeichnet.

## Brief 13 (17. Dezember 1865) von Franz Kettner aus Foley's Crossing an seine Eltern

Liebe Eltern!

Da ich einen ausführlichen Brief per Gelegenheit durch einen Herrn Clamor Brockmann (senden werde), welcher in kurzer Zeit nach Deutschland reisen wollte, aber jetzt noch nicht abgereist ist, so versuche ich Ihnen diese Zeilen durch unsere bis jetzt noch nicht geregelte Postverbindung, zukommen zu lassen.

Wir sind noch alle gesund und am Leben und haben die schauerlichen Kriegszeiten hinter uns. Durch Clamor Brockmann erhalten Sie einen ausführlichen Brief über alle Begebenheiten, die wir während dieser 4½ Jahre durchzumachen hatten.

Meine Familie besteht aus Louis 7 Jahre alt, Ida 5 Jahre alt, Elise 3½ und ein kleiner Junge von 1½ Jahren mit Namen Wilhelm. Die Kinder sind alle gesund und stark für ihr Alter. In meinem ausführlichen Brief, welchen Sie durch Clamor Brockmann etwas später erhalten werden, ersuche ich Sie um einzelne Kleinigkeiten, die Sie mir durch denselben Herrn hierher schicken möchten. Denn wir sind durch den Krieg, wenigstens in unserer Haushaltung, so ziemlich verarmt, da uns beinahe alle Schlachtochsen, von denen wir zu leben haben, gepreßt wurden und Bezahlung haben wir niemals erhalten.

Nun fehlt es uns nämlich an Weißzeug. Ich wünschte deshalb, daß Sie mir ein Dutzend leinene Bettücher, Handtücher, Taschentücher, Kragen und Oberärmel, eine große weiße Bettdecke für ein zweischläfriges Bett, 2 Paar gestickte Unterröckchen für meine beiden Mädchen, einige Tischtücher, einige gute halbwollene Kleider oder Leinenzeug für Kleider für meine Frau und Kinder, etwas gutes Hosenzeug für mich und meine beiden Jungen, ein Arbeitstuch für meine Gemahlin, nicht zu klein, schicken.

Auch ein Verbandszeug nebst Zubehör und ein gutes Taschenmesser für mich, einige kleine Tabakspfeifen, womöglich kleine Holz- oder Meerschaumpfeifen. Ferner ein Korsett, groß genug, daß es meiner Mutter paßt, denn meine Frau ist stark geworden und hat dieselbe Größe wie ich. Ihre Bildnisse namentlich und das der Kinder. Unser aller Daguerreotypie sollen Sie erhalten, sowie wir uns etwas wieder erholt haben. Ich habe in dem anderen Briefe alles ausführlich geschrieben.

Ich reise nach der Hauptstadt Austin, um daselbst als guter Bürger der Vereinigten Staaten ein Amt in Empfang zu nehmen. Nämlich über drei verschiedene County den Wert des Vermögens aufzunehmen, wodurch die Kriegssteuer reguliert wird. Erhalten habe ich dasselbe durch meinen alten Freund Braubach. Dieser flüchtete bei Anfang des Krieges und trat in die nördliche Armee ein. Er kehrte als Captain der Vereinigten Staaten Truppen nach Texas zurück und hatte mich empfohlen. Bei dieser Gelegenheit werde ich den Brief in Austin auf die Post geben und ich hoffe, er wird ankommen.

Durch dieses Amt, welches ich mehrere Jahre behalten kann, werde ich mich einigermaßen erholen von den Verlusten. Ich wohne noch am Llano. Mein Viehstock hat sich nicht so rasch vermehrt, als wenn es Frieden geblieben wäre. Weil ich zuviel

Dienst als Soldat an der Grenze tun mußte, so habe ich in dem Jahr 1865 bloß 70 Kälber gebrannt und gemarkt und ich hätte wenigsten 100 bekommen müssen. Trotzdem sind wir zufrieden, daß wir wenigstens unser Leben erhalten habe.

Ich gebe Ihnen diese Adresse an, weil ein Brief falsch adressiert war und bloß durch Zufall in meine Hände kam. Seit dem Jahre 1861 habe ich keine Briefe von Ihnen erhalten.

Ihr Sohn Franz Kettner
F. Kettner
Hedwigshill
Mason County Texas

Was macht Cholera?
Schreiben Sie mir sofort beim Empfang dieses Briefes.

# Letter / Brief 14

### Letter 14 (March 20, 1866) from Franz Kettner at Foley's Crossing to his Parents

Dear Parents,

Since another good opportunity is available to me, I will send you a third letter without waiting for an answer from my earlier letters. Additionally, I have news to share with you that my family has grown with a new little boy. Second, I have a position with the United States due to my loyalty which I think will bring me 300 dollars a year. That is, as assistant assessor with the Internal Revenue.[131] It is my job to list the taxpayers in six different counties so the tax collector can contact them. It will cost me approximately two months' time. I can spare this without hurting my household affairs.

The only expense that I have is to maintain three horses instead of two which I have already purchased. It was very cheap at an auction in San Antonio where 500 head of military horses were auctioned. I was already present because I had driven cattle there. It was the first silver money in five years that I had received in my hand from the sale of oxen.

I bought the most essential items of clothing for me and my family but always at very high prices.

You will receive this letter through a good friend of mine named Wilhelm Cook.[132] He will share with you his address and specify how long he will be in Ger-

---

[131] Stella G. Polk, (Polk, 168) lists "Francis Kettner Assessor and Tax Collector" under "Appointments Under Provisional Government, 1865."

[132] Franz most likely is referring to William Koock. The German population was not sure of the spelling of "Koock" (Terry Jordan, *personal communication*). William Koock kept a diary of his travels in Germany which is still in the possession of the Koock family and is published in "The Southwest Collection, Special Collection Library", Texas Tech University, Lubbock, TX 79409. His trip to Germany correlates with Franz's letter. [Gertrude Earnest "William and Minna Jordan Koock" in *Mason County Historical Book*, 144 (Mason, Texas: Mason Historical Commission 1976).]

William Koock was an early business man in Mason County, establishing a merchandise store, a cotton gin, and a flour mill at Koockville, several miles northwest of the present day city of Mason. After the Civil War, his store and accompanying stock pens served as a staging area for cattle drives

many. In any case, several months, and he is willing to bring me everything if the need arises that you would wish to send me. You will win more time through the help of Mr. W. Cook than when you would send me something through Clamor Brockman. In addition, it is preferable to me. Send me the portraits, when possible, of our entire family. Our children speak a lot about the German grandparents and Louis thinks that grandfather in Germany could indeed send wonderful toys and picture books. Since I am mentioning books, if you still have them, send me Rotteck's General World History with the pictures and further scientific books which I very much lack. Regarding linen items, send me those which you yourselves find useful. Likewise, when cotton material for dresses is too expensive, instead choose a light-weight half-wool or also linen.

Our state is again completely peaceful, only the trade and business still remain flat. However, I think it will again be better in a year. My family is always healthy except for some small illnesses which occur everywhere. When I go to San Antonio again and have some cash, my first activity will be to get myself photographed and send it to you. I think you will not find me looking much older. My friends here claim that I keep myself very well. I have an iron constitution. I had a small attack of gout or rheumatism in the right shoulder but it has considerably improved since it has become warm.

I have already planted my field with grain and sugar beets from which I make molasses or syrup for the children. Otherwise, the main purpose of my land is to grow grain and feed for my horses and melons for the children. Throughout the winter I feed one horse steadily in the stable that I use for riding. The others I let run until spring when the grass is again good. I do not have to ride much in the winter.

If you have yet not sent ahead the items which I have described upon receipt of this letter, take this opportunity. Wilhelm Cook will give you his address and the length of time.

We all greet you many times, my wife and the children and I love you,

Son Franz Kettner

Llano River, 20 March 1866

---

leaving the area. Koock's role in Mason history is underscored by his kindness, generosity, and civil mindedness. The following is quote from J. Marvin Hunter, "A Brief History of the Early Days in Mason County," *Frontier Times*, 6 January 1929, 153-156:

> But there are things other than the building and improvements that proves the remarkable individuality of Wm Koock. He was a most generous man, a friend of children, and a friend of all mankind. White people and Mexicans alike were his loyal friends. He was the kind of man that could have gone among savages and made himself a power and a benefactor.

## Brief 14 (20. März 1866) von Franz Kettner aus Foley's Crossing an seine Eltern

Liebe Eltern,

Da sich mir noch eine gute Gelegenheit darbietet, so sende ich Ihnen den dritten Brief, ohne Antwort auf meine vorhergehenden abzuwarten. Außerdem habe ich Ihnen eine Neuigkeit mitzuteilen, daß sich meine Familie um einen kleinen Jungen erweitert hat. Zweitens, daß ich eine Anstellung bei den Vereinigten Staaten erhalten habe, durch meine Loyalität zu denselben, welche mir 300 Dollars jährlich einbringen wird, denke ich. Nämlich Assistant Assessor über die Internal Revenue. Mein Geschäft ist es, in 6 verschiedenen County, die Steuerpflichtigen aufzunehmen, wonach der Steuereinnehmer sich zu richten hat. Es wird mich ungefähr 2 Monate Zeit kosten. Diese kann ich entbehren, ohne mir in meinen häuslichen Angelegenheiten zu schaden. Die einzige Auslage, welche ich habe, ist, mir statt zwei Pferde, drei zu halten, welches ich mir bereits angeschafft habe. Es war sehr billig, bei einer Versteigerung in San Antonio, woselbst an 500 Stück Militärpferde versteigert wurden. Und ich war gerade anwesend, da ich Ochsen dahin getrieben habe. Seit 5 Jahren war es das erste Silbergeld, welches ich durch den Verkauf von Ochsen in die Finger bekommen habe.

Das Allernötigste an Kleidungsstücken für mich und meine Familie habe ich auch daselbst gekauft, aber noch immer zu sehr hohen Preisen.

Diesen Brief erhalten Sie durch einen guten Bekannten von mir namens Wilhelm Cook.[133] Derselbe wird Ihnen seine Adresse mitteilen, ebenso die Zeit bestimmen, wie lange er sich in Deutschland aufhält. Auf jeden Fall, einige Monate, und ist erbötig alles mir mitzubringen, was Sie mir allenfalls zu schicken wünschten. Sie würden durch die Vermittlung des Herrn W. Cook mehr Zeit gewinnen, als wenn Sie mir etwas durch Clamor Brockmann schicken würden. Außerdem wäre es mir auch lieber. Schicken Sie mir ja die Portraits, womöglich von unserer ganzen Familie. Unsere Kinder sprechen viel von den deutschen Großeltern und Louis meint der Großpapa von Deutschland könnte uns doch auch schön Spielsachen schicken und Bilderbücher. Da ich doch gerade an Büchern bin, schicken Sie mir doch, wenn Sie dieselbe noch haben, Rottecks allgemeine Weltgeschichte mit Bildergalerie und sonstige wissenschaftliche Bücher; an denen es mir sehr mangelt. Was das leinene Weißzeug anbelangt, so schicken Sie mir von dem, was Sie selbst im Gebrauch haben. Ebenso, wenn Baumwollenzeug für Kleider einen hohen Preis haben sollte, so nehmen Sie lieber leichtes Halbwollenes oder auch Leinenes.

Die Ruhe in unserem Staate ist wieder vollständig hergestellt, nur der Verkehr und die Geschäfte gehen noch flau. Aber ich denke in einem Jahre wird es wieder besser gehen. Meine Familie ist immer gesund, ausgenommen manchmal kleine Kinderkrankheiten, die aber überall vorkommen. So wie ich wieder nach San

---

[133] Wilhelm Cook hat über seine Deutschlandreise ein Tagebuch geführt. Dieses ist veröffentlicht in "The Southwest Collection, Special Collection Library," Texas Tech University, Lubbock, Texas 79409.

Antonio komme, und einigermaßen bei Kasse bin, soll es mein Erstes sein, mich fotografieren zu lassen und es Ihnen zu schicken. Ich glaube Sie werden mich nicht viel älter aussehend finden. Meine Freunde hier behaupten, ich konserviere mich sehr gut. Meine Konstitution ist eine eiserne. Bloß diesen Winter hatte ich einen kleinen Anfall von Podagra[134] oder Rheumatismus in der rechten Schulter, was sich aber bedeutend gebessert hat, seit es warm geworden ist.

Mein Feld habe ich bereits bestellt mit Korn und Zuckerrohr, aus welchem ich Melasse oder Sirup für die Kinder bereite. Sonst ist der Hauptzweck von meinem Feld, Korn und Futter für meine Pferde zu ziehen und Melonen für die Kinder. Den Winter hindurch füttere ich ein Pferd beständig in dem Stall, was ich zum Reiten brauche. Die anderen lasse ich laufen bis Frühjahr, bis das Gras wieder gut ist. Im Winter habe ich wenig zu reiten.

Sollten Sie also bei Empfang dieses Briefe die Sachen, um welche ich geschrieben habe, noch nicht fortgeschickt haben, so nehmen Sie diese Gelegenheit in Angriff. Wilhelm Cook wird seinen Aufenthalt und die Länge der Zeit angeben.

Wir alle grüßen Sie vielmals, meine Frau und die Kinder
und ich verbleibe Ihr.
Sohn Franz Kettner
Llanoriver, 20. März 1866

---

[134] Podagra = Gicht.

# Letter / Brief 15

## Letter 15 (Autumn 1866[135]) Letter from Dr. Franz Lambert Kettner in Oberkirch to his Son Franz Kettner in Texas

[The first pages are missing.]

Across from our home stands the most beautiful house in Oberkirch, that of Borsig, the innkeeper of the old Eagle Inn. The inner furnishings are as lovely as the house. The cloister garden is already built upon; the evangelic church as well as 5 other fine buildings stand there. Businessman Stockle is dead. His old maid daughter along with her mother run the poor business. We have 8 beer breweries here, but despite that, no good beer to drink.

Mother waits longingly for the photograph of your whole family and I wait already a long time for a small smoked bear ham.

Military service has been introduced here.[136] Each man who is fit must be a soldier for 3 years, 4 years in reserve and up to 32 years for state defense. Allegedly an improvement, but which costs a lot of money.

Things are more expensive this year. A pound of beef costs 18 kronen, pork 18 kr, veal 15 kr, a pound of butter 25 to 30 kr., 1 eugo?[137] 2 kr., l load of beech wood 18 to 20 gulden, etc. And so in relationship stands everything. Trade and business are not good. Government loans are 8 to 10 guldens under their true value.

For 9 years we have had a wine yield. The vintage from 1865 was a particularly fine one. Yesterday the last of 3 great casks in my cellar was emptied. As a result of

---

[135] The first page of this letter is missing so the date is an approximation. This letter was in the possession of Patsy Kothmann Ziriax, Mason, TX. (Patsy is a great-granddaughter of Franz Kettner).

[136] Most likely the military service was for the Austro-Prussian War, also called the German War. The war was fought between the Austrian and Prussian Empires and German allies on each side. It ended August 23, 1866 with the Treaty of Prague, leaving Prussia as the predominant power. This led to the formation of the North German Confederation a year later. (*The Grosse Knaur, Encyclopedia in 4 Volumes*, s.v. "Deutscher Krieg".) Since the war began and also ended in 1866, one can safely assume Letter 15 was written in this year.

[137] Here the handwriting is very illegible and the term is unclear.

wine speculation, I have lost about 200 gulden and have remaining only wine for my duration of life.

Mother and I have made wills for one another, each inherits from the other. You will inherit your share from the stated order, totally without deduction and without a reduction and if no unfortunate experience intrudes; your share should run from 3 to 5000,[138] which you would receive first after our deaths.

Professor Juelg[139] was here in May. He could have been elected to the city council but did not take part in the election. He plays an important role in Constance and is much admired. The teacher Johannes Woerner[140] has died and left behind a 27 year-old unmarried daughter.

Franz Kissel has wanted to travel to America for two years. I wrote this to my sister in Wisconsin and to his aunt in Washington. The replies were not favorable. His aunt had already invited him to stay with her as long as needed until he had a suitable place. My sister, however, did not invite him if he traveled there. Since this time, I have broken off writing to her.

Nicolai has been elected to the second chamber (lower house) and has received the Order of the Lion from Grand Duke Zaehringer[141] and Saint Michael's Order from Bayern. He is a Saint Michael's wearer as a protestant. These are probably state loyalty awards that must be given back after the death of the recipient, purely honorary.

The businessman Fischer from Rastatt also visited us this summer.[142] The number of his children from his second marriage increase. Koehler has moved his paper business into a factory of the newest design.[143] His daughter, who married Fischer from Ifetsheim[144] and lives in Rastatt, is here sick and will soon die from consumption.

There are many young people from the state of Baden who had emigrated to America where I notice that the death rate is very high. I do not know what else to

---

138 The currency was probably guldens.

139 Dr. Bernhard Juelg, University Professor and Language Researcher, 1825-1886. In the year 1843, Bernhard Juelg went to Mannheim, in order to complete the last two years of the higher education there. See Hans-Martin Pillin, *Oberkirch. Die Geschichte der Stadt in großherzoglich badischer Zeit 1803-1918* (Oberkirch: Die Stadt Oberkirch, 1978), 309. Franz Kettner and Bernhard Juelg probably were classmates in Mannhein.

140 Johannes Woerner was probably an elementary school teacher since an elementary school had been established as early as 1802. Higher education private schools were not started until 1880 in Oberkirch. See Hans-Martin Pillin, 237-238.

141 Zaehringer, German royal line from the 10th century Counts in Bresisgan. The landed estate branch of the Zaehringers founded the state of Baden. Baden was from 1806 a grand dukedom. See *The Grosse Knaur, Encyclopedia in 4 Volumes*, s.v. "Zaehringer."

142 This suggests that this letter was written in the late summer or autumn.

143 Ignaz Koehler finally discontinued the production of paper by hand in September 1865 and founded a paper manufacturing factory. He handed this business over to his son August on October 31, 1868. Ref: Hans-Martin Pillin, 316.

144 "Ifetsheim" was probably the phonetic spelling of "Iffezheim."

write which will interest you so I will stop with many greetings from us to you and your family.

Keep well. Your Father Kettner

**Fig. 34. Three Views of Oberkirch**: Lower Hauptstrasse (Main Street) before 1866 (first picture). The spire in the middle of the picture is the old spire of the Catholic church, which burned down in 1871. Hauptstrasse in 1873 (second picture) with the spire of the new Catholic church. Hotel and Inn "Linde" around 1889 (last picture). Taken from Hans-Martin Pillin, *Oberkirch, Die Geschichte der Stadt in großherzoglich badischer Zeit 1803-1918*, Volume II (Oberkirch: Die Stadt Oberkirch, 1978), pages 142, 165, and 213.

**Abb. 34. Drei Ansichten von Oberkirch.** Blick in die untere Hauptstraße vor 1866 (erstes Bild). Der Turm in der Mitte des Bildes ist der alte Kirchturm der katholichen Kirche, dessen oberer Teil 1871 ausbrannte. Mittleres Bild: Hauptstraße im Jahre 1873 mit dem Turm der neuen katholischen Kirche. Unteres Bild: Hotel und Gasthaus zur "Linde" um 1880. Entnommen aus Hans-Martin Pillin, *Oberkirch, Die Geschichte der Stadt in großherzoglich badischer Zeit 1803-1918*, Band II (Oberkirch: Die Stadt Oberkirch, 1978), Seiten 142, 165 und 213.

## Brief 15 (Herbst 1866[145]) von Dr. Franz Lambert Kettner aus Oberkirch an seinen Sohn Franz Kettner in Texas[146]

[Die ersten Seiten fehlen.]

Gegenüber unserer Wohnung steht das schönste Haus in Oberkirch, des alten Adlerwirt Börsig. Sowie das Haus ebenso ist auch die innere Einrichtung. Der Klostergarten ist bereits überbaut, die evangelische Kirche nebst 5 anderen schönen Gebäuden ruhen darauf. Kaufmann Stöckle ist gestorben, die Tochter als alte Jungfrau mit ihrer Mutter führen das schwache Geschäft. Bierbrauer haben wir hier gegen 8, und doch kein gutes Bier zum Trinken.

Die Mutter wartet sehnlichst auf die Photographie von Deiner ganzen Familie und ich warte schon längst auf einen kleinen geräucherten Bärenschinken.

Die Wehrpflicht wird hier eingeführt,[147] jeder taugliche muß 3 Jahre Soldat, 4 Jahre Resedit[148] und bis zu 32 Jahre Landwehrmann sein. Lauter Verbesserungen, die viel Geld kosten.

Wir haben [es in diesem] Jahr teuer, 1 Pfund Ochsenfleisch 18 kr, Schweinefleisch 18 kr, Kalbfleisch 15 kr, 1 Pfund Butter 25 bis 30 kr, 1 Eugo?[149] 2 kr, 1 Klafter Buchenholz 18 bis 20 Gulden etc. Und so steht alles im Verhältnis. Handel und Wandel nicht gut. Staatsanleihen 8 bis 10 Gulden unter wahrem Wert.

Seit 9 Jahren hat es einen Wein gegeben, 1865 besonders ein vorzüglicher. Gestern ist mein Keller von 3 großen Faß, die letzen, entleert worden. Am Schluss der Weinspekulation habe ich gegen 200 Gulden verloren, habe auch nur noch auf meine Lebensdauer Wein.

Die Mutter und ich haben wechselweise testamentiert, einer erbt das andere. Du erhältst Dein Anteil nach der bestehenden Verordnung ganz ohne Abzug und ohne Verschmälerung und wenn kein unglückliches Ereignis eintritt, so könnte Dein Anteil von 3 bis 5000[150] belaufen, was Du erst nach unserm Ableben erhalten werdest.

Professor Jülg[151] war diesen Mai hier. Derselbe sollte in die Ständekammer gewählt werden. Er hat die Wahl nicht angenommen. Derselbe spielt in Konstanz

---

[145] Wahrscheinlich Spätsommer oder Herbst 1866

[146] Original des Briefes befindet sich im Besitz von Patsy Kothmann Ziriax, Mason, Texas.

[147] Vermutlich steht die Wehrpflicht mit dem Deutschen Krieg, der Auflösung des Deutschen Bundes oder der Gründung des Norddeutschen Bundes im Zusammenhang. Zwischen Preußen und den süddeutschen Staaten wurden nach Gründung des Norddeutschen Bundes enge Militärbündnisse geschlossen. (*Der Große Knaur, Lexikon in 4 Bänden*, unter dem Stichwort "Deutscher Krieg".) Alle Ereignisse spielten im Jahre 1866. Demnach wurde der vorliegende Brief im Jahre 1866 geschrieben.

[148] Dieser Begriff könnte Reservist bedeuten. Der Begriff Resedit könnte aber auch mit der Art der Wehrpflicht zusammenhängen, wie sie in jener Zeit im Großherzogtum Baden Gesetz war.

[149] Hier ist die Handschrift sehr unleserlich und der Begriff ist unklar.

[150] Ohne Währungsangabe, vermutlich Gulden.

[151] Dr. Bernhard Jülg, Universitätsprofessor und Sprachenforscher, 1825-1886. Im Jahre 1843 begab sich Bernhard Jülg nach Mannheim, um dort die letzten beiden Jahre der höheren Schulausbildung zu absolvieren. Vgl. Hans-Martin Pillin, *Oberkirch. Die Geschichte der Stadt in großherzoglich badischer Zeit 1803-1918, Band II*, (Oberkirch: Die Stadt Oberkirch,1978), 309.

eine große Rolle und ist sehr beliebt. Lehrer Johannes Wörner[152] ist gestorben und hat eine 27 Jahre alte ledige Tochter zurückgelassen.

Franz Kissel wollte vor 2 Jahren nach Amerika reisen, ich erkundigte mich bei meiner Schwester in Wiskonsin[153] und bei seiner Tante in Wasington.[154] Die Antworten waren nicht günstig. Die Tante hat denselben eingeladen und so lange bei ihr zu verbleiben, bis er einen geeigneten Platz habe. Meine Schwester aber hat denselben nicht eingeladen, wenn er dahin komme. Seit dieser Zeit habe ich den Briefwechsel abgebrochen.

Nicolai ist in die 2. Kammer gewählt worden und hat den Großh. Zähringer[155] Löwenorden und von Bäuern[156] den heiligen Michaelorden erhalten. Als Protestant ist er heiliger Michaelträger geworden. Dies sind lauter Staatstreuegelder, die nach dem Tode des Trägers zurückgegeben werden müßten, lauter Ehrensachen.

Herr Kaufmann Fischer von Rastatt hat uns diesen Sommer auch besucht.[157] Seine Nachkommenschaft [aus] 2. Ehe mehrt sich. Köhler hat sein Papiergeschäft in eine Fabrik neuester Art verwandelt.[158] Die Tochter, die an den Fischer von Ifetsheim[159] verheiratet und in Rastatt wohnt, ist hier krank, und wird alsbald an der Auszehrung sterben.

Es sind aus dem badischen Lande sehr viel junge Leute nach Amerika gewandert, wo ich wahrnahm, daß die Sterblichkeit sehr sehr groß ist. Ich weiß nun nicht mehr zu schreiben, was Dir willkommen sein kann, weswegen ich schließe nebst vielen Grüßen von uns allen an Dich und Deine Angehörigen.

Lebet alle wohl Dein Vater

Kettner.

---

Dies legt die Vermutung nahe, daß Franz Kettner und Bernhard Jülg sich von einer gemeinsamen höheren Schulausbildung in Mannheim her kannten.

152 In Oberkirch gibt es seit dem Jahre 1802 eine Volksschule. Eine Höhere Privatschule gab es erst ab 1880. Vgl. Hans-Martin Pillin., S.237-238.

153 Wisconsin

154 Washington

155 Zähringer, alemannisches Fürstengeschlecht. Ab dem 10. Jahrhundert Grafen im Breisgau. Der markgräfliche Zweig der Zähringer begründete den bad. Territorialstaat. Baden war ab 1806 Großherzogtum. Vgl. *Der Große Knaur in 4 Bänden*, diverse Stichworte.

156 Bayern?

157 Dies läßt darauf schließen, daß der Brief im Spätsommer oder Herbst geschrieben wurde.

158 Ignaz Köhler hatte die Handpapiermacherei im September 1865 endgültig eingestellt und einen Papierherstellungsbetrieb gegründet. Diesen übergab er am 31. Oktober 1868 seinem Sohn August. Vgl. Hans-Martin Pillin, S. 316. Auch dies läßt auf das Jahr 1866 als Briefdatum schließen.

159 Wahrscheinlich phonetisch geschrieben. Iffezheim

# Letter / Brief 16

**Letter 16 (July 26 1868, August 6, and September 26, 1868) from Francis Kettner at Foley's Crossing to his Parents**

Assistant Assessor's Office
United States Internal Revenue
____ Division, Third District, Texas

My dear parents,

I received your last letter in time and you must not think badly of me that you have not heard from me sooner. I myself have been in many ways overloaded with work. In addition, there has been illness in the family. My wife has suffered for over a year from stomach spasms and all medicine has so far been in vain. Also, if it does stop for 4 to 6 weeks, it comes back again. Dear father, if you should perhaps know of a medicine, please tell me about it. Morphine is the only helpful medication so far that at least calms the cramps for a short while.

The children are now all healthy. Our little Karl is now two years and six months old and Louis, the oldest, is ten years old and makes very fine progress in school, in the German language as well as in English.

The year 1868 was a hard one for me. Because the district for my travel route as United States assessor is as large as two Baden counties, I no longer travel alone. Fort Mason with its cavalry troops lies 6 miles from my farm so I have taken along a 2-man escort with a pack mule for the past two years. This year a so-called throat sickness broke out among the military horses that was very contagious. Because I had no knowledge about the existence of this illness, both of my horses became infected and kicked the bucket. I could only shoulder the loss and quickly bought two other horses. Then these were stolen from me on the night of July 16 by Indians and I was again without horses. Until now I have only bought myself one horse but I am still compelled still to buy another.

In addition, I have to pay 50 gulden school fees for Louis. The boarding fee will cost me almost as much. I have also lost 500 florins for horses in this year, a huge loss for my family. However, I am holding tightly onto the proverb: "A person is happy who is able to forget what cannot be changed."

Both of my horses had pulled my light horse carriage very well and were not more than four and a half years old. We have had a lot of rain the entire summer (an exception) and I harvested a very good corn (grain) crop. We have thousands of melons. Also my flock of sheep has increased. We lambed almost 40 head and I have sold wool this year. That is in addition to my household needs which are considerable for we make wool mattresses and I wear wool stockings in summer and winter. I believe that raising sheep will, in time, drive out raising cattle. We also have some goats. They require no care and come home by themselves every evening. When the herd becomes more than a hundred, though, a person must begin to tend them. I have two sheep, a wether and a ram, that gave 15 pounds of wool in shearing. The average is only 5 pounds per sheep.

The American situation is still not the same as it was before the war; the terrible administration of President Johnson is to blame. Texas is still under military rule and the course of business is still slow. However, the times will be better. The Germans achieved an advantageous showing for themselves during this war. There was an entire division of only Germans in the army, even under German command and our German generals. Among those was our Baden compatriot Franz Siegel who especially stood out since he commanded an army corps of 50,000. I have spoken to old Willich, well-known from the Baden revolution, in San Antonio where he was with a brigade of infantry that he commanded as general.

I do not know anything else new to write you. Next time I will write you a longer letter when I have more time. This one you should take just as a sign of life from me. In the hope that these few lines will reach you still in good health, I give greetings to all my relatives and remain your grateful son.

Franz Kettner

August 6, 1868

Because my letter has not been sent yet and it is a rainy day right now and I have had to put aside making feed, I will grip the pen instead in order to converse with you.

What is the aunt in Mannheim doing? Greet her many times and I request a picture from her. What are Marie and her husband doing and what is the name of the little girl? Give me the address of August Nicolai in your next letter; I will start a correspondence with him. Likewise, greet Emil Schauenburg for me and tell him that if he wishes to write me one time, I would answer him immediately and tell him to my best about many hunting adventures.

Although I am no longer a passionate hunter now, I can truthfully say that I am still a master with the rifle. Next winter several friends from San Antonio will come as agreed to go on a buffalo hunt. The buffalo, which still number in the millions, move southward each winter and come in great herds to Texas some 500 English miles away from me. The hunt on horseback should be a very exciting event. Naturally, it requires a very nimble horse, a good rider, and a pretty good shooter with his revolver in order to have success. By itself, when a person has lived 20 years in Texas and ridden so much on horseback, it seems as if the man was born as a rider. And despite all the daring riding, accidents seldom happen. The horses are much more sure of foot through their free range roaming than horses are in Germany.

I cannot get the two horses that the Indians stole from me out of my mind, not so much because of their worth as because I tamed them myself and have ridden and gotten used to them. We usually drove on Friday evening around 4 from the house, the whole family, in order to pick Louis up from the school. Likewise, we took him back on Sunday evenings.

I immediately bought a 4-year-old horse for 50 dollars, 125 florins in German money, and this week I bought still another for 5 dollars less. In the future, I will keep my horses under lock and key each night in the stable which I built for this purpose and which stands in the middle of the house. I have harvested enough feed and grain in order to reasonably feed my horses.

I wanted to build more this year. My compatriots from Baden had delivered the shingles for me from Fredericksburg, naturally for the usual price. I had ordered these from them in order to get good shingles but had to postpone the building because of the losses I experienced.

I believe that the stomach cramps that my wife suffers from come mainly from colds, perhaps also sometimes from particular foods. We are using at this time a German Doctor Keidel in Fredericksburg. He has already changed medicines many times.

That is enough for today. It is evening and I need to get my horses in the stable; I have become fearful now. My neighbors have already lost all their horses several times in the last 8 years that I have lived here, but I was always lucky.

September 26, 1868

When someone is unlucky, says a proverb, it all comes at once. I have been exceptionally careful about my horses since the last theft and have kept the horses under lock and key after I built a stable. However, my horses were stolen in broad daylight some hundred feet in front of the house between 1 and 2 o'clock by the Indians without being seen by anyone in the house. The Indians left behind a horse that had been ridden until it was lame. This one is still in my possession but it is probably also a stolen horse whose owner, in time, will find it.

The Indians have been unstoppable this year with murder and thievery and it is about time for the government to start a defensive war against them since they are a terrible plague for the country. My wife and children cannot comfort themselves over our losses, but how can lamenting help. Naturally, this has set me back more than an entire year, but a person must not let his courage drop, nevertheless.

The stomach cramps have not bothered my wife for two months; perhaps it will be better. At this time I will buy myself only one horse and feed it all the time in the stable.

However, by springtime I will have to buy myself still another horse because I cannot get by with only one horse.

I was just building on the houses and had been occupied with this for 8 days and did not need the horses. I simply let them graze in daytime close by the house and I believe that it was during lunchtime that these red dogs sneaked up on my horses and stole them.

I will mail this letter now, however, otherwise even more unpleasant happenings could come along with it.

Francis Kettner

**Fig. 35. Countryside Around Foley's Crossing.** This is a westward view of the terrain located between Todd Mountain and Foley's Crossing along FM Road 2389. See Fig. 25, Letter 10. The bluffs in the center of the photograph are on James River.

**Abb. 35. Landschaft um Foley's Crossing.** Dieses ist eine Westansicht der Gegend, die zwischen Todd Mountain und Foley's Crossing entlang der Landstraße 2389 liegt. Siehe Abb. 25, Brief 10. Die Steilufer in der Mitte des Fotos liegen am James River.

## Brief 16 (26. Juli, 6. August und 26. September 1868) von Franz Kettner aus Foley's Crossing an seine Eltern

Assistant Assessor's Office,
United States Internal Revenue,
....Division, Third District, Texas

Meine Lieben Eltern.

Ihren letzten Brief habe ich seiner Zeit erhalten und Sie müßten es mir nicht übel nehmen, nicht früher etwas von mir zu hören. Allein ich bin in mancher Art mit Arbeit überladen. Dazu kommen noch Krankheiten in der Familie. Außerdem leidet meine Frau schon seit einem Jahre an dem Magenkrampf und alles Medizinieren war bis jetzt vergebens. Wenn es auch vier bis sechs Wochen ausbleibt, so kommt es wieder. Sollten Sie lieber Vater vielleicht ein Mittel wissen, so teilen Sie mir solches mit. Morphin war bis jetzt das einzig wirksame, was wenigstens augenblicklich den Krampf stillte.

Die Kinder sind jetzt alle gesund, unser kleiner Karl ist jetzt zwei Jahre 6 Monate alt und der Louis der Älteste 10 Jahre alt und macht sehr schöne Fortschritte in der Schule, sowohl in der deutschen wie in der englischen Sprache.

Das Jahr 1868 ist für mich ein hartes Jahr geworden. Da ich meine Reisetour als Vereinigter Staaten Assessor in meinem Distrikt, welcher so groß ist, wie zwei badische Kreise, nicht mehr allein reise, und 6 Englische Meilen von meiner Farm Fort Mason mit Kavallerie Besatzung liegt; so hatte ich die letzten zwei Jahre zwei Mann Eskorte mit einem Packesel mitgenommen. Dieses Jahr war nun unter den Militärpferden eine sogenannte Halskrankheit ausgebrochen, welche sehr ansteckend war. Und da ich keine Ahnung von der Existenz der Krankheit hatte, so wurden meine beiden Pferde angesteckt und krepierten. Dieser Schaden war nun noch zu ertragen, denn ich kaufte mir rasch zwei andere. Allein diese wurden mir den 16. Juli des Nachts von Indianern gestohlen, und nun war ich abermals ohne Pferde. Bis jetzt habe ich mir erst ein Pferd gekauft, bin aber gezwungen, noch eines zu kaufen.

Außerdem muß ich für Louis 50 Gulden Schulgeld bezahlen. Das Kostgeld wird mich beinahe ebenso hoch kommen. Ich habe also in diesem Jahre für 500 fl Pferde verloren; ein großer Ausfall in meiner Familie. Jedoch ich halte an dem Sprichwort fest: Glücklich ist, wer das vergißt, was einmal nicht zu ändern ist.

Meine beiden Pferde gingen sehr schön in meinem leichten Pferdewagen und waren nicht älter als 4 ½ Jahre. Wir haben dieses Jahr den ganzen Sommer (ausnahmsweise) sehr viel Regen und ich mache eine sehr gute Kornernte. Melonen haben wir zu Tausenden. Meine Schafe vermehren sich auch. Die Zucht beläuft sich bald auf 40 Stück, und ich habe dieses Jahr Wolle verkauft. Außerdem meinen Hausbedarf, welcher nicht unbedeutend ist, da wir Wollmatratzen machen und ich im Sommer und Winter wollene Strümpfe trage. Ich glaube, die Schafzucht wird seinerzeit die Viehzucht verdrängen. Einige Ziegen haben wir auch darunter. Sie machen gar keine Last und kommen jeden Abend von selbst nach Hause. Wenn die

Herde größer wird über hundert Stück, dann muß man allerdings anfangen, dieselben hüten zu lassen. Ich habe von zwei Schafen, einem Hammel und einem Bock 15 Pfund Wolle geschoren, im Durchschnitt aber bloß 5 Pfund per Schaf.

Unsere amerikanischen Zustände sind immer noch nicht ganz so, wie vor dem Kriege, woran die schlechte Administration des Präsidenten Johnson schuld ist. Texas ist noch immer unter Militärherrschaft, und der Geschäftsgang ist noch lau. Jedoch die Zeiten werden besser werden. Die Deutschen haben sich durch diesen Krieg eine vorteilhafte Stellung erschwungen.[160] Da in der Armee ganze Divisionen rein deutsche, sogar unter deutschem Kommando und unseren deutschen Generälen sind. Worunter unser Landsmann Franz Siegel sich besonders auszeichnete, welcher ein Armeecorps von 50.000 kommandierte. Den alten Willich, aus der badischen Revolution bekannt, habe ich in San Antonio gesprochen, wo er mit einer Brigade Infanterie lag, welche er als General befehligte.

Neues weiß ich Ihnen weiter nicht zu schreiben. Ich werde Ihnen das nächste mal einen längeren Brief schreiben, wenn ich besser Zeit haben werde. Dies sollten Sie bloß als ein Lebenszeichen von mir erfahren. In der Hoffnung, daß diese paar Zeilen Sie noch gesund antreffen, grüße ich alle meine Verwandten und bleibe Ihr dankbarer Sohn

Franz Kettner

6. August 1868

Da mein Brief noch nicht fort ist, es gerade ein Regentag ist und ich mit meinem Futtermachen aussetzen muß, so ergreife ich abermals die Feder, um mich mit Ihnen zu unterhalten.

Was macht die Tante in Mannheim, grüßen Sie dieselbe vielmals und ich ließe sie um Ihr Bild ersuchen. Was macht Marie und ihr Mann und wie heißt das kleine Mädchen? Ihrem nächsten Briefe geben Sie mir die Adresse an von August Nicolai, ich werde mich in Korrespondenz mit ihm setzen. Ebenfalls grüßen Sie mir Emil Schauenburg, und sagen Sie ihm, er möchte mir einmal schreiben, ich würde ihm sofort antworten und manches Jagdabenteuer zum besten geben.

Obgleich ich jetzt kein passionierter Jäger mehr bin, so kann ich wohl sagen, ich bin noch immer ein Meister mit der Büchse. Nächsten Winter werden einige Bekannte von San Antonio erscheinen, um verabredungsgemäß auf die Büffeljagd zu gehen. Die Büffel, davon es noch Millionen gibt, ziehen jeden Winter südwärts und kommen in großen Herden nach Texas etwa fünfhundert englische Meilen entfernt von mir. Und die Jagd zu Pferde soll sehr aufregender Natur sein. Natürlich es gehört ein flinkes Pferd, ein guter Reiter, und ein ziemlich guter Schütze mit dem Revolver dazu, um Erfolg zu haben. Allein, wenn man zwanzig Jahre in Texas gelebt hat und so viel zu Pferde zubringt, so kommt es einem vor, als wäre man zu Pferde geboren. Und trotz des tollen Reitens kommen äußerst selten Unglücksfälle vor. Die

[160] geschaffen

Pferde sind durch das freie Herumlaufen viel sicherer auf den Füßen als in Deutschland.

Die beiden Pferde, die mir die Indianer gestohlen haben, können mir nicht aus dem Gedächtnis kommen, weniger wegen des Wertes, als weil ich sie selbst gezähmt und eingeritten und zuletzt eingefahren hatte. Wir fuhren gewöhnlich am Freitag abends um 4 von Hause weg, die ganze Familie, und holten Louis von der Schule ab. Ebenso brachten wir ihn sonntags abends zurück.

Ich habe ein 4 Jahre altes Pferd für 50 Dollars, in deutschem Geld fl 125, gleich wieder gekauft, und diese Woche habe ich noch ein anderes gekauft, 5 Dollars billiger. Ich werde in der folgenden Zeit meine Pferde jede Nacht unter Schloß und Riegel stellen in den Stall, welchen ich zu diesem Zwecke gebaut habe und der sich mitten im Hause befindet. Ich habe Futter und Korn genug geerntet, um meine Pferde vernünftig füttern zu können.

Ich wollte dieses Jahr noch bauen. Und meine Landsleute von Haßlach[161] hatten mir die Schindeln nach Friedrichsburg geliefert natürlicherweise für den gewöhnlichen Preis. Ich hatte dieselben deshalb bei Jenen bestellt, um gute Schindeln zu bekommen, werde aber das Bauen aufschieben müssen wegen der erhaltenen Verluste.

Der Magenkrampf, von dem meine Frau gequält wird, glaube ich wenigstens, kommt meistens von Erkältungen, vielleicht auch manchmal von gewissen Speisen her. Wir haben bis zu dieser Zeit einen deutschen Doktor Keidel in Friedrichsburg gebraucht. Derselbe hat auch jetzt schon mehrmals die Medizin gewechselt.

Doch genug für heute, es ist Abend und ich muß meine Pferde in den Stall holen, ich bin jetzt ängstlich geworden. Meine Nachbarn haben schon alle mehrmals Ihre Pferde verloren seit den 8 Jahren, die ich hier wohne, und ich war immer glücklich.

26. September 1868

Wenn jemand Unglück hat, sagt ein Sprichwort, so kommt alles auf einmal. Ich bin seit dem letzten Stehlen meiner Pferde äußerst vorsichtig geworden und habe die Pferde jede Nacht unter Schloß und Riegel gebracht, nachdem ich mir einen Stall gebaut habe. Dennoch wurden mir die Pferde abermals, und das am hellen Tage einige hundert Schritte vor dem Hause zwischen 1 und 2 Uhr von den Indianern gestohlen, ohne daß es jemand vom Hause aus gesehen hätte. Die Indianer ließen ein Pferd stehen, was lahm geritten war. Dasselbe ist bis jetzt noch in meinem Besitz, wird aber wohl auch ein gestohlenes sein, wozu sich der Eigentümer mit der Zeit finden wird.

Die Indianer sind dieses Jahr unausstehlich mit Stehlen und Morden und es wäre anfangs Zeit, daß die Regierung einen Vertilgungskrieg gegen dieselben anfing, denn dieselben sind eine schreckliche Plage für das Land. Meine Frau und Kinder können

---

[161] Gemeint ist Haslach, eine Gemeinde, die im Jahre 1803 in den badischen Staatsverband überging und später Gemeinde des neugeschaffenen großherzoglich-badischen Amtsbezirks Oberkirch wurde. Vgl. Hans-Martin Pillin, S. 335.

sich gar nicht trösten über diesen unseren Verlust, aber was kann das Lamento helfen. Es hat mich natürlicherweise mehr wie ein ganzes Jahr zurückgebracht, allein man muß deshalb den Mut nicht sinken lassen.

Der Magenkrampf bei meiner Frau ist seit zwei Monaten ausgeblieben, vielleicht wird es besser. Ich werde mir im Augenblick bloß 1 Pferd kaufen und dasselbe beständig im Stall füttern. Bis zum Frühjahr aber muß ich mir doch noch eines kaufen, da ich mit einem Pferde nicht fertig werden kann.

Ich war gerade am Häuser aufschlagen und war schon acht Tage damit beschäftigt, brauchte die Pferde nicht, und ließ dieselben bloß im Hellen dicht beim Hause Gras fressen, und gerade, ich glaube, es war während des Mittagessens, daß diese roten Hunde sich heranschlichen und meine Pferde stehlen.

Jetzt will ich aber diesen Brief der Post übergeben, sonst könnte noch mehr Unangenehmes dazu kommen.

Francis Kettner

# Letter / Brief 17

### Letter 17 (August 12, 1869) from Marie Erdrich in Oberkirch to her Uncle Franz Kettner at Foley's Crossing[162]

Oberkirch, August 12, 1869

Dear Uncle,

You will certainly be surprised to receive a letter from me and will surely fear that that a sad change has happened in your father's home. I cannot take this belief from you and must unfortunately inform you that our dear grandmother passed away quietly on August 9th after long and hard suffering.

Grandfather has surely informed you before that she especially suffered during the last year and she was hardly able to walk to me nearby. It was remarkable that she felt much better from her severe illness about 14 days earlier and we had the hope that she would recover her health.

Her chest was healthy, but her heart was the site of her illness. Either she had an enlarged heart or arteriosclerosis of the main arteries around the heart.

She was bedridden for 9 weeks and was severely endemic the last 4 weeks. We engaged a compassionate nurse to care for her because she could not take care of herself in any way. Her death was easy. Now she rests in the grave of my mother.

It is very difficult for all of us but especially for Grandfather who needs all his strength to bear this misfortune. He continues to live in his normal fashion. Our little Ida, a lively and vivacious child of 2 ½ years is now his constant companion.

My family has also again increased with a little son who was born on Whitsuntide and who was baptized with the name Franz[163] to honor his godfathers, his great-uncle and uncle. At that time our Grandmother was doing well. She was able to visit me every day for the first 8 days which she could not do before.

---

[162] Patsy Kothmann Ziriax, Mason , TX, provided this letter.

[163] Franz Erdrich, born May 16, 1869, died January 23, 1870 in Oberkirch.

You already know that my brother Franz was married in Switzerland. He has a very sweet little girl named Maria and now hopes for a son and heir. This month his associate will marry the sister of his wife.

Klara has returned home from the school and has also already become an adult.

It would give me much pleasure to receive your photograph sometime as well as that of your wife and children because, quite frankly, I can no longer picture how you look.

Grandfather is quite well and still takes care of his practice which is not as large as before. This is not displeasing to us because otherwise it would be too exhausting for him.

There is still no real unity in Oberkirch. Now there are the reds and the blacks. Who was red before is now black, especially our neighbor, Marks Becker, who has influence on businesses and the citizens of Oberkirch always take the side that has the most interest. Grandfather belongs to the reds; we stay neutral.

The little town of Oberkirch has become much finer. There are many new houses and also much luxury is displayed.

Grandfather's sister in Mannheim is also still quite well, but I doubt that she will come here again.

Please write us immediately after receiving my letter. The next time Grandfather will again write, but it would have affected him too much to write you about this death.

I am truly worried about this winter. The evenings will be very long for him because he does not have any of the so-called bad habits, for example, games, etc., which now, if he had the interest, would take his mind off things. When he reads in the evenings, his good friend sleep is there and closes his eyes and when he goes to bed early he is not able to sleep through the night which afterward is more unpleasant. I try my best to amuse him. If I were still at home, it would be much easier for him.

I hope you are all healthy and well.

I am writing you in a hurry because my little son, whom I care for by myself, seldom allows me peace.

Sending my best regards to you, your wife and children, also from Grandfather and my husband, I remain

Your devoted niece,

Maria Erdrich

Grandfather sent his last letter on July 12th.

**Fig. 36. Franz's Niece, Maria Kissel Erdrich** (born June 28, 1844 and died October 2, 1879 in Oberkirch). She is the daughter of Ida Leopoldine Kissel (Franz's sister) and Karl Friedrich Kissel.

**Abb. 36. Maria Erdrich, geb. Kissel, die Nichte von Franz** (geb. 28. Juni 1844 und gest. 2. Oktober 1879 in Oberkirch). Sie ist die Tochter von Ida Leopoldine Kissel (Schwester von Franz) und Karl Friedrich Kissel.

**Fig. 37. Leopold Erdrich** (born May 4, 1838, died February 2, 1877, in Oberkirch). He and Maria are the great-grandparents of the author, Ilse Wurster. Photographs are in the possession of Ilse Wurster.

**Abb. 37. Leopold Erdrich** (geb. 4. Mai 1838, gest. 2. Februar 1877 in Oberkirch). Er und Maria sind die Urgroßeltern der Autorin Ilse Wurster. Die Fotos befinden sich im Besitz von Ilse Wurster.

**Brief 17 (12. August 1869) von Marie Erdrich aus Oberkirch an ihren Onkel Franz Kettner in Foley's Crossing[164]**

Oberkirch, den 12. August 1869

Lieber Onkel!

Du bist gewiß sehr erstaunt, ein Schreiben von mir zu erhalten und befürchtest gewiß, es möchte eine traurige Änderung im väterlichen Hause eingetreten sein. Ich kann Dir diesen Glauben nicht nehmen und muß Dir leider berichten, daß unsere liebe Großmutter am 9. August nach langem schwerem Leiden sanft entschlafen ist.

Großvater wird Dir früher schon mitgeteilt haben, daß sie die letzen Jahre besonders sehr leidend war, und beinahe nicht mehr zu mir herüber zu laufen im Stande war. Auffallend war es, daß ungefähr 14 Tage vor ihrem schweren Leiden es viel besser ging und wir Hoffnung hatten auf Wiederherstellung ihrer Gesundheit.

Ihre Brust war ganz gesund, aber das Herz war der Sitz des Übels. Entweder hat sie ein Fettherz gehabt oder eine Verknöcherung in den großen Adern ums Herz herum.

9 Wochen war sie gelegen und die letzten 4 Wochen ist sie arg wassersüchtig geworden. Wir haben zur Pflege eine barmherzige Schwester gehabt, denn sie konnte sich nicht mehr die leichteste Hilfe geben. Ihr Tod war leicht. Sie ruht jetzt aus im Grabe meiner Mutter.

Für uns alle ist es sehr hart, aber besonders für den Großvater, welcher aller Energie bedarf, um dieses Unglück zu ertragen. Seine Lebensweise führt er in gewohnter Weise fort. Unsere kleine Ida, ein wildes, lebhaftes Kind von 2 ½ Jahren, ist nun seine beständige Gesellschafterin.

Meine Familie hat sich auch wieder um ein Söhnchen vermehrt. Am Pfingsten kam es auf die Welt und erhielt in der heiligen Taufe zu Ehren seiner Taufpaten Großonkel und Onkel den Namen Franz.[165] In jener Zeit ging es unserer Großmutter recht ordentlich. Sie konnte in den ersten 8 Tagen mich jeden Tag besuchen, was ihr zuvor nicht möglich gewesen wäre.

Daß mein Bruder Franz in der Schweiz verheiratet ist, wirst Du bereits wissen. Er hat ein sehr nettes Mädele mit namens Marie und hofft nun auf einen Stammhalter. Sein Associe heiratet diesen Monat noch die Schwester seiner Frau.

Klara ist nun aus einem Institut nach Hause zurückgekehrt und ist nun auch schon erwachsen.

Ich hatte mich schon längst gefreut, einmal Deine Photographie zu erhalten, sowie auch die Deiner Frau und Kinder, denn offen gestanden kann ich mir Dich gar nicht mehr vorstellen.

Großvater befindet sich ganz wohl, besorgt auch noch seine Praxis, welche jedoch nicht mehr so stark ist, was uns nicht unangenehm ist, denn sonst würde es ihn zu sehr anstrengen.

---

[164] Original des Briefes befindet sich im Besitz von Patsy Kothmann Ziriax, Mason, Texas.

[165] Franz Erdrich, geb. 16.05.1869, gest. 23.01.1870 in Oberkirch

In Oberkirch ist immer noch keine rechte Einigkeit. Jetzt gibt es rote und schwarze. Was früher rot war ist nun schwarz, besonders unser Nachbar Marks Becker, da er auf die Geschäfte Einfluß hat und die Bürger Oberkirchs sich immer auf die Seite neigen, wo am mehrsten Interesse ist. Großvater gehört zu den roten, wir bleiben neutral.

Das Städtchen Oberkirch hat sich recht verschönert, es sind viele neue Häuser entstanden, und auch viel Luxus wird getrieben.

Die Schwester von Großvater in Mannheim befindet sich auch noch recht wohl. Ich glaube schwerlich, daß sie wieder einmal hierher kommt.

Schreibe uns recht bald nach Erhalt meines Briefes. Das nächste Mal wird der Großvater wieder schreiben. Da es ihn doch wieder sehr angegriffen hätte, Dir über diesen Todesfall zu schreiben.

Ich habe wirklich bang für diesen Winter. Da werden ihm die Abende recht lang werden, denn er hat auch keine von den sogenannten bösen Gewohnheiten an sich. Zum Beispiel spielen, etc., was jetzt, wenn er Sinn dafür hätte, ihn vielfach zerstreuen würde. Will er abends lesen, so ist sein guter Freund Schlaf da und drückt ihm die Augen zu, und geht er früh zu Bett, so kann er die Nacht nicht durchschlafen, was nachher noch unangenehmer ist. Ich gebe mir alle Mühe, ihn zu zerstreuen, allein wenn ich noch zu Hause wäre, so würde es für ihn nur leichter sein.

Bei Dir ist doch auch alles gesund und wohl.

Ich habe sehr in Eile geschrieben, denn mein kleiner Bub, welchen ich allein besorgen muß, läßt mir selten Ruhe.

Indem ich nun Dich, Deine liebe Frau und Kinder herzlich grüße, sowie auch Großvater und mein Mann Euch freundliche Grüße senden, verbleibe ich

Deine
ergebene
Nichte
Maria Erdrich.

Der letzte Brief von Großvater ist am 12. Juli abgesendet worden.

# Letter / Brief 18

## Letter 18 (November 1869) from Franz Kettner at Foley's Crossing to his Father

Dear Father,

Please forgive my despondency, caused by the unexpected event of Marie's announcement about the death of our good mother, that I only now can let you hear something from me. I had received your letter in which you had feared something of this nature, but at the end of your letter it seemed as though you had hope and that a change for the better was occurring. I took it for certain that mother would again become healthy so that the news came to me unexpectedly.

Indeed, I was traveling on one Sunday with my whole family to the small town of Mason, which is two hours away from me, in order to have us photographed. My sister-in-law who had moved there shortly before informed us that a photographer was there. Since Mason is also where I get my mail, I picked up the sad news at the same time and afterward no longer considered the portrait session. Instead, without staying, we drove back to our home again.

Your last letter, in which you were so inconsolable before the event had occurred, hurt me deeply. You must not allow your courage as a man to sink. Every person experiences this loss and it is granted to so few to be able to remain together for fifty years. How many must leave their families without having their goal fulfilled of having their children grown up. Therefore, take new heart and consider yourself one who is fortunate in destiny and enjoy in peace the days which are still left to you. Man's life has such a short duration that one should not live in bitterness and not fight against such a occurrence.

On my part, I would be content when my life span lasted long enough that my children, whom I dearly hold onto, are grown and independent enough that they are able to take care of themselves. That should not be too hard for them in a country like the United States.

Above all, it would be beneficial for you when your home remains running the same as before. I think it would be good when you could convince your sister to give up her home in Mannheim and the two of you live together if it is possible (comfortable) for you to live with her. I believe it would work out if you allowed her to run the household without interference. It would also be thrifty. You would at the same time have the (household) matters taken care of that you had not worried about earlier and that now would be difficult for you. Write me your thoughts about this plan.

Concerning my family we are all healthy except for my wife's digestive problems which now occur at most every one or two months. My oldest son Louis already shoots the shotgun and rides very well. He is also large for his age. He now goes to Mason to stay with my brother-in-law Hunter and attend a completely English school.[166] He is a youngster with great competence and willpower. In his eleven years, he is as developed in every way as a 14-year-old would be in Germany. Children in a southern climate become mature much sooner.

My two girls are exactly like twins, healthy and thriving and my darlings. The two younger boys are strong figures for their age.

Although I am 43 years old, I have not changed much and always pass for a 30-year-old. Next time I will send you the pictures of my entire family and I will make a trip for this purpose.

I still have my job, but the question is how long I can hold onto it because changes are coming from above. The person who has the most important influence at the top will get the job. I believe, however, that I can hold onto it for another two years.

I made my last trip in the summer with a guard of twelve black cavalrymen because the Indians, who have almost all been driven out of Kansas toward Texas, made the region very unsafe. It has now become somewhat quieter. There is probably nothing left for the United States to do except to start an extermination war against the red scoundrels because they stand in the way of the progress of civilization and will not become civilized themselves. Our border areas suffer not only the loss of horses which the Indians steal, but also the murder of the white people who fall into their hands.

My harvest has turned out well this year. I have cooked up an entire barrel of syrup and raised so much feed and grain that my horses can be fed the entire year in their stalls. Also, I have grown good sweet potatoes. If I should lose my job, I will concentrate especially on raising hogs because one can make a good profit because a good mast (wild feed) grows every two or three years.[167] The hogs become as fat as if they were (farm) fed. Last winter I slaughtered 14 large hogs without spending much attention on them. Although I sold the best rear hams and shoulder hams and produced an uncountable amount of bratwurst and kept enough bacon to last the entire year, I still earned 50 dollars from bacon. I now have about 100 swine, large and small. Until now it was Louis' chore every time to feed them some corn when-

---

166 Franz's brother-in-law was Major James M. Hunter. From 1869-1883, he was the proprietor of the Southern Hotel (Fig. 39). [Mrs. Bill Lemburg, "Major James M. Hunter" in *Mason County Historical Book*, 111 (Mason: Mason County Historical Commission, 1976).] This is probably the location where Louis boarded while attending school.

167 Franz is referring to the acorn crop from live oak trees which are abundant in this area of Texas.

ever they came home as a herd. That is sufficient to keep them tame. When a sow comes home with piglets, they are enclosed and fed for a while in order to make the piglets tame and to castrate them. That is the only work that is necessary.

I have begun to expand my field and to fence it with a stone wall.[168] We have the assured news that a second railroad will be built to California that will run 500 miles through the western part of Texas. This will improve Texas immediately. We can get our beef cattle to market in San Francisco in a short time. Now it takes a year to drive them there.

If you have not given up the idea to leave me an inheritance, I would like it to be arranged as you choose.

I will mention again to you, not to allow your head to hang down. I remain your son Franz Kettner.

Say hello to Marie for me and tell her to write again soon.

**Fig. 38. Town of Mason 1876.** This photograph is reproduced from a picture postcard in possession of The Mason Historical Commission and was provided by Jane Hoerster.

**Abb. 38. Die Stadt Mason 1876.** Dieses Foto wurde reproduziert von einer Bildpostkarte im Besitz der Mason Historical Commission und wurde von Jane Hoerster zur Verfügung gestellt.

[168] The field that Franz mentions here is still in cultivation today and remnants of the stone fence surrounding it are still visible.

## Brief 18 (November 1869[169]) von Franz Kettner aus Foley's Crossing an seinen Vater

Lieber Vater!

Entschuldigen Sie meine Niedergeschlagenheit, in die mich das unerwartete Ereignis setzte, nämlich Maries Anzeige über den Verlust unserer guten Mutter, daß ich jetzt erst etwas von mir hören lasse. Ich hatte Ihren Brief erhalten, worin Sie etwas derartiges befürchteten. Aber am Ende Ihres Briefes schien es, als ob Sie Hoffnung hätten und daß eine Krisis[170] zum Besseren eingetreten wäre. Ich nahm für sicher an, daß die Mutter wieder gesund wäre, um so unerwarteter kam mir die Nachricht.

Ich war nämlich an einem Sonntag nach der kleinen Stadt Mason, zwei Stunden von mir entfernt, mit meiner ganzen Familie gefahren, um uns fotografieren zu lassen. Meine Schwägerin, welche jetzt da kürzlich hingezogen ist, ließ uns sagen, daß ein Fotograf da wäre. Da Mason auch meine Post ist, so erhielt ich gleich die traurige Nachricht und an das Abnehmen lassen wurde gar nicht mehr gedacht. Sondern ohne Aufenthalt wieder nach Hause gefahren.

Ihr letzter Brief, worin Sie, ehe das Ereignis eingetreten war, so trostlos waren, hat mich tief geschmerzt. Sie müssen aber den Mut als Mann nicht sinken lassen. Jeder Mensch geht diesem Los entgegen und wie wenigen ist es vergönnt über fünfzig Jahre beisammen bleiben zu können. Wie viele müssen Ihre Familien verlassen, ohne Ihre Bestimmung erfüllt zu haben, nämlich Ihre Kinder großgezogen zu haben. Deshalb fassen Sie frischen Mut und bedenken Sie, ohnehin ein vom Schicksal begünstigter zu sein, und verleben Sie Ihre Tage, die Ihnen noch bestimmt sind, in Frieden. Das menschliche Leben hat überhaupt so kurze Dauer, deshalb soll der Mensch sich nicht diese noch verbittern; gegen solche Geschicke läßt sich nicht ankämpfen.

Ich für meinen Teil bin zufrieden, wenn meine Lebenszeit so lange dauert, bis ich meine Kinder, an welchen ich leidenschaftlich hänge, selbständig und erwachsen weiß, so daß dieselben sich selbst forthelfen können. Das kann Ihnen in einem Lande wie den Vereinigten Staaten nie schwer fallen.

Vor allen Dingen wäre es Ihnen zuträglich, wenn Ihr Hausstand noch wie vor geregelt bliebe. Ich hielt es für gut, wenn Sie die Tante, Ihre Schwester, überreden könnten, daß dieselbe ihre Wirtschaft in Mannheim aufgibt, und Sie zusammen lebten; wenn nämlich die Möglichkeit da wäre, mit ihr leben zu können. Ich sollte es glauben; wenn Sie derselben die Hauswirtschaft unbeschränkt überließen. Äußerst sparsam ist dieselbe. So wären Sie zugleich der Angelegenheiten überhoben, um die Sie sich früher nicht bekümmert haben, und was Ihnen jetzt schwer fallen würde. Schreiben Sie mir Ihre Gedanken über diesen Plan.

Was meine Familie anbelangt, so sind wir alle gesund, bis auf das Magenleiden meiner Frau, welches aber höchstens alle 1 bis 2 Monate jetzt sich einmal einstellt.

---

169 Datum nach Vermutung der Autorin.

170 Wendung

Mein ältester Sohn Louis führt schon die Doppelflinte und reitet ganz gut. Er ist auch groß für sein Alter. Derselbe kommt jetzt nach Mason zu meinem Schwager Hunter und wird eine rein Englische Schule besuchen. Er ist ein Junge von großer Fähigkeit und Willenskraft. Er ist mit seinem elften Jahre in jeder Hinsicht so weit vorangeschritten, als in Deutschland ein Junge von 14 Jahren. Die Kinder werden im südlichen Klima viel rascher reif.

Meine beiden Mädchen sind gerade wie Zwillinge, gesund und blühend und meine Lieblinge. Die beiden kleinen Jungen, sind kräftige Gestalten für ihr Alter.

Ich habe mich, obgleich 43 Jahre alt, sehr wenig verändert, und passiere immer als Dreißiger. Ich werde Ihnen jetzt nächstens die Bilder meiner ganzen Familie schicken, und wenn ich dieserhalb eine Reise unternehmen sollte.

Das Amt habe ich bis jetzt noch immer, ob ich es aber noch lange halten kann, ist die Frage, da von oben herab Veränderungen vorgenommen sind. Derjenige, der oben die gewichtigsten Empfehlungen hat, wird dann angestellt. Ich glaube aber, daß ich es vielleicht noch zwei Jahre halten kann.

Meine letzte Reise im Sommer machte ich unter einer Bedeckung von 12 Mann schwarzer Kavallerie, da die Indianer, welche von Kansas aus beinahe alle nach Texas getrieben wurden, die Gegend sehr unsicher machen. Jetzt ist es etwas ruhiger geworden. Allein es wird wahrscheinlich den Vereinigten Staaten nichts übrigbleiben, als einen Vernichtungskrieg gegen die roten Canaillen zu beginnen, da sie dem Vorschreiten der Zivilisation im Wege stehen und sich nicht zivilisieren lassen. Unsere Grenze leidet zu sehr, nicht allein der Verlust von Pferden, denn dieselben stehlen, auch das Morden der Weißen, welche in ihre Hände fallen.

Meine Ernte ist dieses Jahr gut ausgefallen. Ich habe ein ganzes Faß Sirup gekocht, so viel Futter und Korn gezogen, um meine Pferde das ganze Jahr im Stalle zu füttern, auch gute süße Kartoffeln gezogen. Sollte ich einmal mein Amt verlieren, werde ich auf Schweinezucht besondere Aufmerksamkeit verwenden, indem eine große Einnahme daraus erzielt werden kann, wenn es alle zwei bis drei Jahre eine gute Mast wachsen sollte. Die Schweine werden so fett, als wenn sie gemästet würden. Ich habe letzten Winter 14 große Schweine geschlachtet, ohne große Aufmerksamkeit darauf zu verwenden. Und ich habe, obgleich ich feinen Hinterschinken und Vorderschinken verkaufte und unzählige Quantität Bratwürste fabrizierte auch hinreichend Speck für das ganze Jahr zurückbehielt, 50 Dollars für Speck eingenommen. Ich habe jetzt große und kleine, ungefähr 100 Stück. Es war bis daher Louis seine Aufgabe, so wie dieselben truppweise nach Hause kamen, diese jedesmal mit etwas Körnern zu füttern. Dies ist hinreichend, um dieselben zahm zu erhalten. Kommt eine Sau nach Hause mit jungen Ferkeln, so wird dieselbe eine Zeitlang eingesperrt und gefüttert, um die jungen zahm zu machen und zu schneiden. Dies ist die ganze Last, die dabei ist.

Ich habe angefangen, mein Feld zu vergrößern und mit einer Steinmauer zu umgeben; Wir haben die Gewißheit, daß eine zweite Eisenbahn nach Kalifornien gebaut wird und dieselbe kommt 500 Meilen durch Texas durch den westlichen Teil. Dies würde Texas auf einmal heben. Unsere Schlachtochsen könnten wir in kurzer

Zeit nach San Francisco zu Markte bringen, wo es jetzt ein Jahr dauert, sie dahin zu treiben.

Sollten Sie die Idee nicht aufgegeben haben, für mich einen Bevollmächtigten zu ernennen, so wünsche ich, daß derselbe nach Ihren Anordnungen handelt.

Indem ich Sie nochmals ermahne, den Kopf nicht allzu sehr hängen zu lassen, verbleibe.

Ihr Sohn Franz Kettner

Grüßen Sie mir die Marie und dieselbe soll bald wieder schreiben.

# Letter / Brief 19

## Letter 19 (January 10, 1870) from Francis Kettner at Foley's Crossing to his Father

Dear Father,

I have received your letter and I hope that you will have received my letter (the answer to Marie's important news). It pains me to no end that you are still so devastated over the terrible loss. I hope, however, that this will become eased over time.

We are all healthy and my Louis now finds himself in a completely English school where not a single German word is spoken. I hope that in a short time with his aptitude that he will speak the language perfectly. For Christmas this year, as with all the past ones, we celebrated with a Christmas tree following traditional German customs. My wife received a new women's saddle, Louis a shotgun, the other children toys, and I was remembered with a box of cigars.

My brother-in-law Hunter[171] who lives in Mason, six miles from my farm, has taken Louis in as a boarder and we drive there about every 14 days. He is an American.

You will find some lines enclosed for the Aunt if you would send it to her address. It would be very desirable, less for me than for my children, if you could convince her in a kind way, to simply name me or my children to the capital inheritance according to the laws because no inheritance treaty exists between Texas and Baden. Indeed, I have no idea what the Aunt actually has or what her intentions are for her estate. I would think you might have an idea about this, whether my children have something of a possibility and whether it is of any use to draw this to the Aunt's attention.

Regarding our share of our blessed mother's clothing, ship it in a chest with a list and explanation that these are used items and address it to Louis Delius and Cie, Bremen. Additionally, put the address of Friederich Groos and Cie, San Antonio, Texas and send it through the services of the usual agent with the contract that it be

[171] See Letters 12 and 18.

sent by steamship via New Orleans. It makes me truly sad that, among all the items, there is nothing that I can use as a remembrance. Do not forget to provide the Bremen firm with a list of contents and that they are used items. I believe that they will then be duty free. I think it would be best if you let yourself be advised by the Bremen firm about what steps are necessary in order for it to arrive duty free.

We all greet you many times as well as the Erdrichs, and I hope, that your next letter will reassure me more.

Your son
Francis Kettner

**Fig. 39. The Southern Hotel**. This photograph is in possession of The Mason Historical Commission and was provided by Jane Hoerster.

**Abb. 39. Das Southern Hotel**. Dieses Foto befindet sich im Besitz der Mason Historical Commission und wurde von Jane Hoerster zur Verfügung gestellt.

## Brief 19 (10. Januar 1870) von Franz Kettner aus Foley's Crossing an seinen Vater

United States Internal Revenue
Assistant Assessor's Office, Division, District,.....
Mason, 10. Januar 1870

Lieber Vater

Ihren Brief habe ich erhalten und ich hoffe, Sie werden meinen Brief (die Antwort auf Maries werte Zeilen) erhalten haben. Es tut mir unendlich leid, daß Sie noch so trostlos über den harten Verlust sind. Ich hoffe aber, die Zeit wird denselben mildern.

Wir sind alle gesund und mein Louis befindet sich jetzt in einer rein englischen Schule, wo er kein deutsches Wort zu hören bekommt, und bei seinen Anlagen hoffe ich, er wird in kurzer Zeit der Sprache perfekt mächtig sein. Die diesjährigen Weihnachten haben wir, wie alle früheren nach rechter deutscher Weise gefeiert, mit einem Christbaum. Meine Frau bekam einen neuen Damensattel, Louis eine Büchse, die übrigen Kinder Spielsachen und ich wurde mit einer Kiste Zigarren bedacht.

Mein Schwager Hunter, welcher jetzt in Mason wohnt, 6 Meilen von meiner Farm, hat den Louis in Kost genommen, und wir fahren beinahe alle 14 Tage dahin. Er ist ein Amerikaner.

Einliegend finden sich einige Zeilen für die Tante, welche Sie an die Adresse derselben gefälligst zusenden wollen. Es wäre sehr wünschenswert, weniger für mich, als für meine Nachkommen, wenn Sie der Tante auf eine zarte Weise beibringen könnten, daß nach den Gesetzen, ich oder meine Nachkommen bloß berechtigt sind, vom Kapitalvermögen zu erben, da kein Cardell Vertrag[172] zwischen Texas und Baden existiert. Ich habe zwar keine Idee, was die Tante überhaupt vorhat oder wie dieselbe gesonnen ist über Ihre Hinterlassenschaft zu verfügen. Ich dächte, Sie hätten darüber eher eine Idee, ob meine Nachkommen irgendwelche Aussicht haben, und ob es überhaupt nötig ist, die Tante darauf aufmerksam zu machen.

Was unseren Anteil an der seligen Mutter Ihrer Garderobe anbelangt, so übersende denselben in einem Kistchen mit einem Verzeichnis und dem Bemerken, daß es gebrauchte Gegenstände sind an die Adresse Louis Delius & Cie, Bremen. Außerdem mit der Anmerkung, das Kistchen unter der Adresse Friederich Groos & Cie, San Antonio, Texas durch Vermittlung der gewöhnlichen Agenten zu senden und mit dem Auftrage es per Dampfschiff via New Orleans zu senden. Es tut mir bloß leid, daß unter den ganzen Gegenständen sich nichts befindet, daß ich als Angedenken gebrauchen kann. Versehen Sie das Bremer Haus mit einem Inhaltsverzeichnis und daß es gebrauchte Gegenstände sind. Ich glaube, es wird als dann zollfrei sein. Ich glaube, es wäre das Beste, wenn Sie sich dieserhalb bei dem Bremer Haus unterrichten ließen, was für Schritte notwendig sind, um es zollfrei herübergelangen zu lassen.

---

[172] Auslieferungsvertrag

Wir alle grüßen Sie vielmals so wie Erdrichs und ich hoffe, Ihr nächster Brief wird mich mehr beruhigen.

Ihr Sohn

Francis Kettner

# Letter / Brief 20

**Letter 20 (March 29, 1870) from Francis Kettner at Foley's Crossing to his Father**

My dear Father,

Because I, by chance, had the opportunity to have my picture taken during my March trip this year, and these opportunities happen seldom, I am sending you three pictures. One of them is for the Aunt, the other for Marie or Nicolai. The photographs of my family will come later as soon as the opportunity becomes available.

We are all doing well and we are healthy. I have just returned home after an absence of three weeks. I have ridden 50 English miles over the last few days in order to arrive home on the expected day.

Unfortunately, I had to have my picture taken in my riding clothes. The photos are quite well made.

In the hope that these lines find all of you in good health, I will close my letter due to being in a great hurry. Also, I am waiting each day for an answer to my last letter. Then I will write you in complete details.

Your faithful son,
Francis Kettner

**Fig. 40. Catherine Keller Kettner**. The date of this photograph and the one of Franz below are unknown. However, I believe they were probably taken at a date considerably later than 1870.

**Abb. 40. Catherine Keller Kettner.** Das Datum dieses Fotos sowie des unteren von Franz ist unbekannt. Ich denke jedoch, dass sie bedeutend später als 1870 aufgenommen wurden.

**Fig. 41. Franz Kettner.**

**Abb. 41 Franz Kettner.**

## Brief 20 (29. März 1870) von Franz Kettner aus Foley's Crossing[173] an seinen Vater

Mein Lieber Vater!

Da ich auf meiner diesjährigen Märzreise zufällig Gelegenheit hatte, mich abnehmen[174] zu lassen, und diese Gelegenheiten sehr selten sind, so übersende ich Ihnen drei Bilder. Davon eines für die Tante, das andere der Marie oder Nicolai. Die Bilder meiner Familie werden nachfolgen, sobald Gelegenheit vorhanden ist.

Es geht uns allen sehr gut und wir sind gesund. Nach 3 wöchentlicher Abwesenheit bin ich soeben erst nach Hause zurückgekehrt. Ich habe den letzten Tag 50 englische Meilen geritten, um auf den bestimmten Tag nach Hause zu kommen.

Leider mußte ich mich in meinem Reisekostüm abnehmen lassen. Die Bilder sind so ziemlich gut getroffen.

In der Hoffnung, daß diese Zeilen Sie alle bei guter Gesundheit antreffen, schließe ich meinen Brief wegen allzu großer Eile. Auch da ich jeden Tag Antwort auf meinen letzten Brief erwarte. Dann werde ich Ihnen ausführlicher schreiben.

Ihr treuer Sohn
Francis Kettner

29. März 1870

---

[173] Ort nach Vermutung der Autorin.

[174] fotografieren

# Letter / Brief 21

### Letter 21 (May 20, 1870) from Francis Kettner at Foley's Crossing to his Father

Dear Father,

Find enclosed the photographs of my entire family, as good as we were able to get them made. Of the two girls, the one who sits on the chair is the younger, Elise, and Ida is standing. Of the two boys, Karl the youngest sits and Willy is standing. Louis is alone and my wife is alone. I hope that you received my picture when it was sent.

I have received your letter in which you advised me that the goods have been shipped. However, the chest has not arrived so far. I have kept the list of contents in duplicate.

We are still so far all healthy. Let the pictures be copied several times and send them to the Aunt, Nicolai, Marie and Franz, otherwise, the postage will cost too much. If we have the opportunity to come across a better artist, then you will again receive pictures.

I greet you all many times and remain your son

Francis Kettner

## Brief 21 (20. Mai 1870) von Franz Kettner aus Foley's Crossing[175] an seinen Vater

United States Internal Revenue,
Assistant Assessor's Office, .... Division, ....District, ....
20. Mai 1870

Lieber Vater.

Einliegend erhältst Du die Bilder meiner ganzen Familie, so gut, wie wir sie gemacht bekommen konnten. Die beiden Mädchen, dasjenige welches auf dem Stuhle sitzt ist die Elise, die Jüngere, die Ida steht. Die beiden Jungen, Karl der Jüngste sitzt und Willy steht. Der Louis allein und meine Frau allein. Ich hoffe, Sie werden meine Bilder seinerzeit erhalten haben.

Ihren Brief, worin Sie mir anzeigten, daß die Sachen abgeschickt seien, habe ich erhalten. Aber das Kistchen ist bis jetzt noch nicht angekommen. Das Inhaltsverzeichnis habe ich doppelt erhalten.

Wir sind bis jetzt noch alle gesund. Lassen Sie die Bilder verschiedene Male abnehmen und schicken der Tante, Nicolai, Marie und Franz die Bilder, das Porto würde sonst zu viel kosten. Sollten wir Gelegenheit haben, einen besseren Künstler zu treffen, so werdet Ihr die Bilder noch einmal erhalten.

Euch alle vielmals grüßend verbleibe ich Ihr Sohn
Francis Kettner.

175 Ort nach Vermutung der Autorin.

# Letter / Brief 22

### Letter 22 (Fall 1870) from Francis Kettner at Foley's Crossing to his Father

Dear Father,

Your letter which told of the death of my aunt arrived on time. Also, the chest arrived with all the goods within. It seems from your writing that the Aunt died a blessed death, that is, without great pain.

All of us assessors were called to a conference in the capitol Austin in the month of July. I had to ride 160 English miles in the great heat of July. It did me some good. The legislature was already in session and I met many old acquaintances there. As the dispatch came by telegraph on the 20th of July that the French had declared war on Prussia,[176] many bottles of Wiener Beer with ice were passed around (ice is artificially produced daily in all the large cities in Texas) and an eventual victory was drunk to, for Germany must win without question. This enthusiasm is without exception among the entire German population.

I hope that this war, which I, by the way, have prophesied for 10 years, will have no terrible consequences for you and your affairs. If I were ten years younger and without a family, I would enlist immediately as a volunteer. However, these times are in the past. It only takes a week before we have all the news in the newspaper.

I was paid 90 dollars for my trip to Austin. I have in addition to my job as revenue assessor for the United States still another job for the state of Texas. That is, as inspector for all the cattle which are driven out of the county.[177],[178],[179] This spring, at

---

[176] German-French War, 1870-1871.

[177] Stella Polk (Polk, 170) indicates that Franz was elected Cattle and Hide Inspector Dec. 1869.

[178] W.T. Wheeler, a pioneer cattleman in Mason County provided a description of the early cattle business in this "open range era." Immediately following the Civil War, there were large numbers of cattle, many of them unbranded, in the county. Herds had been abandoned when the owners joined the army and the cattle drifted into the area. As a result, cattle were very cheap and often killed for their hides. This practice was stopped, however, due to indiscriminate killing of cattle belonging to local ranches and due to the fact that cattle were becoming more valuable.

least 10,000 cattle were driven out of our county, some to California, New Mexico, and to the California railroad. I myself have shipped 33 head, mostly three and four-year-old cattle, and am waiting for the man to return soon with the earned payment.

I should tell you about which way you should send me money. In the usual manner. An old friend of mine, Frank van der Stucken, presently lives in Antwerp. He owns here significant holdings here and always receives interest from here. A postal order to his brother Felix van der Stucken in Fredericksburg is sufficient for what-

---

Wheeler also provided a description of the "cattle drifts" and big round-ups. Range land was not fenced until after 1871 and it was not completely fenced until much later. During the winter, "drift herds" of cattle from northern ranges would move south. Each norther (cold front accompanied by a strong north wind) cattle would drift further south, usually to a river. Cattle would accumulate at the Colorado River and after the next severe norther, they would move to the San Saba River and eventually to the Rio Grande. Both horses and cattle would be weak and poor after the winter. Spring hunts or roundups would start when there was sufficient grass for saddle horses and cattle to recover from the winter. Cattle gathered in the south were driven north to large ranches as far away as Oklahoma and New Mexico in a large drive. Cattlemen from all over the state cooperated in the roundups by dividing the state into districts and having a boss to oversee the gathering of cattle in their district. As the herds were driven north, cattle would be cut out of herd in their own range or territory. (J. Marvin Hunter, "Brief History of the Early Days in Mason County," *Frontier Times*, 6 December 1928, 113-134.)

Also, during the open range era, it was an unwritten law that stray cattle picked up in cattle drives to market would be sold with the main herd and the owner would be paid for his cattle which were sold. There were numerous abuses which eventually led to the creation of position of Inspector of Cattle and Hide. This is best described by the following direct quote from *Frontier Times* (J. Marvin Hunter, 129).

> But the "co-operative marketing" business had to be handled in a different way, so an inspection law was passed, and every county had from one, two, three or four inspectors. [Mason County only had one elected inspector according to the election results published by Stella G. Polk (Polk, 170).] These inspectors were selected and usually had deputies. When a man had got ready to drive a herd of cattle out of the county he must have this herd inspected. The inspector could use his own judgment in making the inspection. He could have the cattle driven through a chute, an inspector on each side, he could have them strung out along the trail, or he could ride among the herd and satisfy himself. Whether these cattle had one or a dozen brands, the inspector must put on record every brand he found in the herd, and the herd would be inspected in each county through which it passed, and at their destination, the cattle usually inspected by a Texas inspector, this inspector having permission to make this inspection by courtesy of the state into which the cattle went, if they were driven out of Texas. In this way, there was a record of the brand of the every animal in the herd from the time it started up the trail until it reached its destination. If a man lost any cattle, he could go to the records and see if any inspector had put his brand on record after inspecting any trail herd. And the inspector at the last station where the cattle had been sold, could advise any owner whether cattle in his brand had been sold there, and, if so, by whom. That put an end to promiscuous co-operative or accommodation marketing of the kind that resulted to the loss of the real owner of the cattle. After the inspection law was passed, stray cattle would find their way into big herds and be to market, but the owner invariably got a prompt report and remittance.

[179] In this open range era, Cattle and Hide Inspector was an esteemed position since most residents' livelihood was based on the cattle industry. The result of the breakdown of the system is seen in the range wars that broke out in 1874. [David Johnson, *The Mason County "Hoo Doo" War, 1874-1902* (Denton, TX: University of North Texas Press, 2006)].

ever sum. Therefore, I have written to Frank van der Stucken[180] in order that he will give you his address and tell you in what way you should send the money to him. Additionally, I have spoken with Felix Stucken who advised me that whatever sum is sent him from his brother will immediately be paid out. This postal order must be written out in duplicate and sent in two different letters in case one of them becomes lost.

When I receive the money, I will change my home. I will sell all but 25 milk cows in order to increase my sheep to 800 head and employ a shepherd. I will move somewhat closer to the town of Mason. I am in negotiations over a very good place with a garden which is irrigated and is outstanding for raising sheep.

Because I am held back by my jobs from spending much time on the cattle and because Louis has at least another two years to spend in school, I think it is better to stick the money which I will receive from the cattle into raising sheep.

Wuelfing, the former Prussian artillery captain, has come again to me and will undertake the education of both my girls. The little boys still have vacation before them. I brought Louis a new revolver from Austin. This has made him very happy. He also shoots very well with it. At the moment, he has two months of vacation at home and amuses himself with fishing, riding, and hunting. The childhoods of Texas youths are truly enviable in comparison to Germany. The children also become larger and stronger, what the free movements and natural growing up must contribute to.

The stomach spasms which have plagued my wife seem to have gone away. We only know children's diseases by name. Our borders, which have suffered greatly from the Indians, are now protected by a company of 20 volunteers who are enlisted for a period of one year. One definitely expects more protection from our Texas youths than from the regular military.

My brother-in-law Hunter is the Captain of one company. A company was offered to me, but because the position is only for one year at 120 dollars a month, I did not want to give up my other job that I can probably hold for four years.

You have not said to me whether or not you have received the photographs of my entire family (although they are quite average).

Is it not strange that Franz Kissel does not have any time left over in order to write to his uncle? Tell Marie Erdrich that she should write me a short letter from time to time, at least four times a year and share with me all the news from Oberkirch that could interest me. The postage is now so cheap and I should think that a person could find some time available.

Write me right away again. I hope that your health has become better. I would let go of all the strenuous works and especially helping with births. When a person has

---

[180] Frank van der Stucken emigrated from Antwerp, Belgium to Fredericksburg, Texas. He married Sophie Schoenewolf in 1852. He was a freight contractor and merchant who served as a captain in the First Texas Cavalry during the Civil War. He returned to Antwerp with his family in 1866. *Handbook of Texas Online*, s.v. "Frank Van Der Stucken," http://www.tsha.utexas.edu/handbook/-online/articles/VV/fva4.html (accessed July 9, 2007).

struggled to your age and worked for mankind, I believe he has the right as a person to dedicate the remaining years entirely to his health. You are now in such a condition where you do not need to do so.

All of us send you the best greetings.

Your son

Francis Kettner

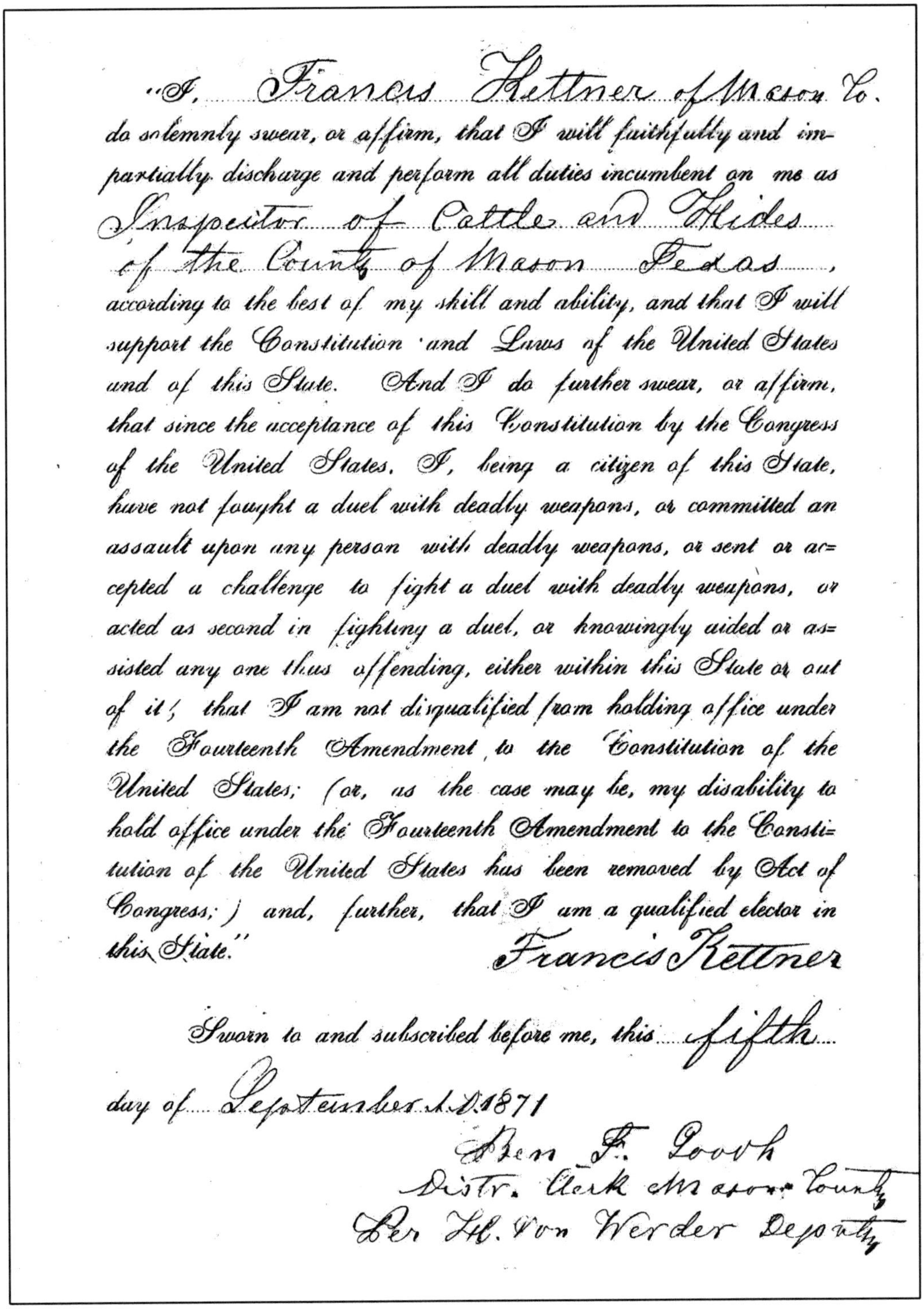

"I, Frances Kettner of Mason Co.
do solemnly swear, or affirm, that I will faithfully and impartially discharge and perform all duties incumbent on me as Inspector of Cattle and Hides of the County of Mason Texas, according to the best of my skill and ability, and that I will support the Constitution and Laws of the United States and of this State. And I do further swear, or affirm, that since the acceptance of this Constitution by the Congress of the United States, I, being a citizen of this State, have not fought a duel with deadly weapons, or committed an assault upon any person with deadly weapons, or sent or accepted a challenge to fight a duel with deadly weapons, or acted as second in fighting a duel, or knowingly aided or assisted any one thus offending, either within this State or out of it; that I am not disqualified from holding office under the Fourteenth Amendment to the Constitution of the United States; (or, as the case may be, my disability to hold office under the Fourteenth Amendment to the Constitution of the United States has been removed by Act of Congress;) and, further, that I am a qualified elector in this State."

Francis Kettner

Sworn to and subscribed before me, this fifth day of September A.D. 1871

Ben F. Gooch
Distr. Clerk Mason County
Per H. von Werder Deputy

**Fig. 42. Oath of Office for Inspector of Cattle and Hides of the County of Mason, Texas**. This document was obtained from the Texas State Archives.

**Abb. 42. Amtseid als Inspektor für Vieh und Häute des Mason County, Texas.** Dieses Dokument wurde von den Texas State Archives erhalten.

## Brief 22 (Herbst 1870[181]) von Franz Kettner aus Foley's Crossing an seinen Vater

Lieber Vater!

Ihr Brief, den Tod meiner Tante anzeigend, kam richtig an. Ebenso das Kistchen mit allem wohlbehalten. Es scheint aus Ihren Zeilen, daß die Tante einen beneidenswerten Tod gestorben ist, nämlich ohne große Schmerzen.

Den Monat Juli waren wir Assessoren alle nach der Hauptstadt Austin zu einer Konferenz beordert. Ich hatte 160 englische Meilen zu reiten in der größten Hitze (Juli). Dafür tat ich mir etwas zugute. Die Legislatur war gerade in Sitzung und ich traf mehrere alte Bekannte dabei. Als aber den 20. Juli die telegrafische Depesche ankam, daß Frankreich Preußen den Krieg erklärt habe,[182] so wurde manche Flasche Wiener Bier mit Eis vertilgt (Eis wird nämlich in allen größeren Städten in Texas täglich künstlich fabriziert) und auf den endfolgenden Sieg getrunken, den Deutschland unwiderruflich gewinnen muß. Und dieser Enthusiasmus ist unter der ganzen deutschen Bevölkerung ohne Ausnahme.

Ich hoffe, dieser Krieg, den ich übrigens schon 10 Jahre vorher prophezeit habe, wird auf Sie und Ihre Angelegenheiten von keinen nachtheiligen Folgen sein. Wäre ich zehn Jahre jünger und ohne Familie, ich würde sofort als Freiwilliger eintreten. Doch diese Zeiten sind vorbei. Es dauert bloß eine Woche, so haben wir alle Nachrichten in den Zeitungen.

Für die Reise nach Austin wurden mir 90 Dollars vergütet. Ich habe neben meiner Anstellung als Revenue Assessor der Vereinigten Staaten noch eine andere Anstellung erhalten für den Staat Texas. Nämlich Inspektor für alles Vieh, was aus dem County getrieben wird. Es sind in diesem Frühjahr aus unserem County wenigstens 10.000 Stück Vieh, teils nach Kalifornien, New Mexico und nach der kalifornischen Eisenbahn getrieben worden. Ich habe selbst 33 Stück mittreiben lassen, meistens drei und vier Jahre alte Ochsen, und erwarte den Mann in Bälde retour mit dem erlösten Geld.

Ich sollte Ihnen angeben, auf welche Art Sie mir Geld senden sollten. Auf folgende. Es wohnt gegenwärtig ein alter Bekannter von mir in Antwerpen, Frank van der Stucken.[183] Der von hier immer Zinsen zugeschickt bekommt und der hier bedeutendes Vermögen besitzt. Eine Anweisung an seinen Bruder Felix van der Stucken in Friedrichsburg ist hinreichend für irgendeine Summe. Ich habe deshalb an Frank van der Stucken geschrieben, damit er Ihnen seine Adresse angibt und auf welche Art Sie demselben das Geld übersenden sollten. Ebenfalls habe ich mit Felix Stucken gesprochen, welcher mir erklärte, irgendeine Summe auf eine Anweisung

---

[181] Ort und Datum nach Vermutung der Autorin.

[182] Deutsch-französischer Krieg 1870-1871.

[183] Frank van der Stucken war aus Antwerpen, Belgien nach Texas immigriert, hatte in Friedrichsburg 1852 Sophie Schönewolf geheiratet, diente während des Bürgerkrieges als Captain in der First Texas Cavalry, und kehrte mit seiner Familie 1866 nach Antwerpen zurück. Quelle: *Handbook of Texas Online*, unter dem Stichwort "Van Der Stucken, Frank Valentine", http://www.tsha.-utexas.edu/handbook/online/articles/ VV/fva4.html, (Zugriff 23.10.2003).

hin von seinem Bruder sogleich auszubezahlen. Solche Anweisung müßte im Duplikat ausgestellt werden und in zwei verschiedenen Briefen abgesandt werden, falls einer verlorenginge.

Wenn ich das Geld erhalte, werde ich meinen Wohnsitz verändern. Mein Vieh bis auf 25 Milchkühe verkaufen, dafür meine Schafe auf 800 Stück vermehren und einen Hüter halten. Ich werde etwas näher nach der Stadt Mason ziehen. Ich bin nämlich am Handeln um einen sehr gut eingerichteten Platz, mit einem Garten der bewässert wird und ausgezeichnet für Schafzucht ist.

Da ich durch meine Anstellungen verhindert bin, mich viel um das Vieh zu kümmern, und Louis zum wenigstens noch zwei Jahre die Schule besuchen muß, so halte ich es für besser das Geld in Schafe zu stecken, was ich aus dem Vieh erhalte.

Wülfing, ehemaliger Preußischer Artilleriehauptmann, kommt wieder zu mir und wird die Erziehung meiner beiden Fräuleins übernehmen. Die kleinen Jungens haben vor der Hand noch Ferien. Ich brachte Louis einen neuen Revolver mit von Austin. Dies machte den Jungen überglücklich. Er schießt auch sehr gut damit. Derselbe ist im Augenblick auf zwei Monate Ferien zu Hause und amüsiert sich mit Fischen, Reiten und Jagen. Die Kinderjahre von texanischen Jungens sind wirklich beneidenswert, gegen Deutschland. Dieselben werden auch größer und kräftiger, was die freie Bewegung und naturgemäßes Aufwachsen bewirken muß.

Der Magenkrampf, mit dem meine Frau geplagt war, hat sich ziemlich gegeben. Kinderkrankheiten kennen wir bloß dem Namen nach. Unsere Grenze, welche sehr viel von Indianern zu leiden hatte, wird jetzt durch 20 Kompanien Freiwilliger beschützt werden, welche auf ein Jahr eingemustert sind. Man hofft bedeutend mehr Schutz von unseren Texaner Jungens als von dem regulären Militär.

Mein Schwager Hunter ist Captain von einer Kompanie. Eine Kompanie wurde mir angeboten, da es aber eine Stellung bloß für ein Jahr ist mit 120 Dollar per Monat, so wollte ich meine andere Stellung nicht aufgeben, welche ich möglicherweise 4 Jahre halten kann.

Sie haben mir nicht angezeigt, ob Sie die Bilder meiner ganzen Familie (allerdings sehr mittelmäßige) empfangen haben oder nicht.

Sehr sonderbar ist es, daß Franz Kissel keine Zeit erübrigen kann, um an seinen Onkel zu schreiben? Sagen Sie der Marie Erdrich, sie sollte mir von Zeit zu Zeit einen kurzen Brief schreiben, alle Jahre 4 mal wenigstens, und mir alle Neuigkeiten aus Oberkirch mitteilen, die mich interessieren könnten. Das Porto ist jetzt so billig und ich sollte denken, etwas Zeit könnte man auch noch erübrigen.

Schreiben Sie mir recht bald wieder. Ihre Gesundheit, hoffe ich, wird sich gebessert haben. Ich würde übrigens alle anstrengenden Geschäfte unterlassen und namentlich die Geburtshilfe. Denn, wenn man sich bis zu Ihrem Alter gequält und für die Menschheit gewirkt hat, so glaube ich, hat der Mensch als Mensch ein Recht, die noch übrige Zeit ausschließlich seiner Gesundheit zu widmen. Sie sind außerdem jetzt in solchen Verhältnissen, wo Sie es nicht gebrauchen.

Wir alle grüßen Sie bestens. Ihr Sohn,
Francis Kettner.

# Letter / Brief 23

**Letter 23 (January 30, 1871) from Francis Kettner at the Foley's Crossing, Mason County, to his Father**

United States Internal Revenue,
Ass't. Assessor's Office, 3d District, Texas

Mason, January 30, 1870[184]

Dear Father,

Today we received the news by telegram that Paris has fallen. The Leipziger Gartenlaube (newspaper) also arrived which I am receiving since this war. Hopefully, this war will soon end. The wounded have received 25 gulden from me. There has been approximately a million dollars sent to Germany, the equivalent to two million fifty-thousand gulden. You can see from this what the Germans are capable of, that is, those who live outside the old homeland.

On the 24th of January, 1871 my office as assessor ceased to exist because the taxes were significantly reduced and many districts shrunk and consolidated. I held it for five years. The only job that I still have is inspector of all the cattle that are driven out of the county. This brings me approximately 500 dollars over a time period of 4 years. When you shared with me in your first letter shortly after the death of the aunt that I should let you know how you should send me the promised 2000 florins, I had no idea about events in the meantime. I have bought, because a good opportunity was offered me, a beautiful farm, very valuable, quite near to the town of Mason where I can send my children to school. (Until now, I have had a home teacher for both my girls, Captain Wuelfing Duelmen of the Prussian artillery, a man almost 60 years old, very sprightly, an outstanding teacher.) Louis is with my sister-in-law in Mason and goes to an English school. The way I organized the

---

184 This is probably a mistake. See paragraph 2 where the date is January 30, 1871.

education of my children at this time is too expensive for me; and therefore, the aforementioned purchase. The last session comes in the summer and I have counted on the promised money for this payment. Since the (farm) purchase was made, if you could make it sooner, that would be very desirable for me; otherwise, I must borrow the money at 12 to 15 percent. That is the interest here.

I have no more news from you since the person in Mannheim had played a trick on you. Since then, I sent a picture of me and Louis to Marie. Otherwise, there is nothing new here. We are all healthy and the children flourish bodily as well as mentally.

Have the kindness to answer this letter as soon as possible so that I will have the time to make arrangements accordingly. I could, in emergency, put off the due date until late in the year. I hope that Frank van der Stucken from Antwerp has given you his address and that all you pay to him will be paid to me by his brother in Fredericksburg without charges. It is the safest way and the fastest. You simply have a money order made out to Felix van der Stucken, Fredericksburg, and send it to me. In addition, Stucken in Antwerp can write his brother in case the money order or the letter is lost.

My next letter will be more detailed since I am very much taken up with work at the moment. In the hope that you and all my still existing relatives are well, I remain your son.

Francis Kettner

My wife and children greet you many times.

## Brief 23 (30. Januar 1871[185]) von Franz Kettner aus Foley's Crossing an seinen Vater

United States Internal Revenue,
Ass't. Assessor's Office, 3d District, Texas.

Mason, 30. Januar 1870[186]

Lieber Vater!

Heute erhalten wir per Telegramm die Nachricht, daß Paris gefallen ist. Ebenso trifft die Leipziger Gartenlaube ein, welche ich seit diesem Kriege erhalte. Hoffentlich wird dieser Krieg bald zu Ende sein. Die Verwundeten haben von mir auch 25 Gulden erhalten. Es ist ungefähr eine Million Dollars nach Deutschland gegangen, gleichbedeutend mit zwei Millionen 50.000 Gulden. Sie können daraus ersehen, zu was Deutsche fähig sind, auch außerhalb der alten Heimat wohnend.

Mit dem 24. Januar 1871 hat mein Office als Assessor aufgehört zu existieren, da die Steuern bedeutend reduziert wurden und sehr viele Distrikte eingingen.[187] Ich hatte dasselbe fünf Jahre. Die einzige Anstellung, die ich noch habe, ist Inspektor über alles Vieh, das aus dem County getrieben wird. Dies bringt mir ungefähr 500 Dollars ein für einen Zeitraum von 4 Jahren.

Als Sie mir in Ihrem ersten Brief kurz nach dem Tode der Tante mitteilten, daß ich Sie benachrichtigen solle, auf welche Weise Sie mir die versprochenen 2000 fl senden sollten, hatte ich keine Ahnung von Zwischenfällen. Ich kaufte, da mir eine gute Gelegenheit geboten war, ganz in der Nähe des Städtchens Mason, eine schöne Farm, sehr wertvoll, wo ich meine Kinder nach Mason in die Schule schicken konnte. (Bis jetzt habe ich für meine beiden Mädchen einen Hauslehrer, Hauptmann Wülfing Dülmen von der preußischen Artillerie, ein Mann von fast 60 Jahren, sehr rüstig, ein ausgezeichneter Lehrer.) Und Louis ist bei meiner Schwägerin in Mason und besucht die englische Schule. So wie ich die Erziehung meiner Kinder im Augenblick betreibe, ist es für mich zu kostspielig, deshalb der besagte Kauf. Der letzte Termin fällt in den Sommer und mit dieser Zahlung habe ich mich auf das besagte Geld verlassen, gleich wie der Kauf gemacht wurde. Wenn Sie es daher möglich machen können, so wäre es für mich sehr erwünscht, sonst müßte ich das Geld leihen zu 12 bis 15 Prozent. Dies ist hier der Zinsfuß.

Ich habe keine Nachricht mehr von Ihnen, seit der Jude in Mannheim Ihnen den Streich gespielt hat. Ich hatte nach der Zeit der Marie mein und Louis Bild geschickt. Sonst gibt es hier nichts Neues. Wir sind alle gesund und die Kinder gedeihen körperlich ebenso wohl wie geistig.

Haben Sie die Güte und beantworten Sie mir diesen Brief sobald als möglich, so daß ich Zeit habe, mich drauf zu richten. Ich könnte im Notfall den Termin bis zum Spätjahr verschieben. Ich hoffe Franck van der Stucken von Antwerpen wird Ihnen

---

[185] Jahreszahl 1870 berichtigt auf 1871 gemäß Absatz 2 des Briefes.
[186] Richtig 1871.
[187] Vermutlich im Sinne von "aufgehoben wurden" zu lesen.

seine Adresse angegeben haben, und alles was Sie an denselben bezahlen, wird mir in Friedrichsburg ohne Spesen von seinem Bruder ausbezahlt. Es ist der sicherste Weg und der kürzeste. Sie lassen sich einfach eine Ordre ausstellen an Felix van der Stucken, Friedrichsburg und schicken mir dieselbe. Außerdem kann Stucken in Antwerpen an seinen Bruder schreiben, falls die Ordre oder der Brief verloren ginge.

Mein nächster Brief wird ausführlicher sein, da ich im Augenblick zu sehr von Arbeit in Anspruch genommen bin. In der Hoffnung, daß Sie und alle meine noch vorhandenen Verwandten sich wohl befinden, verbleibe ich Ihr Sohn

Francis Kettner

Meine Frau und Kinder grüßen Sie vielmals.

# Letter / Brief 24

## Letter 24 (June 4, 1871) from Francis Kettner at Foley's Crossing to his Father

My dear Father!

I have received your letter from the 7th of April and it is upsetting to me that you, through haste, have placed yourself and your children partly in an unpleasant situation. In your place, I would not sell the house for less than it is worth but would have rented it and used the income from it. Concerning my situation, I can help myself without receiving money from you because I have up to this time a very good income. Through the office of the Inspector of Cattle to be sold, I sometimes earn 50 dollars in 4 days.

I will change my living place because the Indians steal too many horses from me. In the last two months, 3 head, and once earlier I had a small fight with them. This was approximately 300 steps in front of the house and I took back the horses from them that they already had in their possession. My son Louis,[188] who took part in it,

---

[188] This event was described in the *Frontier Times* (J. Marvin Hunter, "Brief History of the Early Days in Mason County" *Frontier Times* 6, December, 1928, 113-134). Most likely, Louis Kettner provided this information since he was a source for the *Frontier Times* story. The following is a direct quote from the *Frontier Times*.

> One day, about sundown, in 1871, Francis Kettner's horses were grazing in front of his house on James river, the horses being not more than 75 yards from the house, and in plain view. The horses were in the habit of coming up for their feed, but on this occasion they were a little late, so Mrs. Kettner told Louis to go out and drive them in. Louis, accompanied by his dog, started for the horses, but had only gone a few steps when the dog commenced barking at something in a deep ravine not far from where the horses were grazing. Louis had an old pistol, and, although he wasn't thinking about Indians, he got behind a pile of brush, and just then what appeared to be a man wearing a white shirt, came in sight, passed the horses and came toward Louis. Louis drew his pistol, still thinking the approaching party was a white man, when the rider turned suddenly and waved a shield over his head, and it was this white shield that Louis had mistaken for a white shirt. In waving his shield, the Indian knocked off his straw hat, which was kept as a souvenir. As the Indians turned toward the horses, Louis tried to shoot, but his pistol snapped. His mother then

handled himself with courage and we set 5 Indians in flight without becoming wounded. Because of this I will move near the town of Mason where I have bought myself, indeed, 320 acres of land for 320 dollars. I must leave this place standing empty since I have no prospects of putting a good price on it. As long as the Indian raids are not settled and we do not have a long stretch of protection, it will be a long time until I can put a good price on my old land holdings. The government always continues with the crazy idea that these wild Indians can be civilized through missionaries and the Christian religion. They partly feed them, but they steal and murder without respite. They come 500 miles and more from their living quarters and make their attacks in Texas.

Concerning my inheritance share; you told me in your last letter that this would consist of 1933 florins. Included in that was the 450 florins[189] that I had received earlier from mother. I cannot understand this, naturally, because I do not know what this means. Moreover, I hope that you have your affairs in such order, that by your leaving, my children will not be discriminated against. Because they have no claim to material goods, it would please me when you would send me two copies of your will.

Once again, I do not wish that you make yourself any worry over our part or to regard this obligation as a debt. As long as you can use this yourself, it is my wish that you enjoy it. I would not have accepted your offer to send me money if I had not thought that you received more interest that you needed for your household. That was indeed the sense from your letters.

In approximately two months I will begin to build and move into my new place late in the year. The land lays on the main road[190] which goes by all the different

---

called and told him to run to the house. Mr. Kettner, who was working some distance in the rear of the house, heard the calling, and came running to the house. He was met by Mrs. Kettner, who carried to him his Spencer carbine rifle, a breech-loading gun that carried eight shells, and was capable of great destruction. These were government guns, which the soldiers were forbidden to sell, and civilians forbidden to buy or own, but if the government had delivered them free to the citizens it would have given more protection than the soldiers gave. Not withstanding these government prohibitions, the citizens would occasionally manage to get hold of a Spencer carbine. The Indians were driving the horses up the ravine, with Mr. Kettner and Louis, a mere boy, in pursuit. Suddenly, the horses remembered it was late supper time, and dashed toward the house. A few well directed shots from the Spencer caused the Indians to desist in their efforts to head the horses off, and they went away. But two months later perhaps, the same bunch of Indians came drifting along one day, the horses were some farther from the house than on the former occasion, Mr. Kettner was not at home, and this time the Indians got away with the horses.

[189] Note of the Author. Franz received 900 florin from his parents when he emigrated to Texas. Half of this was from his mother's estate.

[190] Franz is referring to the route between Fredericksburg (Fort Scott) and Fort Mason. This road corresponds to present day US 87. Franz's home on Comanche Creek is one and a fourth miles south of US 87. Traces of this old road still can be seen adjacent to US 87. According to the *Frontier Times* (J. Marvin Hunter, "Brief History of the Early Days in Mason County," *Frontier Times*, 6 February 1929, 187), the El Paso and San Antonio stage route or mail line were established soon after the Civil war. From San Antonio, it passed through Boerne, Fredericksburg (Fort Scott), Loyal Valley, Mason, Menardville, Fort McKavett, Fort Concho, Fort Davis, Eagle Springs, and Quitman Canyon.

military posts and I have a plan to run a small store on it. My wife and Louis can take care of it since I am often away from home. I always have a credit for a thousand dollars in San Antonio or Fredericksburg. My name is still always good in western Texas.

On the 8th of May, the inhabitants of Fredericksburg celebrated the founding of the city, a 25-year anniversary. I was also there with my family. The festivities lasted two days; an entire hall was built for this. There was a lot of dancing. The Watch on the Rhein was sung and a lot of (imported) Bock beer and Rhein wine was drunk. Ice was also available in order to cool the drinks. One now finds in all the larger towns mechanical ice machines that make fresh ice every day. The chemical process is entirely simple. The heat is removed from the water so that it becomes ice.

Has Marie Erdrich ever received the portrait of me and my son or not?

Now it will soon be shown whether this bloody war will have any good consequences such as liberal progress and development or whether it simply goes to the glory of the House Hohenzoller (royalty in Baden). I have very little trust in the old King of Prussia. He is still of the old school (by the grace of God).

I have never received a letter from Franz Kissel. The young man appears to want little to do with his uncle. I have a great desire to visit you next summer if I can make it. On my own, I cannot promise to do so since I have to do substantial work with building and the fields.

The health condition of my wife, principally with the stomach, has gotten better. A younger doctor named Schilling, whose father was a notary in Offenburg, has settled in Fredericksburg. We went there this spring and sought his advice. He immediately explained that the stomach cramps were caused by the stomach digesting too slowly. And it appears that the condition has improved through his treatment. That is, my wife feels significantly better and the stomach spasms have stopped.

Both my girls, Ida and Elise, read already and are making fine progress. The children are all very healthy and strong.

In regard to your eye problem, that is very sad. As long as the other eye is still good, I would not undertake this operation.

I hope to learn something more exact about your household in your next letter. Whether you continue following your old habits or not and whether you are still a lover of gardening or, much more, raising fruit.

In the hope that I will soon receive a letter from you and in that way receive pleasant news about your health condition.

I remain your grateful son,<br>
Francis Kettner

Many greetings from my wife and the children.

Should you have already sold the spoken-about house, make a note of the enclosed address for sending money. This is secure and without cost.

**Fig. 43. Remnants of the Road between Fredericksburg and Mason.** In this particular location, one observes what appear to be wagon ruts. This identification is somewhat subjective, since the terrain has changed. However, this area is on a rocky hill top where one would not expect water erosion.

**Abb. 43. Überreste der Straße zwischen Friedrichsburg und Mason.** An dieser besonderen Stelle kann man noch etwas wie Wagenspuren sehen. Wenn auch die Identifizierung etwas subjektiv war, da sich das Terrain verändert hat. Dennoch, dieses Gebiet liegt oben auf einem felsigen Hügel, wo man keine Erosion durch Wasser erwarten würde.

## Brief 24 (4. Juni 1871) von Franz Kettner aus Foley's Crossing an seinen Vater

Mason, 4. Juni 1871

Mein Lieber Vater!

Ihren Brief vom 7. April habe ich erhalten, und es ist mir unangenehm, daß Sie durch Voreiligkeit, sich und Ihre Kinder teilweise in unangenehme Lage versetzt haben. Ich würde an Ihrer Stelle das Haus nicht unter dem Werte verkaufen, sondern es vermieten und die Zinsen davon gebrauchen. Was meine Lage anbelangt, so kann ich mir helfen, ohne Geld von Ihnen zu erhalten; denn ich habe bis zu dieser Zeit sehr gute Einnahmen gehabt. Durch das Amt des Inspektors des zu verkaufenden Viehs, habe ich manchmal in 4 Tagen 50 Dollars verdient.

Ich werde meinen Wohnsitz verändern, da mir die Indianer zu viele Pferde stehlen. In den letzten zwei Monaten 3 Stück und einmal vorher hatte ich ein kleines Gefecht mit denselben. Das war ungefähr 300 Schritte vor dem Hause und ich nahm ihnen die Pferde wieder ab, die sie schon im Besitz hatten. Mein Sohn Louis, welcher sich daran beteiligte, benahm sich mutig und wir schlugen 5 Indianer in die Flucht, ohne verwundet zu werden.[191] Deshalb werde ich in die Nähe des Städtchen

---

[191] Auszug aus *Frontier Times* vom 6. Dezember 1928, S. 122. J. Marvin Hunter, "Brief History of the Early Days in Mason County". S.113-134. Bericht von wahrscheinlich Louis über dieses kleine Gefecht

Eines Tages gegen Sonnenuntergang im Jahre 1871 grasten Franz Kettners Pferde vor seinem Haus am James River, wobei die Pferde nicht mehr als 75 Yards vom Haus entfernt waren und deutlich zu sehen. Die Pferde hatten die Gewohnheit zur Fütterung hereinzukommen, doch bei dieser Gelegenheit hatten sie sich etwas verspätet, deshalb bat Mrs. Kettner Louis, nach draußen zugehen und sie hereinzutreiben. Begleitet von seinem Hund ging Louis auf die Pferde zu, hatte jedoch erst wenige Schritte getan als der Hund irgend etwas in einer tiefen Schlucht anzubellen begann, nicht weit entfernt davon, wo die Pferde grasten. Louis hatte eine alte Pistole und, obgleich er nicht an Indianer dachte, ging er hinter ein Gebüsch und genau in dem Moment kam etwas in Sicht, was ein Mann zu sein schien, der ein weißes Hemd trug, passierte die Pferde und kam auf Louis zu. Louis zog seine Pistole, immer noch denkend, die ankommende Partei wäre ein weißer Mann, als der Reiter sich plötzlich umwandte und ein Schild über seinen Kopf schwang. Und es war dies weiße Schild, das Louis irrtümlich für ein weißes Hemd gehalten hatte. Durch das Schwenken seines Schildes warf der Indianer seinen Strohhut ab, der später als Souvenir aufbewahrt wurde. Als der Indianer sich den Pferden zuwandte, versuchte Louis zu schießen, aber seine Pistole versagte. Darauf rief seine Mutter und wies ihn an zum Haus zu rennen. Mr. Kettner, der in einiger Entfernung hinter dem Haus arbeitete hörte das Rufen und kam zum Haus gelaufen. Er traf auf Mrs. Kettner, die ihm seinen Spencer Karabiner brachte, ein Gewehr mit einem Röhrenmagazin im Kolben, das 8 Patronen enthielt, und das zu großer Zerstörung fähig war. Dies waren Regierungsgewehre, die die Soldaten nicht verkaufen durften und Zivilisten war es verboten sie zu kaufen oder zu besitzen, aber wenn die Regierung sie frei den Bürgern geliefert hätte, hätte dieses mehr Schutz gegeben als die Soldaten gaben. Ohne diesem Regierungsverbot Widerstand zu leisten, schafften die Bürger es gelegentlich, an einen Spencer Karabiner zu gelangen. (Anmerkung der Autorin:Franz Kettner war Assistant Assessor of the United States Internal Revenue und Angehöriger der Miliz und dürfte diese Schwierigkeiten nicht gehabt haben.) Die Indianer trieben die Pferde die Schlucht hinauf, verfolgt von Mr. Kettner und Louis, nur einem

Mason ziehen, woselbst ich mich angekauft habe. Nämlich 320 Acre Land für 320 Dollars. Ich muß natürlicherweise meinen Wohnsitz vorderhand leer stehen lassen, da ich keine Aussicht habe, denselben verwerten zu können. So lange die Indianerangelegenheit nicht geordnet ist und wir hinlänglichen Schutz erhalten; so lange wird es dauern, bis ich meinen alten Wohnsitz mit 320 Acre Land verwerten kann. Das Gouvernement geht nämlich immer mit der verrückten Idee um, diese wilden Indianer durch Missionare und Christliche Religion zu zivilisieren. Es füttert sie teilweise, dabei stehlen und morden sie ohne Unterlaß. Sie kommen von ihren Niederlassungen 500 Meilen und mehr und machen ihre Einfälle in Texas.

Was meinen Teilzettel anbelangt; so teilten Sie mir in Ihrem letzen Briefe mit, daß sich derselbe auf 1933 fl beläuft. Davon geht ab, Vorempfang des Mutteranteils von 450 fl.[192] Dieses kann ich natürlicherweise nicht verstehen; da ich nicht weiß, was es zu bedeuten hat. Ich hoffe übrigens, daß Sie Ihre Angelegenheiten so geordnet haben, daß bei Ihrem Ableben, meine Kinder nicht benachteiligt werden. Da dieselben an Liegenschaften keine Ansprüche zu machen haben; und es wäre mir lieb, wenn Sie mir zwei Kopien von Ihrem Testament zuschicken würden.

Also noch einmal, ich wünsche nicht, daß Sie sich um unserer halben irgendwie Sorgen machen; oder diesen Pflichtteil als eine Schuld betrachten. So lange Sie denselben gebrauchen können, wünsche ich, daß Sie darüber verfügen. Ich hätte Ihr Anerbieten, mir Geld zu schicken, gar nicht angenommen, wenn ich nicht gedacht hätte, Sie erhalten mehr Zinsen, als Sie zu Ihrem Unterhalt gebrauchten. So war nämlich der Sinn Ihres Schreibens.

In ungefähr zwei Monaten werde ich anfangen zu bauen und bis Spätjahr auf meinen neuen Platz ziehen. Derselbe liegt an der Hauptstrasse, die nach allen den verschiedenen Militärposten geht, und ich habe die Absicht, ein kleines Geschäft dabei zu betreiben. Das können meine Frau und Louis besorgen, da ich oft von Hause fort bin. Ich habe in San Antonio oder Friedrichsburg immer einen Kredit von einigen tausend Dollar. Mein Name ist noch immer gut im westlichen Texas.

Den achten Mai feierten die Bewohner von Friedrichsburg die Gründung der Stadt, 25 jähriges Jubiläum. Auch ich war mit meiner Familie da. Die Festlichkeit dauerte 2 Tage, eine eigene Halle war dazu gebaut. Es wurde viel getanzt. Die Wacht am Rhein gesungen und sehr viel Bockbier (importiertes) und Rheinwein getrunken. Auch war Eis vorhanden, um die Getränke kühl zu machen. Man findet jetzt in allen größeren Städten künstliche Eismaschinen, die jeden Tag frisches Eis machen. Der

---

Jungen. Plötzlich erinnerten sich die Pferde daran, daß schon längst Fütterungszeit sei und stürmten zu dem Haus. Ein paar wohlgezielte Schüsse aus der Spencer veranlaßten die Indianer, ihre Anstrengungen aufzugeben, die Pferde fortzutreiben und sie verschwanden. Aber vielleicht zwei Monate später kam dieselbe Bande von Indianern eines Tages wieder vorbei, die Pferde befanden sich in größerer Entfernung vom Haus als bei der früheren Gelegenheit. Mr. Kettner war nicht zu Hause und diesmal entkamen die Indianer mit den Pferden.

[192] Anmerkung der Autorin: Franz hat bei Auswanderung 900 fl von seinen Eltern mitbekommen. Die Hälfte davon ist der Mutteranteil.

chemische Prozeß ist ganz einfach. Die Wärme wird aus dem Wasser herausgezogen und somit ist das Eis vorhanden.

Hat Marie Erdrich je mein und meines Sohnes gemeinsames Portrait erhalten oder nicht?

Nun wird sich auch bald herausstellen, ob dieser blutige Krieg auch gute Folgen haben wird, nämlich liberales Vorangehen und Entwickelung oder es bloß um den Glanz des Hauses Hohenzollern ging. Ich habe zu dem alten König von Preußen sehr wenig Zutrauen. Er ist noch aus der alten Schule, (von Gottes Gnaden).

Von Franz Kissel habe noch nie einen Brief erhalten. Der junge Mensch scheint sich wenig aus seinem Onkel zu machen. Ich habe große Lust, Sie nächsten Sommer zu besuchen; wenn ich es machen kann. Allein, sicher versprechen läßt sich so etwas nicht, da ich dieses Jahr bedeutende Ausgaben mit Bauen und Feld zu machen habe.

Der Gesundheitszustand, hinsichtlich des Magens meiner Frau hat sich gebessert. Nämlich ein junger Arzt namens Schilling, sein Vater war Notar in Offenburg, hat sich in Friedrichsburg niedergelassen. Wir waren dieses Frühjahr da und gebrauchten seinen Rat. Derselbe erklärte sofort, daß der Magenkrampf entstände, durch zu langsames Verdauen des Magens. Und es scheint, daß durch seine Kur der Zustand gehoben ist. Denn meine Frau fühlt sich bedeutend wohler und die Magenkrämpfe sind ausgeblieben.

Meine beiden Mädchen Ida und Elise lesen schon und machen hübsche Fortschritte. Die Kinder sind alle sehr gesund und kräftig.

Was Ihr Augenübel anbelangt, so ist dies sehr traurig. Allein so lange das eine Auge noch gut ist, würde ich die Operation nicht unternehmen lassen.

Ich wünschte in Ihrem nächsten Briefe etwas näheres über Ihre Haushaltung zu erfahren. Ob Sie dieselbe nach alter Gewohnheit fortführen oder nicht, und ob Sie noch Liebhaber von Gärtnerei oder vielmehr Obstzucht sind.

In der Hoffnung, bald einen Brief von Ihnen zu erhalten, und Angenehmes hinsichtlich Ihres Gesundheitszustandes zu erfahren verbleibe ich Ihr dankbarer

Sohn Francis Kettner.

Viele Grüße von meiner Frau und den Kindern.

Sollten Sie das besagte Haus dennoch verkauft haben, so benötigen Sie die angegebene Adresse für Geldsendung. Dieselbe ist sicher und ohne Kosten.

# Letter / Brief 25

### Letter 25 (July 2, 1871) from Dr. Franz Lambert Kettner in Oberkirch to Francis Kettner[193]

Oberkirch, July 2, 1871

Dear Franz,

At last I can comply with your wish and enclosed send you a money order of six hundred five dollars and 75 cents from a New York House (bank) that merchant Erderich[194] acquired for me in Karlsruhe. Tell me immediately news of its arrival.

Merchant Erderich, Marie Kissel's husband, took care of my entire inheritance business for me in Mannheim and had recommended that the payment by money order was the simplest and least expensive way.

Concerning the distribution from December 15,1869 (mother's estate) there are 1483 gulden to pay to you from your mother's wealth, out of which the enclosed payment comes. Your total distribution from your mother's estate is 1983 gulden,[195] but you received 450 gulden earlier. That leaves 1483 gulden, which you receive in the money order.

The sale of the house took place in Mannheim on the 28th of June for the amount of 10,500 gulden. Of that, 5,500[196] were paid at that time and 5,000 remains standing at 5% interest. It will make it then possible to pay your children their early inheritance without reduction. When the matter is fully completed, it will then show whether I can still give something more. I am not divesting (stripping) myself in that the income is here, but with 78 years in age, a person cannot achieve much.

---

193 This letter was in the possession of Patsy Kothmann Ziriax.

194 Erderich is the older spelling of Erdrich. The author's linkage to Franz Kettner is through the Erdrich family. Her maiden name is Erdrich. See photograph of Leopold Erdrich in Fig. 37.

195 The difference between 1983 (Franz total inheritance) and the sum of 450 and 1483 is 50 gulden. This was probably exchange fees.

196 The number 5 is only partially legible, but it is consistent with the other reported amounts.

The inheritance will amount to 16,000 gulden and now I am finished with this large task. Erderich went 12 times to Mannheim. I also went at the end of March and got diarrhea and stomach pains and had to spend a day with Ameli Wurms, who is still the Ritter innkeeper. After that I had no enthusiasm to return. It took Erderich 3 days for the sale and it required another 2 days until everything was finished.

I have suffered for a year with the eyes. The left eye is totally covered with a cataract (gray star). The right is all reddened but still good. Also, after the death of your mother, I have had another hernia. I was not able to prevent it by careful wearing of a truss and now it cannot be done. It does not cause me a lot of pain, however. Other than these problems, I am healthy.

It is, and remains for me, a sad and boring life. Your mother is in my thoughts every day. I no longer have her and so patience is necessary and one must go forward in his destiny. There is no more desire to work. I have had a housekeeper now for about one year. She is 32 years old and can cook well. Other than a pig, chickens, a (Doberman) pinscher, I do not have anything living and only plant the garden.

Eight days ago we had a large quartering (stay in private homes) of the Wuerttemberg and Baden armies that came from France.[197] They were received in a friendly way and were well taken care of. I had last time 8 men, very rude citizens. They had suffered much and had great losses.

I received a disgraceful letter from Ahrens Schifbauer on behalf of my brother's daughter to whom an inheritance was left because she inherited so little. In the general letter is a small printed note enclosed concerning the Indians. Give me your advice about this in your next letter.

This year does not turn out totally favorable. It has been too cold and too wet. There was no fruit. The grapevines were fine and had begun to bloom but there were only 4 warm days and now there is very [little][198] wine.

The formerly wealthy king has become a poor man through his hubris; in contrast, Emil von Schauenburg has become princely richer and an important figure.

Things go well (orderly) with Franz Kissel in Zurich, as well as with Erderich here. The war caused a small interruption but now things go well again. The family of Nicolai is also healthy.

I was in Karlsruhe at noon for the entrance of our large troops; this [was] a fine parade to see the badly burned, thin, but lively troops. The (flower) wreaths flew like snowflakes on them. The other day they were all served wine, bread, eggs, meats, etc., on the shooting ground. All the officers, hunters of the Werther commandos, took part.

Because your acquaintances are fewer and have scattered, I can write you very little. Old Laura Schrempp still lives, is 8[0] years old, poor, and is cared for by her

---

197 Return from the French-German war. Frieden von Frankfurt a. M. am 10.05.1871.

198 Brackets were added to indicate that the script is unclear.

grandson who also has his father Max and mother to [feed]. I have doubts whether this can continue.

In your next letter which should come immediately after the arrival of the money order, tell me the news about the conditions in Texas and about your son Julius.

We are truly living very expensively. Mutton is 16 kronnen, veal 16, beef 14, oxen meat 21, venison 22, a rabbit 1 gulden 36. Daily wages also rise in proportion. The death rate is high and pleasure-seeking and laziness strong; therefore, also, so many young citizens slide into poverty and die early.

Greetings from me to your wife and children, as well as from Erderich.

Live well, your father

Kettner

**Fig. 44. Present day Oberkirch.** The Ruine Schauenburg (ruins of Schauenburg Castle) overlooks the city and the Rhine valley. The photograph was obtained and reproduced from the Badenpage web site (www.badenpage.de) with their kind permission.

**Abb. 44. Heutiges Oberkirch**. Die Ruine Schauenburg (Reste der Schauenburg) oberhalb der Stadt und des Rheintales. Die Fotografie wurde entnommen und mit freundlicher Genehmigung reproduziert von der Badenpage Webseite (www.badenpage.de)

## Brief 25 (2. Juli 1871) von Dr. Franz Lambert Kettner aus Oberkirch an seinen Sohn Franz Kettner in Texas[199]

Oberkirch, den 2. Juli 1871

Lieber Franz!

Endlich kann ich Deinem Wunsche entsprechen und kann Dir hiermit einen Wechsel von sechshundertundfünf Dolar 75 cents auf ein Neuyorker Haus übersenden, welches Kaufmann Erderich[200] mir in Karlsruhe besorgt hat. Gebe mir bei Eingang desselben sogleich Nachricht.

Kaufmann Erderich, Marie Kissel ihr Mann, hat mir meine ganze Erbsache in Mannheim besorgt und hat die Bezahlung durch Wechsel als die einfachste und wohlfeilste Art anerkannt.

Laut Teilung vom 15. Dezember 1869 habe ich Dir an mütterlichem Vermögen zu bezahlen 1483 Gulden, worauf der anliegende Wechsel lautet. Nach der Teilung hast Du 1983 Gulden[201] zu fordern, werden Dir aber als Vorempfang von 900 Gulden, 450 Gulden abgezogen, bleiben 1483 Gulden, welche Du in Wechsel erhältst.

Der Hausverkauf in Mannheim hat am 28. Juni um die Summe von 10,500 Gulden stattgefunden, wovon 5500[202] sogleich bezahlt wurden, 5000 bleiben zu 5% stehen. Es wurde daher möglich, Euch Kinder euern Voraus ohne Beeinträchtigung zahlen zu können. Wann die Sache vollends geordnet ist, wird es sich zeigen, ob ich noch etwas weiter geben kann. Entblößen tue ich mich nicht, indem der Verdienst dahin ist, denn mit 78 Jahren kann man nicht mehr viel leisten.

Die Erbschaft wird sich auf 16.000 Gulden belaufen und erst bin ich mit große Lasten fertig geworden. Erderich war bei 12mal in Mannheim, auch ich von Ende März und bekam Durchfall und Magenweh und mußte ein Tag bei Ameli Würms, so geizige Ritterwirthin[203] bleiben, habe daher keine Lust mehr bekommen, dahin zu gehen. Erderich hat zu dem Verkauf 3 Tag gebraucht und erfordert noch 2 Tag bis alles fertig ist.

Seit einem Jahr leide ich an den Augen. Am linken ist der graue Star vollkommen ausgebildet. Das rechte ist alles gerötet, aber noch gut. Auch habe ich nach dem Tode der Mutter ein weiteres Gebrechen bekommen, welches ich durch

---

[199] Original des Briefes befindet sich im Besitz von Patsy Kothmann Ziriax, Mason, Texas.

[200] Erderich ist eine veraltete Schreib- und Sprechweise von Erdrich, der Familie von Ilse Wurster, geb. Erdrich.

[201] Wenn man rückwärts rechnet 1483Gulden+ 450 Gulden = 1933 Gulden plus vermutlich 50 Gulden Kosten/Wechselgebühren, die Dr. Franz Lambert Kettner nicht erwähnt = 1983 Gulden. Hier ist ein Zusammenhang mit Franz Kettner Brief 22 vom 4. Juni 1871 herzustellen.

[202] Die Ziffer 5 an zweiter Stelle ist eher erraten als leserlich. Aber nur so stimmt die Rückwärtsrechnung.

[203] Teilweise unleserlich oder Schreibfehler

vorsorgliches Legen eines Bruchbandes nicht verhüten und es jetzt nicht .....[204] kann. Es macht mir aber keine großen Beschwerden. Außer diesen Leiden bin ich gesund.

Es ist und bleibt für mich ein trauriges langweiliges Leben. Die Mutter ist alle Tag in Gedanken bei mir, kann sie nicht mehr habhaft werden und somit ist Geduld notwendig und in sein Schicksal sich zu fügen. Arbeitslust zu haben und geht nicht mehr. Ich habe eine Haushälterin, 1 Jahr erst und rundlich. Dieselbe ist 32 Jahre und kann gut kochen. Außer einem Schwein und Hühnern ein ..... Pinscher, habe ich nicht lebendes und pflanze nur den Garten.

Vor 8 Tagen haben wir starke Einquartierungen von Württemberger und Badische Armee, die aus Frankreich kommen.[205] Dieselben sind freundlich empfangen und gut bewirtet worden. Ich habe letztmal 8 Mann gehabt, sehr grobe Bürger, die auch ordentlich viel zu leiden hatten und starken Verlusten sich ergaben.

Ich habe einen Schandbrief von meines Bruders Tochter namens Ahrens Schifbauer erhalten, welcher die Erbschaft veranlaßt hatte, weil dieselbe ein wenig geerbt haben. In dem gen. Brief ist anliegendes gedrucktes Zettelchen gelegen, die Indianer betreffend. Gebe mir im nächsten Brief hierüber Auskunft.

Das diesjähr. Jahr verläuft nicht ganz günstig. Wir haben zu kalt und zu naß. Obst keines. Reben schön, fingen aber erst an zu blühen, nur 4 Tag warm und schon gibt es wenig[206] Wein.

Der ehemals reiche König[207] ist durch Übermut ein armer Mann geworden, dagegen Emil v. Schauenburg ein äußerst fürstlicher reicher und Mustermann.

Bei Franz Kissel in Zürich geht es ordentlich, ebenso auch bei Erderich hier. Der Krieg hat eine kleine Stockung veranlaßt, geht jetzt aber wieder gut. Familie Nicolai ist auch gesund.

Ich war mittags in Karlsruhe beim Einzug unserer großen Truppen, dies [war][208] ein schöner Zug. Die schwer verbrannte[n], magere[n], aber frisch[en] Truppen zu sehen. Wie Schneeflocken flogen die Kränze auf diese. Den andern Tag wurden diese auf dem Schießplatz mit Wein, Brot, Eier und Fleisch etc. bewirtet, wo alle Offiziere, Jäger des Kommandos von Werther teilnahmen.

Da Deine Kameraden sich vermindert und verstreut haben, so kann ich Dir wenig schreiben. Die alte Laura Schrempp lebt auch noch, ist 8[0] Jahre alt, ist arm und wird von ihrem Enkel ernährt, welcher sein Vater Max und Mutter zu ernähren hat, ob er ferner als zu....[209] es fortführen kann, bezweifle ich.

---

204 Unleserlich.

205 Rückkehr nach Ende des deutsch-französischen Krieges. Frieden von Frankfurt a.M. am 10.05.1871.

206 Die Fotokopie des Briefes schneidet hier nach dem zweiten Buchstaben ab. Das Wort "wenig" wurde aus dem Sinnzusammenhang ergänzt.

207 Welcher König?

208 Text in eckigen Klammern wurde ergänzt.

209 Unleserlich

In Deinem nächsten Brief, der bei Empfang des Wechsel[s] sogleich zu geschehen hat, gebe mir auch Nachricht über die Zustände in Texas und von Deinem Sohn Julius.

Wir leben wirklich sehr teuer. Hammelfl. 16 Kr., Kalbfleisch 16, Rindfleisch 14, Ochsenfleisch 21, Rehfleisch 22, ein Haas 1 Gulden 36. Im Verfällnis stehen auch die Taglöhne. Der Tod ist groß und Genußsucht und Faulheit stark, weswegen auch so viel junge Bürger in Armut geraten und frühzeitig sterben.

Grüße mir Deine Frau und Kinder, ebenso auch von Erderich.

Lebet wohl Dein Vater

Kettner

# Letter / Brief 26

### Letter 26 (August 22, 1871) from Francis Kettner at Foley's Crossing to his Father

Dear Father,

I received your letter with the money order from New York correctly and I hope that you have received my letter during this time.

The Indian adventure with my son Louis occurred as described and you will have found the complete details in my letters. However, during this time the Indians have stolen two horses from me. I believe that I shot one in the fight with Louis; the Indians are vengeful and so I will now change my living place.

I have sold my cattle for a thousand dollars with the exception of the 10 best milk cows. I will bring my swine and sheep with me to the new place. On my new farm are very fine buildings, next to a garden that is irrigated by a spring.

I have at hand (an account) with 1000 dollars at 10 percent interest until I begin with a large sheep raising that, when the Indians are finally driven away, will increase. The Indians here are the same kind of guests that the Arabs in their time were in Algiers. They are here in a moment and then again disappear.

Now it seems serious that a southern railway to California will be built that crosses our region. Through this, Texas will become a prosperous state.

I have already written you that I am no longer the Assistant Assessor. My only job now as Inspector of Cattle and Hides (inspector of all the cattle and raw hides that are shipped out of the county) is a valuable position. I earned 300 dollars in fees during the month of May. When I have something to inspect, I make from 10 to 30 dollars a day. You wrote me in your last letter that you set aside 1000 gulden for financial difficulties for Franz Kissel. Does that amount to 1000 gulden from his legal portion (inheritance)?

It would be desirable for me if you would send me the discussed (inheritance) papers or at least a written form of your and mother's last wills. I find myself charged with 350 guldens, but nothing that says for what it was charged. You know that in the last 20 years that I have received no support, and only once, when I was married,

I had asked you. But this was rejected, as Ida's children had to be raised and supported, because of the wasteful use of their mother's fortune by their father.

I mention this not because the money order is too small. I have written you in my last letter that you need not sell the house on my account and that I can do without anything as long as you need the interest. I only want to know if I am the only one against whom something was charged. And then it fell upon me that Franz Kissel was given 1000 gulden --------,[210] which you honored, and that his share of the inheritance, after my figuring, could not possibly cover this amount.

My wife, through a doctor Schilling, whose father was notary in Offenburg, is relieved from her stomach problems. It was the too slow digesting of the stomach.

I hope that you will not misunderstand the above meaning of the inheritance situation. For example, I could die one day and my wife and children would have no idea what they could expect from my side (of the family) eventually. In addition, it would be necessary for you to make another will because your inheritance relationships would have changed. That is because I can make no claim on material goods.

The nephew of General Werder, Hans von Werder, is a good friend of mine and lives in Mason.

The festivities of the return of the troops are at last over, I hope, and after the enthusiasm has somewhat quieted down, that quiet reason will again take hold and that Germany will ask itself what progress have we reached through this war. Probably something quite meaningless. When a National Assembly with so little (financial?)[211] position authorizes an endowment of 4 million for generals who were never pulled out of their carriers, but only looked after themselves and, in contrast, so little for the soldiers, then a person cannot assume that these lords represent a people's government. Our press chastises this very strongly. Very generous it was that these lord generals did not accept this endowment.

I will describe to you in detail how I am set up and how I live on my new place (later). I think that Louis will soon be strong enough to work about 20 acres of field. I have a press coming in order to press sugarcane for syrup. It is out of iron and is set in motion by a horse. This cost me 80 dollars.

Enclosed is a successful picture of Louis and Ida. Louis has made a name for himself in this region due to his bravery.

In the hope that this letter finds you still in good health, we all greet you, wife and children

Your son
Francis Kettner

[210] Letter is partially destroyed.
[211] Letter is partially destroyed.

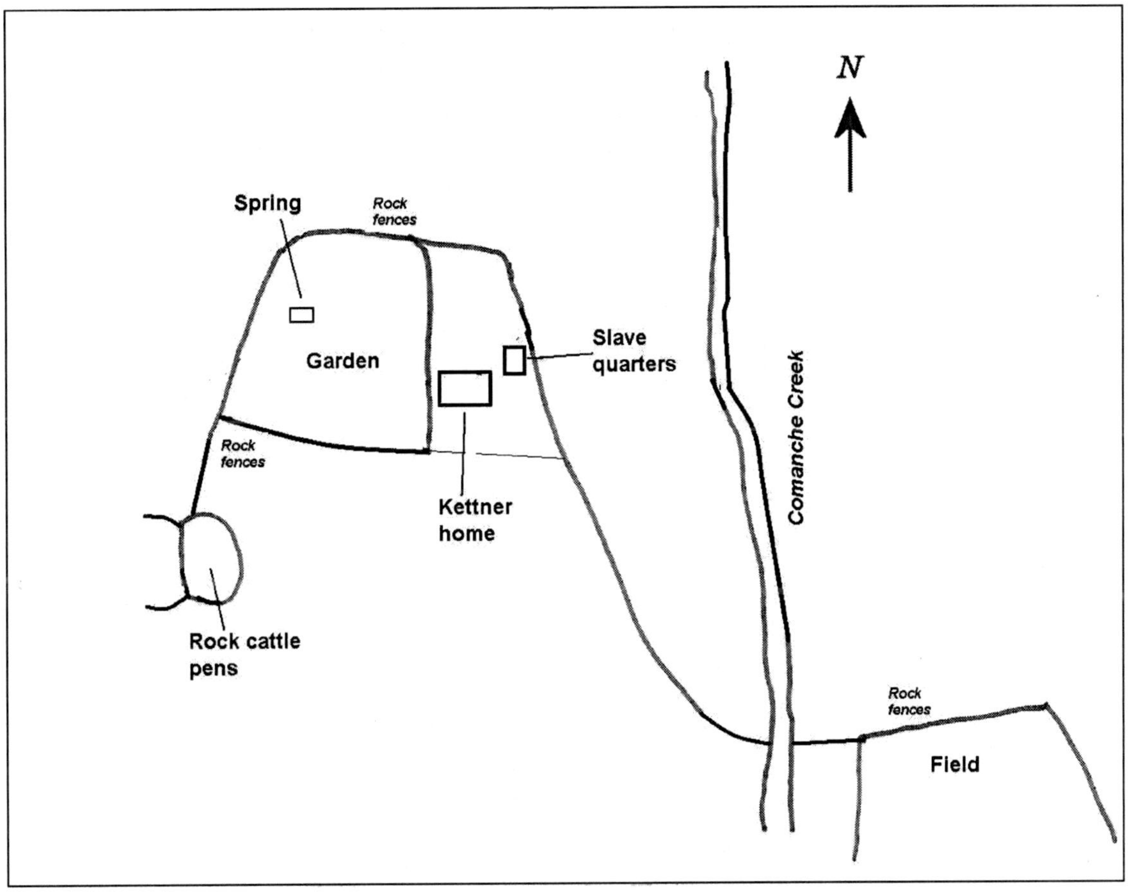


**Fig. 45. Diagram of the McSween Place.**

**Abb. 45. Diagramm des McSween Place.**

**Fig. 46. Spring.** Presently, the spring and garden are pretty much unchanged. The garden area was composed mainly of the field in the photograph below the spring . The far white building is the Kettner home and the slave quarters are behind it. The rock cow pens are right of the spring. Remnants of the rock fence enclosing the garden are still visible. According to Charles A. Kettner, the spring was used to water this vegetable garden area through the 1970s. The original stone and mortar basin was rebuilt by his father Francis F. Kettner (Franz's namesake and grandson) around 1955; however, it is almost identical to the original basin in size and shape. He also recalls using the spring as a swimming pool while growing up, much the same as many others had done.

**Abb. 46. Quelle.** Heutzutage sind die Quelle und der Garten noch ziemlich unverändert. Die Gartenfläche bestand hauptsächlich aus dem Feld, das auf dem Foto unterhalb der Quelle liegt. Das Gebäude im Hintergrund ist das Kettner Haus und das Sklavenquartier liegt dahinter. Die steinernen Kuhpferche befinden sich rechts von der Quelle. Überreste der steinernen Garteneinfassung sind immer noch sichtbar. Nach Aussage von Charles A. Kettner wurde die Quelle noch bis in die 1970er Jahre zum Bewässern des Gemüsegartens genutzt. Das Originalbassin aus Stein und Mörtel wurde von seinem Vater Frances F. Kettner (Namensvetter von Franz und sein Enkel) um 1955 erneuert, jedoch ist es ziemlich identisch mit dem Originalbassin, sowohl in Größe als auch Form. Er erinnert sich noch daran, dass er als Heranwachsender die Quelle als Schwimmbecken genutzt hat, ähnlich wie viele andere auch.

## Brief 26 (22. August 1871) von Franz Kettner aus Foley's Crossing an seinen Vater

Lieber Vater.

Ihren Brief, nebst Wechsel auf New York habe ich richtig erhalten, und ich hoffe, Sie werden während dieser Zeit, meinen Brief erhalten haben.

Das Indianerabenteuer mit meinem Sohn Louis hat seine Richtigkeit und Sie werden in meinem Briefe die näheren Details gefunden haben. Die Indianer haben während dieser Zeit mir abermals zwei Pferde gestohlen, und da ich glaube, daß ich in dem Gefecht mit Louis einen geschossen habe, die Indianer äußerst rachsüchtig sind, so werde jetzt meinen Wohnsitz ändern.

Mein Vieh habe ich mit Ausnahme der 10 besten Milchkühe für tausend Dollars verkauft. Meine Schweine und Schafe werde ich an den neuen Platz mitnehmen. Auf meiner neuen Farm sind sehr schöne Gebäudlichkeiten, nebst einem Garten, der von einer Quelle bewässert wird.

Ich habe vor der Hand 1000 Dollars auf Zinsen zu 10 Prozent, bis ich mit großer Schafzucht beginnen werde; welche, wenn die Indianer einmal beseitigt sind, hier in Aufschwung kommen wird. Die Indianer sind hier gerade solche Gäste als seiner Zeit die Araber in Algier. Auf einmal sind Sie dagewesen und auch wieder verschwunden. Allein es scheint jetzt Ernst damit gemacht zu werden, namentlich durch den Bau der südlichen Eisenbahn nach Kalifornien, welche unsere Gegend berührt. Dadurch wird Texas ein wohlhabender Staat werden.

Daß ich nicht mehr Assissant Assessor bin, habe ich Ihnen früher schon geschrieben. Allein meine jetzige Stellung als Inspector of Cattle and Hides (Inspektor von allem Vieh und Rohhäute, welche aus dem County gehen) ist eine wertvollere Stellung. Ich habe während des Monats Mai 300 Dollars verdient an Gebühren. Wenn ich etwas zu inspizieren habe, so mache von 10 bis zu 30 Dollars per Tag. Sie schrieben mir in Ihrem vorletzten Briefe, daß Sie durch Franz Kissel, wegen 1000 Gulden in Verlegenheit gesetzt wurden. Beträgt denn der Pflichtteil desselben 1000 Gulden? –

Es wäre doch wünschenswert für mich, wenn Sie mir die besagten Teilungspapiere zuschicken würden, oder wenigstens eine Abschrift Ihrer und der Mutter letzten Willens. Ich finde mir 350 Gulden angerechnet, aber nichts gesagt für was berechnet. Sie wissen, daß ich in den letzten zwanzig Jahren keine Unterstützung erhalten, und bloß einmal, als ich mich verheiratete, Sie um eine angegangen habe. Welches mir aber abgeschlagen wurde, da der Ida Kinder, welche durch die Liederlichkeit ihres Vaters um ihr mütterliches Vermögen gebracht wurden, erzogen werden mußten.

Ich erwähne dies nicht deshalb, daß mir der Wechsel zu klein ist, ich habe Ihnen in meinem letzten Brief geschrieben, daß Sie meinethalben das Haus nicht zu verkaufen brauchen, und daß ich auf alles verzichte, so lange Sie die Zinsen zu gebrauchen gedenken. Allein ich möchte doch wissen, ob ich der einzige bin, dem etwas angerechnet wird. Und dann kam es mir auffallend vor, daß Franz Kissel 1000

Gulden auf .....[212] abgab, welche Sie honorierten, da doch dessen Pflichtteil, nach meinem berechnet, unmöglich diese Summe betragen kann.

Meine Frau ist durch einen Arzt, namens Schilling, dessen Vater war Notar in Offenburg, von ihrem Magenübel so ziemlich hergestellt worden. Es war zu langsame Verdauung des Magens.

Ich hoffe, daß Sie die obige Andeutung der Vermögensverhältnisse, nicht mißverstehen. Ich könnte zum Beispiel eines Tages sterben, meine Frau und Kinder hätten gar keine Idee, was sie einmal von meiner Seite zu erwarten hätten. Außerdem wird es nötig sein, da sich Ihre Vermögensverhältnisse geändert haben, daß Sie ein anderes Testament machen. Da ich auf Liegenschaften keinen Anspruch machen kann.

Der Neffe des Generals von Werder, Hans von Werder, ist ein intimer Bekannter von mir und wohnt in Mason.

Die Einzugsfeierlichkeiten sind, hoffe ich, endlich vorbei, und nach dem der Enthusiasmus sich etwas verdunstet hat, wird auch die ruhige Vernunft wieder an das Ruder kommen und Deutschland wird sich fragen, was haben wir für einen Fortschritt durch diesen Krieg erzielt. Wahrscheinlich einen sehr unbedeutenden. Denn wenn eine Nationalversammlung mit so wenig ...position[213] 4 Millionen für Dotationen bewilligt, für Generäle, welche nicht aus ihrer Karriere herausgerissen wurden, sondern sich verbesserten, und im Verhältnis so wenig für Soldaten (Landwehr) so [kann] man nicht annehmen, daß diese Herren eine Volksregierung repräsentieren. Unsere Presse geißelt dies sehr stark. Sehr generös war, daß diese Herren Generale diese Dotation nicht annahmen.

So wie ich auf meinem neuen Platze wohne, und einigermaßen eingerichtet bin, werde ich Ihnen denselben ganz genau beschreiben. Ich werde, da Louis jetzt bald kräftig genug ist, circa 20 Acre zu Feld machen. Eine Presse, um Zuckerrohr für Sirup zu bereiten, habe ich mir kommen lassen. Sie ist aus Eisen und wird von einem Pferd in Bewegung gesetzt. Dieselbe kostet mich an 80 Dollars.

Anbei erhalten Sie ein gelungenes Bildnis von Louis und Ida. Louis hat sich durch seine Tapferkeit einen Namen in dieser Gegend erworben.

In der Hoffnung, daß Sie dieser Brief noch bei guter Gesundheit trifft, grüßen wir Sie alle, Frau und Kinder

Ihr Sohn

Francis Kettner

[212] Brief teilweise zerstört.

[213] Brief teilweise zerstört.

# Letter / Brief 27

### Letter 27 (December 24, 1871[214]) from Francis Kettner at the McSween Place[215] (Mason County, Texas) to his Father

Dear Father

I received your last letter with the inheritance documents and the confusion in the matter is now cleared up for me. In regard to my illness of that time which you probably noticed, I can only assure you that in my whole life, I will not forget this time. First a high fever, then I fell into the hands of an American quack healer who totally ruined me with a too strong a dose of calomel.[216] And then immediately the cold fever which I had for 9 months without treatment. This was the probable illness. So let us just forget about these matters.

I have been living on my new lands for about 3 months, have good buildings, mostly stone houses, and am occupying myself now with a stone fence for the field of 30 acres.[217] I have built three hundred feet so far myself with the help of a Mr. Hans von Werder, the cousin of our famous general, who was earlier also a lieutenant in the Prussian army. The other I have given out in contract.

In addition, I have a garden quite near the house which I irrigate with a spring. You have no idea what sort of harvest a person in this land can achieve with irrigation since we hardly have a winter here. I have two large mules to work the land that

---

[214] This author assumes that this letter was written on Christmas Eve, 1871. The original letter is dated January 18, 1872, but the date is in a handwriting different than Franz's. It could have been the date that the letter was received in Oberkirch.

[215] The McSween Place is located on the banks of Comanche Creek approximately 6 miles southwest of the town of Mason. Dr. John McSween, an early settler and founder of Mason County, obtained this property by a land grant from the state of Texas Nov. 21, 1857. He sold it to Henry and Cathrine Morris Feb. 2, 1870 and they in turn sold it to Francis Kettner Sept. 2, 1871. The source of this information are the original deeds in possession of Charles A. Kettner (a great-grandson of Franz.)

[216] Mercuric chloride, an old medical remedy used primarily as a laxative.

[217] This field is still in cultivation and remnants of the rock fence remain.

cost me 230 dollars in addition to two horses. Louis had gathered up nuts[218] from the new place and from this bought himself a beloved little horse of which he is very proud, because it is very quick.

We have not yet been troubled on this land by Indians. I simply keep the mules in the stall. The horses run free and live from the grass.

My wife has become fairly cured from her stomach spasms through Doctor Schilling from Offenburg. That was caused by too slow digestion in the stomach. Other than that we are all healthy. Our little boy Karl now is 5 years old.

In addition to the peach trees which were already in the garden, I will plant apple trees, plums, and pears. It appears that the worth of Texas is climbing since it already has begun to build a railroad. The raw land (value) goes higher. When the southern railroad, which goes through Texas to California, connects us with the northern (line), the Indian attacks and murders will stop. Then western Texas will be the healthiest and best part for living. Competent workers and people with small capital can make a living here easier than anywhere else.

Hans von Werder, who ten years earlier went from here to South America, thanks our Creator that he, even with nothing, is again in Texas. There was no money used in trade there, only exchanges in goods. It took him many years to get enough money together simply to be able to travel back to Texas. You can advise anyone who will work to come to Texas. We need more immigrants.

Louis is home for this winter and helps me with the work. This summer he will return again to school. The girls Ida and Elise are beautiful, healthy children and read and write the German language. I have not yet had them start English. This evening the Christmas tree will be lighted and Christmas presents given out. The Germans keep their customs in foreign lands and the Americans follow many of them, such as drinking beer. There are very many varieties of beer in bottles imported from Germany such as Bremer and Wiener beer and Rhein wine.

My family is always healthy. The children do not know what illness is.

Although I purchased it quite cheaply, because of improvements on the houses and stone fences, my new farm cost over 1,500 dollars, but it is now worth 2,000 dollars. The 600 dollars from my blessed mother I have out for interest at 10 percent with good security. I will leave this in interest and will not use it for the farm.

My new, lighter horse wagon with spring-mounted seats and new tack, along with the two large mules, cost me 400 dollars, that is to say, a thousand gulden. The mules handle work better and are easier to keep in feed and live to be 50 years old. They are outstanding for plowing. It is truly a pleasure for me to plow with good animals.

The children are gradually becoming restless because it has become evening and they wait for the little Christ Child. Therefore, I need to close.

---

[218] The nuts that Franz mentions are, without a doubt, pecans. Even today they are very plentiful along the banks of Comanche Creek.

In the hope that you still find some pleasure in life at your age and that you keep good enough health to have an enjoyment of life, I wish you a good new year.

All of us, wife as well as children, greet you many times. Louis will write you an extra letter next time, because yesterday, accompanied by an older man, he rode out to hunt and has just now returned home.

In the hope that these lines find you in good health, I love you

Your loving son

Francis Kettner

**Fig. 47. Live Oak Tree.** This is the present day southern view from the Kettner home. The tree has changed very little since 1871 according to family lore.

**Abb. 47. Lebende Eiche**. Dies ist heutzutage der südliche Blick vom Kettner Haus. Der Baum hat sich der Familienerzählung nach sehr wenig verändert seit 1871.

## Brief 27 (24. Dezember 1871[219]) von Franz Kettner vom McSween Place in Mason County/Texas an seinen Vater

Lieber Vater

Ihren letzten Brief, mit den Teilungsdokumenten habe ich richtig erhalten und das Unklare in der Sache ist mir klar geworden. Was meine damalige Krankheit anbelangt, welche Sie mit angeblich bemerkten, so kann ich Ihnen bloß versichern, daß ich in meinem ganzen Leben diese Zeit nicht vergessen werde. Zuerst das hitzige Fieber, dabei in die Hände eines amerikanischen Quacksalbers gefallen, welcher mich durch zu starke Dosis Kalomel[220] total ruinierte. Und dann gleich das kalte Fieber, welches ich 9 Monate behielt, ohne Pflege. Das war die angebliche Krankheit. Doch lassen Sie uns diese Sache übergehen.

Ich wohne seit ungefähr 3 Monaten auf meinem neuen Lande, bin gut eingerichtet, beinahe alles Steinhäuser, und beschäftige mich im Augenblick mit Steinfenz für das Feld von 30 Acres. Dreihundert Schritte habe ich bis jetzt selbst gemacht mit Hilfe eines Herrn Hans von Werder, Cousin unseres berühmten Generals, früher auch Leutnant in der Preußischen Armee. Das andere habe ich in Kontrakt gegeben.

Außerdem habe einen Garten dicht beim Hause, welchen ich mit einer Quelle bewässere. Sie haben keine Idee, welche Ernten man in diesem Lande mit Bewässerung erzielen kann, da wir beinahe keinen Winter haben. Ich habe zur Bearbeitung des Landes zwei große Maultiere, welche mich 230 Dollars kosteten, außerdem zwei Pferde. Louis hat auf dem neuen Platze Nüsse gesammelt, und dafür sich ein allerliebstes kleines Pferd gekauft, auf welches er, da es sehr flink ist, ungeheure Stücke hält.

Von Indianer sind wir auf diesem Platze noch nicht belästigt worden. Ich halte bloß die Maultiere im Stalle. Die Pferde laufen frei, und leben von Gras.

Meine Frau ist durch Doktor Schilling von Offenburg so ziemlich von ihrem Magenkrampf kuriert worden. Derselbe entstand durch zu langsame Verdauung des Magens. Sonst sind wir alle gesund. Unser kleiner Junge Karl geht jetzt ins 5. Jahr.

Ich werde außer Pfirsichbäumen, welche bereits in dem Garten gestanden haben, Apfelbäume, Pflaumen und Birnen pflanzen. Texas scheint jetzt, da bereits angefangen ist, an Eisenbahnen zu bauen, im Werte zu steigen. Das rohe Land geht in die Höhe. Wenn die südliche Eisenbahn, welche durch Texas nach Kalifornien geht, uns mit dem Norden verbindet, so hören die Indianerräubereien und Mordtaten auf. Dann ist das westliche Texas der gesündeste und beste Teil zum Wohnen. Tüchtige Arbeiter und Leute mit geringem Kapital können leichter als sonstwo ihr Leben machen.

Hans von Werder, welcher vor zehn Jahren von hier nach Zentralamerika ging, dankt unsrem Schöpfer, daß er, wenn auch mit nichts, doch wieder in Texas ist. Denn da ist kein Geld im Verkehr, sondern bloß Tauschhandel. Es kostete ihn viele

---

[219] Ort und Datum nach Vermutung der Autorin, 18. Januar 72 von fremder Hand hinzugefügt, wahrscheinlich Empfangsdatum.

[220] Quecksilberchlorid. Früher angewendet als Entwässerungsmittel und Abführmittel.

Jahre, um soviel Geld zusammen zu bringen, um bloß wieder nach Texas reisen zu können. Sie können jedem, der arbeiten will, anraten, nach Texas zu kommen. Denn wir haben Einwanderung nötig.

Louis ist diesen Winter zu Hause und hilft mit zu arbeiten. Diesen Sommer kommt er wieder in die Schule. Die Mädchen Ida und Elise sind hübsche gesunde Kinder, lesen und schreiben die deutsche Sprache. Im Englischen habe ich noch keinen Anfang machen lassen. Heute abend wird der Christbaum den Kindern angezündet und beschert. Die Deutschen behalten ihre Sitten im Auslande bei, und die Amerikaner machen manches nach, namentlich das Biertrinken. Es werden von Deutschland sehr viele Sorten Bier auf Flaschen importiert. Namentlich Bremer und Wiener Biere und Rheinwein.

Meine Familie ist immer wohl. Namentlich die Kinder wissen nicht was Kranksein heißt.

Meine neue Farm kostet mich doch, obgleich ich sehr billig gekauft habe, durch Verbesserungen an den Häusern und Steinfenzen über Fünfzehnhundert Dollars, ist aber dann auch 2000 wert. Die 600 Dollars von der Mutter selig, habe ich auf Interessen zu 10 Prozent mit guter Sicherheit. Dieses lasse ich auf Interessen und werde es nicht auf die Farm verwenden.

Mein neuer leichter Pferdewagen mit Springfeder-Sitzen und neuem Geschirr, nebst den beiden großen Maultieren, kostet mich 400 Dollars, sage tausend Gulden. Die Maultiere halten Arbeit besser aus, sind leichter im Futter zu halten und werden 50 Jahre alt. Sie gehen ausgezeichnet im Pflug. Es ist mir wirklich ein Vergnügen, mit guten Tieren zu pflügen.

Die Kinder werden allmählich unruhig, da es Abend wird und das Christkindchen erwartet wird. Deshalb muß ich schließen.

In der Hoffnung, daß Sie in Ihrem Alter noch einigen Geschmack am Leben finden und Ihre Gesundheit dermaßen sich erhält, daß Sie Genuß am Leben haben, wünsche Ihnen ein gutes neues Jahr.

Wir alle, Frau sowohl wie Kinder, grüßen Sie vielmals, und Louis wird Ihnen nächstens einen Extrabrief schreiben, da er gestern in Begleitung eines älteren Mannes auf die Jagd ritt und soeben erst nach Hause gekommen ist.

In der Hoffung, daß diese Zeilen Sie in guter Gesundheit antreffen, verbleibe ich Ihr

Sie liebender Sohn
Francis Kettner.

# Letter / Brief 28

## Letter 28 (July 21, 1872) from Dr. Franz Lambert Kettner in Oberkirch to Francis Kettner[221]

Dear Franz!

I received your letter without a date and take from it that all goes well with you and your family and that you, after your long stay in America, are now for the first time a working farmer and have just now begun to lend out money, which should have occurred much earlier.

Concerning my health, it is good for this age; my eyes are better, no longer painful and red. I do not have any more business; it seems that I appear too old to the people. On the other hand, I also do not want to treat patients any more and so in the long, useless, boring (times), I putter around in the garden where I have beautiful plants such as espaliered fruit.

My right eye remains somewhat better for vision and so if it continues (I can live with it).

We are having an unusual number of thunderstorms with downpours and great flooding. Despite this, the year has gone well, although it is just the middle of fall. We are having hot days of 22 to 27 degrees in the shade. Things are expensive – 22 kreuzer for 1 pound of oxen meat, beef 20, veal 18, pork 20, 7 eggs for 12 kr., butter 35. The fruit is still the cheapest.

Six weeks ago, Nicolai, with his wife who is very sick, wanted to spend 14 days with me for a recovery period. I had barely received the news when Kissel's wife came with a 3-year old child. They wanted to get away from scarlet fever, from which 8 days earlier, they had lost two children, one and a half and five years old. The child was here three days and then also came down with scarlet fever, so she remained here with her mother until yesterday. Since she was healthy, they traveled back to Zurich. According to talk, Kissel is doing fine. The two brothers-in-law have a

[221] The original letter is in the possession of Patsy Kothmann Ziriax.

business together, employ two traveling salesmen and work in total with 6 in a small linen or notions shop.

My house was as if quarantined. I did not go to the Erderich's and he could not come to my house in order to avoid spreading the disease.

Also, Klara Nicolai was not able to make her usual summer visit, but had to wait until September until the house was totally cleaned.

------ has been here for 14 days. I have not yet spoken to him. What I hear is that he has a horrible, angry wife and a new baby and will probably no longer go to Texas because he still has an inheritance share remaining here. He is supposed to look pretty worn out.

I have learned from ----when I spoke to him that he lived and worked as ---. He told me that among you (in America) neither diligence nor saving is much valued. From that also stems your fortune and prosperity. Whether he himself returns to Texas, he does not yet know. He still has holdings here.

Greetings to all of you

Your father Kettner

28 degrees warm in the shade.

## Brief 28 (21. Juli 1872) von Dr. Franz Lambert Kettner aus Oberkirch an seinen Sohn Franz Kettner in Texas[222]

Oberkirch, 21. Juli 1872

Lieber Franz!

Dein Brief ohne Datum habe ich erhalten und daraus vernommen, daß [es] Dir und Deiner Familie gut geht, und Du nach dem langen Aufenthalt in Amerika jetzt erst ein arbeitsamer Bauer wirst und jetzt erst anfängst Geld auszulehnen, was schon früher hätte geschehen sollen?

Was meine Gesundheit anbelangt, ist vermög[223] des Alters gut, meine Augen sind besser, nicht mehr schmerzhaft und nicht mehr rot. Ich habe keine Geschäften mehr, es scheint mir den Leuten zu alt zu sein. Andererseits will ich auch keine Patienten mehr behandeln und so treibe ich mich in der langen [Zeit] nutzlos langweilig mit dem Garten herum, in welchem ich schöne Pflanzen namentlich Spalierobst habe.

Mein rechtes noch etwas besseres Auge läßt auch an Sehkraft nach, wenn es auch immer noch so bleibt.[224]

Wir haben außerordentlich viel Donnerwetter mit Wolkenbrüchen und große Überschwemmungen. Dagegen wird das Jahr doch gut ausfallen, jedoch nur ein halber Herbst. Wir haben heiße Tage 22 bis 27 Grad im Schatten. Wir haben teuer, 22 kr (Kreuzer) 1 Pfund Ochsenfleisch, Rindfleisch 20, Kalbfleisch 18, Schweinefleisch 20, 7 Eier 12 kr, Butter 35. Die Früchte sind noch am billigsten.

Vor 6 Wochen wollte Nicolai mit seiner Frau auf 14 Tage zu mir zur Erholung kommen, welche sehr krank war. Kaum hatte ich die Nachricht erhalten gehabt, kam dem Kissel seine Frau mit einem 3 Jahr alten Kind. Sie wollten dem Scharlachfieber entrinnen, an welchem dieselben vor 8 Tagen 2 Kinder von 1 ½ und 5 Jahren verloren haben. Es war 3 Tag hier, so ist auch es von Scharlach befallen und blieb samt der Mutter bis gestern hier. Wo[rauf] sie gesund nach Zürich gereist sind. Nach der Sage desselben geht es ihm gut.[225] Die 2 Schwäger haben ein gemeinschaftliches Geschäft, unterhalten 2 Reisende und arbeiten im ganzen zu 6 im kleinen Weiß- oder Kurzwarengeschäft.

Mein Haus war wie abgesperrt. Ich ging nicht zu Erderich und so durfte auch derselbe nicht zu mir kommen, um die Verbreitung der Krankheit zu vermeiden.

Auch die Klara Nicolai durfte nicht ihren gewöhnlichen Sommerbesuch machen, sondern muß bis September [warten] bis das Haus ganz gereinigt ist.

..... ist seit 14 Tagen hier. Ich habe denselben noch nicht gesprochen. ..... Wie ich höre, hat er eine gräßlich böse Frau und ein neues Kind und wird wahrscheinlich

---

[222] Original des Briefes befindet sich im Besitz von Patsy Kothmann Ziriax, Mason, Texas.

[223] In Anbetracht

[224] Dr. F.L. Kettner meint wahrscheinlich, wenn es so bleibt, kann er damit leben.

[225] Dem Kaufmann Kissel

nicht mehr nach Texas gehen, indem er noch Erbesgebühr[226] hier stehen haben soll. Er soll ziemlich abgearbeitet aussehen.

Soeben habe ich erfahren von ....., den ich gesprochen habe, er wohnt und betreibt ...... Er hat mir erzählt, daß unter Euch weder Fleiß noch Sparsamkeit geherrscht habe. Daher rührt auch Dein Reichtum, Wohlhabenh[eit]. Ob derselbe wieder nach Texas gehe, weiß er noch nicht. Er hat noch Vermögen hier.

Grüße an Euch alle

Dein Vater Kettner

28 Grad warm im Schatten.

226 Einen Erbschaftsanteil

# Letter / Brief 29

### Letter 29 (December 4, 1872) Unknown Writer (probably Wuelfing Duelmen) at Sisterdale, Kendall County, Texas to Francis Kettner

Dec. 4th A.D. 1872

My good Kettner:

I received your letter from 26 November and am hurrying to answer you. I am not surprised about your experience with Morris, Eckert, Reichenau, etc. and only say to your comfort as I earlier remarked if you remember, that candidates for offices should have a thick skin; that it is their damn duty and fault and for that you also receive a good income. I wonder that you have again run for the office of inspector; I thought that your decision was then already made to give up the office. In the story with Morris about the swine, I am completely convinced that everything happened how you said. The way in which you openly drove out the swine and slaughtered them a person cannot call thievery.

The discussion with Morris over the said situation I am not capable of remembering exactly; however, I can testify over what I do remember. At any rate, Morris told you that he had given you permission to dispose of the swine which he was not in position to drive out to the stand (market) that fall.

My vacation begins the 21st of March and lasts until the 7th of April; if the court is in session during this time I can come, otherwise not. Concerning myself, I live here very satisfied with the people who treat me courteously, are friendly, and include me. From troubles and gossip, nothing has come to me up to this date. Whether I will receive payment for my service as public school teacher, the future will decide. Under the prevailing conditions, my prospects appear to be quite doubtful.

My children in the school are good and well-behaved, although I find there are no great talents among them. Only the devil knows how it is that I can get along well with the people here without difficulty, while such is not the case where I absolutely would prefer to live otherwise; that is in your region. In any case, the fault cannot fall only on me that I could not feel at home, and naturally also, not on you. I have to wait six months for the first payment from Europe, according to the received letters. My pearls are luckily lost along with the letters concerning them. I will not write anything further about what I am able to testify in regard to your trial. However, it is in any case a relief to you if other witnesses fail (to show), out of necessity. I leave no friend –

[The letter stops here and the next page is missing.][227]

---

[227] One is intrigued by the events discussed presumably by Wuelfing Duelmen. Old records indicate that Franz purchased his farm on Comanche Creek from H. Morris (see footnotes Letter 27). It is possible that a conflict arose from the disposal of hogs still on the property after the sale.

Also during this period, Franz was suspended as Cattle and Hide Inspector. Stella G. Polk (Polk 170) lists the following: "December 1869 Results of Election", Franz Kettner, Cattle & Hide Inspector; "May, 1871 Results of Election", Franz Kettner, Inspector of Hides and Animals (removed in 1872) and Wilson Hey appointed in February, 1872. Kettner reappointed in May, 1872, "September 1872 Results of Election" Francis Kettner, Inspector of Hides and Animals. David Johnson (Johnson 17) states: "On January 18, 1872, Ben Gooch, James Ranck, and W.P. Lockhart, the country treasurer, wrote to Reconstruction governor E.J. Davis claiming that Kettner was "bold and bitter" against Republicans and requested removal in order to install Wilson Hey in his place." Johnson also says that Franz's removal was successful, but he was reinstated after citizens rose to his defense. "James M. Hunter defended Franz. Hunter went on to state that the appointment of Hey was objectionable since he was also serving as Deputy County Clerk and was in the employ of B.F. Gooch & Co. in a large cattle company."

## Brief 29 (4. Dezember 1872) von Unbekannt[228] aus Sisterdale in Kendall County/Texas an Franz Kettner in Texas[229]

Sisterdale,[230] Kendall Co. Texas

Dec. 4th A.D. 1872

Mein bester Kettner!

Ihren Brief vom 26. Nov. habe ich erhalten und beeile mich, Ihnen zu antworten. Ihre Erfahrungen mit Morris, Eckert, Reichenau etc. haben mich nicht gewundert, und kann ich zu Ihrem Troste nur wie bereits früher bemerkt daran erinnern, daß Kandidaten für Ämter ein dickes Fell haben müssen, das ist ihre verdammte Pflicht und Schuldigkeit und dafür beziehen Sie ja auch nachher gute Bezahlung. Daß Sie sich wiederum um das Amt des Inspektors beworben haben, wundert mich, ich glaubte Ihr Entschluß wäre schon damals gefaßt gewesen, diese Office aufzugeben. In der Schweinegeschichte mit Morris bin ich vollkommen überzeugt, daß Alles sich so verhält, wie Sie angeben. Als Diebstahl kann man ja die Art und Weise, wie Sie die Schweine öffentlich auftrieben und schlachteten, jedenfalls nicht hinstellen.

Der Unterhaltungen mit Morris über besagten Gegenstand vermag ich mich nicht wörtlich zu erinnern, jedoch vermag ich zu bezeugen, daß nach allem, was mir erinnerlich, Morris Ihnen allerdings Erlaubnis erteilt hat, über die Schweine verfügen zu dürfen, welche er in jenem Herbste in der Range nicht aufzutreiben im Stande war.

Meine Ferien beginnen im März am 21ten und dauern bis 7ten April, wenn die Court in diese Zeit fällt, kann ich kommen, sonst nicht. Was mich anbetrifft, so lebe ich hier ganz zufrieden bei Leuten, die mich zuvorkommend, freundlich und teilnehmend behandeln. Von Stänkereien und Klatschereien ist mir bis dato noch nichts vorgekommen. Ob ich je Bezahlung für meine Dienste als Freischullehrer erhalten werde, ist der Zukunft vorbehalten zu entscheiden, unter den jetzt obwaltenden Umständen scheinen meine Aussichten sehr zweifelhafter Natur zu sein.

Meine Kinder in der Schule sind gut und wohlerzogen, wenn auch keine großen Talente sich darunter befinden. Der Teufel weiß, wie es zugeht, daß ich mich hier mit den Leuten ganz gut vertragen kann, ohne Diffikultäten[231] zu haben und solches nicht da der Fall ist, wo ich sonst unbedingt vorziehen würde zu leben, das ist in

---

[228] Vermutlich Wülfing Dülmen. In den Briefen Nr. 12, 22 und 23 schreibt Franz Kettner von Herrn Wülfing Dülmen, einem ehemaligen preußischen Artillerieoffizier. Gem. Brief 22 kommt Herr Wülfing wieder zu ihm, um seine beiden Mädchen zu unterrichten. Vielleicht handelt es sich um diesen Lehrer?

[229] Original des Briefes befindet sich im Besitz von Patsy Kothmann Ziriax, Mason, Texas.

[230] Sisterdale wurde 1847 von Nicolaus Zink gegründet, einem deutschen Freidenker. In den nächsten zwei Jahren schlossen sich ihm einige "48er" an, die nach der gescheiterten Revolution von 1848 aus Europa flohen. Quelle: *Handbook of Texas Online*, unter dem Stichwort "Sisterdale, Texas," http://www.tsha.utexas.edu/handbook/online/articles/SS/hns51.html, (Zugriff 23.10.2003).

[231] Deutsch-englisch. Schwierigkeiten

Eurer Gegend. Jedenfalls muß der Fehler nicht nur an mir gelegen haben, daß ich mich aber nicht heimisch fühlen konnte, an Ihnen natürlich auch nicht. Auf die erste Zahlung von Europa habe ich noch zufolge erhaltener Briefe 6 Monat zu warten. Meine Perlen sind glücklich verlorengegangen mit samt dem betreffenden Briefe. Über das was ich in betreff Ihres Prozesses auszusagen vermag, schreibe ich weiter Nichts, jedoch ist es für Sie jedenfalls entlastend und da Ihnen andere Zeugen fehlen, von Wichtigkeit. Ich lasse keinen Freund -

- - [der Brief bricht hier ab, die nächste Seite fehlt]

# Letter / Brief 30

### Letter 30 (December 10, 1872) from Francis Kettner at the McSween Place to his Father

Mason, December 10, 1872

Dear Father!

I received your letter from last summer and it mentioned that a letter of mine was lost.

I did not want to write you until our presidential election was over because I was very interested in this election. Indeed, I was also voted in for my office as inspector and I had two opponents against me, an American and a German. I was voted in again for a two-year term and had three votes more than both of my opponents combined. You can see from that how I stand in my county.

I had a good harvest last year with approximately 300 bushels of corn and we made 200 gallons of syrup. We sold 150 gallons and kept 50 gallons for our household use. Now I am eager to bring more land under stone fencing with (the help) of a black worker and, also, to enlarge my garden, but all with a good stone fence.

I believe my farm is one of the best. Last summer I bought 130 more sheep for my small herd so that now I can sell wool for 300 dollars each spring. Likewise, I have a very good swine stock and fine, pure (bred) swine. We raised about 100 head last summer. And every evening when the swine were called for feeding time, you could see them running from all directions to the farm.

Louis, Ida, and Elise ride every morning to school and come home each evening. I keep two horses just for school because the school is over a half hour away. Elise is ten years old but larger and heavier than Ida. She weighs over 100 pounds and is almost grown up. At 13 years old, here in this country, the girls are almost grown up.

I have close neighbors where I now live. At the moment, I am in negotiations to buy 640 acres of land that borders on mine because I have the plan to run the sheep business in a larger number.

You remarked in your last letter that it seems as if I now save more. It is in America exactly as in Germany, without funds one cannot make much. And I can say that for the first time in the last two years, I have some money in my hand in order to progress forward faster. The raising of children costs a lot here and I am just beginning to have some help from Louis. At any rate, people here have no worries over food; everyone has enough to eat.

I have a spring in my garden and I have it enclosed with a stone wall. I believe I wrote you about it in my last letter. I can keep the water in a fairly large quantity which at the present time makes a refreshing bathing place for the children. In dry weather, I can water the garden. We had more vegetables last summer than 3 families could use. Almost every Saturday, people came from the town of Mason to buy vegetables, mainly for the boarding houses. I have, however, put a lot of money into the farm already and I still need a year until the buildings are exactly what I want. The living house consists of three spacious rooms including a kitchen that is large enough in which to eat.[232] In addition, there is a stall out of stone and a smoke house for the bacon, also from stone.[233] Concerning my family, I can truly say that we are living very satisfied and happy. We have not had any sickness among our children and the stomach spasms of my wife are almost entirely gone. Our children are healthy and strong. Captain Braubach, an old acquaintance, visited me four weeks ago from San Antonio. While he was here, we went on a turkey hunt. We drove out in the evening with my team, Louis accompanied us, and returned home again the

---

[232] The original home Franz described is still in use today by his descendants. In 1917, the outside of house was plastered and the plaster was etched to make it look like cement blocks (a popular building material at the time). Probably at this time a bathroom and an additional room was added. In January 1995, the home partially burned. It has been restored close to its original condition. Franz's youngest son, Karl (later called Charlie) lived in the house until his death in 1943. His son Francis F. Kettner continued to live in the house until his death in 1972. It is presently owned by his son, Dr. Charles Kettner. The property originally owned by Franz is still in the possession of his descendants.

[233] This building is probably the old slave quarters which is also still in use. The original owner of the farm, Dr. McSween, was one of the few slave owners in area. The outside of the slave quarters was plastered like the house to make it look like cement blocks. The original slave quarters consisted of a single room with a fire place on each end and lean-to shed. Early on, the dirt floor was replaced with a concrete floor and a partition wall was added to divide the single room. Much later around 1960, the shed was closed in and the floor was added to make an additional bedroom. The fire place on the north end of the house was closed and this room was used as a smoke house for generations and is probably the same house that Franz is describing to his father.

In the *Frontier Times* (J. Marvin Hunter "Brief History of the Early Days in Mason County," *Frontier Times*, 6 Novernber, 1928, 65-78), Louis Kettner provided the following information: "Dr. John McSween was among the early settlers, and he was the first justice of the county. He owned a few slaves, and the old Negro slave quarters he built for his slaves are still standing on the place owned by Charlie Kettner. Dr. McSween moved to Burnet County and died there." When Louis Kettner mentions Charlie Kettner, he is referring to his youngest brother, called Karl by his parents. Louis was surprised that the slave quarters were still standing in 1928. One wonders what his reaction would be to the slave quarters and the McSween house still existing almost 90 years later.

next morning at 9 and we had shot 27 wild turkeys.[234] The passion for hunting has left me but Louis is a passionate Nimrod and the cartridges which he always uses, cost me quite a lot.

We have not had a frost yet and today while I am writing these lines, we are having a thunderstorm and I am writing in shirt sleeves. I hope and wish that little Klara would send me her photograph because she is now grown up and one could see, in any case, whether she resembles her mother.

In the hope that these lines reach you in good health, we all wish you a happy New Year. Louis, Ida, and Elise will write their own letters in a few days so that you can see that they have already learned something.

Greeting you many times

I remain your son Francis Kettner

[234] A personal account published in the *Frontier Times* (J. Marvin Hunter, 6 December, 1929, 113-134), presumably by W.E. Wheeler, describes the abundance of game in Mason County. There were large herds of both deer and antelope and huge flocks of turkeys. The large surplus of turkeys lasted until the late 1880's. "Turkeys were coming in great droves from every direction and soon the whole country was black with them." Buffalo were occasionally seen, but they were primarily west of Mason County.

**Fig. 48. Kettner Home on the McSween Place.** This photograph was taken around 1910. Louise, Mary, and Ruby Kettner are shown. Mary (Mary Kothmann) is Patsy Kothmann Ziriax's mother. Mary and Patsy are responsible for preserving Dr. Franz Lambert Kettner's letters. Two rooms have doors opening to the front porch. The kitchen Franz describes is at the back of the house.

**Abb. 48. Kettner Haus auf dem McSween Place.** Dieses Foto wurde um 1910 aufgenommen. Es zeigt Louise, Mary und Ruby Kettner. Mary (Mary Kothmann) ist die Mutter von Patsy Kothmann Ziriax. Dank Mary und Patsy wurden die Briefe von Dr. Franz Lambert Kettner aufbewahrt. Zwei Räume haben Türen, die sich zur Frontveranda öffnen. Die Küche, die Franz beschreibt, befindet sich auf der Rückseite des Hauses.

**Fig. 49. The Slave Quarters.** The old slave quarters are shown in the background. Francis F. Kettner (Franz's grandson) is shown on his donkey. This photograph was also taken around 1910.

**Abb. 49. Das Sklavenquartier.** Das alte Sklavenquartier ist im Hintergrund zu sehen. Francis F. Kettner (Enkel von Franz) wird auf seinem Esel gezeigt. Diese Aufnahme entstand ebenfalls um 1910.

**Fig. 50. Restored Kettner Home 2006.** If one compares the restored home with that in Fig. 48, a room was added on the right with a door opening to the porch. The remaining two doors are the same as shown in Fig. 48. The other addition is a room on the porch to the left.

**Abb. 50. Wieder aufgebautes Kettner Haus 2006.** Vergleicht man das erneuerte Haus mit dem von Abb. 48, so wurde ein Raum auf der rechten Seite hinzugefügt mit einer Tür zur Frontveranda. Die anderen zwei Türen entsprechen denen der Abb. 48. Außerdem wurde links ebenfalls noch ein Raum an die Veranda angefügt.

**Fig. 51. Old Slave Quarters 2006.**

**Abb. 51. Altes Sklavenquartier 2006.**

## Brief 30 (10. Dezember 1872) von Francis Kettner vom McSween Place an seinen Vater

Mason, 10. Dezember 1872

Lieber Vater!

Ihren Brief habe ich letzten Sommer erhalten, und es geht daraus hervor, daß ein Brief von mir verloren gegangen ist.

Ich wollte Ihnen nicht eher schreiben als bis unsere Präsidentenwahl vorüber war, da auch ich in dieser Wahl sehr interessiert war. Es wurde nämlich auch für mein Amt als Inspektor gewählt, und ich hatte zwei Gegner gegen mich, einen Amerikaner und einen Deutschen. Ich wurde für einen Zeitraum von zwei Jahren wiedererwählt und hatte drei Stimmen mehr als meine beiden Gegner zusammen hatten. Sie können daraus ersehen, wie ich in meinem County stehe.

Ich habe letztes Jahr eine gute Ernte gemacht, ungefähr 300 Büschel Korn und wir machten 200 Gallonen Sirup; verkauften 150 Gallonen und behielten 50 Gallonen für den Hausgebrauch. Jetzt bin ich eifrig daran, mit einem schwarzen Arbeiter mehr Land in Stein-Umzäumung zu bringen, auch meinen Garten zu vergrößern, alles aber mit gutem Steinfenz.

Ich halte meine Farm für eine der Besten. Letzten Sommer habe ich noch 130 Stück Schafe zu meiner kleinen Herde gekauft, so daß ich jetzt jedes Frühjahr für 300 Dollars Wolle verkaufen kann. Ebenfalls habe ich eine sehr gute Schweinezucht und lauter feine Schweine. Wir haben letzten Sommer ungefähr 100 Stück aufgezogen. Und jeden Abend, wenn die Schweine gerufen werden zur Fütterungszeit, so können Sie dieselben von allen Richtungen laufen sehen, um nach der Farm zu kommen.

Louis, Ida und Elise reiten jeden Morgen nach der Schule und kommen abends nach Hause. Ich halte zwei Pferde bloß für die Schule. Da die Schule über ½ Stunde entfernt ist. Elise ist zehn Jahre alt, aber größer und schwerer als die Ida. Dieselbe wiegt über 100 Pfund und ist beinahe ausgewachsen. Mit 13 Jahren sind hier zu Lande die Mädchen beinahe ausgewachsen.

Ich habe nahe Nachbarn, wo ich jetzt wohne. Ich bin im Augenblick in Unterhandlungen 640 Acre Land zu kaufen, welches an mein Land anstößt, da ich die Absicht habe, die Schäferei in größerem Maßstabe zu betreiben.

Sie bemerkten in Ihrem letzten Briefe, daß es den Anschein habe, daß ich jetzt etwas erübrige. Es ist in Amerika gerade wie in Deutschland, ohne Mittel läßt sich nicht viel machen. Und ich kann wohl sagen daß ich seit 2 Jahren erst etwas Mittel in der Hand hatte, um rascher vorwärts zu kommen. Denn die Erziehung von Kindern kostet hier sehr viel und jetzt fange ich erst an, etwas Hilfe an Louis zu haben. Nahrungssorgen kennt man hier allerdings nicht, jeder hat genug zu essen.

Daß ich eine Quelle in meinem Garten habe, und dieselbe eingefaßt habe mit einer Steinmauer, glaube habe ich Ihnen in meinem letzten Briefe geschrieben. Ich kann das Wasser in ziemlicher Quantität aufhalten, was zu gleicher Zeit ein erfrischender Badeplatz für die Kinder ist, und bei trockener Witterung bewässere ich die Gemüse. Wir hatten letzten Sommer mehr Gemüse als 3 Familien gebrauchen konnten und beinahe jeden Samstag kamen Leute von der Stadt Mason, um sich Gemüse zu kaufen, namentlich für die Gasthäuser. Ich habe aber auch schon viel Geld in die Farm gesteckt, und ich brauche noch ein Jahr, bis die Einrichtung so ist, wie ich dieselbe wünsche. Das Wohnhaus besteht aus 3 geräumigen Zimmern, nebst einer Küche, groß genug, daß darin gespeist wird. Außerdem einen Stall von Stein und ein Räucherhaus für den Speck ebenfalls von Stein. Was meine Familie anbelangt, so kann ich wohl sagen, wir leben sehr zufrieden und glücklich. Krankheiten haben wir noch keine unter unseren Kindern gehabt und das Magenübel von meiner Frau hat sich beinahe ganz behoben. Unsere Kinder sind gesund und kräftig. Captain Braubach, ein alter Bekannter, besuchte mich vor 4 Wochen von San Antonio. Wir machten während seinem Dasein eine Puterjagd, fuhren abends mit meinem Gespann los, Louis begleitete uns, und kamen den nächsten Morgen 9 Uhr wieder nach Hause und hatten 27 Stück wilde Puter geschossen. Die Leidenschaft der Jagd hat bei mir aufgehört, aber Louis ist ein leidenschaftlicher Nimrod und die Patronen, die derselbe immer gebraucht, kosten mich ziemlich viel.

Wir haben bis jetzt noch keinen Frost gehabt und heute während ich diese Zeilen schreibe, haben wir ein Donnerwetter und ich schreibe in Hemdsärmeln. Ich erwarte und wünsche, daß mir Klärchen Ihre Photographie sendet, da dieselbe jetzt ausgewachsen ist und man jetzt auf jeden Fall erkennen kann ob sie ihrer Mutter gleicht.

In der Hoffung, daß diese Zeilen Sie bei guter Gesundheit antreffen, wünschen wir alle Ihnen ein glückliches Neues Jahr. Louis, Ida und Elise werden in einigen Tagen einen eigenen Brief folgen lassen, damit Sie sehen sollen, daß dieselben schon etwas gelernt haben.

Sie vielmals grüßend
Verbleibe ich Ihr Sohn
Francis Kettner

Mason, 10. Dezember 1872

# Letter / Brief 31

### Letter 31 (May 12, 1873) from Dr. Franz Lambert Kettner to Francis Kettner at the McSween Place[235]

Oberkirch, May 12, 1873

Dear Franz!

I want to now answer your letter from December 10, 1872 because I wrote to you five days before the arrival of this letter.

This time I have enough stuff to write and will start at once with my own self. On the 20th of January of this year when I had my 80th birthday quietly, I have sought my pension. This I have received with a full income of 500 guldens a year along with a flattering note.[236]

I realized in autumn on a house call (as doctor) to Petersthal in deep snow, that I was too old and weak to be able to undertake strenuous business. Because of that, I have decided on retirement which I also find very boring. I must accept the situation, however, because I cannot change it and I am no longer capable of present work.

Outside of old age, I am healthy. My eye infection is gone, I am still weaker which you can notice from my letter. There is nothing for me in life; it has no more worth for me; I can only work a little still.

Also the conditions of the times are not good. The spring was beautiful, the outlook was hopeful. Then followed on the 21st, 22nd, and 23rd, cold nights of minus 1 to 2 degrees (Celsius) by which the grapes, nuts, and cherries were frozen. And since then, we have had wet, cold weather and cannot expect a good year which does not fit the expensive [unreadable]. A pound ox meat 25 kr., pork 24, butter 36 to 40, a cord of wood 22 to 40, a pair of average oxen 500 gulden, etc., and it leads to a terrible year for the ruined and growing number of riff-fall (communists).

---

235 The original letter is in the possession of Patsy Kothmann Ziriax, Mason, TX.

236 See "Introduction."

What is going to happen? Nicolai was also here yesterday and he complained about too many businesses and inflation. With a yearly income of 2000 gulden, he is not making it because he has 5 children to feed and to educate. Klara is home [again]. She is 20 years old and would very much like to [marry], but that is not so easy to do.

It is going well with Erderich and with Kissel in Switzerland. Kissel's business has 2 traveling salesmen and another 4 in the shop. He had begun with nothing and earned it with his [---hard work], without having to go to the silver men (bankers or money lenders).

[----] has been here since fall; he lives in New Braunfels and has married, according to his description, a vile and bad wife. When he has received his inheritance share, he will return to Texas with his wife and daughter. I have learned from him how terrible and lazy you both were. Therefore, he works very hard for his brother. When he has received his share of the inheritance, he will again go to Texas. He says that in your area a lot of cotton is planted which you have not yet written about.

The freedom for trade here is disadvantageous. Everyone wants to become an inn keeper or businessman. To the left of my home is Mark's Buder, a wine and beer inn. To the right is the Schell Haus. Wine and beer. Now the two there are totally ruined and a second has begun.

Directly across lives the inn keeper Haiz of the Adler, a wine and brandy trader. He lives in a newly built elegant home and it looks as though he possesses a large fortune. This man is very respectable and industrious. He has an elegant team and driver and is the son of Palmerfranz from Loecherberg.

How I take it from [-----] is that it is not customary with you in Texas to set money aside but that it is used up from year to year.

The old widow Schrempp has died at 83 and her son Max at 60, completely poor.

The emigration to America is very strong, especially in order to avoid going into the army, because everyone must become a soldier. The majority of emigrants who go there are prosperous people who support their needy ones here; however, the real republicans have already returned here and are on the surface cured (of their ideology). I would not have given these men the permission to come (back) and carry on their cause.

We are coming against a very unfavorable year. Today, on the 14th of May, we have 4 degrees warm and outside on the mountains there is ice. What will come next? After the rainy weather, still cold weather is coming.

Outwardly it looks like great wealth rules. There is the glitz of feather hats, silk and velvet but when one asks about the fortune, there is mostly little in hand.

I have said enough so I want to close with the wish that you will become a large landowner; however, you probably need to learn the field work first before you become too old.

Many greetings to your family. May you all live well and contented.

Your father

Kettner

## Brief 31 (12. Mai 1873) von Dr. Franz Lambert Kettner aus Oberkirch an seinen Sohn Franz Kettner im McSween Place[237]

Oberkirch, den 12. Mai 1873

Lieber Franz!

Deinen Brief vom 10. Dezember 1872 will ich Dir nun jetzt beantworten, weil ich vor Ankunft Deines Briefes 5 Tage zuvor an Dich geschrieben habe.

Diesmal habe ich Stoff genug zum Schreiben und will gleich mit meiner Person den Anfang machen. Seit dem 20. Januar des Jahres, wo ich meinen 80. Geburtstag im Stillen begangen habe, habe ich um meine Pensionierung nachgesucht. Diese habe ich mit vollem Gehalt zu 500 Gulden jährlich erhalten nebst einem schmeichelha[f]ten Nachruf.[238]

Ich habe im Spätjahr[239] bei einer Dienstreise bei starkem Schnee nach Petersthal wahrgenommen, daß ich zu alt und zu schwach bin, anstrengende Geschäfte mehr verrichten zu können. Deswegen habe ich um Ruhe nachgesucht, welche ich auch zur Langweile erhalten habe. Ich muß [mich] aber in die Lage fügen, weil ich es nicht ändern kann und zum jetzigen[240] Dienst nicht mehr tauglich bin.

Ausgenommen des Alters bin ich gesund. Meine Augenzündung hat sich verloren, mir ist noch Schwäche vorhanden, was Du aus meinem Brief ersehen kannst. Aus dem Leben mache ich mir gar nichts, es hat für mich keinen Wert mehr, ich kann nur noch wenig arbeiten.

Auch sind die Zeitverhältnisse nicht gut. Der Frühling war schön, die Aussichten waren hoffnungsvoll. Da erfolgten am 21., 22., 23. kalte Nächte zu 1 bis 2 Grad kalt,[241] wodurch der Weinstock, Nüsse und Kirschen erfroren sind. Und [da wir] seitdem naßkalte Witterung haben und kein gutes Jahr zu erwarten haben, was zu der ....[242] teuren nicht paßt. Ein Pfund Ochsenfleisch 25 kr, Schweinefleisch 24, Butter 36 bis 40, Klafter Holz 22 bis 40, ein paar mit[t]lere Ochsen 500 Gulden, etc. und geht noch ein schlechtes Jahr hinzu bei dem verdorbenen und [in] großer Zahl befindlichen Gesindel: {Kommunisten}.[243]

Was wird da kommen? Nicolai war gestern auch hier, der jam[m]ert wegen zu vielen Geschäften,[244] wegen der großen Teuerung. Mit jährlich 2000 Gulden kommt er nicht aus, weil er 5 Kinder zu ernähren und zu erlirnen[245] habe. Die Klara ist ....[246]

---

[237] Original des Briefes befindet sich im Besitz von Patsy Kothmann Ziriax, Mason, Texas.

[238] Siehe Einführung.

[239] 1872

[240] Im Sinne von derzeitigen

[241] Minusgrade

[242] Unleserlich

[243] Geschweifte Klammern von Dr. F.L.K.

[244] Nach Einführung der Gewerbefreiheit wurden zu viele konkurrierende Geschäfte eröffnet

[245] Wahrscheinlich "auszubilden"

[246] Unleserlich

[wieder] zu Haus, ist 20 Jahre und wünscht sich gerne zu verh[eirat]en,[247] was aber nicht so leicht geht.

Bei Erderich und bei Kissel in der Schweiz geht es gut. Kissels Geschäft sind 2 Reisende und noch 4 im Geschäft. Der hat mit nichts angefangen, und bringt es mit seinem ....,[248] ohne bei den Silbermännern zu sein.

..... ist seit Spätjahr hier, er ist in Neu Braunfels wohnhaft und verehelicht, hat nach seinem Geständnis eine wüste und böse Frau bekommen. Wenn er seine Erbgebühr erhalten hat, geht er wieder nach Texas zu seiner Frau und Tochter. Von [ihm] habe ich erfahren, wie häßlich und sparsam fleißig ihr gehabt habt. Deshalb arbeitet er fleißig bei seinem Bruder. Wie er seine Erbgebühr[249] bekommen hat, geht er wieder fort nach Texas. Der sagt, daß bei seiner Heimat viel Baumwolle gepflanzt wird, wo Du noch nicht geschrieben hast.

Die Gewerbefreiheit ist hier recht nachteilig. Alles will Wirt werden und Kaufmann. Zur linken meiner Wohnung ist Marks Büder? mit ....[250] Wein und Bierwirt. Zur rechten das Schellsche Haus. Wein und Bier. Jetzt sind 2 dort ganz verdorben und ein 2ter fängt an.

Gegenüber wohnt Adlerwirt Haiz, Wein und Branntweinhändler, wohnt in einem neuerbauten eleganten Haus und scheint ein großes Vermögen zu besitzen. Dieser Mann ist sehr solid und fleißig. Hat ein elegantes Gespann und Führer, ist der Sohn vom Palmerfranz vom Löcherberg.

Wie ich von .... vernommen, ist es bei Euch in Texas nicht üblich Kapitalien anzulegen, sondern wird von Jahr zu Jahr aufgezehrt.

Die alte Wittfrau Schrempp ist im 83 und ihr Sohn Max mit 60 Jahren, ganz arm gestorben.

Die Auswanderung nach Nordamerika ist sehr stark, besonders um dem Militär zu entgehen, weil alles Soldat sein muß. Die meisten dort Eingewanderten sind wohlhabende Leute, die ihre Notleidenden hier ....[251] unterstützen, jedoch sind die echten Reblikaner[252] bereits alle wieder zurückgekommen und sind äußerlich geheilt. Diesen Männern hätte ich die Erlaubnis nicht erteilt, zu kommen und ihr Sach auszuüben.

Wir gehen einem sehr ungünstigen Jahr entgegen. Heute den 14. Mai haben wir um 4 Grad warm, mithin auf dem Gebirge Eis. Was wird darauf folgen? Auf das viele Regenwetter noch kaltes Wetter bringen werde.[253]

Äußerlich scheint [es], als herrsche großer Reichtum. Federhüte, Seide und Samt glänzt, und wenn ein[254] nach dem Vermögen fragt, so ist meistens nur wenig vorhanden.

---

[247] Unleserlich, aber wahrscheinlich verheiraten
[248] Mehrere Worte unleserlich
[249] Seinen Erbteil
[250] Unleserlich
[251] Unleserlich
[252] Republikaner
[253] Wenn auf das viele Regenwetter noch kaltes Wetter folgen wird.

Da ich nun genug gesprochen, so will ich schließen mit dem Wunsche, daß Du ein großer Ekonom[255] werden wirst, wirst aber wahrscheinlich Feldarbeit erst erlernen müssen, wes[256] Du zu alt bist.

Viele Grüße an die Deinigen. Lebet alle recht wohl und zufrieden.

Dein Vater

Kettner

---

[254] Man

[255] Ökonom im Sinne von Landwirt

[256] Wozu

# Letter / Brief 32

**Letter 32 (Early Summer 1873[257]) from Francis Kettner at the McSween Place, to his Father**

Dear Father!

Because I have until now not received an answer from my last letter that I wrote you last Christmas and New Year, I am assuming that either my letter did not arrive or that your answer has been lost. Concerning my family and myself, we are all lively. I have made a very good harvest from the 16 acres that I brought within a stone fence last winter. My sheep have sheared very well and the wool has never before been so high in price. I now have almost 200 head of sheep. However, I had a lot of work so that I was absent from home almost the entire spring in order to inspect the cattle that would be driven out for sale.

Louis had plowed during my absence. And afterward, when I returned home, we plowed with two plow teams and the harvest was secure. My garden, which I irrigate from a spring, is the best in the entire county.

I had to make a trip to Austin (the governor's home) in the spring of this year where the railroad now goes. Texas now has a future.

In the hope that I will soon hear from you, greet all my relatives and I remain your grateful son

Francis Kettner

You must excuse me for writing so briefly, but I am still overwhelmed with work and would like to know why I have not received a reply.

[257] The date is approximated by the author.

**Fig. 52. Rock Pens.** These livestock pens have been associated with the Kettner place for generations and were used to work livestock until the mid-1970s. They are approximately 100 yards west of the Kettner home. It is possible that a portion of the pens were constructed by McSween before Franz purchased the property.

**Abb. 52. Steinerner Pferch.** Diese Vieheinfriedungen gehörten seit Generationen zu dem Kettnerplatz und wurden zur Viehhaltung bis Mitte der 1970er Jahre genutzt. Sie befinden sich ca. 100 Yards westlich des Kettner Hauses. Es ist möglich, dass ein Teil der Mauer bereits von McSween errichtet wurde bevor Franz das Anwesen kaufte.

## Brief 32 (Frühsommer 1873[258]) von Franz Kettner vom McSween Place an seinen Vater

Lieber Vater!

Da ich auf meinen letzten Brief, welchen ich Ihnen letzten Weihnachten und Neujahr geschrieben habe, bis jetzt noch ohne Antwort bin, so vermute ich, daß entweder mein Brief nicht angekommen, oder aber Ihre Antwort verloren gegangen ist. Was meine Familie und mich anbelangt so sind wir alle munter. Ich mache eine sehr gute Ernte von 16 Acres, welche ich letzten Winter in Steinfenz gebracht habe. Meine Schafe haben sehr gut geschoren und die Wolle war noch nie so hoch im Preis. Ich habe jetzt nahe an zweihundert Stück Schafe. Aber ich hatte sehr viel Arbeit, da ich beinahe das ganze Frühjahr von Hause abwesend war, um das Vieh zu inspizieren, welches zum Verkauf fortgetrieben wurde.

Louis hat während meiner Abwesenheit gepflügt. Und nachher, als ich nach Hause kam, pflügten wir mit zwei Pflügen und die Ernte ist gesichert. Mein Garten, den ich mit einer Quelle bewässere, ist der schönste in dem ganzen County.

Ich hatte dieses Jahr im Frühjahr eine Reise nach Austin (Gouverneurssitz) gemacht, bis wohin die Eisenbahn schon geht. Texas geht jetzt erst einer Zukunft entgegen.

In der Hoffnung, bald von Ihnen zu hören, grüße ich alle meine Verwandten und verbleibe Ihr

dankbarer Sohn

Francis Kettner.

Sie müssen entschuldigen, daß ich so kurz schreibe, aber ich bin noch mit Geschäften überhäuft, und möchte wissen, weshalb ich keine Antwort erhalte.

[258] Ort und Datum nach Vermutung der Autorin.

# Letter / Brief 33

### Letter 33 (September 18, 1873) from Francis Kettner at the McSween Place to his Father

Mason County, September, 1873

Dear Father!

Just now I can spare enough time in order to answer your letter from the 12th of May, 1873. My entire family is doing well and all are healthy except for my little problem. I overexerted myself last winter with building the stone fence and suffer from that until now. Especially because I cannot give myself (time to recover) on account of my job as inspector of all the cattle and all the raw hides that leave the county. For example, there were 14,000 living cattle this year and summer that came under my hand, all of which were driven to Kansas.[259]

I had to make a note of the brand and the ear markings of each one and keep a book for that. Therefore, I was most of the time away from home, at least during the spring.

Louis had plowed and had sown part of the field. On top of that, I have begun to build and to equip my farm to be comfortable. My farm, without the sheep, swine, cattle, and inventory, I could have sold already this summer for 2,000 dollars, that is, 5,000 gulden.

My garden, which borders on the house yard and is watered by a fine spring, is an impressive little place with splendid nut trees and weeping willows and bee hives. The spring flows into a stone-walled cistern in which it is held until evening and then it is used to irrigate the garden. It is sufficient for the entire garden at the dry periods during the months of June, July, and August.

---

[259] Note that in Letter 22, Fall of 1870, that 10,000 head of cattle are driven to California, New Mexico, and to the California railroad. In 1873, all cattle (14,000 head) were driven to Kansas.

In your last letter you mentioned [....] many times. I have not seen this man since 1850, therefore 23 years. Once I simply asked about him from someone from New Braunfels who was in our area. I learned that his wife and her grown children had sometimes thoroughly beaten him and that he, anyhow, does not have a fit mind.

Louis will go again this winter to an English school in Mason (our town) in order to perfect his English language. You were surprised that the Texans do not put much emphasis on piling up their capital. That is completely understandable. As long as my invested money, for example, in sheep, cattle, swine, or land earns 30 percent, then you will find no one who will loan out his money at 8 percent interest. Therefore, 10 to 12 and a half percent interest is paid for a hundred because the Texans can also figure.

We do not have any worries about food here, each raises his own meat and bread and I raise, at the minimum, enough vegetables every year for certain through my irrigation. If we have the desire for mutton, then we slaughter a wether, or for pork, then a pig, or poultry.

I have all the ham for my family and usually another 1,000 to 1,500 pounds of bacon, a crock of lard, so that we, in our normal lives, do not know anything about having to shut off our mouths from food. In fall, we fill up a stone crock with butter so that we can eat from it to our heart's desire the entire winter. Bratwurst is also produced in large number. I also keep aside a little cask of syrup for our household use. Indeed, I make enough syrup each year, since I plant sugar cane[260] and have an iron press which is turned by a horse (it cost 100 dollars), that over 100 gallons is always sold. Last year, as I bought the sugar press, I sold 150 gallons at one dollar per gallon since I wanted to earn the money back again from it.

Germany, as well as the rest of Europe, will come to its downfall through the overdone luxury. The middle class will disappear in time and only the very rich and the very poor people (continue to) exist. Moreover, the poor will be 100 times greater and the communists will cause even more troubles. It had pleased me that our old Friedrich Hecker[261] was so well received by the Mannheim citizens; you can imagine that his Stuttgart speech somewhat displeased.

We Americans can no long adapt ourselves to such conditions like the Germans. In our country where the newspaper is free, the speech is free. It is a country in which I can expose the mistakes of the president if he makes a false step and through the press openly chastise him and make fun of him. Naturally, we can see no progress in a law for the press like the one the National Assembly has been presented by Prince Bismark. And furthermore, after my 25-year experience here in the United States, progress could not be stopped. No one believed twenty years earlier that this

---

[260] This is sorghum sugar cane.

[261] Friedrich Karl Franz Hecker (September 9, 1811 to March 3, 1881) was a revolutionary politician. He organized the Rebellion of 1848 in Southwest Germany and had to flee to USA where he fought for the Union in the Civil War. Ref: *The Grosse Knaur, Encyclopedia in 4 Volumes*, Volume 2, Stuttgart, Hamburg, 1967.

generation would experience the halt of slavery. Even fewer (believed) on the political equality between the white and the black races. And so on. Luxury has also begun to work and spoil things somewhat here. However, it cannot ruin any families and it causes no starvation.

Both of my young ladies make my head heavy sometimes on account of luxury articles. Elise is more vanity-inclined than Ida. Ida, however, is much wilder. She prefers to ride a horse until it looks like a wet cat or she jumps over ditches, while Elise, the younger, has developed a more domestic sense. Elise is a head taller than Ida and one and a half years younger. The children are all healthy and strong.

The old widow Schrempp had reached a fine age and it pains me that she died poor. She was not, in any case, responsible for the ruin to poverty of her family. Here in Texas everyone comes ahead with each year. The one quickly, the other slowly, but everyone improves without exception. I know no poverty-fallen. Already through the increase in the cattle, sheep, and swine, one comes each year into better circumstances.

I have never seen a beggar here in 25 years and I could only explain to my children what sort of trade a beggar has. They were very shocked that there were such people and that they were not ashamed of themselves to beg from other people. Now compare our circumstances with the European ones. Here, no worries; there, bitter poverty. It would pain me to see such people before my eyes while one can read the need, the deprivation, the cares from their eyes and their faces; while again another part (of society) enjoys the finest luxuries, in eating and drinking as well as in homes and clothing.

In each letter you give me the meat, butter, and wood prices, articles which are unavoidably necessary for living, and the lack of which the poorest here do not suffer, and which so many must do without in your praised Baden. So has every country its different sides. Germany is, above all, over-populated.

Cotton is planted here in all of Texas, only not in my region, because the people can make their living easier with raising cattle, etc., etc. It is also because cotton requires much more work and it must be planted in the hottest time (of the year).

I will write a letter to Marie Erdrich in 14 days. Greet her and all of the relatives and answer this letter quickly.

Your son<br>
Francis Kettner

What is the family Fachon doing? I'd like to hear about them.

## Brief 33 (18. September 1873) von Franz Kettner vom McSween Place an seinen Vater

Mason County, 18. September 1873

Lieber Vater!

Jetzt erst kann ich mir etwas Zeit erübrigen, um Ihren Brief vom 12. Mai 1873 zu beantworten. Meiner ganzen Familie geht es gut, und alles ist gesund, bis auf meine Wenigkeit. Ich habe mich letzten Winter bei Steinfenzungen etwas überhoben und habe bis dato daran zu leiden. Besonders, da ich mich nicht schonen konnte, wegen meiner Anstellung als Inspektor von allem Vieh und allen Rohhäuten, die aus dem County gehen. So sind zum Beispiel 14,000 Stück lebendiges Rindvieh dieses Frühjahr und Sommer durch meine Finger gegangen, welche alle nach Kansas getrieben wurden.

Ich mußte von jedem Stück den Brand und das Ohrenmark aufnotieren und halte ein Buch darüber. Deshalb war ich sehr oft beinahe die meiste Zeit von Hause, wenigstens während des Frühjahres.

Louis hat gepflügt und zum Teil das Feld bestellt. Darauf habe ich angefangen zu bauen und mich bequem einzurichten. Meine Farm ohne Schafe und Schweine und Vieh, und Inventarium könnte ich schon für die Summe von 2000 Dollars sage 5000 Gulden verkaufen.

Mein Garten, dicht an den Hofraum grenzend, mit einer schönen Quelle eingefaßt, von den prachtvollsten Nußbäumen und Trauerweiden mit Bienenzucht ist ein reizendes Plätzchen. Die Quelle fließt in einen gemauerten Behälter, in welchem das Wasser aufgehalten wird bis zum Abend und alsdann zum Bewässern des Gartens verwendet wird. Sie ist hinreichend für den ganzen Garten bei trockener Zeit, während des Monats Juni, Juli, August.

In Ihrem letzten Brief erwähnten Sie mehrmals..... Ich habe den Menschen seit dem Jahre 1850 also 23 Jahre nicht mehr gesehen, bloß einmal habe ich mich nach demselben erkundigt, als jemand von Neu Braunfels in unserer Gegend war. Ich erfuhr, daß seine Frau und deren erwachsene Kinder, den Herrn .... manchmal gehörig durchgeprügelt haben, und derselbe sowieso nicht den richtigen Verstand habe.

Louis kommt diesen Winter wieder in eine englische Schule nach Mason (unsere Stadt), um sich in der englischen Sprache zu vervollkommnen. Sie wundern sich, daß die Texaner nicht darauf sind Kapitalien aufzuhäufen? Das ist ganz natürlich, solange mir angelegtes Geld z.B. in Schafe, Rindvieh, Schweine oder Land 30 Prozent Zinsen abwerfen, so wird sich wohl niemand finden, der zu 8 % sein Geld verleiht. Deshalb werden sogar 10% und 12 ½ Prozent bezahlt für das Hundert, allein die Texaner können auch rechnen.

Nahrungssorgen kennen wir hier keine, jeder zieht sein eigenes Fleisch und Brot und Gemüse ziehe ich wenigstens jedes Jahr sicher, durch meine Bewässerung. Haben wir Lust nach Hammelfleisch, so schlachten wir einen Hammel oder nach Schweinefleisch ein Schwein, oder Federvieh.

Ich halte für meine Familie alle Schinken und gewöhnlich noch 1000 bis 1500 Pfund Speck, ein Faß voll Schmalz, so daß wir im gewöhnlichen Leben von an dem Munde abzwacken nichts wissen. Butter machen wir im Spätjahr ein in Steintöpfen, daß wir den ganzen Winter nach Herzenslust davon essen können. Bratwürste werden ebenfalls die schwere Menge produziert. Sirup behalte ich auch ein Fäßchen voll retour für Hausgebrauch. Ich mache nämlich jedes Jahr Sirup, da ich das Zuckerrohr pflanze und eine eiserne Maschine habe durch ein Tier gezogen (kostet 100 Dollars), so werden immer etwas über hundert Gallonen verkauft. Das letzte Jahr, als ich die Zuckerpresse kaufte, habe ich sogar 150 Gallonen verkauft à 1 Dollar per Gallone, weil ich das Geld wieder heraus verdienen wollte.

Deutschland wird durch den übertriebenen Luxus, sowie das übrige Europa, seinem Verfall entgegengehen. Der Mittelstand wird mit der Zeit verschwinden und bloß sehr reiche und sehr arme Leute werden existieren. Aber die Armen in der 100fachen Mehrzahl und der Kommunismus wird noch einmal viel Unheil anrichten. Es hat mich gefreut, daß unser alter Friedrich Hecker[262] so gut von den Mannheimern empfangen wurde, daß seine Stuttgarter Rede etwas mißfiel, läßt sich wohl denken.

Wir Amerikaner können uns solchen Verhältnissen, wie den deutschen, nicht mehr anpassen. In einem Lande, wo die Zeitung frei, die Rede frei, in einem Land in welchem ich den Präsidenten, so wie er einen Schnitzer macht, durch die Presse gehörig geißeln, lächerlich machen, seine Fehler aufdecken kann. Natürlicherweise können wir in einem Pressegesetz, wie das des Fürsten Bismarck der Reichsversammlung vorgelegte, keinen Fortschritt erblicken. Und dennoch nach meinen 25 jährigen Erfahrungen hier in den Vereinigten Staaten konnte der Fortschritt nicht aufgehalten werden. Sklaverei, so glaubte vor zwanzig Jahren niemand, daß die jetzige Generation es erleben würde, daß dieselbe abgeschafft würde. Viel weniger an politische Gleichstellung zwischen der weißen und schwarzen Rasse. Und dennoch. Der Luxus fängt auch schon hier an, etwas störend zu wirken. Aber er kann keine Familie ruinieren und keine Hungersnot erzeugen.

Meine beiden jungen Ladies machen mir auch manchmal den Kopf schwer von wegen Luxusartikel. Die Elise ist viel putzsüchtiger als die Ida. Die Ida ist aber auch viel wilder. Dieselbe reitet lieber ein Pferd, bis es wie eine gebadete Katze aussieht, oder setzt über einen Graben, während die Elise, die jüngere, einen mehr häuslichen Sinn entwickelt. Die Elise ist einen Kopf größer als die Ida und 1 ½ Jahr jünger. Die Kinder sind alle gesund und kräftig.

Die alte Witwe Schrempp hat ein hübsches Alter erreicht und es tut mir leid, daß die Frau arm gestorben ist. Dieselbe war in keinem Falle Schuld an der Verarmung ihrer Familie. Hier in Texas kommt ein jeder vorwärts mit jedem Jahre. Der eine schnell, der andere langsam, aber verbessern tut sich ein jeder ohne Ausnahme.

---

[262] Hecker, Friedrich Karl Franz, revolutionärer Politiker. 28.09.1811 – 24.03.1881. Organisierte den Aufstand von 1848 in Südwestdeutschland, mußte nach den USA fliehen, kämpfte im Sezessionskrieg für die Nordstaaten. Vgl. *Der Große Knaur, Lexikon in 4 Bänden*, Bd.2, Stuttgart/Hamburg 1967.

Verarmungen kenne ich keine. Schon durch das Vermehren des Viehstockes, Schafe und Schweine kommt ein jeder jedes Jahr in bessere Verhältnisse.

Ich habe in den 25 Jahren hier noch nie einen Bettler gesehen und ich mußte meinen Kindern auseinander setzen, was ein Bettler für ein Gewerbe hat. Dieselben waren sehr erstaunt darüber, daß es solche Menschen gibt, die sich nicht schämen, von anderen Menschen zu betteln. Vergleichen Sie nun unsere Zustände mit den europäischen. Hier keine Sorgen, da drüben bittere Not. Es würde mir leid tun, solche Menschen vor Augen zu sehen, denen man den Mangel, die Entbehrung und Sorgen aus den Augen und aus dem Gesicht lesen könnte; während wieder ein anderer Teil den raffiniertesten Luxus treibt, sowohl im Essen und Trinken sowie auch in Wohnung und Kleidung.

Sie geben mir in jedem Ihrer Briefe die Fleisch-, Butter- und Holzpreise an, Artikel, welche zum Leben unumgänglich notwendig sind, und an welchen der Allerärmste hier nicht Not leidet, und welche so viele in Ihrem gepriesenen Baden entbehren müssen. Deshalb hat jedes Land seine verschiedene Seiten. Deutschland ist überhaupt übervölkert.

Baumwolle wird hier in ganz Texas gepflanzt, bloß in meiner Gegend noch nicht, weil die Bevölkerung ihr Leben leichter macht mit Viehzucht, etc. etc. Es wird aber noch kommen. Die Baumwolle kostet sehr viel Arbeit und muß in der heißesten Zeit gepflügt werden.

Der Marie Erdrich werde ich in ungefähr 14 Tagen einen Brief schreiben. Grüßen Sie mir dieselbe so wie alle Verwandten und beantworten Sie mir diesen Brief recht bald.

Ihr Sohn<br>
Francis Kettner

Was macht die Familie Fachon? Ich habe noch nie etwas darüber vernommen.

# Letter / Brief 34

### Letter 34 (October 29, 1873) from Niece Klara Nicolai in Oberkirch to Francis Kettner[263]

Oberkirch, 29.10.1873

My dear Uncle!

You will be surprised to receive an answer from me to your last letter to Grandfather. He has had me take over this duty because I am presently here to visit and at his age and weakness, he is not able to write. After all this, you know me well. Certainly you remember little Klara who is now 21 years old; therefore, an introduction is not required.

Grandfather was very sick in the previous weeks. He had an abdominal infection and we really had little hope over his recovery, but his good, strong nature has helped him. He is [----] and finds himself very well, but at 81 years of age, one does not spring back and so it is that everything is not yet totally fine.

I was in northern Germany during the time when I received the news of his sickness. Naturally, I returned immediately and am now here in order to take care of him.

He says to give you the best greetings as well as your wife and the children, but the news he thinks you can get better through me.

Erdrich is also doing well. They have three children and two died. The business is profitable and Marie is happy. Her brother Franz lives in Zurich and is also blessed with children. He finds himself, so far as I hear, very well.

From my family, also, I can only report things are good. We continue to live in Karlsruhe. Papa has fairly well (progressed) and has a high government office. I still have 4 siblings, the youngest child is 7 years old. You will not have a good knowledge of all our German relations. So little as I have of you. I have thought that you lived in the middle of wilderness, I was (surprised) that you asked in your letter

---

263 The original letter is in the possession of Patsy Kothmann Ziriax, Mason, TX.

about the (effect) the American politics has in (Germany?). I mean, you must, indeed, rather live in our civilized Germany. It is so fine overall. We had always hoped to get to know you one day. However, it does not seem that we will ever have the opportunity. You would be certainly astonished about all the changes and perhaps would not feel yourself to be at home anymore.

You asked in your letter about the Fachons. I can only tell you a little. We are no longer (in contact) so I only know the main things. The parents live in Kontanz and he is, as far as I know, retired; his older son died of consumption (tuberculosis) and the younger son is a salesman; earlier he used to come here often as a traveling salesman for a large business firm.

Now we are having fall. Unfortunately, the yield is not what was desired, the quality was good but the quantity was very little. The grapes had bloomed well in the spring when a frost came and brought all the good hopes to nothing.

Your friend Emil von Schauenburg has built himself a princely house in Gaisbach. The building is totally designed like a castle and is called the castle by everyone in Gaisbach.

Grandfather in now completely in retirement, he never makes house calls and, at most, he shares his medical advice still here at home. He can still be lively, and he often enjoys it when he can still annoy us.

Actually, I had wanted to write you in English at first, but did not dare it and thought it better to write the first letter to my godfather in my mother tongue. The impressions then would be more favorable. I allow myself to enclose my photograph, also. It was taken not long ago in northern Germany. Therefore, quite similar. You only have to imagine the hair lighter, a little younger looking, and then you have the whole person in front of you. Grandfather told me that you have already asked for our picture sometimes and since I have it here right now, I will not neglect to fulfill your wish. We are living, truly, in a very serious time; the government fights again the papacy with force and all the Jesuit monasteries were closed. It is good when we are at last freed from this gang that only cause problems everywhere.

I will now close. I think that I have shared with you all that could interest you and I wish to impart from everyone many greetings on you and your worthy family.

With friendly greetings I remain your devoted Klara Nicolai

## Brief 34 (29. Oktober 1873) von Nichte Klara (Klärchen) Nicolai aus Oberkirch an ihren Patenonkel Franz Kettner in Texas[264]

Oberkirch, 29.10.1873

Mein lieber Onkel!

Du wirst erstaunt sein, von mir eine Antwort auf Deinen letzten Brief an Großvater zu erhalten. Allein da ich wirklich hier zu Besuch bin hat er mir dieses Amt überlassen, da das Alter und die Schwäche ihn zu keinem Schreiben mehr kommen lassen. Dem Ganzen nach kennst Du mich wohl, Du erinnerst Dich gewiß an das kleine Klärchen, das jetzt 21 Jahre alt ist, also einer Vorstellung bedarf es jetzt nicht.

Großvater war in den letzten Wochen sehr krank, er hatte eine Unterleibsentzündung und wir eigentlich wenig Hoffnung auf seine Wiederherstellung, doch seine gute kräftige Natur hat ihm geholfen. Er ist ....[265] und befindet sich ganz gut ...... in einem [Alter] von 81 Jahren macht man keine Sprünge mehr und das ist eben was ihm noch nicht recht gefallen will.

Ich war während einiger [Zeit] in Norddeutschland, woselbst ich Nachricht von seiner Krankheit erhielt. Natürlich kehrte ich sofort zurück und bin nun hier um ihn zu pflegen.

Er läßt Dich bestens grüßen, sowie Deine Frau und die Kinder, allein die Neuigkeiten, meint er, könntest Du besser durch [ihn erhalten].

Erdrich geht es auch gut. 3 Kinder haben [sie] [und] 2 sind verstorben. Das Geschäft ist sehr einträglich und Marie recht glücklich. Ihr Bruder Franz lebt in Zürich ....., ist auch mit Kindern gesegnet. [Er] befindet sich, so viel ich höre, ganz gut.

Von meiner Familie kann ich Dir auch nur Gutes berichten. Wir wohnen immer noch in Karlsruhe. Papa ist ziemlich weit ...... und hat eine hohe Beamtenstellung. 4 Geschwister habe ich noch, der jüngste Bub ist 7? Jahre alt. Du wirst von all unseren deutschen Verhältnissen keinen rechten Begriff mehr haben. So wenig wie ich von euch. Ich denke mir, daß Ihr halb in der Wildnis wohnt, mir war ..... daß Du Dich in Deinem Briefe fragst, .... die Amerikanische Politik ins ..... hast. Ich meine, Du müßtest doch auch lieber in unserem geregelten Deutschland leben. Es ist zu schön überall. Wir hatten immer gehofft, Dich auch einmal kennen zu lernen. Doch scheint es nicht, daß wir jemals die Aussicht dazu haben werden. Du wärst gewiß auch über all die Veränderungen erstaunt und würdest Dich vielleicht nicht mehr zurechtfinden.

Du fragst in Deinem Briefe nach Fachons. Ich kann Dir nur wenig von ihnen sagen. Wir haben uns [inzwischen] auch nicht in ...., also ist mir [nur] die Hauptsache bekannt. Die Alten leben in Konstanz, er ist, so viel ich weiß, pensioniert; sein ältester Sohn ist an der Schwindsucht gestorben und der jüngere

---

264 Original des Briefes befindet sich im Besitz von Patsy Kothmann Ziriax, Mason, Texas.

265 Brief teilweise zerstört.

ist Kaufmann, kam auch früher öfter als Reisender eines großen Geschäftshauses hier her.

Wirklich haben wir Herbst. Leider ist das Erträgnis nicht nach Wunsch ausgefallen, die Qualität ginge noch, aber die Quantität ist sehr gering. Die Reben waren sehr schön gestanden, als im Frühjahr ein Frost eintrat und all die schönen Hoffnungen zunichte machte.

Dein Freund Emil von Schauenburg hat sich in Gaisbach ein fürstliches Haus gebaut, ganz burgenartig ist das Gebäude angelegt, wird auch überall das Schloß von Gaisbach genannt.

Großvater ist nun vollständig in Ruhestand gesetzt, auch privatim[266] geht er nicht mehr fort, höchstens erteilt er noch seinen ärztlich Rat hier im Hause. Lebhaft kann er immer noch sein und freut sich oft sehr, wenn er uns recht ärgern kann.

Eigentlich wollte ich Dir zuerst englisch schreiben, doch traute ich nicht recht, es ist doch besser, wenn man den ersten Brief, den man an ein[en] Paten richtet, in seiner Muttersprache losläßt. Der Eindruck wird dann jedenfalls ein günstigerer. Ich erlaube mir auch meine Photographie beizulegen. Es ist kürzlich noch in Norddeutschland gemacht worden. Also sehr ähnlich. Du mußt Dir nur das Haar hell denken, ein bißchen jünger aussehend, dann hast Du die ganze Person vor Dir. Großvater sagt mir, Du hattest schon manchmal um unsere Bilder geschrieben, da ich es nun gerade hier habe, will ich nicht versäumen, Deinen Wunsch zu erfüllen. Wir leben wirklich in einer sehr ernsten Zeit, der Staat kämpft mit Macht gegen [das] Papsttum, alle Jesuitenklöster werden [geschlossen] und es ist gut, wenn wir einmal von dieser Bande erlöst sind, die überall nur Unheil stiftet.

Doch nun will ich schließen, ich glaube Dir so ziemlich alles mitgeteilt zu haben, was Dich interessieren könnte, und möchte nun von allen noch viele Grüße an Dich und Deine werte Familie beifügen.

Mit freundlichem Gruß verbleibe ich Deine ergebene Klara Nicolai

---

[266] Privat.

# Letter / Brief 35

### Letter 35 (April 29, 1874) from Francis Kettner at the McSween Place to his Niece Marie Erdrich in Oberkirch and to his Father

Mason, April 29, 1874

Precious Marie!

I have not yet received an answer from my last letter to Klara, addressed to Papa, that I sent 8 days before Christmas 1873. Could it be that your letter was lost?

My family enjoys good health and Louis, who went to school last winter in Mason, is again at home. We needed to use everyone this spring, partly because my fields have been considerably enlarged and partly because the lambing time came right then. We have received 100 lambs. They are very fine sheep and I was mostly away from home, occupied as inspector.

Now I have sufficient time in order to care for my household tasks. Throughout last winter we ate green cabbage because the winter was so unusually mild. My garden is now in full bloom and we always have the reputation of having the finest garden in the county. Picture this (in your mind), close by the house, on a very gentle rise, is a walled-in spring, shaded by magnificent nut trees and weeping willows. The basin that holds a large amount of water, is an outstanding bathing (swimming) place. Every evening and morning, the water is allowed to run into the different beds, so that we have vegetables throughout the longest dry periods.

It is a favorite activity of mine to work in the garden every morning before breakfast and to observe my bees since I possess quite a lot of them. The bees swarm here three times a year. My fruit trees already have begun their fruit. My open porch on the front of the house is graced with climbing plants, the yard of the house with roses and evergreens and various splendid oleander which are brought into the house each winter. Oleander is, without question, the most beautiful plant that I know. My girls, who have a great love of flowers, spend a lot of work in order to grow as many flowers as possible. My Ida, who would rather ride a horse than do housework, is now overjoyed. Indeed, I have bought a fine apple-white stallion for a hundred and fifty dollars, about 250 gulden, that she usually rides and regards as her own, although almost always in a short gallop. The girl makes a lovely figure on the horse and is a skilled rider, jumps over ditches and other obstacles and understands how to ride a horse.

My official term as government employee, at which I have already worked about 10 years, takes the greatest part of my time. Upon the expiration of my term, I will stop because it prevents me from getting my own work done. That is, I need my whole time for myself and I no longer need the additional income.

The property that I own, figuring at the very lowest prices, is now worth 15,000 florins and I started out with nothing. Because the oak mast (acorns) is certain, I will be able to sell bacon or swine this winter for about 1000 florins. I will use all the remaining money to buy all the land around me so that my farm will consist of 1000 to 1500 acres. Because there will be a completed railroad in about 2 years, Texas will be quickly populated and the land (prices) will climb.

I hope that you will quickly reply after the receipt of this letter and share with me all the new local news. In addition, I am waiting for some lines from Papa, and I hope, that because I have been so long without an answer from you, that his health has stabilized and that he's again lively.

I hope that this letter finds you and your entire family in good health, many greetings to all of you and I remain your uncle.

Francis Kettner

Many greetings to Papa and to Erdrich

Mason, 29 April 1874

Dear Papa,

At the same time as Marie's letter, I am writing you a few lines, also. You will see from Marie's letter that everything is fine with us. Regarding the health condition of my wife, the stomach spasms totally disappeared two years ago and, since then, everything is fine. I have been and continue to be occupied with building and improving my ranch. I have earned a lot of money during the last two years as inspector, but my improvements also cost me a lot. However, most of them are completed now and I will focus on buying the adjoining land because I must employ a shepherd next year to herd my sheep and the time will come when one must herd the sheep on his own land.

Raising bees is more profitable here than in Germany. The bees swarm twice in the spring and once in the late summer, that is, three swarms for each hive and they are always very rich in honey. I do not like to camp out in bad weather any more on account of rheumatism. Other than that, all of my old friends here claim that I do not look older than 20 years old. Perhaps there is a bit of flattery. Next time I will write you in more detail.

Your son Francis Kettner

**Fig. 53. Oil Painting of the Kettner Home by Lena Klingelhefer Lewis (Early 1940s).**
**Abb. 53. Ölgemälde des Kettner Hauses von Lena Klingelhefer Lewis (frühe 1940er).**

**Brief 35 (29. April 1874) von Franz Kettner vom McSween Place an seine Nichte Marie Erdrich und an seinen Vater in Oberkirch**

Mason, 29. April 1874

Teure Marie!

Auf meinen letzten Brief an Klärchen, adressiert an Papa, welchen ich acht Tage vor Weihnachten 73 abgeschickt habe, bin bis jetzt ohne Antwort. Sollte vielleicht Euer Brief verloren gegangen sein?

Meine Familie erfreut sich guter Gesundheit und Louis, welcher während des letzten Winters in Mason zur Schule ging, ist auch wieder zu Hause. Wir waren dieses Frühjahr alle sehr in Anspruch genommen, teilweise weil mein Feld bedeutend vergrößert worden ist, und anderenteils kam gerade die Lammzeit. Ich habe 100 Lämmer erhalten. Sehr feine Schafe, und ich war meistens von Hause entfernt, als Inspektor beschäftigt.

Jetzt habe ich hinreichend Zeit, meine Häuslichkeiten zu besorgen. Letzten Winter haben wir fortwährend grünen Kohl gegessen, so ausnehmend gelinde war der Winter. Mein Garten steht auch jetzt in schönem Schmucke, und wir haben das Renommee, immer den schönsten Garten im County zu haben. Stelle Dir vor, dicht beim Hause, auf einer ganz kleinen Erhöhung, ist eine Quelle ausgemauert, beschattet von prachtvollen Nußbäumen und Trauerweiden. Das Bassin, welches bedeutend Wasser hält, ist ein ausgezeichneter Badeplatz. Jeden Abend und Morgen wird das Wasser in die verschiedenen Beete laufen gelassen, so daß wir in der größten Trockenheit fortwährend Gemüse haben.

Es ist ein Liebhaberei von mir, jeden Morgen vor dem Frühstück mich im Garten zu beschäftigen und meine Bienen zu beobachten, deren ich ziemlich viel besitze. Die Bienen schwärmen hier dreimal jährlich. Meine Obstbäume tragen auch schon. Meine offene Galerie an der Front des Hauses ist mit Schlingenpflanzen versehen, der Hofraum mit Rosen und Immergrün und verschiedenen prachtvollen Oleander, welche jeden Winter ins Haus geschafft werden. Oleander ist unstreitig das schönste Gewächs, was ich kenne. Meine Mädchen, welche große Liebhaberei an Blumen haben, wenden viel Arbeit darauf, alle möglichen Blumen zu ziehen. Meine Ida, welche viel lieber ein Pferd reitet als Hausarbeit besorgt, ist jetzt überglücklich. Ich habe nämlich eine feine Apfelschimmelstute gekauft für hundert und fünfzig Dollars, nach Gulden 250 fl, welche dieselbe als ihr Eigentum betrachtet und gewöhnlich reitet, aber beinahe immer im kurzen Galopp. Das Mädchen macht eine hübsche Figur zu Pferde und ist eine gewandte Reiterin, setzt über Gräben und sonstige Hindernisse und versteht ein Pferd zu führen.

Meine öffentliche Laufbahn als Beamter, als welcher ich jetzt schon circa zehn Jahre einen großen Teil meiner Zeit widmete, werde ich nach Ablauf meiner Dienstzeit beschließen, da ich durch meine eigenen Interessen davon abgehalten werde. Nämlich ich gebrauche meine ganze Zeit für mich selbst und habe es nicht mehr nötig von wegen dem Einkommen.

Mein Eigentum, was ich besitze, ist nach den allerniedrigsten Preisen berechnet ungefähr fl 15.000 wert und ich habe mit nichts angefangen. Da die Eichelmast gesichert ist, so werde ich diesen Winter für nahe an fl 1000 Speck oder Schweine verkaufen. Alles übrige Geld werde ich dazu verwenden, alles Land um mich herum anzukaufen, so daß meine Farm an tausend bis 1500 Acre enthält. Denn da wir in circa zwei Jahren ein komplettes Eisenbahnnetz haben werden, so wird Texas sich rasch bevölkern und das Land wird steigen.

Ich wünsche, daß Du mir nach Empfang dieses Briefes rasch antwortest, mir alle Lokalneuigkeiten mitteilst, außerdem erwarte ich einige Zeilen von Papa, ich hoffe, da ich so lange ohne Antwort von Euch bin, daß seine Gesundheit sich befestigt hat, und er wieder munter ist.

Indem ich hoffe, daß dieser Brief Dich und Deine ganze Familie bei guter Gesundheit antrifft, grüße Euch vielmals und verbleibe Dein Onkel

Francis Kettner

Viele Grüße an Papa und den Erdrich.

Mason, 29. April 1874

Lieber Papa.

Gleichzeitig mit Maries Brief, will ich auch einige Zeilen an Sie schreiben. Aus Maries Brief werden Sie ersehen, daß bei uns alles munter ist. Der Gesundheitszustand meiner Frau, nämlich der Magenkrampf, ist seit zwei Jahren gänzlich verschwunden und seitdem ist alles wohl. Ich war und bin noch immer am Bauen und Einrichten meines Gutes beschäftigt. Ich habe die letzten zwei Jahre als Beamter viel Geld verdient, aber meine Einrichtungen kosten mich ebenfalls sehr viel. Doch jetzt ist das meiste fertig, und ich beschränke mich jetzt darauf, angrenzende Ländereien aufzukaufen; denn meine Schafe werde ich im Zeitraum von einem Jahr durch einen Hirten hüten lassen müssen; und die Zeit wird kommen, wo man auf seinem eigenen Lande hüten muß.

Die Bienenzucht ist hier viel ergiebiger als in Deutschland. Im Frühjahr schwärmen dieselben zweimal und im Nachsommer einmal, also drei Schwärme von jedem Stock und sind immer sehr reich an Honig. Das Biwakieren bei schlechtem Wetter will mir nicht mehr recht behagen, von wegen Rheumatismus, sonst behaupten alle meine alten Bekannten hier, daß ich nicht älter aussehe als vor zwanzig Jahren. Vielleicht etwas Schmeichelei dabei. Nächstens werde ich an Sie ausführlicher schreiben.

Ihr Sohn Francis Kettner.

# Letter / Brief 36

### Letter 36 (Fall 1874[267]) from Francis Kettner at the McSween Place, to his Father

My dear Father,

I received the letter from Marie in good time and I am making haste so that you will hear something from me. We are all still healthy and lively. The summer was unusually hot and dry and afterward we made a good harvest because the rain still arrived at the right time. The trees are full of acorns and nuts and we will have very good swine to slaughter. I have around 40 head of swine to slaughter that I will sell, either living or slaughtered and with the bacon to sell. In addition, I have 200 bushels of corn to sell.

I was away from home much of this summer due to my position as inspector, but my official term comes to an end this year. I will probably not take on a public office any more because I need all of my time myself for the farm work. My sheep increase every year; I have a large swine-raising operation. The cattle also increase and I make a larger area of cultivated ground every year so that I seek to use my time at home. In addition, I cannot stand to camp outside much anymore because I suffer quite a lot of back pain since the time that I fenced in my fields two years ago with stone that I dug up and laid on myself. Over all, I am at the age in which a man cannot rip out a tree any more.

I can ride on a horse all day long, that does not tire me at all. So I will use the largest part of my time working on horseback, riding after my swine and gathering them into groups where I find them and driving them home to feed them so that they will remain tame.

In addition, I am beginning to raise horses. I have purchased three stallions. The Indian situation is coming to a close, at last. The tribes must either come into order or they will be exterminated. The war is already in full force and there have already

[267] The date of this letter is approximated by the author.

been battles won. The Indians, who are very well armed, will be beaten this time, however, because they cannot withstand the artillery fire. The state of Texas is coming into its development quickly.

Elise, who is now twelve and a half years old, is fully grown-up and as tall as me and a head taller as her older sister Ida. Both of my little boys, Willy and Karl,[268] are completely happy since they now have their own horses.

About 14 days ago, millions of traveling grasshoppers came through here. Fortunately, they have left us. They came from the north and were traveling south and the whole sky was white.

An old comrade-in-arms who had served with me in a company twenty-two years ago visited me a few days ago as a traveling salesman and flattered me by saying that I had changed very little. He had had his own business worth several thousand dollars, but was ruined because of speculation. Now he starts again from the first as a traveling salesman. I would rather start slowly and be safe. I think I would be unhappy if I had to start again from the beginning with nothing. The times have also changed. It requires more of a bankroll in order to start a livelihood than it did 25 years ago. Then a log cabin was enough. Now it has to be a good stone house and luxuries. Louis wears a silver pocket watch with a silver chain that he bought with his own money. In order to improve my farm to how I want it to be, it will cost me two more years in work and strength. It is necessary for me to enclose about 250 acres of meadowland for my sheep for lambing in the spring and later to allow the rams to run in there. Best suited for this purpose and for a lifetime are stone fences, but these cost so much money and hard work. Fortunately, suitable stone is found very close by.

I have also sought to make something with grapes. I have the hope that the climate here is suitable. My peach trees were so full this year that I had to support them. Apple and pear trees[269] are also planted but they have not yet born fruit.

The grasshoppers have totally ruined my fall garden. Last year we ate fresh cabbage from the garden until New Year. In addition, we had green lettuce through the entire winter. We will produce bratwurst this winter for the entire year. We will keep all the ham for our own use and only sell the bacon.

I surprised my wife with a sewing machine that makes outstanding work. I wish that you would answer this letter right away and write me everything new that could interest me, mainly however, how you are doing. Enclosed you will find the seal of my office for curiosity's sake.

---

[268] The original pantry from the kitchen is still in use in the Kettner home. It has a lock on the door with a bell that rings when the key is turned. According to family lore, Karl had a real sweet tooth and had a habit of stealing sugar from the pantry. Mrs. Kettner had the lock installed to safe guard her sugar supply.

[269] The predominate trees in Franz's garden have been pear trees since the early 1900s and up to the present day. Neighbors recall picking a pear when they rode past the Kettner place. Personal communication with Charles A. Kettner.

I hope that you will find the opportunity to send me a small, genuine Meerschaum pipe. I have already bought for myself several so-called Meerschaum pipes, but have been regularly misled. Smoking is my only unnecessary habit, but I cannot give it up.

From time to time, I am drinking a bottle of good imported Wiener beer, but it is somewhat too expensive. Coffee is our main drink and we drink it strong and good. The climate requires it. In summer, we nap after lunch until 2 and then drink a strong cup of coffee. Then one is again lively, despite the heat.

In the hope that this letter finds you still healthy and lively, I remain

Your grateful son, F. Kettner

(greetings on all the relatives)

**Fig. 54. Remnants of the Rock Fence.** This photograph was taken on southern boundry of Franz's property. The fence was probably built to enclose the 250 acres of meadowland for lambing sheep that Franz describes to his Father. It is appoximately one half mile from the Kettner home.

**Abb. 54. Überreste der Natursteinmauer**. Dieses Foto wurde an der südlichen Grenze des Besitzes von Franz aufgenommen. Die Mauer wurde wahrscheinlich errichtet, um 250 acres Weideland für trächtige Schafe einzuzäunen wie Franz an seinen Vater schreibt. Es befindet sich ca. eine halbe Meile vom Kettner Haus entfernt.

## Brief 36 (Herbst 1874[270]) von Franz Kettner vom McSween Place an seinen Vater

Mein lieber Vater!

Den Brief von Marie habe ich seinerzeit erhalten und ich beeile mich, etwas von mir hören zu lassen. Wir alle sind noch immer gesund und munter. Der Sommer war ausnehmend heiß und trocken und dennoch haben wir eine gute Ernte erhalten, indem der Regen immer noch zur rechten Zeit eintraf. Die Bäume sind voll von Eicheln und Nüssen und wir werden sehr gute Schweine zu schlachten haben. Ich habe circa 40 Stück Schlachtschweine, die ich verwerten werde. Entweder lebendig oder schlachten und den Speck verkaufen. Ebenfalls habe ich 200 Büschel Maiskorn zu verkaufen.

Ich war diesen Sommer noch viel abwesend von Hause in meiner Stellung als Inspektor, aber dieses Jahr geht meine Amtszeit zu Ende. Ich werde wahrscheinlich kein öffentliches Amt mehr annehmen, da meine Wirtschaft meine Zeit selbst in Anspruch nimmt. Meine Schafe vermehren sich mit jedem Jahre, ich habe eine große Schweinezucht. Das Vieh vermehrt sich auch, mein Feld wird auch mit jedem Jahr größer gemacht und kultiviert, so daß ich meine Zeit zu Hause zu verwerten suche. Außerdem bekommt mir das draußen Kampieren nicht mehr recht gut, weil ich viel von Rückenschmerzen zu leiden habe seit der Zeit ich zur Einfriedigung meines Feldes zwei Winter hindurch Steine gefahren habe, alleine aufgeladen und abgeladen. Überhaupt bin ich in dem Alter, wo man keine Bäume mehr ausreißen kann.

Zu Pferde kann ich den ganzen Tag sein, das ermüdet mich nicht im mindesten. So werde ich von nun an den größten Teil meiner Zeit zu Pferde arbeiten, nach meinen Schweinen reiten und dieselben gelegentlich in Partien, so wie ich sie finde, nach Hause treiben und füttern, damit sie zahm bleiben.

Außerdem fange ich etwas Pferdezucht an. Ich habe mir drei Stuten angeschafft. Die Indianerfrage geht ihrer endlichen Lösung entgegeben. Dieselben müssen jetzt Ordre parieren oder werden ausgerottet. Der Krieg ist schon in vollem Gange und es werden schon Gefechte geliefert. Die Indianer, welche sehr gut bewaffnet sind, werden aber jedesmal geschlagen; da dieselben das Artilleriefeuer nicht ertragen können. Der Staat Texas geht rasch seiner Entwicklung entgegen.

Elise welche jetzt 12 ½ Jahre alt ist, ist völlig ausgewachsen und so groß als ich selbst, und einen Kopf größer als ihre ältere Schwester Ida. Meine beiden kleinen Jungen Willy und Carl sind ganz glücklich, daß sie jetzt eigene Pferde besitzen.

Vor ungefähr 14 Tagen kamen die wandernden Heuschrecken hier durch zu Millionen. Haben uns aber glücklich verlassen. Dieselben kamen von Norden und zogen südlich, die ganze Luft war weiß.

Ein alter Waffengefährte, welcher mit mir in einer Kompanie diente, 22 ½ Jahre her, besuchte mich dieser Tage als Handlungsreisender und sagte mir die Schmeichelei, daß ich mich sehr wenig verändert hätte. Derselbe hatte sein eigenes

---

[270] Ort und Datum nach Vermutung der Autorin.

Geschäft gehabt, war einige tausend Dollars wert, aber durch Spekulation gebrochen worden. Jetzt fängt er wieder von neuem an als Reisender. Ich gehe doch lieber langsam voran und sicher. Ich glaube, ich wäre unglücklich, wenn ich wieder von vorne so mit nichts anfangen sollte. Die Zeiten haben sich auch geändert. Es gehören jetzt mehr Mittel dazu, sich eine Existenz zu gründen als vor 25 Jahren. Da war ein Blockhaus gut genug. Jetzt müssen es gute Steinhäuser sein und der Luxus. Louis trägt schon ein silbernes Zylinderührchen mit Silberkette, welche er sich aus eigenen Mitteln angeschafft hat. Mein Gut völlig einzurichten, so wie ich es wünsche, kostet mich noch zwei Jahre Arbeit und Arbeitskräfte. Ich muß notwendig ungefähr 250 Morgen Wiesenland einfriedigen, um die Schafe im Frühjahr mit ihren Lämmern und später die Böcke darin laufen zu lassen. Am besten dazu und für Lebenszeit eignen sich Steineinfenzungen. Aber dieselben kosten viel Geld und Arbeitskraft. Die dazu geeigneten Steine befinden sich glücklicherweise ganz in meiner Nähe.

Ich habe auch einige Versuche gemacht mit Reben, ich habe Hoffnung, daß das Klima dazu geeignet ist. Meine Pfirsichbäume waren dieses Jahr so voll, daß ich dieselben stützen mußte. Apfel und Birnen habe auch gepflanzt, haben aber noch nicht getragen.

Die Heuschrecken haben meinen Spätjahr-Garten total ruiniert. Letztes Jahr aßen wir bis Neujahr frischen Kohl aus dem Garten. Ebenso hatten wir grünen Salat den ganzen Winter hindurch. Wir werden diesen Winter Bratwurst fürs ganze Jahr fabrizieren, ebenso alle Schinken für den Selbstgebrauch behalten und bloß den Speck verkaufen.

Ich habe meine Frau mit einer Nähmaschine überrascht, welche ausgezeichnete Dienste verrichtet. Ich wünsche, daß Sie mir diesen Brief recht bald beantworten und mir alles Neue schreiben, was mich interessieren könnte, namentlich aber, wie Sie sich befinden. Beiliegend finden Sie meinen Amtssiegel der Kuriosität halber.

Ich wünschte, Sie würden eine Gelegenheit finden, mir eine kleine echte Meerschaumpfeife zu senden. Ich habe mir bereits mehrere angebliche Meerschaumpfeifen gekauft, bin aber regelmäßig angeführt worden. Das Rauchen ist meine einzige unnötige Ausgabe, aber ich kann es nicht lassen.

Zuweilen trinke ich eine gute Flasche importiertes Wiener-Bier, welches aber etwas zu teuer kommt. Kaffee ist unser Hauptgetränk und denselben trinken wir stark und gut. Das Klima verlangt es. Im Sommer wird nach dem Essen bis zwei Uhr geschlafen und dann eine starke Tasse Kaffee getrunken. Dann ist man wieder munter, trotz der Hitze.

In der Hoffnung, daß dieser Brief Sie noch gesund und munter antrifft verbleibe ich

Ihr dankbarer Sohn F. Kettner

(Grüße an alle Verwandte).

# Letter / Brief 37

**Letter 37 (March 26, 1875[271]) from August Nicolai in Karlsruhe to Franz Kettner in Texas[272]**

Karlsruhe, March 26, 1875

Dear Brother-in-law!

I received your letter of the 15th February this year on the 11th of March, a few days later I received the notarized power-of-attorney with the covering letter of the Consul of the German Reich from Galveston, the February 22, 1875.

I sent the power-of-attorney immediately to the Grand Duke's Notary in Oberkirch with whom I have worked for the quickest possible settlement of the inheritance shares. I have already been three times to Oberkirch for this purpose.

The first time for two days, the entire estate was taken up and taxed.

Fourteen days later came the required notification and necessary preparations for the auctioning of the (medical) practice, the house, and the fields in back of the house. Three days were needed for these tasks; I was present for two of them.

Franz Kissel, from here, also went there for the entire auction and yesterday the distribution of the sum of the inheritance took place. It only remains for the cost of the distribution to be figured and to complete the estate notes which the notary said required 14 days to 4 weeks.

In my next letter I will tell you at least a summary of your designated share notice; therefore, today I will hold back from telling you. Some of the most important bequests I can tell you earlier.

On the second day of the proceedings, we found among grandfather's documents a personally written will, whose authenticity cannot be denied. In it he had, as he

[271] Since the last page is missing, there is no signature, but it is clear to the author from the handwriting and contents that this letter is from August Nicolai, the husband of Elise Nicolai.

[272] Original letter is in the possession of Patsy Kothmann Ziriax, Mason, TX.

had earlier also told you, declared a large number of his moveable belongings as legacies for remembrance.

So for you, his golden watch with the hair chain; for Klara, the mirror in the open room; I received a 4-ohm (about 600 liters) cask of sherry and the faithful and kind servant girl Katharina received her bed and two bedspreads.

The best legacies went to the Kissel family.

Maria received the alabaster standing clock, 6 silver coffee spoons, Grandfather's pocket watch that he carried for 60 years, and various painted coffee sets.

Franz Kissel received his fur coat, 6 silver coffee spoons, and 6 good shirts.

Maria's husband, Leopold Erdrich received 4-ohm wine casks as well, and then, probably because of his efforts in the sale of Mrs. Sartory's[273] house in Mannheim, an additional cash gift of 200 gulden.

And to conclude, Maria's oldest daughter Ida received a dozen silver tablespoons and a silver serving spoon.

The auction of the remaining moveable property and real estate came out well in general. The house, garden, and fields yielded about 15,000 marks (8750 gulden), more than grandfather had ever expected. The now-planned construction of a railroad from Appenweier through Oberkirch to Oppenau has affected these favorable proceeds.

The existing securities were divided, as well as possible, into shares. The value was computed exactly after the current rate on the day grandfather died. Apart from the above-mentioned small personal bequests that Grandfather wanted to make after the death of your mother, here and there, on account of the (performed) support and care, the division is computed completely according to justice and the law.

Following this, one inheritance share fell to you, one to Clara, and the third to Franz Kissel and Marie Erdrich as the grandchildren of your sister Ida.[274]

The costs of (settling) the estate have not yet been determined as earlier noted. Also, some other parties have not yet made their amount exact. I can, therefore, not figure your share to the penny now, (but) probably you will receive something between 15,000 and 16,000 marks which in the former, well-known southern German currency would be about 9000 gulden. Your early inheritance share, which was the same as both the other two inheritance shares, that was computed as half of your father's fortune, was already subtracted.

The great distance from your domicile and the difficulty of valuing the Baden State bonds according to use, makes the mailing of these bonds not seem advisable. Therefore, I will take over the shares that fall to you, at a given price, either for Clara or one of the other heirs.

[*The letter breaks off here and the following pages are lost.]*

---

[273] Maria Magdalena Sartorius, her maiden name was Kettner.

[274] Children of Ida are the grandchildren of Dr. Franz Lambert Kettner.

## Brief 37 (26. März 1875) von August Nicolai[275] aus Karlsruhe an Franz Kettner in Texas[276]

Karlsruhe, 26. März 1875

Lieber Schwager!

Deinen lieben Brief vom 15. Februar d. J.[277] habe ich am 11ten d. M. erhalten, einige Tage später erhielt ich auch die avisierte Vollmacht mit Begleitschreiben des Consulats des Deutschen Reiches d. d. Galveston den 22. Februar 1875.

Ich habe die Vollmacht sofort dem Großh.[278] Notar in Oberkirch gesendet, bei welchem ich überhaupt auf die möglichst rasche Erledigung der Erbschaftsteilung hingewirkt habe. Ich war zu diesem Behufe bereits dreimal in Oberkirch.

Das erste Mal wurde an zwei Tagen die gesamte Habe aufgenommen und taxiert.

14 Tage später erfolgte nach den erforderlichen Bekanntmachungen und sonstigen Vorbereitungen die Versteigerung der Praxis, des Hauses und des hinter demselben liegenden Feldes. Zu diesem Akte waren drei Tage nötig, an zwei derselben war ich anwesend.

Bei der ganzen Versteigerung war auch Franz Kissel von hier zugegen, und gestern fand die Verteilung der Erbschaftsmasse statt. Es sind nun noch die Teilungskosten festzustellen und die Teilungszettel zu fertigen, worüber nach Angabe des Notars noch immer 14 Tage bis 4 Wochen vergehen mögen.

Ich werde Dir mit meinem nächsten Briefe den für Dich bestimmten Teilzettel mindestens im Auszuge mitteilen, ich will mich deshalb für heute darauf beschränken, Dir einige wichtigere Notizen vorläufig mitzuteilen.

Am zweiten Tage der Aufnahme fanden wir unter Großvaters Wertpapieren ein eigenhändig geschriebenes Testament, dessen Echtheit nicht bestritten werden konnte. Danach hat er, wie er auch Dir früher mitgeteilt hat, eine größere Anzahl Fahrnisgegenstände[279] als Legate zur Erinnerung vermacht.

So an Dich seine goldene Uhr mit Haarkette, an Klara den Spiegel im offenen Zimmer, ich erhielt ein vier ohmiges[280] Cerres[281] Weinfaß und das treue und brave Dienstmädchen Katharina ihr Bett mit zwei Anzügen.

Die besten Legate fielen der Kisselschen Familie zu.

Maria erhielt die Alabaster-Stockuhr, 6 silberne Kaffeelöffel, Großvaters silberne Taschenuhr, die er 60 Jahre lang getragen hat und verschiedenes gemaltes Kaffeegeschirr.

---

275 Der Handschrift und dem Inhalt nach stammt dieser Brief von August Nicolai, Ehemann von Elise Nicolai.

276 Original des Briefes befindet sich im Besitz von Patsy Kothmann Ziriax, Mason, Texas.

277 Anmerkung der Autorin: Brief von Franz Kettner aus Mason/Texas vom 15. Februar 1875 an August Nicolai nach dem Tode seines Vaters am 16. Januar 1875 fehlt.

278 Großherzoglich

279 Fahrnis = bewegliche Güter

280 Ohm = von lat. ama "Eimer" (auch Ahm oder Aam), altes Flüssigkeitsmaß zwischen 134 und 174,75 Liter. Vgl. *Der Große Knaur, Lexikon in 4 Bänden*, Bd.3, Stuttgart/Hamburg 1967, S.443.

281 Spanisch Xeres, englisch Sherry

Franz Kissel erhielt den Pelzmantel, 6 silberne Kaffeelöffel und 6 bessere Hemden.

Der Mann von Maria, Leopold Erdrich erhielt ebenfalls 4 Ohm große Weinfässer, sodann angeblich wegen Bemühungen bei der Versteigerung des Hauses von Frau Sartory[282] in Mannheim noch ein Geldgeschenk von 200 Gulden.

Endlich erhielt Marias älteste Tochter Ida ein Dutzend silberne Eßlöffel und einen silbernen Vorleglöffel.

Die Versteigerung der übrigen Fahrnisse und der Liegenschaften ist im allgemeinen befriedigend ausgefallen. Aus Haus und Garten und Feld wurden ca. 15000 Mark (8750 Gulden.) gelöst, mehr als Großvater sich je erwartet hätte. Der nun in Angriff genommene Bau einer Eisenbahn von Appenweier über Oberkirch nach Oppenau hat auf diesen günstigen Erlös eingewirkt.

Die vorhandenen Wertpapiere wurden so weit als möglich in Stück geteilt. Deren Wert ist genau nach dem Tageskurs von Großvaters Sterbetag berechnet. Abgesehen von der oben erwähnten kleinen Begünstigung in den Legaten, wozu Großvater durch die ihm in den letzten Jahren seit Deiner Mutter Tod da und dort zu Teil gewordene Unterstützung und Pflege veranlaßt sein mochte, ist die Teilung der Gerechtigkeit und den Gesetzen entsprechend vollzogen worden.

Danach fällt ein Erbteil auf Dich, einer auf Clara und der Dritte auf Franz Kissel und Marie Erdrich als Enkel Deiner Schwester Ida.[283]

Wie bereits bemerkt, sind die Teilungslasten noch nicht festgestellt. Auch einige andere Partien sind ihrer Größe nach noch nicht genau bekannt. Ich kann deshalb auf den Kreuzer[284] Deinen Erbanfall jetzt noch nicht bezeichnen, annähernd wirst Du indessen zwischen 15000 und 16000 Mark, d. i. in dem Dir wohl noch bekannten Voremfang, der gleich war jenen bei den beiden andern Erbteilen, zur Hälfte auf des Vaters Vermögen aufgerechnet wird, schon abgezogen.

Die weite Entfernung nach Deinem Wohnsitze und die Schwierigkeit badische Staatspapiere u. dgl. dorten entsprechend zu verwerten, läßt die Übersendung dieser Stücke entschieden nicht ratsam erscheinen. Ich werde deshalb die Dir zugefallenen Stücke um den aufgerechneten Preis entweder für Clara oder sonst übernehmen.

[*Der Brief bricht hier ab, das Nachfolgende fehlt.*]

---

[282] Maria Magdalena Sartorius, geb. Kettner.

[283] Kinder von Ida sind die Enkel von Vater Dr. Franz Lambert Kettner.

[284] Heute: "Auf den Pfennig genau."

# Letter / Brief 38

## Letter 38 (March 29, 1875) from Marie Erdrich[285] in Oberkirch to her Uncle Franz Kettner[286]

Oberkirch, the 29th of March 1875

Dear Uncle!

As you have heard from Uncle Nicolai, we all have a very sad loss to deplore. I can easily imagine that you were deeply shocked by this unexpected news and that it would be of great interest for you to know more completely about the last days of his life. I am convinced that a letter from me has been lost because you write that you have had no more news from us for ¾ of a year. Also, your last letters do not mention anything that was covered in my letter. I even had said to Grandfather at that time that you did not think it was worth the trouble to answer my letter although I had taken all the trouble to give you a detailed picture of all the local conditions.

At the start of last year Grandfather was still fairly sprightly and during the summer he still came to us over here. Then he got stomach pains once again and recovered very slowly. Since last fall, he could hardly walk alone any more; his feet lost their ability and also his memory failed a lot. In the last months, he fantasized (hallucinated) often in the evenings. When I came to visit him, he recognized me totally, but in the next minute he began to say, "if I were only in my own home now; now I must remain overnight in a strange home."

It was truly fortunate that he had a servant girl who was here in the time of Grandmother, and who had so outstandingly cared for him that his own children couldn not have taken care of him better. I was doubly pleased because this summer

---

[285] Since the last page is missing, there is no signature. However, the writer is without a doubt Marie Erdrich since she refers to her daughter, Ida, in the third to last paragraph. She is Franz's only niece who has a daughter named Ida.

[286] The original letter is in the possession of Patsy Kothmann Ziriax, Mason, TX.

I was so occupied with business that it was not possible, with the best of will, to visit him as often as I had wanted to.

Our Ida was the apple of his eye. She is extremely lively and merry and mentally ahead of herself in years but she caused us a lot of trouble in her growing up due to her wildness.

Grandfather did not have a true illness. A few days before his end came, he suddenly fainted on Sunday after lunch. We thought that he would stay in our arms. After he again became conscious and we had brought him to his bed, he had felt very well again except for coughing which he already had (been doing) for some time.

We had (engaged) still another attendant and also wrote to Karlsruhe at the same time so that Klara would come here immediately. Every evening he hallucinated and was in general very seldom himself; still we believed that this condition could continue for weeks, until on the 5th day after his fainting spell, the pulse

[*The letter ends on the fourth page and the rest of the text is missing.*]

## Brief 38 (29. März 1875) von Marie Erdrich[287] aus Oberkirch an ihren Onkel Franz Kettner in Texas[288]

Oberkirch, den 29. März 1875

Lieber Onkel!

Wie Dir durch Onkel Nicolai mitgeteilt wurde, haben wir alle einen sehr traurigen Verlust zu beklagen. Ich kann mir leicht vorstellen, daß Dich diese unerwartete Nachricht tief erschüttert hat und ist es für Dich gewiß von größtem Interesse, noch näheres über die letzte Zeit seines Lebens zu hören. Ich bin überzeugt, daß ein Brief von mir verloren gegangen ist, denn Du schreibst, seit etwa 3/4 Jahren hättest Du keine Nachrichten mehr von uns. Und auch Deine letzten Briefe erwähnen nichts, was auf meinen Brief Bezug gehabt hätte. Ich äußerte sogar bereits damals gegen Großvater, daß Du es gar nicht der Mühe wert hältst, von meinem Brief Notiz zu nehmen, zudem[289] ich mir alle mögliche Mühe gegeben habe, Dir von den hiesigen Verhältnissen ein genaues Bild zu geben.

Anfangs des verflossenen Jahres war Großvater noch ziemlich rüstig und auch während des Sommers kam er noch zu uns herüber. Dann bekam er wieder einmal Magenweh und erholte sich wieder sehr langsam. Seit dem letzten Spätjahr konnte er kaum mehr allein gehen, die Füße versagten ihren Dienst und auch das Gedächtnis nahm sehr ab. In letzterer Zeit fantasierte er gegen Abend sehr oft. Wenn ich ihn da besuchte, erkannte er mich vollständig, aber in der nächsten Minute fing er an, "wenn ich nur zu Hause wäre, jetzt muß ich auch noch in einem fremden Hause über Nacht bleiben."

Ein wahres Glück war es, daß er ein Mädchen hatte, welche noch zu Zeiten der Großmutter da gewesen ist, und welche ihn so außerordentlich gut gepflegt hatte, daß seine eigenen Kinder nicht besser hätten für ihn sorgen können. Ich bin doppelt froh, denn wie ich diesen Sommer im Geschäft angestrengt war, ist es mir beim besten Willen nicht möglich gewesen, ihn so oft zu besuchen als mein Wille gewesen wäre.

Unsere Ida war sein Augapfel. Sie ist äußerst lebhaft und lustig und in geistiger Hinsicht ihren Jahren voraus, macht uns aber in der Erziehung viele Mühe durch ihre große Wildheit.

Eigentliche Krankheit hatte Großvater nicht. Ein paar Tage vor seinem Ende bekam er plötzlich Sonntags nach dem Mittagessen eine Ohnmacht. Wir glaubten er bleibt uns in den Armen. Nachdem das Bewußtsein wieder da war und wir ihn zu Bett gebracht hatten, fühlte er sich wieder ganz wohl, außer Husten, welchen er schon einige Zeit hatte.

Wir hatten noch eine Obwärterin und auch nach Karlsruhe schrieben wir gleich, worauf Klara umgehend hierher gekommen ist. Abends fantasierte er beständig und

---

[287] Brief von Marie Erdrich ohne Unterschrift, da die letzte Seite fehlt. Sie erwähnt Ihre Tochter Ida im drittletzten Absatz.

[288] Original des Briefes befindet sich im Besitz von Patsy Kothmann Ziriax, Mason, Texas.

[289] "zudem" im Sinne von "insbesondere da"

war überhaupt sehr selten bei sich, doch glaubten wir, daß dieser Zustand noch einige Wochen könnte dauern, bis am 5. Tag nach seiner Ohnmacht der Puls.

Hier bricht der Brief nach der 4. Seite ab, der folgende Text fehlt.

# Letter / Brief 39

### Letter 39 (July 2, 1875) from August Nicolai in Karlsruhe to Francis Kettner[290]

Dear Brother-in-law!

Since some time I have been waiting for a letter from you with the acknowledgment that your inheritance letter, my figuring sheet, and the first exchange note for the entire sum of your inheritance in currency has been received by you in full.

Yesterday I received your worthy writing from the 27th of May of this year and was not a little surprised to learn that this letter was first an answer to my letter of the 26th of March this year and that you, also, on the day of posting this letter in question, had not yet received either of my last letters.

I repeat, therefore, that I already on the 7th of May this year sent you in a registered letter the (inheritance) share notice, my computation, and the first exchange note from a New York house (bank) for the total sum of your inheritance. I have, however, used caution to have issued both first and second exchange notes. Likewise, I have sent the second in a registered letter on the 15th of May this year and in it I also said that I had already sent the packet from the 7th of May, upon the receipt of your note on account of a Mainz House (Bank). You will learn from the exchange note that you will obtain gold in relation to the value of the gold in your currency. I also identified for you the business house in San Antonio, which I believe is the headquarters of the German Consulate with which the referred-to, very stable New York currency house has a business connection. Hopefully, when you receive this letter, both of my last mailings from the 7th and 15th of May will have reached you and I ask now the urgent request from you that you notify me as soon as possible about the correct arrival.

According to your request, I will send your father's watch to R. Moureau in Bremen and it will please me, also, when you notify me that you have received it.

---

290 The original letter is in the possession of Patsy Kothmann Ziriax, Mason, TX.

That you would like to return to Germany once more in about two years, makes me very happy; I think that you will first stay with me.

Since the completion of the inheritance business, I have not been in Oberkirch. I think that sometime in the summer that I will go there once again.

A few days ago, I got the news that Fanny, the oldest daughter of the earlier innkeeper Fischer of the Adler, is engaged to a salesman from Freiburg. You may know that the Frau Fischer, across from Grandfather's house, has been married now[291] for a long time to Salesman Borsig.

At present, they are working energetically on the railroad from Appenweier to Oppenau; next year it will be completed.

Greet your entire family for me and, as I hope, if a letter from you is already on its way, let me hear something soon again from you.

Your faithful brother-in-law

A. Nicolai *[The letter exchange stops here.]*

**Fig. 55. August Nicolai.** This photograph, labeled Nicolai, was in the collection of the Gamel family and was provided by Deloris and Clay Lindsay. The back of the photograph identified F. Halm, Constanz, Augustinerstrafse, as the photographer. The photograph was mistakenly labeled "Great Grandfather Kettner" by Franz's granddaughter. However, we are reasonably certain that the portrait is of August Nicolai since Constanz is near Nicolai's home in Karlsruhe.

**Abb. 55. August Nicolai.** Dieses Foto, beschriftet Nicolai, wurde in der Sammlung des Gamel Familie und wurde von Deloris und Clay Lindsay zur Verfügung gestellt. Die Rückseite des Fotos identifiziert F. Halm, Konstanz, Augustinerstrafse, wie der Fotograf. Das Foto wurde fälschlicherweise mit der Bezeichnung "Great Grandfather Kettner" von Franz Enkelin. Aber wir sind ziemlich sicher, dass das Porträt von August Nicolai, da ist in der Nähe von Konstanz nach Hause Nicolai in Karlsruhe.

[291] The letter is only partially legible at the fold. "now" could also be interpreted as "again".

## Brief 39 (2. Juli 1875) von August Nicolai aus Karlsruhe an Franz Kettner in Texas[292]

Karlsruhe, 2. Juli 1875

Lieber Schwager!

Schon seit einiger Zeit erwarte ich einen Brief von Dir mit der Anzeige, daß Dein Teilzettel, meine Abrechnung und der Primawechsel über den ganzen in bar umgesetzten Betrag Deiner Erbschaft wohlbehalten bei Dir eingetroffen sind.

Gestern erhielt ich Dein wertes Schreiben vom 27. Mai d. J. und war nicht wenig überrascht zu erfahren, daß dieser Brief erst eine Antwort auf meinen Brief zum 26. März d. J. ist und Dir also am Tage der Absendung des fraglichen Briefes meine beiden letzten Zusendungen noch nicht zugekommen waren.

Ich wiederhole deshalb, daß ich schon am 7. Mai d. J. in rekommandiertem Schreiben die Teilzettel, meine Abrechnung und Primawechsel auf ein New Yorker Haus über den ganzen Betrag Deines Erbteils Dir zugesendet habe. Ich habe allerdings die Vorsicht gebraucht, Prima und Secunda Wechsel ausstellen zu lassen. Die Secunda habe ich ebenfalls mit rekommandiertem Schreiben am 15. Mai d. J. abgesendet und darin Dir auch mitgeteilt, daß ich bei Empfang Deiner Notiz wegen eines Mainzer Hauses die Sendung vom 7 ten Mai schon expethiert[293] hatte. Du wirst aus den Wechseln erfahren, daß Du Gold zu empfangen hast, beziehungsweise den Goldwert in Eurer Valuta. Ich hatte Dir auch die Geschäftshäuser in San Antonio und ich meine auch am Sitze des Deutschen Konsulats bezeichnet, mit welchem das bezogene sehr solide New-Yorker Contierhaus in Geschäftsverbindung steht. Hoffentlich sind bei Ankunft dieses Briefes meine beiden letzen Sendungen vom 7ten und 15. Mai bei Dir angekommen und ich richte nun noch die dringende Bitte an Dich, mich baldigst von der richtigen Ankunft zu benachrichtigen.

Deinem Wunsche gemäß werde ich Deines Vaters Uhr Ende ....[294] an R. Moureau in Bremen senden und wird es mich freuen, s. Z. auch über den richtigen Empfang derselben von Dir benachrichtigt zu werden.

Daß Du in etwa 2 Jahren einmal nach Deutschland zurückkehren willst, freut mich sehr, ich denke, Du kehrst dann zunächst hier bei mir ein.

Seit Vollendung der Teilungsgeschichte war ich nicht mehr in Oberkirch. Ich denke indessen, daß ich im Laufe des Sommers noch einmal hinkommen werde.

Vor wenigen Tagen erhielt ich die Nachricht, daß die älteste Tochter von dem früheren Adlerwirt Fischer, Fanny sich mit einem Kaufmann von Freiburg verlobt hat. Es wird Dir bekannt sein, daß die Frau Fischer seit langer Zeit an Kaufmann Börsig, vis a vis von Großvaters Haus wie[295] verheiratet ist.

---

292 Original des Briefes befindet sich im Besitz von Patsy Kothmann Ziriax, Mason, Texas.

293 Expediert = aufgegeben.

294 Brief zerstört.

295 Teilweise unleserlich wegen Brieffaltung. In alternativer Interpretation könnte hier auch "wieder" stehen.

Es wird gegenwärtig fleißig an der Eisenbahn von Appenweier nach Oppenau gearbeitet, im nächsten Jahr wird sie wohl fertig werden.

Grüße mir Deine ganze Familie und lasse, auch wenn, wie ich wünschen möchte, schon wieder ein Brief von Dir unterwegs ist, doch bald wieder etwas von Dir hören.

Dein treuer Schwager

A. Nicolai

*[Der Briefwechsel bricht hier ab.]*

# Kettner Family Genealogy / Genealogie der Kettner Familie

**Dr. Franz Lambert and Maria Clara Kettner.** This original photograph was in the possession of Edna Kettner Kothmann (Louis Kettner's daughter) who gave it to Charles A. Kettner to be kept in the Kettner home. See Fig. 7, p. 11 for colored prints of Franz Lambert and Maria Clara.

**Dr. Franz Lambert und Maria Clara Kettner.** Dies Originalfoto befand sich im Besitz von Edna Kettner Kothmann (Tochter von Louis Kettner), die es Charles A. Kettner gab, damit es im Hause der Familie Kettner aufbewahrt werde. S. Abb. 7, S. 11, kolorierte Bilder von Franz Lambert und Maria Clara.

**Franz and Katherine Kettner on their 50th Wedding Anniversary.** The children, Louis, Ida Keller, Charlie, Alice Gamel, and William are standing behind their parents.

**Familie Kettner anläßlich des 50. Hochzeitstages von Franz und Katharina Kettner.** Die Kinder Louis, Ida Keller, Karl, Alice (Elise) Gamel und William stehend hinter ihren Eltern.

## *Hourglass Tree of Dr. Franz Lambert Kettner*

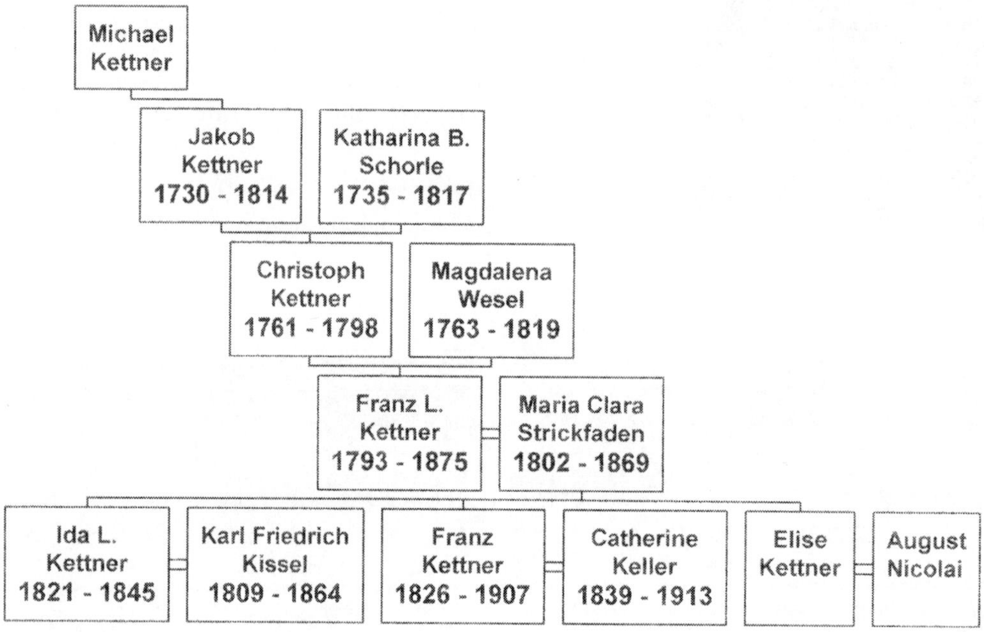


Elise and August Nicolai were married in Karlsruhe and had five children, one of which was Klara Nicolai. Letter 37 and 39 were written by August Nicolai.

## *Descendants of Ida Leopoldine Kettner*

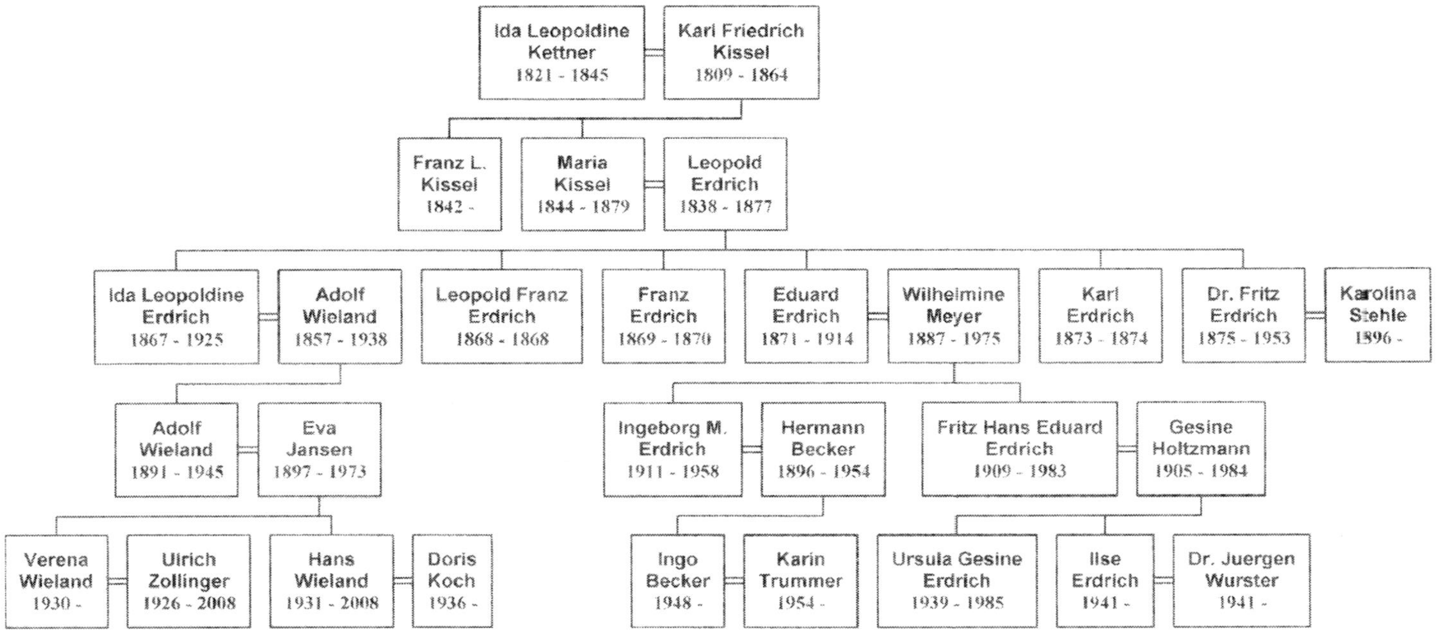

## *Descendants of Franz Kettner (1 of 2)*

cont. p. 267 below

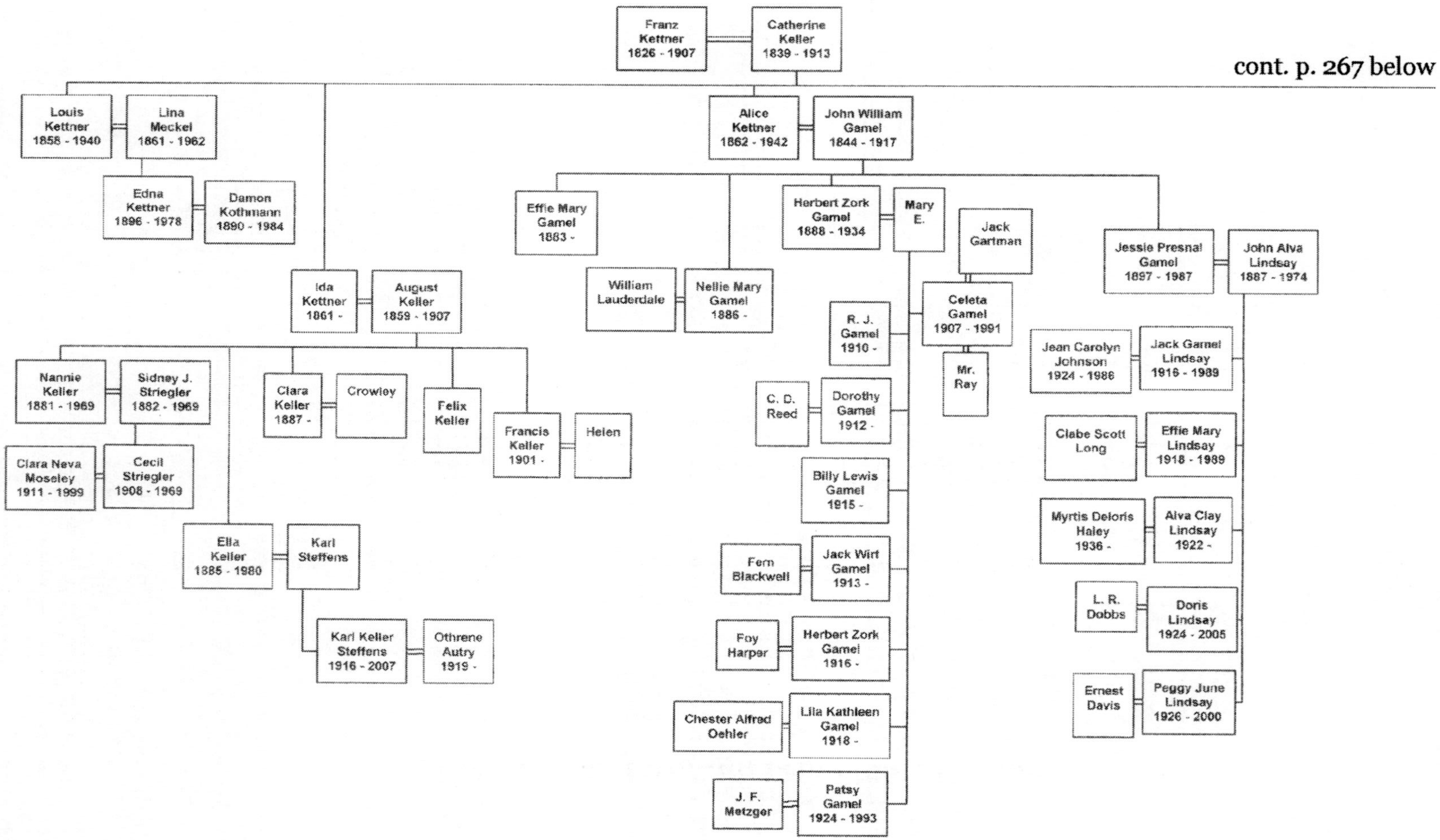

cont. from p. 266 above

## *Descendants of Franz Kettner (2 of 2)*

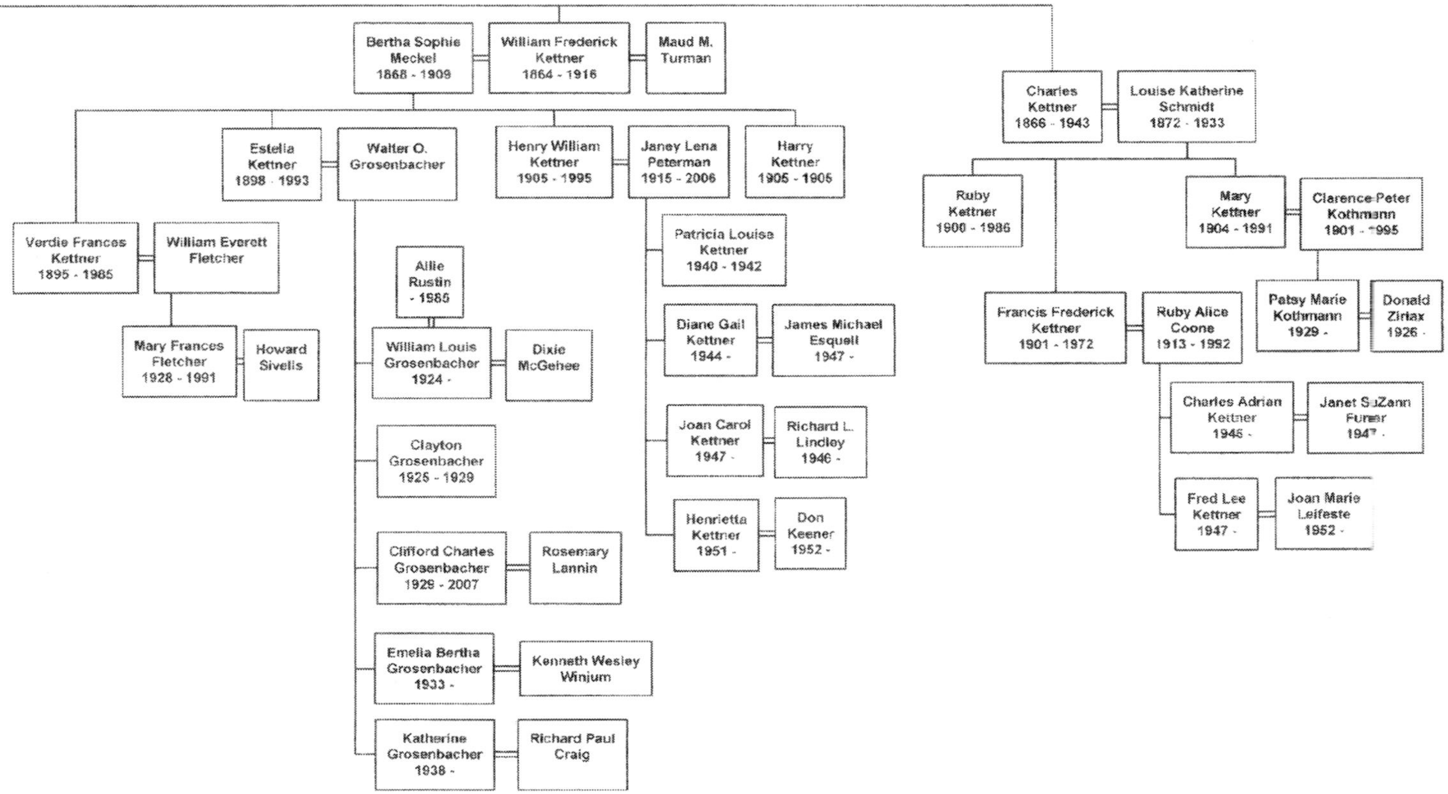

# Selected Bibliography / Ausgewählte Bibliographie


Bieberstein, H.R. v. "The First Lynching in Fredericksburg." In *Fredericksburg the First 50 Years,* trans. C.L Wisseman, 47-48. Fredericksburg, Texas: Fredericksburg Publishing Co., Inc, 1971.

Bierschwale, Margaret. *History of Mason County Texas through 1964.* Mason, Texas: The Mason County Historical Commission, 1998.

Blum, B. "The History of the Development of Gillespie County According to Information Taken from the County Records" In *Fredericksburg, Texas, the First Fifty Years*, trans. C.L. Wisseman, 52. Fredericksburg, TX: Fredericksburg Publishing Co., Inc, 1971.

Hunter, J. Marvin. "Major James M. Hunter." *Frontier Times*, 6 October 1928, 1-2. Jim Rodgers at http://www.frontiertimesmagazine.com/index.html. is a current source of back issues of the magazine.

Hunter, J. Marvin. "A Brief History of the Early Days in Mason County." *Frontier Times* 6, (Nov 1928. Dec. 1928, Jan. 1929, Feb. 1929, and Mar. 1929).

Johnson, David. *The Mason County "Hoo Doo" War*, 1874-1902. Denton, TX: University of North Texas Press, 2006.

Jordan, Terry G. *German Seeds in Texas Soil, Immigrant Farmers in Nineteenth Century Texas.* Austin, Texas: University of Texas Press, 1998.

Jordan, Terry G. and Jordan, Marlis A. "Letters of a German Pioneer in Texas."*Southwestern Historical Quarterly* 69, (1966): 463-472.

Klotzbach, Kurt. *Wagenspur nach Westen.* Goettingen: W. Fischer-Verlag, 1974.

Kothmann, Mary. "Francis (Franz) Kettner." In *Mason County Historical Book*, 134. Mason, Texas: Mason Historical Commission, 1976.

Kowert, Elise. "First Courthouse Remembered," Fredericksburg Standard Radio Post, June 23, 1993

Kriewitz, Emil. "Recollections from Indian Times." In *Fredericksburg, Texas, The First Fifty Years*, trans. Charles L Wisseman, Sr., 48-49. Fredericksburg, TX: Fredericksburg Publishing Co., Inc, 1971.

Lemburg, Mrs. Bill. "Major James M. Hunter." In *Mason County Historical Book*, 111. Mason, TX: Mason County Historical Commission, 1976).

Lc May, Alan. *The Searchers*. New York: Curtis Publishing Co., 1954.

Peters, Arno. *Synchronoptische Weltgeschichte*. München-Hamburg: Universum-Verlag,. 1965.

Pfister, Patty Schneider. *Castell, Texas, One Hundred Sixty Years, 1847-2007*. In preparation.

Pillin, Hans-Martin. *Oberkirch, Die Geschichte der Stadt von den Anfängen bis zum Jahre 1803*. Volume I, Oberkirch: Die Stadt Oberkirch, 1976.

Pillin, Hans-Martin. *Oberkirch, Die Geschichte der Stadt in großherzoglich-badischer Zeit, 1803-1918*. Volume II, Oberkirch: Die Stadt Oberkirch, 1978.

Polk, Stella Gibson. *Mason and Mason County: A History*. Burnet, TX: Eakin Press, 1980.

Runge, R. "Obituary Francis Kettner" *Mason County News*, September 13, 1907.

CPSIA information can be obtained at www.ICGtesting.com
Printed in the USA
BVOW04s2301180416

444704BV00017B/80/P

9 781463 705985